GLOBAL JOURNALISM

LONGMAN SERIES IN
PUBLIC COMMUNICATION

SERIES EDITOR: RAY ELDON HIEBERT

GLOBAL JOURNALISM

A SURVEY OF THE WORLD'S MASS MEDIA

JOHN C. MERRILL, Editor

Containing Contributions By:

John C. Merrill
  Louisiana State University
Paul S. Underwood
  Ohio State University
John Luter
  University of Hawaii
Jim Richstad
  University of Oklahoma
L. John Martin
  University of Maryland
Marvin Alisky
  Arizona State University
Ralph D. Barney
  Brigham Young University

Longman

New York & London

Global Journalism

Longman Inc., 95 Church Street,
White Plains, N.Y. 10601
Associated companies, branches, and representatives
throughout the world.

Developmental Editor: Gordon T. Anderson
Editorial and Design Supervisor: Frances Althaus
Interior Designer: Antler & Baldwin, Inc.
Production Supervisor: Ferne Kawahara
Manufacturing Supervisor: Marion Hess

Library of Congress Cataloging in Publication Data

Main entry under title:

Global Journalism.
 (Longman series in public communication)
 Bibliography: p.
 Includes index.
 Contents: Introduction — the global perspective /
John C. Merrill — Europe and the Middle East / Paul S.
Underwood — Asia and the Pacific / John Luter and
Jim Richstad — [etc.]
  1. Journalism. I. Merrill, John Calhoun, 1924–
II. Underwood, Paul S. III. Series.
PN4775.G56 1983   070   82-17214
ISBN 0-582-28338-8
ISBN 0-582-28339-6 (pbk.)

Printing: 9 8 7 6 5 4 3   Year: 91 90 89 88 87

Manufactured in the United States of America

CONTENTS

PREFACE

Not always to the delight of everyone, and certainly not always with resulting international harmony, the nations of the world are communicating increasingly and having an impact on one another. Contributing greatly to this cosmopolitan babel are the media of mass communication which are growing in number and potency. Supplementing the global media is a mushrooming array of conferences, seminars, symposia, clinics and workshops—many under the sponsorship of UNESCO—dealing with a wide assortment of journalistic and communications issues and problems.

Anyone today who is involved in mass communications or plans to enter this vast enterprise knows that a familiarity with at least the rudiments of global mass communications is essential for success. The days are now behind us when American journalism students, for example, could study only the American press and its practices and concerns. Like it or not, journalists everywhere must break out of their provincial shells and enter the broader world of international communication, thus becoming, in a very real sense, *international* journalists and mass communicators.

Back in 1959 when I wrote the *Handbook of the Foreign Press* there was really nothing, with the possible exception of my friend Robert Desmond's *Press and World Affairs* (1937), which could be used as a textbook in international communications or comparative press systems. Material was sparse and scattered in bits and pieces here and there in the journals. Throughout the 1960s articles and books on press problems around the world increased steadily, and in the 1970s and 1980s the outpouring of such literature was turning into a wide and deepening river. Now, in the 1980s, when it comes to a textbook in the area, the problem is not too little but too much information.

Books abound on the media systems of various countries and regions of the world; anthologies are available that deal with many aspects of international communications, Third World concerns, the New World Information Order, news agencies, and the like (see Bibliography). Unlike the 1950s, '60s and '70s, the decade of the 1980s provides the serious student of international communication and the world press an abundance of excellent material. But in a real sense it is still either scattered and unsynthesized, or it is contained in expensive encyclopedic volumes unsuitable for classroom use as a textbook.

From such a recognition of the continued need for a discrete text encompassing the world's press, the present authors determined to undertake such a project. This new book is not an attempt to update and rewrite the Merrill, Bryan, and Alisky *Foreign Press* editions of 1964 and 1970. Rather than trying to deal with the mass media of every country of the world individually as did the ambitious (perhaps overly ambitious) *Foreign Press*, the present volume deals with global journalism and mass communication by regions of the world and by special topics related to each region. And these regional sections are written by six authors, each with particular interests and expertise.

The reader will be able to find in the pages of this single book a great amount of pertinent data about the journalism of the world, by region and by topic. Of necessity, the material is abbreviated and perhaps (to some) superficial. But, after all, we are trying to cover the journalism of the entire world—no easy task for a single volume designed for classroom use by students.

Certainly the present volume does not pretend to be an exhaustive treatment of national press systems; such a treatment would, of course, necessitate many volumes and would defeat the purpose of this work—to provide a survey of international communication. This book is mainly for the neophyte, the inquisitive beginner, and not for the specialist who concentrates on the journalism of one nation or one area of the world. It is for the person desiring an overview, a survey of global journalism in its main aspects. We believe that it can be used advantageously in a course dealing with comparative world journalism and/or international communication or as a supplemental text for several basic journalism and social science courses.

All journalism students need at least an introduction to the world's press so that they may better appreciate and evaluate the press of their own country. Such an introduction should go a long way in helping students shed their provincialism and begin thinking of their own press system in an international context. During the past several decades, study of global communication has been growing rapidly in schools and departments of journalism and mass communication. Courses in this broad area have become important fixtures in most curricula. It is now generally recognized, for example, that an American studying journalism or communication should no more limit himself or herself to American journalism than a history student should study only American history. This present volume is presented as such an introduction to the world's journalism and, if used intelligently with collateral readings, guest lectures, etc., should give the student a good insight into the scope, characteristics, and issues of global journalism.

Many specifics of world journalism—which tend to become dated rather quickly—have been purposely ignored or minimized in this book, for we see this volume not as a reference work but as a panoramic picture of world journalism and an introduction to global communications problems and issues.

Information for this book has been obtained from innumerable sources—from analysis of foreign publications, lectures, scholarly papers, articles, books, governmental pamphlets, embassy materials, journals and magazines of all types, and newspapers. All the authors have traveled extensively abroad; at least three have been foreign correspondents; and all have had occasion to see press systems firsthand and to have had numerous interviews and conversations with leading journalistic figures (in the media and in academia) the world over.

We are indebted to many persons, known and unknown, for their valuable aid in making this book possible. Encouragement, suggestions, and material have been supplied by so many (both at home and abroad) that it is impossible to make individual acknowledgments. We do, however, wish to express our sincere appreciation to all these people.

One final note: In a very real sense all the collaborators in this work are co-authors; the regional sections of the book were designed and written especially for *Global Journalism* and are not reprints from other publications. As editor, I would like to express my deep appreciation to the contributors who have worked so diligently with me to bring out this book. In my long introductory part of the book I have retained some portions of what I wrote in *The Foreign Press* (now out of print) where this material was thought to be still relevant; with this material I have added new data intended to help provide a general and global perspective for the substantive regional sections which follow. This is a big project, to be sure, and we hope that it will fill the needs of those who have been looking for such a book.

John C. Merrill

PART 1

THE GLOBAL PERSPECTIVE

JOHN C. MERRILL

In this rather long introductory part of the book we attempt to bring before the reader at least a few of the most important contemporary issues and problems in international journalism and some of the major aspects of communications developments in a worldwide context. The more specific and substantive matters of global journalism will be taken up in the main body of the book by five of the coauthors who will each survey a major region of the world.

Some readers prefer to deal in generalities and broad overviews; they should find this introductory global perspective of interest. What is presented in this initial part of the book should introduce certain controversial dimensions of global journalism and to set the stage for more intensive study of particular mass-media systems. Theoretical considerations are given some attention in this introduction as are some of the issues which loom large on the global scene—e.g., the growing debate about the New World Information Order and international communications problems among nations generally.

Since this is an attempt to give a panoramic view of global journalism, we purposely use rather broad strokes to paint our picture in this introductory part. Also we eschew the more pronounced symbols of scholarship (footnotes) in order to move readers rapidly forward and to acquaint them with some of the generally agreed upon ideas and data relative to international journalism. In fact, in this entire book we have made an effort to keep overt (and certainly pretentious) scholarship out of sight as much as possible so that the basics of the work will be easily assimilated and the dangers of the book becoming quickly dated will be minimized.

Specific quotations and statistical data, of course, are important, but it was felt that these should be deemphasized here in favor of a more general treatment. Readers desiring to fill gaps in the book or to compensate for what they may see as statistical or evidential deficiencies are encouraged to consult either reference works in international communication or more topical books (see our Bibliography).

Now let us get on with our more general introductory problem: the presentation of the global dimensions of journalism interlaced with some basic and important concerns of those involved in the many facets of transnational communication.

WORLD CRISIS AND THE PRESS

Distrust and misunderstanding among peoples everywhere are commonplace today; and in this climate of suspicious anxiety and unrest, the world's mass media of communication are reaching more people with more messages than ever before. All who are in positions to think about such things are aware that the world is in crisis and that one hasty or irresponsible action might plunge the world into a disasterous, even catastropic, war. Representatives of many nations come increasingly to conference tables to talk about the multitude of world problems and dangers, and ostensibly they desire to establish peace, allay fears, gain global justice, and improve world understanding through better communication.

But seated with these men and women at United Nations forums and elsewhere are deep-rooted prejudices and suspicions, strong national feelings and vested interests; beneath the smooth patina of the words are long-simmering antagonisms, traditional power politics, and fundamental misunderstandings. And all the while, the media of mass communication are pouring a glut of messages over vast audiences. The global press—the giant organism holding together cultural and nationalistic groups—is busy "reporting" and "interpreting" the constant succession of world crises and the conferences dealing with them.

The global press wields tremendous power today as a purveyor of vital information. It has the potential to help erase erroneous impressions and stereotypes and to ease tensions; it can also create fears and needlessly perpetuate anxieties. It can shake people from complacency, or it can lull them into an unthinking and dangerous sleep. With psychological warfare raging fiercely, the press finds itself in a place of tremendous responsibility today. Modern technology has created a small world, and human beings are locked together in the same tiny room where everyone is forced to share the consequences of one another's action.

Physical means of communicating news and interpretation throughout the world are well-developed and capable of providing the quantity of messages needed for proper understanding among peoples. But while messages flow more rapidly and in greater quantity than ever before, questions of quality of impact, of significance, of balance, of truth, and of motive come to the forefront. And while on the surface there appears to be adequate information moving through most parts of the world, governmental pressures, secrecy, censorship, and propaganda impede the meaningful and free flow of news.

As governments get larger and more complex in bureaucratic structure, the problems of press access to basic and relevant information gets more difficult. At the same time, sincere and normally cooperative governmental representatives find that with more exposure to the mass media they are increasingly misrepresented—their statements are twisted and their meaning is distorted, all of which can lead toward a climate of suspicion and mistrust on the part of public officials and in turn to a reluctance on their part to say very much for public dissemination. As governments become more sensitive and cautious when confronted by the press, the universe of frank and open news reporting is restricted, and honest and thoroughgoing dialogue becomes more difficult.

An informed public opinion is needed throughout the world if judicious decisions are to be made; a free-flowing and intelligent supply of news and views must nourish this public opinion. Lester Markel, long-time Sunday editor of the *New York Times*, has said:

> We live in a mine-trapped and fogbound world, a world in which facts are few and hunches difficult. . . . We shall not be able to reach sound judgments that are so urgent unless we have an informed and alert public opinion, unless our information is good. . . . For an informed opinion is a weapon without which we cannot be truly armed, a torch without which we cannot find our way through the darkness.

And, speaking later on this general subject, Markel had this to say about the concept of the "flow of the news":

> We cannot have understanding—and thus peace—among the peoples of the world unless they come to know one another better, unless they have better, truer, information about one another; the main instrument for communicating such information, for bringing about such understanding is the newspaper; it is not the Voice of America, the BBC, Radio Moscow, that matters in the long run; it is the day-by-day flow of the news.

On the world scene as on the national scene, a truthful and unfettered press can best serve the people. At least this is the view from the libertarian standpoint of the Western democracies. Such a free press can go far to mend differences among nationalities, classes, and groups; it can frustrate the plans of war-hungry leaders and rulers. The accomplishment of these possibilities is a prodigious task for the press, one that requires the acceptance and application of the free-press theory; for only with a free press can people have more than a foggy or lopsided picture of what is happening around them.

Throughout the world, press freedom is really an ideal; no country has actually achieved it. This ideal is simply on a continuum somewhere between absolute control and complete freedom. Recent surveys and studies tend to indicate that in many ways freedom of the press is eroding slowly in a worldwide context. Press laws are proliferating, sanctions of many kinds are hindering the free workings of the press, and press councils and other groups are moving in to guide activities of the press.

The world is full of would-be press controllers, whether in so-called libertarian or in authoritarian countries. Governments—at least their leadership—desire political and social stability and realize that press freedom, or too much of it, endangers this stability and the general national status quo. Hence, it is quite understandable that the natural national tendency is toward more regulations for the control of the press. A controlled press, then, is the common—not the exceptional—state of things in the world, and a relatively free press today may be highly restricted tomorrow. And even the so-called relatively free press, if examined closely is found to be encompassed by a multitude of restrictions, subtle or overt. This basic pull toward authoritarianism within governments makes it extremely difficult for the press to fulfil its responsibilities under a free-press theory; in fact, it would seem to make it an impossibility.

In the light of the foregoing situation, the idea of the press having free access to factual and significant information may understandably appear to many thoughtful persons as only the dream of unrealistic optimists. Certainly, few observers could fail to see the difficulties of implementing such an idea in these days when the world is divided into numerous nationalistic camps, each with its own governmental and press philosophy. And it might be added at this point that each nation's press system and philosophy is usually very closely in step with that nation's basic political and social system and ideology. So in one very real sense, every country's press system is more often than not truly a "branch of government" or a cooperating part of the total national establishment.

Even the casual observer will note that the world press today is subjecting men's minds to a ceaseless and terrific bombardment of messages calculated to influence and control. Internally a nation's press tries to mold the state into a consolidated, smooth-running machine ready to repel any outside danger, and externally the press directs its broadsides at potential enemies. This may be a practical course in times of danger, but it does not make for objective, information-oriented communication within or among countries.

Perhaps the press has come in for too great a share of blame for this situation. Press responsibility to all men of all nations is a fine concept, but a responsible press in an irresponsible social or governmental context is hardly to be hoped for except by those too uninformed or too idealistic to know better. And it may be that the individual citizen is to blame for the bias and government propaganda which permeate large segments of the world press today.

Many critics say that the press is actually hindering world understanding and cooperation, and that the world press is stretching animosities among nations to dangerous dimensions and thereby worsening the international psychic crisis. This does not seem an un-likely thesis. It would imply great amounts of propaganda in the news stream—propaganda aimed at perpetuating the psychological tug of war among nations and peoples; it would also imply that "exception-al" incidents which are even further exaggerated by the newspapers are then disseminated as important news; it would further imply that "eccentric" and "dangerous" people are the subject of much of the news. In short, it would imply that "unreal" and "alarmist" news dominates the newspaper columns and the television screen. It is not difficult to see how critics feel that this is the case.

When we examine the world press today, we get the feeling that the jangled nerves of the world's populations can hardly be eased by the newspapers—and certainly not by TV. On the contrary, anxieties are created, magnified, and perpetuated; religion is set against reli-gion, social class against social class, race against race, and national-ity against nationality. Instead of being conveyors of enlightenment and harmony, the national press systems tend too often to be "press agents" for individual nations or special groups, thus doing a good job of increasing irritations and suspicions among governments and giv-ing distorted pictures of various nations.

Very few observant critics of the press would deny that news media—printed and electronic—are mainly instruments of propagan-da on the international level and are involved largely in creating and destroying images. Certainly the world's communication channels have been all but choked in recent years by inflammatory and slanted messages concerning explosive situations in the Middle East, in the emerging nations of Africa, in divided Berlin, in Afghanistan and Po-land, in Cuba and Central America. The reader, listener, and viewer searching for truth and the "real story" is left oftentimes in bewilder-ment. He or she notes contradictions in the news, discrepancies among world news agencies, and opinions creeping more and more into news columns and network newscasts and is indeed puzzled—and frustrated.

All indications are that the world's consumers of news and views are in for a long siege of ideological messages. There have been few truces in international psychological warfare. As technology pushes mass messages into the more remote regions and saturates ever-growing populations, the world's psychosis is bound to worsen. Truth in the messages is no assurance of enlightenment or emotional stabi-lization; recent history has shown clearly that even the most truthful statement can boomerang, that it can appear as something quite different when viewed from the perspective of a particular audience's traditional beliefs, desires, and expectations.

The mass media should not be looked upon as a panacea for the world's problems. The most powerful radio transmitters and the most enterprising and honest newspapers and magazines will not be able to substitute for international cooperation and progress on the diplomatic level. Mass communication is obviously no substitute for direct involvement of persons and their technologies in the world crisis; international action certainly speaks louder than mass-oriented words.

Worldwide envy, resentment, suspicion, and hatred build emotional walls against the most objective and well-intentioned printed word and erect mental jamming stations against the most honest broadcast. And when one considers that in every nation the government uses news as a weapon, with no real attempt at honesty and objectivity, the task of the mass media in the fight for peace and understanding appears hopeless. As government management of the news grows (and while administrative and diplomatic representatives persist in their game of brinkmanship), the more dismal the future looks for world journalism.

THE PROBLEM OF NATIONAL IMAGES

Day after day the press of all nations grind out a stream of news, views, pictures, advertisements, and headlines which go a long way in creating and reinforcing images or stereotypes not only of their home countries but of other nations as well. Most students of international journalism will agree that these national stereotypes perpetuated in the world's press pose a serious problem to global communication and understanding. Although there are many theories or concepts of national images and what should be done about them—from breaking them down or eliminating them completely to changing them to more favorable ones—very few realistic suggestions have been made.

It seems appropriate while dealing with the world press in general to discuss briefly at least some aspects of this very important problem of national images or stereotypes.

First, one is faced with definitional problems which lead into dense semantic thickets. Just what does national image mean? Although a precise definition is impossible to formulate, many people have attempted it. They at least are able to present a kind of image of an image—or an abstracted picture of one—and thereby do succeed, perhaps without realizing it, in providing a kind of operational definition.

"Image" is often said to be roughly equivalent to "sterotype," and national image is therefore often called a national stereotype, or a generalized, abstracted profile of a nation or its people. One writer tells us that an image stands for "the whole realm of material objects, happenings, relations" connected with another country. While few persons would disagree with Frederick T. C. Yu's statement that all images "are infinitely simpler than reality," this really says little about them.

A descriptive short-cut, a composite or consolidated characterization of the people and the government of a country, is what national image is to some; however, there are those who consider such a concept far too limited. One writer feels that national image is not simply one but rather a series of images.

Today we witness, especially on the part of the developing, or Third World, countries, a tremendous concern with the problem of national images. Many of the new and understandably sensitive nations, supported by bureaucrats of UNESCO, are convinced that the images presented by the information media of the big Western countries through their journalism are harmful, biased, and unrealistic. Critics in the Third World charge that news about them, especially from Western wire services, is distorted and concerned only with bad news—catastrophe, corruption, social disorder, and national failure.

Not only qualitatively, but quantitatively, is the image bad, they charge. Critics say that there is very little news on the global news wires about Third World nations, thereby furnishing a fragmented picture of their nations, an image of chaos, negativism, sensationalism, and juvenilism. Far too much of Western reporting is simplistic, say the critics, resulting in a false image built largely on ideological labels. The Western image-makers, the charge goes, leave far too much important information out about the overall plight of the developing nations and the frightening odds which they face. All this leads to a negative and false image and to widespread apathy and ignorance in the West.

Presumably an image of a country involves a great many factors, and overabstraction, overgeneralization, and oversimplification constitutes a real and present danger for the governmental leaders and decision-makers as well as for nondecision-makers in the mass public. The belief is widespread among sociologists and political scientists, to name but two groups, that national images are dangerous concepts in that they lead to improper conclusions and assumptions about other peoples—that national images obstruct international understanding, are basically negative and misleading, and generally cause international (and national) friction.

The temptation is naturally great to launch into some type of idealistic program that is often camouflaged as a "practical" blueprint for improving understanding among nations. In other words, there are those among us who would always go around changing images so as to create more harmony in human relations. Certainly international understanding—or misunderstanding—is a natural concern of serious, humanistic-oriented persons. Without a doubt many citizens of all nations have images or stereotypes of other nations which they wish—or perhaps would wish if they thought much about these images—to eliminate. And certainly these images do lead to misunderstanding and even to friction among certain persons (and nations) at some times, in some places, under some circumstances. Today seemingly more than ever before, we hear of concrete programs or proposals to eliminate harmful images of nations which are believed to cause misunderstanding and friction.

It is at this point that we come in contact with *information control*, or the "process" consideration mentioned earlier. It is here that management (or manipulation) becomes a concern and leads to some kind of plan or program for solving the image problem.

An organized and definite program as such which would presumably eliminate the stereotypes and the myths thought harmful to international peace is at best highly idealistic and perhaps even inadvisable. This does not mean, of course, that basic misunderstandings are not to be deplored. It simply means that a *program* to correct them is open to question.

The concept of a program is itself filled with the potentialities of the stereotype: It is suspect, it is generalized, and it is a cliché which linguistically projects a well-constructed and idealized image. It is a semantic label which tends to simplify reality and cause uncritical people to expect more than can be delivered.

Nations, especially those segments of them which are sophisticated enough to be concerned about images, have come to the point where they are suspicious of organized attempts to correct their generalized ways of thinking about other countries—or about their own countries for that matter. Such attempts are considered by sensitive citizens to be false, hypocritical, and socially and politically dishonest. Unspontaneous and largely managed, or directed, image-making is the reaction of sophisticated citizens.

It is natural for Americans to have stereotypes of other nations, and vice versa, however unfortunate we may feel this to be. Are we to assume that the present stereotypes relative to different countries are any more damaging or more erroneous than would be *new* stereotypes promulgated by a conscious program?

The whole matter might be considered from the perspective of stereotype analysis itself. We certainly know that there is a stereotype of a stereotype, a sort of generalization about a generalization. And we must admit that usually a stereotype is negative. Stereotypes are visualized as "bad," "unfortunate," "incomplete," "damaging to good will," "harmful," "biased," and so forth. In effect, we see stereotypes as vicious and unrealistic walls which separate peoples and keep them from getting along together. This is basically the stereotype of the stereotype.

But an interesting question comes up at this point: What is the alternative? Is there any way to eliminate one stereotype without imposing another one in its place? Is not the process of eliminating stereotypes simply the changing or modification of stereotypes? The new or revised stereotype may prove to be more effective for certain purposes than the older one, but one wonders if it will be more accurate, more real, or more stabilizing to society.

How can Mexicans, for instance, think of the United States *without* thinking in stereotypes? How can citizens of the United States think of Mexico in any other manner? Thinking itself is abstracting, selecting, focusing on certain dominant characteristics or certain aspects of reality which fit a person's preconceived notions. Thinking, in effect, *is* stereotyping—and certainly *mass* thinking is. So we run into an imposing problem in the matter of changing *people's* stereotypes about other people—the problem inherent in the mass mind itself. Now, there are those who would immediately challenge the use of such an abstract term as mass mind. Perhaps it should be challenged; the point is, however, that it is used quite often and is frequently equated with public opinion. Since these two terms—fuzzy though they may be—are in actual use and thus in a sense take their place in social relations, we must deal with them.

To influence public opinion we must be concerned with the troublesome concept of the mass mind. To be concerned with the mass mind is to be concerned with stereotypes. To be concerned with stereotypes is to be concerned with generalizations. To be concerned with generalizations is to be concerned with images one country might have of another.

But again the problem of generalization itself confronts us and reemphasizes for us the importance of stereotypes in anything we attempt to say. *Countries*, as we know, do not have images of other countries—or of *anything* for that matter. Their *citizens* individually may have images, and it is well to remember that "citizens" is plural, as is "images." If we are not careful in talking about countries, we will fall into the trap of using supergeneralizations. In fact, when we speak of countries having images of other countries, we use a sort of massive stereotype. Perhaps this usage has grown out of the marriage of public relations to political science with the concept of corporate image as best man. Today many people appear to feel that a nation (or corporation) not only can *hold* an image, but can *be* the image of something else.

It is necessary always to break down such generalizations into parts. *Which persons* within country *A* have *what kind of* stereotypes of *which segments or aspects* of country *B*? When we begin thinking of national stereotypes in this fashion, we begin thinking of them as relative and individualized, and we begin wondering if they are not altogether meaningless.

But we know that they are not completely meaningless because some persons talk as if they *know* these stereotypes, as if stereotypes have meaning for them. So perhaps we must say that certain stereotypes of nations do in fact exist, although nobody has ever quite succeeded in getting at them even in individuals much less in entire nations.

Assuming the existence of national stereotypes in individual members of a society, a further question arises: Is the stereotype one has of another nation basically erroneous or basically valid? We cannot logically assume that negative or unfavourable stereotypes are per se more erroneous than positive or favorable ones. However, we frequently tend to make such an assumption, a fact which indicates something of our stereotype of the stereotype. Perhaps we need to realize that all is not fresh air and light in international relations or with individual nations, and that nations can have largely unfavorable characters (or images) just as specific persons can. We cannot really change the nation by manipulating its image any more than we can make a blind man read by constantly picturing him facing an open book.

Perhaps what we need in the area of international images or stereotypes is a splintered, or pluralistic, concept which is, indeed, indescribable. Little purpose can be seen in institutionalized destruction of national stereotypes. For the destroyer of the stereotypes places himself in the position of truth holder—in the position of having the proper insights into what the stereo type *ought to be*. When he demolishes a stereotype, one would expect him to put something more valid in its place, and he himself implies the necessity of doing so.

We read that school children in the Soviet Union and in the United States have distorted ideas of one another. This is not surprising; they undoubtedly have distorted ideas of their own classmates and of their own parents—even of themselves. It might be said that everyone everywhere has distorted ideas about reality in general or about any piece of it. But what about these school children? It seems that they must change their concepts slowly through formal education and natural maturation. And they must learn to live with the knowledge that they will always, at all times in their lives, have distorted images of one another and of other countries. This is a fact of human societies, and of the process of communication itself. Or to state this another way: They must recognize their own humanness and proceed on a personal basis to open their minds to ever more humanizing stereotypes. What more can they do?

It would be rather simple and greatly satisfying to suggest such panaceas as having more news in the press about the respective nations, more exchange of students, more appreciative and knowledgeable tourists, better motion pictures, and more books of a representative type. Such proposals, however, are not only trite but smack too much of a trend toward stultifying consensus and a sort of universalistic morality. In fact, it relegates personal, cultural, and national differences and decisions to some negative outcast status.

What is rather pitiful about this national stereotype concept is that the people most often concerned about it are the very ones who hold the most simplistic views. They picture whole nations or the nation's children or the people as having common impressions about whole groups or nations. This appears to be a rather basic form of stereotype building in itself. It is much easier to think of the nation as having a stereotype of another nation than of thinking about individual persons in the nation as having differing ideas, impressions, and attitudes about another nation.

Many persons will feel that this discussion completely ignores the question, that it is concerned with peripheral matters and does not squarely face the tedious job of restructuring our images of other nations. This is very far from the case. What we are saying here is that the restructuring job is a *personal* matter which each citizen of every country must undertake on his own. He must not, and should not, rely upon an organized campaign of restructuring. He cannot assume that at any time he has the correct or right stereotype or image of any other nation—or even of his own nation. He will have misconceptions that are often based on misinformation, biases, ignorance, censorship, information from interest groups, and the like.

He may feel justified if he desires to blame his misconceptions on the communications media, the communications gap, the credibility gap, or whatever he desires to call it. But the fact is, he will always have this problem with him. He will always have divergent images fed to him by the media and by nature itself. He will always need to select, sift, clean, and reconstruct information for his own satisfaction and in accord with his maturity and education at that particular time. He must realize that he will always be faced with choices—in facts, opinions, experts, emphases. He must choose. And *what* he chooses determines his stereotypes, which, in turn, will help him to make further choices.

The alternative to our rather confused system of multiple stereotypes is a closed society, an authoritarian system, in which stereotypes have been corrected and citizens have the same (and right) images of other nations and of their own nation. But as long as a nation is free and open, it will be pluralistic and will have erroneous (or they will so appear to some persons) stereotypes. Whose stereotype is correct is not the question: Let us assume that *all* stereotypes are wrong—in the sense of being incomplete and nonobjective. Otherwise, they would not be stereotypes.

In spite of the inadequacies of stereotypes, it is the main contention here that these partial images—if we may call them that—are indispensable to public thinking, and possibly even to private thinking, about other countries. We must consider other countries in generalizations; we cannot think about the multifaceted societies as they are in actuality or about the individual citizens within them. We must think in broad strokes, in vivid colors, in lumps and pieces. Whether or not this is a commendable practice is not the issue; the fact remains, a human being *must* think about other nations in this way. Otherwise he can say little more about other countries than, "It's too complex and differentiated for me to say anything about it."

If we are going to talk (and think) about other nations, we must make use of stereotypes. If we want to have only favorable stereotypes, which is one thing, we surely have the right to have them. But this does not mean that these stereotypes will be very close to the truth of the matter; in fact, a favorable stereotype may be far more misleading (and dangerous) than an unfavorable one. And there is no evidence to lead us to believe that favorable stereotypes existing among nations lead to more understanding and harmony than do unfavorable ones.

In any discussion of relations between two nations, human values are naturally deemed to be extremely important. One such human value is independent determination of one's own opinions—or forming one's own stereotypes, if you will. This stereotype may be imperfect (it will be), but it is essential to human rights and a free society. And, to repeat, there is no reason to believe that it is *more* imperfect than it would be if it were more favourable.

The best way that the people of any nation can understand those of another nation is to develop on an individual basis a more sophisticated attitude toward the realities of language and a more patient stance toward each other. At the very root of this understanding will be a changed attitude toward stereotypes—an attitude which shuns the very stereotyping of stereotypes as automatically and necessarily dangerous and vicious. The citizens of every nation must constantly attempt to think in particulars while realizing that the overriding tendency is for us to think in clusters, generalizations, or stereotypes.

Of course, if we take this line of thought very far we will find ourselves in the curious position of having destereotyped our thinking about one another's nations to the point that we are forced to be silent. And, perhaps *more silence* and *less communication* is really what international relations is in need of today. At least silence precipitated by a conscious determination to destereotype our conceptions of one another would be an intellectually healthy silence.

GLOBAL NEWS FLOW

The flow of international news and information is largely in the hands of the big world news agencies. This fact in itself is a cause of alarm and a point of contention within large segments of the global community. Most of the criticism of the worldwide flow of news comes from the so-called Third World—the developing, or nonaligned, countries. Charges of inadequate and biased reporting and news dissemination by the international news agencies are heard on every hand, especially in media conferences sponsored by UNESCO.

Chief targets of this criticism are the news agencies of the West —the United States' Associated Press (AP) and United Press International (UPI), Britain's Reuters, and France's Agence France-Presse (AFP). Quite simply, the Third World is concerned over what it sees as the unenlightened, biased, and inadequate journalistic theory and practice of the capitalistic Western nations—especially the United States. Hardly a day goes by that some editor or political leader in the Third World does not take a public swing at Western journalism for its injustices in the area of news coverage.

News Flow: Basic Issues

According to Third World spokesmen, the Western news agencies are disrupting the free flow of news, are distorting the realities of the developing nations, and are presenting negative images of the Third World. The leaders of these developing countries are justifiably sensitive to the kind of press treatment they receive. And, by and large, they feel they do not fare well in the Western press—especially in stories from the big news agencies.

They wish to eliminate the impediments they see blocking the flow of information throughout the world. In other words, they want to see news flow as freely from the Third World to the West as it flows from the West to the Third World. The big Western agencies, they say, have a virtual monopoly on news dissemination and fail to provide the world with a realistic picture of what is really happening. News is too biased, they say, especially in respect to the Third World; it is too heavy on items of poverty, illiteracy, riots, revolutions, volcano eruptions, antics of national leaders, skyjackings, etc. They ask: Why is there not more news about good things that are going on—bridge building, highway constuction, new schools, and the like? Why is it that the AP and UPI, and to a lesser degree Reuters and AFP, so grossly neglect these aspects of the Third World?

Western journalists, by and large, believe that what the Third World critics really want is not a free flow of news and information but a balanced flow. The Western newsmen put the emphasis on freedom in the flow, they contend; and Third World journalists and government officials place the emphasis elsewhere—on the flow being balanced, or equilibrated, in their parlance.

Briefly, what the Third World does seem to want from Western journalism is this: (1) a kind of balanced flow of news in and out of the Third World; (2) more thorough, incisive, and unbiased news coverage of their countries on a continuing basis, and (3) more emphasis on good, or positive, news of the Third World, including largely educational news of a progress type which has come to be called "development" news.

Western journalists admit that there is some truth in the indictments of Western journalism. Certainly there is an unevenness in news flow among nations—but Western newsmen say that this is also true of news flow within countries. And certainly much global coverage can be said to contain bias—but *all* reporting can be so indicted. Also, what the Third World means by development news is really not considered particularly newsworthy by Western journalists.

But one thing *is* clear: the West does dominate the worldwide flow of communications. Although more than 120 news agencies exist globally (representing some 68 percent of all nations), a few large ones dwarf the rest in terms of personnel, facilities, and technology. Most of the developing world must rely for global and regional news on the four big Western agencies named earlier—plus, in some instances, the other international agency, TASS of the Soviet Union. A Third World newspaper receiving the Big Four of the West and TASS would have some some half-million words pouring across its desks every day.

Third World countries' displeasure with the big transnational news agencies has led to the creation of their own press agency pool to exchange news of common interest and develop a new style of journalism that gives priority to nonsensational and more positive events and processes. Since 1976, the nonaligned movement of the Third World has operated the News Agencies Pool of Nonaligned Countries.

Tanjug, the Yugoslav government news agency, transmits most of the daily file, including reports to and from some 40 national agencies.

The pool is not a news agency such as Reuters or AFP; it does not have a central headquarters, a general manager, or even a budget. Member nations have a self-financing structure—the sender of the news paying for its transmission. The news they exchange is mainly composed of communiqués, protocol visits of diplomats, and texts of speeches. Also represented in the file are economic, ecological, and cultural items.

In addition to the nonaligned news pool, there is also Interpress, which calls itself a "Third World news service." Government agencies pay it to rewrite and process their news reports and to provide them with an incoming file of reports. Interpress also gets UNESCO funds to promote its special activities and interests; in a sense, Interpress is a kind of globally oriented public relations firm.

Much of the news sent by both the nonaligned news pool and Interpress is of the constructive type—news of cultural and economic development; of agricultural, technological and industrial progress; and of items that promote trade and cooperative relations among the Third World nations. Largely it takes the form of features, special articles, speeches, analytical pieces, and backgrounders.

A typical Western reaction to the pool and Interpress is that the majority of the Third World nations involved in both have authoritarian regimes and that most of the information flowing through these organizations is made up of governmental propaganda and handouts from autocratic leaders; the news, therefore, cannot be objective or credible.

So the debate goes on. There seems to be no end in sight. Differing concepts of journalism are embraced by nations around the world, and conceptual dedication largely determines the pragmatic, everyday practices of the communications media. It is no wonder that disagreements about journalistic objectives abound throughout the world.

Methods and Dimensions of Flow

As has been said earlier, some 100 nations of the world make use of their own national news agencies, many of which are doing excellent jobs of intranational collection and distribution of news. And some are actually regional agencies, supplying and receiving news from other nations. A few of the leaders among these national and regional news agencies are: Australian Associated Press; Agence Belga of Belgium; Canadian Press; Hsin Hua (New China) of China; Ritzau of Denmark; South African Press Association; Deutsche Presse-Agentur of West Germany; Kyodo of Japan; EFE of Spain; MENA (Middle East News Agency) of Egypt; and CANA of the Caribbean area. More of these agencies will be discussed later in the regional sections of this book.

Most of the news transmitted throughout the world is what is generally referred to as "headline news", "straight news", or "spot news"; and there has long been realization among world journalists that too little interpretive or explanatory writing finds its way into the international communications stream. Most news agencies are trying to remedy this situation, and increasingly the *why* of the news is being emphasized by international reporters as they try to put their communiqués into a meaningful context for the reader.

There are three main foreign news sources used by the press of the world. They are news agencies; special news services, syndicates, and "stringers"; and staff correspondents of newspapers and broadcast entities. The news agencies account for more than three-fourths of the news transmitted globally. Only the larger and more progressive of the world's newspapers can maintain full-time correspondents abroad, but scores of journals have special-assignment correspondents or roaming reporters throughout the world or writers on a "stringer" basis in various countries. Many newspapers also share correspondents with other publications. The bulk of the world news flow is made up of political, military, and foreign relations items, as might be expected. Human interest news follows in fourth place.

Making possible the great glut of global press messages are four main communications systems—submarine cables, telegraph and telephone lines, radio (including radio-telephone, point-to-point radio, and omnidirectional radio), and the communication satellites for live on-the-spot television coverage. In addition, of course, many feature stories and background articles are sent through the mails.

There are certain cities throughout the world which because of their location, size, or political importance are especially prominent as collecting centers and transmission points for world news. These cities are London, Paris, Zurich, Madrid, Rome, Copenhagen, Stockholm, Berlin, Bonn, Brussels, Amsterdam, Tokyo, Calcutta, Bombay, New Delhi, Peking, Hong Kong, Moscow, Cairo, Ankara, Sidney, Brisbane, Montreal, Toronto, Havana, Buenos Aires, Rio de Janeiro, Caracas, Mexico City, Honolulu, Manila, San Francisco, New York, and Washington, D.C.

All the big news agencies have bureaus in these cities or, in a few cases, special correspondents who cover them regularly. In addition, most of the larger newspapers of the world keep their own employees in these strategic centers. The same can be said of the big broadcasting organizations of the world.

It would seem safe to say that quantitatively the news flow around the world is adequate, although unbalanced and spotty from time to time, and the big job facing the world press is the improvement of the quality of news as it moves in increasing bulk from country to country.

News-gathering Development

The modern, systematic gathering of global news has developed and grown along with communications facilities. From courier-carried newsletters sent by persons and groups across national boundaries, special messenger services, and the slow transmittal of news by horse and coach, international news gathering and disseminating has made slow but tremendous advances.

In the early 1800s light signals and the use of carrier pigeons made their advent, but it was the telegraph's appearance on the communications scene a little before midcentury that did most to clear the way for a speedier and freer flow of news among nations and to precipitate the growth of the news-gathering organizations.

By the late 1960s, continents had been linked by undersea cables, and land and submarine telegraph communication had caught the interest of governments and business enterprises; and, of course, newspapers were fascinated by this chance to use this new and speedy telegraphic method. Great Britain early took the lead in international communication, and even in the first part of the present century its cable interests exceeded those of all the rest of the world combined.

With the advent of the telegraph, the modern news agencies came into existence. The first to be established was Havas of France. By 1840 the organization had already joined its continental service to Britain by carrier pigeon, and after the telegraph's invention, the agency's services were expanded rapidly.

A Havas employee, Israel J. Beer (later known in Britain as Paul Julius Reuter), left the agency and in 1848 began his own service, first in Aix-la-Chapelle and soon afterward in Brussels. In 1851, he moved his headquarters across the English Channel to London. Here, after a slow beginning, he secured the respect and cooperation of the British press. By the end of the nineteenth century, Reuter's agency (as it was then called) was the world's most important.

Another Havas worker who deserted the French agency (in 1848) to set up his own was Bernard Wolff. He returned to his native Germany, and by 1860 his agency was regularly sending commercial news and political dispatches to German business firms and newspapers. The Wolff agency [Wolffische Telegraphen-Buro (WTB)] thereby took its place among the early news-gathering organizations of the world.

In 1870 the big agencies (Havas, Wolff, and Reuters), after a period of heated competition, entered into an agreement by which each was to have news rights in certain areas of the world and must share with the others its daily news file. These areas were actually news preserves in which each of the agencies (the United States' Associated Press soon became a part of the plan) had a collecting and distributing monopoly.

The news preserves of the alliance (generally known as the European Agency Alliance or the International News Cartel) were as follows: Wolff would operate in Germany, Scandinavia, Austria, Hungary, the German colonies, and in parts of the Balkans and Switzerland; Havas would cover France and the French colonies, Spain, Portugal, Italy, Belgium, Rumania, Serbia, Turkey, and most of Latin America; Reuters had the biggest slice of the world—the Middle and Far East, most of Africa and part of the Balkans, the East Indies, and part of South America; and the Associated Press (of the United States) got North and Central America as its special area.

This alliance broke up in the 1930s because of pressure from many sources and because it was directly challenged by the American United Press, which early in the postwar period was expanding its world news service into such cartel areas as Latin America and Japan. Actually, the alliance began to dissolve in 1924 when Mussolini took the Italian agency (Stefani) from French control; the cartel further crumbled a few years later when Hitler's government bought the Wolff agency and turned it into a propaganda instrument. The final blow was given the alliance in 1934 when the Associated Press declared complete independence of the cartel; this opened a new era in which all agencies became independent and free to operate everywhere.

The Wolff and Havas agencies kept their names until World War II when Wolff's agency became Hitler's Deutsches Nachrichten-Buro, and France's postwar agency emerged under the name of Agence France-Presse.

In the twentieth century, with the help of complex networks of telegraph, telephone, radio, radiotelephone, radio-telegraph, and international satellite systems (e.g., Telstar), the news-gathering-and-distributing organizations have become tremendously powerful on the world scene. A *world news agency* is an organization, comprehensive in scope, which offers extensive world news coverage and large-scale distribution to subscribers in many nations.

A strictly *national* agency, on the other hand, is mainly local in scope, offering news coverage and distribution to the press of the country in which it is based, or serving as a sending agency for news coming from a world agency. At present there are five major world news agencies; they represent four major nations of the world—two of the agencies being based in the United States and one each in Britain, France, and the Soviet Union. These five agencies handle the great bulk of international news that appears in the press of the world.

World News Agencies

The following five international or world news agencies have networks of correspondents to gather news in a large number of countries and headquarters staffs to edit this news and transmit it to (1) their bureaus abroad for local distribution, (2) national news agencies with whom they have agreements, and (3) subscribing print and electronic media throughout the world. These agencies make extensive use of telecommunications in receiving and transmitting their messages. All these agencies originated in nations where the press was highly developed; the agencies came into being between 1835 and 1918.

Reuters. Founded in 1851 by Paul Julius Reuter in London, the agency was a family concern until 1916 when it became a private company with Sir Roderick Jones as managing director until 1941. It then became a cooperative agency or trust owned by the British press (with the Australian and New Zealand dailies also owning stock). Reuters has since been governed by 11 trustees, eight of whom represent the press of the United Kingdom.

Reuters is a nonprofit agency, with operating costs derived from subscribing media. Its service is received in almost every country. Its largest offices are in New York, Paris, Rome, Buenos Aires, Cairo, Frankfurt, Stockholm, and Geneva—and in London, of course.

Reuters is known for its reliable, alert reporting; its wiring is not as colorful and lively as that of some of its competitors, but it has a quality of seriousness and conciseness that has long made it a leader in its field. All the Reuter service is transmitted in English.

TASS. Telegrafnoie Agenstvo Sovetskavo Soiuza (TASS) was founded in 1918 under the name of ROSTA; it took its present name in 1925. This agency, like Agence France-Press and the two United States agencies, acts as a national agency as well as a world agency. TASS is state-controlled and is the main organization for collecting and transmitting news within the Soviet Union. News is sent not only in Russian, but in English, French, German, Spanish, and Arabic to its subscribers abroad. As a government agency, TASS is dependent on the Council of Ministers of the Soviet Union for its economic and editorial direction. Its headquarters are in Moscow, and its sprawling network of thousands of full-time and part-time correspondents stretches throughout the Soviet Union. It maintains bureaus or correspondents in all the major countries of the world. TASS has arrangements, sometimes informal, to exchange domestic news with several other world agencies.

TASS is the main source of news for national agencies in nations politically associated with the Soviet Union. It also provides news to agencies outside the Soviet bloc, such as Pars (Iran), Kyodo (Japan), and Bakhtar (Afghanistan), the last named perhaps now realistically within the Soviet bloc. For news collection, TASS uses mainly ordinary commercial telecommunication channels, and for news distribution it relies heavily on voice radio. As the official Soviet news agency, TASS is widely quoted throughout the world.

Associated Press. The oldest of the American agencies, AP was founded in 1848 and was called the New York Associated Press. The New York AP went out of business in 1892 and a new AP—founded in the Midwest and incorporated in Illinois—took over and became the present Associated Press. In 1900 it reorganized and incorporated in New York, where its headquarters have been ever since.

Today the AP, a cooperative agency owned by its member newspapers, provides news to subscribers in some 100 nations. It employs some 2,500 newsgatherers around the world, about 560 of them full-timers working outside the United States. AP has about 50 bureaus in foreign countries and has exchange agreements with agencies of about a dozen countries.

Agence France-Presse. This French agency was founded in 1835 by Charles Havas as Agence Havas with headquarters in Paris. By 1860 the agency had subscribers in most parts of Europe, and had drawn up contracts with Reuters and the German Wolff agency for cooperative news exchange. Faced by Nazi agression in 1940 the French government bought the agency's information branch and set up a propaganda office at Vichy. When the Germans came, they took over the agency and turned it into a part of the official Nazi news agency, DNB.

After France was liberated at the end of World War II, several interim war agencies were merged to form the Agence France-Presse (AFP), which was set up in the old Havas headquarters and took over most of the prewar agency's employees.

In 1944 AFP was forced to ask for financial aid from the government—with subsequent government slanting of news—because the struggling Paris dailies could not finance its operations. Thus, until 1957, AFP was the only major news agency of the free world to be largely government-supported. In January, 1957, AFP got an autonomous board of directors, controlled by editors of French newspapers.

AFP has a staff of some 3,000 and about as many clients around the world. Transmission of news is mainly by wire, but radio is being used increasingly. The agency has some 70 bureaus abroad and about 20 in France. Nearly half of AFP's daily transmission is world news. It has exchange agreements with agencies in some 30 nations and with the other big world agencies.

United Press International. In May, 1958, the United Press International (UPI) was formed in the United States when the United Press Association (founded in 1907 by E. W. Scripps) and the International News Service (founded in 1909 by William Randolph Hearst) were consolidated.

The UPI, like its forerunners UP and INS, has been known for its lively and colorful writing through the years. Unlike the Associated Press, the UPI is a private profit-making corporation. In recent years it has been plagued by serious economic problems, and there is still considerable speculation about its viability.

In the summer of 1982 UPI was bought by Media News Corp., owned by four newspaper and television executives from the South and the Midwest. It was bought from the E. W. Scripps Co. At that time UPI had some 6,000 newspaper and broadcast clients worldwide (in about 80 countries) and about 2,000 reporters.

GLOBAL PRESS PHILOSOPHIES

The world today is a giant arena in which large and small press systems are actively engaged in a strange kind of game. It is obvious to the onlooker that the participants are not certain just what it is they are supposed to be doing. Some are fighting among themselves; others are parading placidly about, oblivious to the rather frenzied activity about them. Some appear to be rushing madly around, shouting and kicking at their less active neighbors. Others stand in neat rows awaiting an order which will send them marching as one toward a certain goal, and some—their rows sagging rather wearily—seem to be ready to give up independent action and join the ranks of a bigger neighbor.

What is guiding these activities? How do the participants—press systems and units thereof—know what it is they are trying to do? In the main, they all have rather specific sets of directions, but these directions vary considerably. However, it may be said that all these participants—regardless of their peculiarities—have guiding concepts which are tied rather tightly to the traditional types of govern-ments they represent. These concepts, or philosophies—in many cases unwritten—serve to give some type of reason for the participants being in the arena.

Probably as many press philosophies or theories exist in the world today as there are media managers; certainly an observer can see many, and often quite significant, variations in basic media types from country to country and, in many cases, among sections of one country. However, when he looks down on the giant arena—to con-tinue the metaphor—he will notice that out of the wide and intricate press design a few ideological patterns take shape and stand out. Four such principal patterns have been isolated and have been fully dis-cussed in an interesting and scholarly little book (*Four Theories of the Press*). These ideological patterns formed among the world's press systems are classified as:

1 The authoritarian theory
2 The communistic theory
3 The libertarian theory
4 The social responsibility theory

The first two of these theories, or concepts, are really quite simi-lar, and it is difficult to differentiate many of the basic character-istics; for example, both are primarily totalitarian in their insistence on control and careful regimentation of the press. The press systems of Hitler's Germany in the 1930s and 1940s and of Franco's Spain in the 1950s are good examples of the authoritarian theory in practice; in a totalitarian sense they differ little from today's prime example of a communistic press system—that of the Soviet Union.

The other two theories—the libertarian and the social respon-sibility—overlap also in many respects. In fact, most nations which accept the libertarian theory today consider responsibility of the press to the public a part of this theory. Of course, the idea of social responsi-bility brings up many philosophical questions which cannot be exam-ined here; but since in any country the organization of society—its social and political structure—determines to a large extent what re-sponsibilities the press (and the citizen) owes this society, one must conclude that every country's press quite naturally considers itself as being socially responsible.

If it is realized that these four concepts, or theories, have evolved over many years and are still evolving, and that they overlap in many respects when applied, then as a method of systematizing a discussion of press concepts this four-way classification is quite helpful. Very briefly, here are a few important aspects of the four theories.

Authoritarian Theory

Under the authoritarian theory, which made its apperance in a clear form in sixteenth-century England, the press was to support the government in every respect and advance the programs of the national leadership. A press system which serves in the main capacity of a governmental propaganda agency under a "strong-man" type of government might be called an authoritarian press system. The theory revolves around the idea that a person engaged in journalism is so engaged as a special privilege granted by the national leader. It follows that this journalist is under an obligation to the leader and the government. This press philosophy has formed, and now forms, the basis for many press systems of the world, and may be observed currently in many African and Latin American nations.

Having the longest tradition, the authoritarian press—although functioning as a private enterprise within the individual country— owes its existence to the state and must operate to support and perpetuate the authority of that state which permits it to survive. The press, in such an authoritarian country, has just as much freedom as the national leadership wants it to have.

Communist Theory

Karl Marx might be called the father of the communistic press theory, which took its roots during the first quarter of the present century. In a Communist society, according to Marx, the functions of the press should come from the central function—the perpetuation and expansion of the socialist system. Means of communications should exist to transmit social policy and not to aid in searching for truth.

Media of communication under this theory are simply instruments of the government; as such they are integral parts of the state. The press must be owned and used by the state and directed by the Communist Party or its agencies. Within the Communist press system, however, self-criticism (i.e., criticism of failure to live up to Communist planning) by the press is permitted; in fact, it is encouraged. The Communist theory is based on the premise that the masses are too fickle and too ignorant and unconcerned with government to be entrusted with details of its operation. Such ideas as "man's inherent rationality," "minority rights," and the "fundamental right of every citizen to know government business" are considered unrealistic and simply "bourgeois concepts" by those adhering to the Communist press philosophy.

This Communist theory is much like the authoritarian one previously discussed; the one big difference between the two in practice is that while the Communist press is owned and operated by the state, the authoritarian press is privately owned. Another difference is that control by government in the Communist system is constant and uncompromising, whereas government control in an authoritarian system can change considerably with the particular leader in power.

Libertarian Theory

The concept of the libertarian press can be traced back to the seventeenth century, where it took roots in England and on the new continent of America. The philosophy of that time viewed man as a rational being having inherent natural rights and thus gave rise to the libertarian press theory. Man, according to this new rationalistic philosophy, had the right to pursue truth, and would-be interferers with this right should be restrained. Exponents of this libertarian press movement during the eighteenth century—characterized by John Milton and John Locke—insisted that governments keep hands off printed material. Individual liberties were emphasized by these philosophers, liberties that have manifested themselves in the American Declaration of Independence and the constitutional guarantees of free speech, free press, and free religious pursuits.

Under the libertarian theory, the press functions to uncover and present the truth, and it cannot function this way if it is controlled by some authority outside itself. The free press in theory will produce reportorial truth because it is regulated by all members of a free society who express their wishes in a free market where they can support or refuse to support certain newspapers or magazines.

Rather than this being a freedom especially for the press, it is really a right of the people to be informed and to choose their informants; in theory, this freedom belongs to the people rather than to the editors, publishers, and news managers. However, since the press must serve as the informational link between government and people, the freedom automatically extends itself to the press. If this informational link is broken by governmental censorship or secrecy—or by other means such as doctored news released by a government press agent—the concept of freedom of information is largely invalidated.

Today the libertarian press measures its social utility by how well the public is kept abreast of government activities. Theoretically at least, the libertarian press is a fourth estate, supplementing the executive, judiciary, and legislative branches of government. This, according to the theory, is one of the main ways the libertarian press accepts its social responsibility.

Social Responsibility Theory

A mid-twentieth century concept, the social responsibility theory of the press (as it is recognized in the Western world) had its roots in the libertarian press system. It goes beyond the libertarian theory, however, in that it places a great many moral restrictions on the press. Instead of emphasizing freedom for the press, it stresses responsibility. The theory has been drawn largely from a report published in 1947 by a private group (the Commission on Freedom of the Press) which studied the American press and came up with a critique.

According to this commission (often called the Hutchins Commission after its chairman Robert M. Hutchins), the mass media, because of their pervasive impact in all areas, have gone beyond such libertarian concepts as the search for truth, and the press's right of access to information. The new theory, as expressed by the commission, maintains that the importance of the press in modern society makes it absolutely necessary that an obligation of social responsibility be imposed on the communications media.

The Hutchins Commission saw press freedom as limited by a social responsibility to report facts accurately and in a meaningful context. Such thinking, of course, leads to the advocacy of a regulatory system to watch the actions of the press and to keep it functioning properly; the Commission on Freedom of the Press did not overlook this, and in its report suggested that some type of government regulation might be needed to ensure that the press accepted its responsibility. It was even suggested that the government might go into the communications business to properly inform the citizens if the private media did not wake up to their obligations to the public.

The social responsibility theory implies a recognition by the media that they must perform a public service to warrant their existence. The main parts of the commission's report which seemed to have antagonized many American editors and publishers were those that intimated government interference in the press system. Journalists in the United States have traditionally advocated social responsibility by the press, but they have seen the government's role of enforcement as a definite trend toward socialism and as a danger to the free press. In recent years Third World countries have gravitated toward a kind of press responsibility concept which would increasingly make journalism a kind of cooperating partner with the governments for the sake of national progress and development. Most Western journalists see this Third World–UNESCO trend, like the Hutchins Commission concept of the 1940s, as a threat to open and free communication.

Discussion of the "Theories"

It is helpful to think about these four concepts, or theories or philosophies, when discussing the structure and practices of the world
press. However, it might be well to make a few observations about
them at this point.

First of all, it might be argued that the social responsibility
theory is *not of the kind*—is not a parallel theory—as the others. In
fact, it might be said that all press systems are socially responsible if
they satisfy the norms, codes, and prerequisites of the press in a particular society. When a press system does not mirror its country's
political philosophy, it is then irresponsible. In other words, a social
responsibility theory does not seem to exist alongside, or in addition to,
the authoritarian, libertarian, and Communist theories. It is a part
of, or an outgrowth of, any or all of these other three.

In this sense the United States press system would be socially responsible, because in American political theory there is supposed to
be room for dissent, for eccentric units—not only persons but press
organizations—to coexist. One person's irresponsible press unit (e.g.,
newspaper) may be another person's responsible unit. The press is not
homogeneous with respect to an agreed-upon concept of responsibility; it is fragmented and pluralistic, often acting in different ways
and supporting different causes and political candidates. The very fact
that the United States press is *responsible* means that for many persons and groups in the country it will be considered *irresponsible*.

In like manner, the press of the Soviet Union might very well be
considered responsible to its society. Its concept of responsibility may
differ from that of the United States, but it is a valid concept. The
Soviet press is responsible when it reinforces the government and
socialist system of the Soviet Union. It is responsible when it pushes
national policy, when it speaks with one voice to help bring about
progress in the form of reaching certain specified goals. It becomes
irresponsible when it becomes a hindrance to the smooth achievement
of these goals, when it fights against governmental or Communist
Party policy. In other words, it becomes *irresponsible* the closer it
comes to doing what in the United States would be considered
responsible.

Many governments throughout the world today, especially in the
so-called nonaligned or developing world, firmly believe in a supportive, or cooperative, press which has moral obligations to help the
governments combat evil and forces which would threaten national
security and stability. It is safe to say that in the Third World at
least, most governments believe—without really having evidence for

such a belief—that a controlled press promotes national development and social and political harmony. And there are even spokesmen in the West representing liberal opinion who contend that new nations with fragile societies needing to progress and to achieve a sense of nationhood cannot really afford to have a free press with open debate. They see their position as one advocating press social responsibility.

Turning now to the authoritarian and Communist theories, we see that in many ways they are quite similar. The main difference seems to be that the authoritarian system permits private ownership of the press while the Communist system does not. Both systems of the press are, to varying degres at various times, authoritarian— perhaps totalitarian. The authoritarian press system knows quite well what it *cannot* print, and beyond that the editors are given considerable freedom and discretion in their editorial decision-making. The Communist system, on the other hand, is oriented to the opposite way. Since it is a part of the government, an agitation and propaganda arm of the state-party apparatus, it is mainly concerned with printing what it is told to print. In short, it knows what it *must* print. So a good argument can be made that the press is potentially freer in an authoritarian country than in a Communist country.

Last, let us look briefly at the libertarian theory or system. There is no doubt that it is under heavy fire from critics of all types. The social responsibility advocates would change it, making it more responsible—forcing it into a definitional straightjacket tailored to fit all press units of the country. These critics, and they are found in the West as well as in socialist and Third World countries, feel that they know what the press should do to be responsible. And they believe that this concept of responsibility should take precedence over the older, traditional concept of freedom. They would define responsibility and have the libertarian press adjust to this definition. We even find this currently being proposed in the international arena; UNESCO and many of its member states, for example, are even pushing for a global code of journalistic ethics.

But these press reformers often fail to see the problem, or at least one problem, which their ideas create: The act of adjusting to somebody's ethical code or concept of responsibility is a conforming act, one which automatically erodes the whole idea of freedom of the press. So a good case may be made for the contention that as a libertarian press system becomes "more responsible" (conforming more and more to a common concept of responsibility), it loses more and more of its freedom. At least this is a danger of which freedom-loving people must be aware. Freedom of the press can slowly, but rather easily, be lost under the popular banner of social responsibility.

GOVERNMENTS AND JOURNALISM

Freedom of expression is the continuation and practical manifestation of freedom of thought and is therefore one of the most fundamental human rights. Consequently, the principle of such freedom is set forth more or less explicitly in every social covenant, regardless of the political system it establishes. Such covenants—whether in the form of written constitutions or, as in the United Kingdom, derived from custom—acknowledge the fundamental nature of this right and assert the right of freedom of expression and, more specifically, freedom of the press.

Nevertheless, throughout the world—regardless of what press theory a country might accept—the right to publish and to get the truth is either denied or under constant attack. Limitations imposed on such rights are often undisguised, but they can be quite subtle. The complex nature of gathering, publishing, and disseminating news is such that the press is brought constantly into contact with the government. In addition, because of the pervasive role of the government in determining the affairs and destinies of men, the press is increasingly dependent on government for a major portion of its most significant news.

Wherever in the world the courageous newspaper exists, serving its reader as the guardian of his interest and the protector of his rights, exposing abuses of power, and criticizing failures and wrong decisions, it is a thorn in the side of government—or could be. It is an ever-present source of concern for government officials; it is a power that must be kept under control if the government is touchy about criticism or adverse news presentation. All this makes press-government relations difficult, and the only place where harmony seems the rule is in the Communist or fascist nations where frictions are not long tolerated.

In the libertarian-press nations, government pressures are usually a gradual application of legal, political, and economic restraints with the lid of secrecy opening and closing from time to time. In the authoritarian-press countries, the government pressures are more direct and less subtle, and press freedom varies (if at all) with the individual strong-man leader. In the Communist nations, of course, the press–government relationship is most stable, for both parties know what to expect of the other. After all, both parties are in reality the same party. Government pressure in Communist press systems amounts to constant and pervasive editorial, economic, and policy direction.

Government Pressures

Government pressures on the press of the world can be placed in the following categories, each of which will be discussed briefly: (1) legal pressures, (2) economic and political pressures, (3) secrecy, (4) direct censorship and force.

Legal Pressures. Legal pressures consist of four main types: (1) constitutional provisions, (2) security laws, (3) press laws, (4) penal laws.

Constitutional Provisions. While almost every national constitution traditionally provides for press freedom, in many cases the same constitutions place certain restrictions on this freedom. In almost identical words the Soviet Union, the People's Republic of China, and the various Communist people's republics of Eastern Europe guarantee the freedom of the press. But in every case the constitutional guarantee or its economic adjunct limits the guarantee and the means (communications facilities, printing equipment, paper, and other materials) to the working people. Since the Communist Party in each of these countries is the self-appointed spokesman for the working people, the effect has been to limit the proclaimed freedoms to itself.

As we have seen, Article 12 of the Spanish Charter of July 19, 1945, one of the fundamental documents of the Spanish constitution, declares that "all Spaniards may freely express their ideas." Appended to this statement, however, is an additional passage that says that this right can be maintained only as long as these ideas "do not advocate the overthrow of the fundamental principles of government."

Article 35 of the Spanish Charter further stipulates that the principles embodied in Article 12 "may be temporarily suspended in part or in whole by the government by means of a decree which must define the scope and duration of this measure." Article 36 warns, "Any violation of any of the rights proclaimed in this charter will be punished by laws which will determine, in each case, the actions that may be taken in its defense before the competent jurisdictions."

In Greece, the birthplace of democracy, Article 14 of the 1911 Constitution as revised by the Fourth Revisionary Assembly and readopted on January 1, 1952, says: "Any person may publish his opinion orally, in writing or in print with due adherence to the laws of the state. The press is free. Censorship and every other preventive measure is prohibited. The seizure of newspapers, either before or after publication, is likewise prohibited."

But, the Constitution continues:

By exception, seizure after publication is permitted (a) because of insult to the Christian religion or indecent publications manifestly offending public decency, in the cases provided by law, (b) because of insult to the person of the King, the successor to the Throne, their wives or their offspring, (c) if the contents of the publication according to the terms of the law be of such a nature as to (1) disclose movements of the armed forces of military significance or fortifications of the country, (2) be manifestly rebellious or directed against the territorial integrity of the nation or constitute an instigation to commit a crime of high treason.

Similarly, the constitution of Ireland by way of exception says, "The publication or utterance of blasphemous, seditious or indecent matter ... shall be punishable according to law." The Belgian constitution reserves the "power to suppress offenses committed in the use of (this) liberty." The constitution of Norway prohibits publication in contempt of religion, morality, or the constitutional power, or false or defamatory accusations against any other person. While the constitutions of Germany, Mexico, Cuba, Nicaragua, Venezuela, and India explicitly forbid the publication of libel, obscenity, or other material harmful to public morality, other constitutions make provision for restrictions through such a phrase as "except as provided by law."

The Indian constitution acknowledges that there cannot be any such thing as absolute and uncontrolled liberty and makes provisions authorizing the state to restrict the exercise of the freedom guaranteed under Clause 1, Article 19, within the limits specified. Thus, Clause 2, Article 19, as subsequently amended under the First Amendment to the Constitution, enables the legislature to impose reasonable restrictions on the exercise of freedom of speech and expression in the interests of the security of the state, friendly relations with foreign states, public order, decency, or morality; or in relation to contempt of court, defamation, or incitement to an offense.

Security Laws. No country allows the press total freedom in the publication of information. Even the publication of truth is not always in society's interest. The publication of news which might endanger national security is everywhere prohibited. Infringement of such prohibition may constitute the crime of treason or espionage, or that of divulging the secrets of national defense, or secrets involving relations with other states, or other official secrets.

All states punish treason, espionage, and violations of state security. Such offenses are of many different kinds, including: betrayal to a foreign power of personnel, military installations, war material, and strategic or technical information pertaining thereto; disclosure of information concerning the government's espionage and counterespionage apparatus and/or activities; and the communication of documents, plans, or other information relating to the national defense or to the safety or order of the country.

Press Laws. Press laws deal specifically with the rights and restrictions of the press. Most of the press laws throughout the world are more restrictive than protective, as exemplified by those in such countries as Turkey, India, and many of the Middle Eastern and Latin American countries. However, some actually stress the press's rights and make them explicit, as is the case in Sweden. Typical of the stricter press laws are the "desacato" laws of Latin America which prevent the press from being "disrespectful" to government officials. The United States, Belgium, Switzerland, and Britain have no press laws.

Penal Laws. The penal laws are usually just and require the press to accept responsibility for its published material; but they do not require censorship. These laws can be restrictive, however, when such phrases as "incitement to disorder" are too strictly interpreted, or when provisions dealing with defamation are too harsh, or when the stamp of "immoral publication" is applied too widely and too often. Moreover, in some nations inaccurate news can be the basis of immediate press punishment.

Freedom of the press exists in varying degrees in most countries, but in all these the journalist who abuses it and goes beyond certain limits commits an offense under civil and/or criminal law. No country allows the press total freedom with respect to information. Prohibition to publish is found to a greater or lesser degree in the press and/or penal laws of every country.

In most countries the law forbids malicious slander or libel—that is, statements, whether true or false, maliciously intended to damage the honor or reputation of private individuals. The Mexican Press Law, Article 9, goes quite far in this matter; it prohibits the publication of information dealing with adultery, indecent behavior, rape, attacks on private life, divorce, paternity or maternity, or annulment of marriage. As is also the case in many states of the United States, Mexican law does not allow the publication of the names of the victims in cases of rape or indecent behavior. Many jurisdictions make it illegal to report offenses committed by juveniles.

In Japan both civil and criminal codes prohibit both libel and obscenity and provide penalties therefor. By the Juvenile Law of 1948, Article 61, Japan prohibits publication of any material identifying juvenile delinquents, and, by Article 148 (Paragraph 2) of the Election Law, Japan forbids the publication of news designed to influence an election. Article 148 (Paragraph 3) of the same law prohibits the publication of the results of election polls.

Nearly all countries forbid publishing information likely to impede the course of justice. Some countries forbid publishing evidence until it is heard in open court; but every country where the press is free permits publishing the actual proceedings. Among the severe restrictions found in most countries are laws prohibiting the publication of news or comment likely to bring a court of law into contempt. In some countries the press may not criticize any legal decision before, during, or after the hearing.

Economic and political pressures. One of the less apparent means of abridging the freedom of the press is through economic controls and pressures. Governments have exerted these economic pressures by offering bribes and subsidies to newspapers and journalists, by granting progovernment publications special favors and privileges, by placing official advertising in friendly papers and withholding it from antigovernment papers, by selectively distributing newsprint, by restricting newspaper distribution in the case of antigovernment papers, and by giving grants of various kinds to selected newspapermen. One or more of these techniques are common in most parts of the world, and are especially prominent in Southeast Asia, Latin America, and the Middle East.

Because of the high costs of production and distribution, the governments of many countries with economies based on private enterprise make available to the press both direct and indirect subsidies. In the United States and most other countries, newspapers and periodicals enjoy lower postal rates. In Italy and several other countries of Europe, journalists are granted reduced railway fares, and publications occasionally receive subsidies and reductions in taxes. Grants are also made to news agencies. In other countries publications often receive preferred exchange treatment, government-subsidized newsprint imports, advertising subsidies, etc.

Obviously all these measures of economic assistance can be used as instruments to exert pressure on the press. The exercise of such pressures is common in many countries of the world and is especially prominent in Southeast Asia, Latin America, and the Middle East.

But there are countries with authoritarian regimes or with authoritarian tendencies that use such economic intervention as an instrument of control. Portugal, for example, has used restrictive or discriminatory measures such as subsidies to government papers and the inequitable distribution of newsprint.

Authoritarian regimes in Latin America often have found economic regulations useful in controlling the press. In Argentina the Perón regime used a wide range of such powers; and in Colombia, the dictator Rojas Pinilla chose these quieter and more subtle methods of muzzling the press—notably through the control of newsprint.

In Bolivia, the government's actual control of newspapers is chiefly exercised through its control of newsprint, which is used as a sword of Damocles over the heads of editors who might be tempted to criticize the government or its officials. The government office for the control of the news is copied from the similar institution create by Perón. Bolivia's state-controlled trade unions (COB) have also been used against nonconformist newspapers, and it is often from this quarter that demands for suppressions and closures originate.

As has been seen in the discussion of the legal position of the press in Communist countries, the economic adjunct of the constitutional guarantee limits the means of production (plant, equipment, paper, and other materials) to the Communist Party or its auxiliaries.

A Soviet law of 1932 which interprets and implements the economic corollary of the constitutional guarantee states that printing offices of any kind, including those using duplicating machines as well as those dealing in printing equipment, may be maintained only by government agencies, cooperatives, and public organizations. Moreover, even government agencies must obtain special permits to acquire printing equipment or to use printing offices and are held strictly accountable for supplies of paper, inks, type metal, and other necessities.

The distribution of newspapers to the appropriate sections of society is also regulated. Only 10 percent of a newspaper's edition is sold in the street. The rest is distributed according to a detailed plan. Each republic and region of the country receives a fixed quota of papers published in Moscow. Local distribution is arranged so that Party and Komsomol officials are first to receive newspapers, and administrative and economic units are next. It is almost impossible for a private person to subscribe to one of the chief newspapers. A Soviet citizen cannot simply buy or subscribe to the paper of his choice; he receives the paper that is specified for him according to the plan.

In China and the Communist states of Eastern Europe the governments have taken firm control of the press, and a major part of this control is exercised by economic means. In each country the regime or the Party has taken ownership of the principal and best printing plants. And even in those nominally independent printing plants, all the materials needed for printing—paper, inks, metals— are owned by the state and may be obtained only by allocations, much in the Soviet pattern.

Secrecy. Of the various forms of secrecy limiting the people's right to know, interference with the right to get information ("first in order of its importance") is the most subtle and at the same time the most erosive. This type of indirect pressure, taking the form of hindering press access to government sources and records, is quite common throughout the world press systems.

Governments attempt to do this in varying degrees everywhere. It has been, and is today, a special irritant to the libertarian press which tries to inform the citizens of government activities. The United States and other libertarian-press nations in recent years have seen increasing government evasiveness and overclassification of documents and papers. Press conferences scheduled and directed by the government are becoming more and more popular, because they may be used to channel such news as it desires to the readers. This tends to place the government in the position of news determiner and relieves the press of most of its initiative and independence in the investigation of government affairs. This situation is often attributable to the press's own inertia; for example, Marquis W. Childs (American columnist) has said that although government "constantly threatens to circumscribe and curtail the right of the people to know" and "secrecy becomes an end in itself," this freedom is "threatened not so much from without as from within." He adds: "The corrosive blight of conformity has spread where nonconformity was once the measure of courageous performance.

Direct Censorship and Force. This is common in the communist and other dictatorial nations. There are various forms of this type of forceful pressure such as official censorship, warnings and instructions to publishers and editors, an obligation of the press—as in Spain—to publish government handouts, use of harassment and violence in dealing with the press—as exemplified by politically inspired mob actions, strikes, and demands for direct intervention of Cuban and Bolivian trade unions, and Perón's tactics in dealing with hostile Argentine newspapers such as *La Prensa*.

PRINT MEDIA: WORLD OVERVIEW

Throughout the world, when one talks of journalism, one predominantly has in mind the press—a term that generally connotes newspapers. Journalism itself is a semantically fuzzy term; and when projected upon a global screen, it takes on special distortions and specialized meanings. But it still retains its core meaning: activities and enterprises concerned with conveying news and interpretation of news —along with liberal doses of promotion, propaganda, entertainment, and human-interest features—to mass and specialized audiences.

When we think of journalism, we think of media of mass communications—mainly newspapers, magazines, radio and television. Further, we think of activities by these media which are related to a news orientation, a concern with informing rather than with entertaining, although it is not possible ever to completely separate the two.

The Press: The Big Picture

A consideration of journalism immediately leads us to a look at the press. Generally, the term "press" connotes the print media—and even more specifically newspapers. So let us say a few general things about newspapers globally.

Nobody really knows how many newspapers are published throughout the world. There are estimates, of course. UNESCO and other organizations from time to time put out figures. Taking many of these estimates into consideration, we would propose that it is reasonable to say that close to 60,000 newspapers are published today, with a total circulation of perhaps 500 million. About 8,000 of these newspapers are dailies. The readership, of course, is likely to be three or four times the circulation because of the practice of passing copies on to others, posting them, and putting them in libraries.

At least one-third of all newspapers are found in North America. Another third are in Europe (including the USSR), and the other third are scattered throughout the rest of the world. Europe probably accounts for about half the world's total newspaper circulation, North America, a quarter; and the rest of the world, another quarter.

When one considers that in addition to newspapers, there is a magazine and assorted periodical press of gigantic proportions, one can readily see that the print media of mass communications have the potential of great power and influence in creating, stabilizing, and changing world opinion. And if, in addition, one takes into consideration the potent electronic media of radio and television that gird the globe and reach even the illiterates, the communications impact on international thought is magnified beyond conception.

Newspapers are being hurt everywhere by the high cost of newsprint, inflated prices for equipment, restraints on press freedom, and difficulties with trade unions. Advertising and subscription rates (in capitalist and mixed societies) are not keeping pace with rising costs in production. So there are serious financial problems on the newspaper scene everywhere.

The world's newspapers are quite diverse with respect to emphases and content, although chain ownership and certain economic facts are making more and more newspapers similar. There are still, however, vast differences among them.

In capitalist nations newspapers normally devote from 40 to 65 percent of their total space to news and editorial matter. The rest is taken up by advertising. In addition to advertising and news, the typical newspaper provides its readers with such items as features, photographs, editorials and essays, columns, letters to the editor, invited and free-lance contributions, news analyses, long verbatim speeches, government announcements, comic strips and cartoons, crosswords and other puzzles, weather reports and maps, horoscopes and other journalistic fluff, stock-market charts and graphs of various kinds, and a potpourri of editorial tidbits.

In Communist countries newspapers are far more serious than are those in capitalist nations. They are puritanical in their news presentation, giving little or no sensational news of crime, disasters, and the like. Usually they are filled with official pronouncements, news of development and progress, and stinging editorial propaganda against the non-Communist world.

In the so-called Third World countries, the papers are normally small and poorly printed and are struggling economically. Some of the papers resemble capitalist journals and others more often resemble those of communist nations. They are certainly inconsistent, by and large: The same paper may play up Western-style sensationalism and also give prominence to long essays and articles about national development. In journalistic techniques, if not always in politics, these nations are really nonaligned.

Growth of newspapers and their readership is stagnant in the developing Third World, according to UNESCO. In Africa there are still countries with no daily newspapers at all; and in all but 10 African countries, the average daily circulation is less than 20 copies per 1,000 people. Newspapers remain an urban and elite form of communication in the developing countries. Even here, however, newspaper defenders insist that newspapers are far more important than the circulations might indicate. For example, citizens reached by newspapers are the most knowledgeable and influential in their countries; what does appear in the press is often repeated by broadcast media, and newspapers pass through many more hands in a developing country than in an advanced Western nation.

Countries with the highest newspaper readership rates are Britain, Norway, Denmark, Sweden, Japan, and the United States. All these have rates of more than 200 copies of dailies published per 1,000 persons. The average circulation of dailies per 1,000 persons (for the world as a whole) is between 90 and 100.

In most of the world's nations, daily newspapers are very small (if they exist at all) and crude, having only four pages. Only in some 25 countries can dailies be found with as many as 12 pages. More than 25 percent of the world's dailies are English-language publications. Next to English the greatest number of dailies are published in Chinese, followed by German and then Spanish.

Despite many barriers to newspaper growth around the world, the press is growing. New publications are springing up on every continent, many of them catering to specialized audiences. In Europe the press has been growing more slowly since 1970, but it is still vigorous in spite of many economic problems. In Africa, South America, and Asia newspapers are generally small and struggling, but their quality is slowly improving as more young people are getting journalistic training.

Cities of the world which might be considered the chief press centers because of the number and quality of the newspapers printed there include London, New York, Paris, Moscow, Amsterdam, Copenhagen, Stockholm, Brussels, Rome, Hamburg, Vienna, Zurich, Peking, Tokyo, Cairo, Johannesburg, Toronto, Melbourne, Havana, Mexico City, Rio de Janeiro, Buenos Aires, and Bogotá.

The world's largest daily papers are found in Britain, Japan, and the Soviet Union, with Britain's *Daily Mirror* and *Daily Express*, Japan's *Asahi* and *Mainichi*, and the USSR's *Pravda* and *Izvestia* having the greatest circulations. Nations having at least one daily newspaper with a circulation of 3 million or more are Great Britain, Japan, West Germany, China, and the USSR.

Following are the cities of the world which have the greatest number of daily newspapers: Tokyo, Buenos Aires, Beirut, Djakarta, Karachi, Lahore, Rio de Janeiro, São Paulo, Bombay, Istanbul, Mexico City, Havana, and Berlin (East and West combined), with 20 to 30 papers; Paris, Tel Aviv, Taipei, Hong Kong, London, New York, Moscow, Rome, Milan, Amsterdam, Vienna, Copenhagen, Stockholm, Calcutta, Cairo, Warsaw, Montevideo, and Santiago, with 10 to 20 papers.

The largest-circulation dailies in some of the major nations are *Daily Mirror* (Britain), *Bild-Zeitung* (West Germany), *Il Corriere della Sera* (Italy), *Asahi* (Japan), *Ren Min Rih Bao* (Red China), *Pravda* (USSR), *Times of India* (India), *France-Soir* (France), *ABC* (Spain), *New York Daily News* (United States), *La Prensa* (Argentina), *Toronto Daily Star* (Canada), *Excélsior* (Mexico), *O Globo* (Brazil), *Le Soir* (Belgium), *Berlingske Tidende* (Denmark), *Het Vrije Volk* (Holland), *Aftenposten* (Norway), *Dagens Nyheter* (Sweden), *Rand Daily Mail* (Union of South Africa), and *Sun News Pictorial* (Australia).

Among the most influential weekly newspapers in the world are the following: *Die Zeit* (West Germany), *Manchester Guardian Weekly* (Britain), *Die Weltwoche* (Switzerland), *Ecclesia* (Spain), *La Patrie du Dimanche* (Canada), *Weekly Star* (Canada), *Sunday Times* (South Africa). Britain has the greatest number of large weekly newspapers of any nation in the world. There are four British weeklies (Sunday papers) which have circulation of 2 million or over. The *News of the World* is the largest of these Sunday papers. Having worldwide prestige among the British Sundays are the *London Observer* and London's *Sunday Times*.

The periodical press of the world is extremely varied in type, quality, and scope. Magazines and journals range from the popular illustrateds of Germany and Italy to the ultraserious journal of the *New Yorker* type. Magazines and journals come and go continuously, are begun and die out; so it is impossible to say how many are published throughout the world. Some of the so-called periodicals really come out irregularly and have no real publishing schedule. But throughout the world, there is a wide variety of journals and magazines catering to many audiences. There are newsmagazines of the *Time* and *Newsweek* pattern such as West Germany's *Der Spiegel* and Japan's *Shukan Asahi*. And here and there around the world one can see magazines of the news variety, but featuring photographic rather than verbal coverage. *Paris-Match* of France is a leading example. Journals of serious intellectual discussion can be found—mainly in Europe and North America.

Leading magazines and other periodicals will be mentioned later in this book as the various world regions are discussed. Here it should be noted that the international publication pattern runs on through the periodical spectrum from the ultraserious and quality journals into the purely entertainment magazines, confessions, hobbies, comics, offbeat art journals, and romance and adventure magazines. The world reader in most countries thus has a wide assortment of periodicals to choose from if he desires to supplement his newspaper reading.

International Quality Newspapers

Quality (or elite) journalism is that which has an impact with intellectuals and opinion leaders throughout the world. It is journalism which diplomats, educators, writers, theologians, economists, and scientists take seriously. It is the kind of journalism which libraries and universities in all countries feel must be made available to their students. It is the kind of journalism, in every country, that serves as a kind of model for the mainstream serious journalists and newspapers. It is that which is most quoted, alluded to, and respected; in short, it is that which has the biggest impact on the serious thinking of a nation, on basic decision-making vis-à-vis a nation's own government and other governments.

Quality journalism is thereby found in so-called quality newspapers of the world. These newspapers are dedicated to being journalistic opinion leaders, to having a real impact on national and world policy, to being respected by serious, educated, and concerned citizens for their thoroughness, balance, integrity; and all desire to serve as role models for other newspapers in their societies.

Quality, or elite, newspapers must have influence—at least they must be taken seriously—not only in their own countries but also in other countries. These elite papers may be essentially of two types: (1) those published in free or libertarian nations, and (2) those published in controlled or authoritarian nations. Each group of elite papers is dedicated to its particular press philosophy and takes its responsibilities, as it sees them, very seriously. Therefore, it is evident that such a binary classification system is too simple in reality and that all papers everywhere are free to varying degress and restricted to varying degrees, although the character of freedom and restraint may differ greatly.

Considerable emphasis is often placed today on social responsibility in determining the elite status of a newspaper. To what degree is the paper socially responsible? The quality or eliteness of a newspaper, many feel, depends on the answer to this question. In the United States and other Western democracies, social responsibility is thought of generally in terms of freedom from governmental control—coupled with some sense of doing the right thing at the right time. In other words, social responsibility is the press utopia through which only libertarian-oriented publications may pass.

Although this concept was propagated by the Hutchins Commission (more properly known as the Commission on Freedom of the Press) in 1947 and more recently in a number of articles and books (e.g., Siebert, Peterson, and Schramm's *Four Theories of the Press*), it is perhaps far too simple a concept and may be unsatisfactory in the modern world of fragmented and pluralistic serious journalism.

The question might be asked, for example, if the authoritarian or Communist presses are not responsible to their societies. In fact, in certain respects, a newspaper would be more responsible if some type of monolithic supervision existed to maintain social harmony and stability. So it is possible to propose that all newspapers (of any political system) which reflect the philosophy of their governmental system and try to present serious educational reading fare are being socially responsible. This, of course, may seem unreasonable or even "treasonable" in the Western democracies, but its unreasonableness tends to fade away when projected onto the screen of international journalism.

With the foregoing considerations in mind, it is well to consider how the elite press is scattered geographically around the world. And if the reader wonders how certain newspapers come to be known as elite journals, it should be simply noted that their names emerge from many types of surveys and studies and from conversations with informed politicians, editors, professors, and the like who are serious students of the world press. A thoroughgoing discussion of the criteria of elite journalism and the members of this distinguished group of newspapers may be found in John Merrill's *The Elite Press* (1968) and *The World's Great Dailies* (by Merrill and Harold Fisher, 1980).

Asia, with the exception of China, Japan, and India, is virtually without an elite press. Japan stands out among the three for its high development of, and progress in, quality journalism—and popular journalism, too, for that matter. *Asahi Shimbun* is certainly the best quality daily in Japan and indicates that an elite paper can, with editorial sagacity, develop a large circulation within a free-market press system. *Pravda* and *Izvestia* (USSR) and their counterpart in Peking, *Ren Min Rih Bao* (People's Daily), of course, have fewer circulation problems, since Communist Party members and many others find that they need these daily journals of guidance and news.

India's problems relative to the elite papers are much more acute than are those in the USSR, China, or Japan. A multiplicity of languages (coupled, of course, with economic deficiencies) seems to be the main barrier to more and better elite journalism. At present the major elite papers of India are published in English, the three most important being the *Statesman* of Calcutta, the *Hindu* of Madras, and the *Times of India* published in Bombay and Delhi. In addition to the language problem, the Indian press must contend with a low literacy rate, an underdeveloped educational system, scarcity of training facilities and trained journalists, and old and crude printing equipment.

The continent of Africa, outside of Egypt in the north and the Republic of South Africa in the south, has no significant elite newspapers. Probably the best dailies of Africa and *Al Ahram* in Egypt and the *Rand Daily Mail* and *Die Burger* of South Africa. In the neighboring Middle East the press systems are mainly transitional—caught between the severe problems of many parts of Asia on the one hand and of Africa on the other. One hindrance to the development of an elite press in this area is that these nations are still not decided on whether they should have their press systems veer toward libertarianism and competition or toward authoritarianism and state planning. This will probably continue to be a real issue as long as the friction between Israeli and Arab forces exists.

When one turns to another underdeveloped region of the world—

Latin America—one is somewhat surprised to find a rather sizable group of good newspapers existing in spite of awesome economic and literacy problems. One explanation may be that Spanish is the almost common language of the Latin American press, whereas in both Asia and Africa the polyglot of languages and dialects makes the press development extremely difficult. Many Latin American dailies—such as Argentina's *La Prensa* and Chile's and Mexico's *Excélsior*—meet the demands of thinking readers for percipient and serious journalism.

In Oceania, Australia alone has a press which includes newspapers of the elite type. Such outstanding dailies as the *Age* of Melbourne, the *Herald* of that same city, and certainly the thriving serious national daily, the *Australian*, must be mentioned.

North America (above the Mexican border) has a large share of the world's elite newspapers. Exemplifying the elite press of Canada are the excellent dailies *Globe and Mail* of Toronto and the *Free Press* of Winnipeg. In the United States elite dailies appear in nearly every major section of the country; however, most of these are concentrated along the East Coast and in the Middle West. In the East are such sophisticated and articulate dailies as the *New York Times*, the *Washington Post*, the *Christian Science Monitor*, the *Baltimore Sun*, and the *Miami Herald*. In the Middle West are published such leading elites as the *St. Louis Post-Dispatch*, the *Minneapolis Tribune*, and *Kansas City Star*. Among southern elite papers there is the *Louisville Courier-Journal* and the *Atlanta Constitution*. Quality papers of national and worldwide prestige tend to fade out in the plains and mountain areas of the American West. Along the West Coast, however, there are the *Los Angeles Times* (undoubtedly the best daily in the West) and a few other near-elite such as the *Portland Oregonian*.

Western Europe has the world's most developed elite press. From Scandinavia to Spain, and from Britain to Russia, elite dailies (and weeklies) saturate the continent with serious journalism and spread their influence into distant lands. The elite dailies of Europe are probably the most erudite and knowledgeable in the world, providing insights available nowhere else.

Many types of quality papers are to be found in Europe. There are the free elite of most of Western Europe—led by the superserious *Neue Zürcher Zeitung* of Switzerland, *Le Monde* of France, *The Times* and the *Guardian* of Britain, and *Die Welt* and *Frankfurter Allgemeine* of West Germany. *ABC, El Pais* of Spain, and the Communist elite such as *Pravda* and *Izvestia* of Russia and *Politika* of Yugoslavia represent the prestigious controlled or authoritarian press of Europe.

The continent has such dailies as the Scandinavian *Aftenposten* of Oslo, *Berlingske Tidende* of Copenhagen, and *Dagens Nyheter* of

Stockholm, which blend their heavy diets of serious news and views with rather flashy typography without loss of influence and dignity. In Italy is the comprehensive *Il Corriere della Sera* of Milan and *La Stampa* of Turin, examples of serious free journalism; and there is also in Vatican City the influential voice of the Papacy—*L'Osservatore Romano*. Without a doubt, the elite press of Europe is the most pluralistic in all the world, with a wide selection of dailies and weeklies providing many political orientations and special appeals demanded by the serious newspaper reader.

Elite newspapers of the world are but one aspect or part of the world's press. Popular or mass-appeal papers are sprinkled liberally across the globe and obviously have their own kind of impact on mass culture and popular taste. They, together with a sizable group of middle-area papers (located somewhere between the mass appeal and the elite), form the great bulk of the world's newspapers. However, it is well to keep in mind as one studies the press of each country that it is really the state of elite newspapers in that country which offers the best insights into the health and general level of journalism.

Press Freedom

Among students of the world press and among institutes and organizations making it their concern to study such matters as freedom of the press, government controls, press responsibility, and press pluralism, there appears to be a consensus that press freedom is losing ground all through the world. Every year the surveys indicate that the press everywhere is becoming more controlled except in a few scattered countries.

Surveys by such organizations as the Associated Press and the InterAmerican Press Association regularly paint a dismal picture of deteriorating press freedom in most parts of the world. These are quick to make the point that Western concepts of press freedom are certainly not accepted everywhere and that there are many semantic problems in dealing with this subject. All the students of press freedom are also quick to note that although press freedom (from a United States viewpoint) is generally being lost throughout the world, there are regions where it is holding its own or even improving slightly.

North America has a great amount of press freedom. Latin America has very little. Europe is highly polarized, with the nations of Western Europe largely enjoying very free press systems and the countries of Eastern Europe going to the other extreme.

Like Europe, the Middle East is polarized into free press and controlled press camps. But unlike Europe the press is facing increased restrictions. Many of the emerging nations of Africa and Asia are in a state of flux, generally gravitating toward more control. This is reflected in their press systems, too, where controls are exerted in the name of responsibility, stability, or national goals. The Australian press system is remarkably free, and so are those of Japan, New Zealand, and Singapore. In Africa no press system can be considered very free. South Africa exhibits characteristics of press freedom, but large percentages of the population have no access to the press at all.

TELECOMMUNICATIONS: WORLD OVERVIEW

The vast majority of the world's people are within listening and viewing range of radio and television stations. And it is probably safe to say that for the first time, more people have access to radio transmissions than those who do not. Despite jamming, censorship, and inadequate reporting, world broadcasting tends to saturate the globe. If freedom of information existed in a majority of the world's nations, then the gigantic system of telecommunications might well be considered a genuine hope for the spreading of information and news of a useful and reliable sort.

But the number of free-radio nations is in the minority. And because of this, a crowded, semiliterate, impoverished world will continue to be partially informed, and thus partially propagandized. Broadcasting can jump mountains, can diminish the isolation of villages without roads, and can penetrate the minds of those who cannot read. But just as with the press, the transmitting media must be free of governmental and private restraints for reporters and editors to fully accomplish their mission—to inform. At least this is the libertarian perspective.

Even in its less-than-perfect state, broadcasting reaches millions of people who otherwise would have no link with the mainstream of global affairs. When one considers the prevalence of group (or public) listening, mobile millions who listen on small transitor sets, plus the countless numbers who have individual receivers inside their homes and offices, it is not difficult to realize how potent and significant broadcasting really is.

Radio is the dominant mass medium in the Third World, having expanded greatly over the past 30 years. Although precise figures are hard to get, it is safe to say that a great majority of people in Latin America have regular access to radio, as do sizable minorities of Asians and Africans. Most are exposed to local and national programming, although millions listen to international shortwave broadcasts. In most countries radio has an urban orientation, often failing to serve rural people's needs. UNESCO has pointed out that in all nations, radio that is oriented toward education and national development averages only about 5 percent of air time; the bulk of programming is entertainment-oriented.

Rise of Television

Television got a limited start in Britain, France, and the United States before World War II, but it did not become a genuine mass medium until after 1945. Not until a decade later did rapid expansion in stations, programs, and receiver distribution take place, even in some of the most economically developed nations.

For example, at the beginning of 1953, there were only 60,000 television sets in France, giving it the lowest ratio of receivers per family of any nation in Europe. The dramatic birth of Eurovision in 1953, with its initial special telecast of the coronation of Britain's Queen Elizabeth II, engendered a French demand for more domestic expansion of video. But during the following year the French National Assembly approved only a 5-year plan for very slow growth of the government network. This plan reflected the government's fear that television newsreels of the unpopular Algerian war might inflame negative public opinion more than would the less graphic radio reports. Since 1958, when General Charles de Gaulle became president, the French government has expanded French TV greatly; and today it is a powerful force in France and on the European continent.

In the mid-1950s, video began to leap forward in other developed nations. In 1955 Parliament finally permitted competition for the BBC-TV; privately owned commercial television stations, serving provincial viewing areas, went on the air and at certain prime-time hours hooked together as a national network. The sluggish BBC noncommercial network then felt it had to add its own second network with revitalized informational and entertainment programs.

The British adoption of commercial TV, in a country which had symbolized noncommercial broadcasting, prompted other prosperous nations similarly oriented to reexamine their own broadcasting postures in terms of harnessing advertising revenue to broadcasting growth.

By the late 1960s, in the more economically developed nations, except for the Soviet Union—even in countries where an older radio pattern had tied broadcasting to governmental noncommercial networks—commercial inroads were made in order to finance some video variety for the viewer. Unlike less expensive radio, television could not multiply its offerings without some private funds to supplement public funds. And even in the USSR, commercial announcements for GUM stores and other governmental sales entities began to appear on the video screen.

In the Third World, radio—not television—remained the major broadcasting medium, but television had become a prestige symbol. Like a national airline, a TV network gave emotional status to nations sensitive about their meager image in a world of rich nations and poor nations. So even in the poorer nations of the world, television is continuing to expand rapidly. Even so, some 25 countries in Asia and Africa have no TV. When television does exist outside the developed West, it is confined mainly to cities and reaches elite populations. Programming in the Third World is largely imported, much of it from the United States. However, there is a trend toward national TV production centers, such as in Mexico and Egypt, which produce programming of increasing appeal to their own people and to neighboring countries. However, television promises to continue for some time being a global medium with a high degree of foreign cultural influence.

Some Asian, African, and Latin American nations might have been wiser to put their scarce funds into radio expansion entirely rather than draining appropriations to the more costly television systems. But the governments in question were more interested in soothing nationalistic inferiority complexes among the have-nots than in doing what might well have been more feasible in purely realistic and pragmatic terms. Television, however, has become a proof, or sign, of modernization throughout the world; and it is as understandable for a poor country to invest in TV as it is for a poor citizen of the Western world to do the same.

Differences: Systems and Languages

Global broadcasting systems vary considerably. Latin American republics have generally adopted the system of the United States—privately owned commercial radio and television stations. The British system, the famed public trust called the BBC, has been adapted with modifications by France, Italy, and several other European and Commonwealth nations.

The governmental broadcasting system, run directly by the regime in power and symbolized by the Soviet Union, China, and other Marxist nations, has been copied with some modifications by many African and Asian countries. American influence can be seen by the coming of regional, commercial, privately owned networks to Britain, existing alongside the BBC-TV. Conversely, British influence can be found in the spread of educational or cultural noncommercial (public) television in the United States.

Even though from time to time France has claimed that its Radio Télévision Française (RTF) resembles the BBC, it differs in one important respect: the BBC is removed from political parties and regimes in office, whereas the RTF is tied to the Minister of Information, a cabinet member of the government in power.

Another variation of broadcasting systems is that of the Dutch. In Holland, listeners' societies own stations on a cooperative basis. There is a labor union broadcast society, as well as both Catholic and Protestant societies. Radio listening and television viewing in Holland measure lower than they do in other European countries, but book and magazine reading and theater attendance rates are among the world's highest.

A country with several languages cannot use radio to integrate and inform as readily as a monolingual nation can. Belgium, for example, broadcasting in Flemish and Walloon to its Dutch speakers and its French speakers, has this additional problem of languages; another example in Europe is Switzerland, broadcasting in German and French. But in an underdeveloped, overpopulated nation such as India, the problem of languages becomes especially acute. Switzerland and Belgium are highly literate and industrialized and have to contend with only a couple of languages. But in a country such as India the people are mostly illiterate and poor and have some 16 different languages and dozens of minor dialects to contend with.

At least half the member nations of the United Nations not only have broadcasting systems for domestic audiences but also deliberately beam programs to one or more foreign nations. We tend to think of international broadcasting in terms of the two most famous exponents: the Voice of America and Radio Moscow's shortwave services. Of course, we remember from time to time the pioneering of the BBC of Britain in global radio with its overseas services. And we are becoming increasingly aware of the extensive international broadcasting being done by China.

Moreover, there are nongovernmental private radio stations parallelling the United States' Voice of America. Radio Free Europe's transmitters beam to the Communist satellites of Eastern Europe. RFE laughs at the Communists and reveals truths they try to hide from the citizens of such countries as Hungary, Bulgaria, Rumania, Poland, and Czechoslovakia. Similarly, Radio Free Asia confronts China.

Every year the global total of radio receivers jumps 100,000 sets or more. With more than half the adults in the world not able to read well enough to decipher a newspaper headline, the importance of radio communication—and to an increasing extent television communication—becomes self-evident.

Television News Agencies

The world's largest television news agency is VISNEWS (Vision News), created in 1957 by the BBC. Its headquarters are in London. The agency has four regular daily satellite feeds of news—three from London and one from New York. This news reaches subscribers in Australia, New Zealand, Japan, Hong Kong, and South America; from some of these points the news flow is expanded through videocassettes sent to other nearby television stations not getting direct satellite transmission.

This news agency permits subscribers to get news the same day it happens, thereby decreasing use of film shipments which have delayed news two or three days. VISNEWS service contains feature and background stories and reports of national success and achievement, not only hard news. Staff members are stationed in most of the major world capitals. The agency is seen as having great potential for equalizing news flow throughout the world; it has been especially welcomed by UNESCO and some third world countries. But it is still too expensive for poorer nations.

VISNEWS is owned by BBC, Reuters, and the triumvirate of Canadian Broadcasting Corporation, the Australian Broadcasting Corporation, and the Broadcasting Corporation of New Zealand. VISNEWS has some 400 (part-time) cameramen in the field. They gather stories on film and videotape from around the world for transmission via satellite. The agency is the world's principal supplier of international news film. It has 16 bureaus globally and a staff of some 400, including about 25 full-time cameramen. It has reciprocal agreements with other television operations all over the world, and claims to cover 99 percent of the world's TV receivers.

The main rival of VISNEWS is UPITN. This is a transnational enterprise which combines UPI and the British Independent Television News (ITN). The agency is growing very rapidly, with its services being used by more than 200 TV stations in more than 70 countries, and its transmissions being accessible to some 90 percent of the world. Like VISNEWS, it uses satellites for news transmission.

UPITN has a newtork of editorial offices in Washington, D.C., New York, London, Paris, Frankfurt, Rome, Salisbury, and Hong Kong. London is UPITN's main center. Through UPI bureaus the agency has representation in almost every country. About 50 camera crews of many nationalities supplemented by nearly 500 free-lancers globally cover the day's news.

Despite the positive aspects of these two big transnational television agencies, they have their critics. Many deplore the whole idea of transnational companies and their dominating effects. Third World nations increasingly complain about the corroding effects of transnational media on their cultures. With the communication electronic technology permitting nations such as the United States to transmit programs directly to receivers over the globe, the complaints are likely to grow. More outside information will flow into a Third World country and such information capable of being received directly will moreover be much harder for governments to examine and control. So concern is expected to grow.

A Word About Satellites

Communication satellites are used today for national and worldwide communication, and are becoming ever more important. The concept of one world through these satellites appears to be growing. A communication satellite is simply a relay station in space that can be used to provide either intranational or international communication.

Most are placed in a circular orbit some 40,000 kilometers above the earth, completing a revolution of their orbit every 24 hours; they are called synchronous satellites. When the orbital path lies entirely within the plane of the earth's equator, the orbit is called equatorial. A synchronous satellite in equatorial orbit is referred to as geostationary because to an observer on the ground it appears to be motionless.

Two well-spaced satellites of this type can see almost all the inhabitable regions of the earth. Because of their flexibility and diversity of applications, satellites are highly effective tools of mass communication; each one normally has a number of transponders or repeaters. A typical satellite has twelve. Usually there is a transponder for each television channel to be distributed; they can be assigned and reassigned from the ground to provide any desired mix of communication services for public and private use.

Intelsat is a system of satellite used by many nations. It began in 1964. A consortium of some 85 nations owns and operates this commercial satellite system, with each member nation voting proportionate to its share of Intelsat traffic. Different countries tend to use Intelsat in proportion to their economic and international relations with other countries, which means that the heaviest use occurs in the Atlantic region. Because the United States has been the biggest user of Intelsat, it has paid more than 50 percent of the total cost of Intelsat since its beginning.

Global "Informatics" Concern

Beyond their concern for satellite transmissions from the more wealthy Western nations, the Third World countries are taking an increased interest in legislation which would control the kind of data that companies and other organizations store in computers. Storage and data flow around the globe is a growing issue as the use of computers and satellites proliferates.

By regulating the information stored in computer banks as well as the flow of data from computers across borders, the Third World hopes to benefit its developing information industries and to at least slow down the domination of those in the industrialized world. The big multinational corporations, especially in the United States, are seen as flooding the world every day with great masses of information.

For one thing, some countries are passing privacy laws that would stipulate the kinds of data that may be computerized and would specify exactly who would be permitted to inspect the data. But the world debate over data flow goes further than privacy. Some nations worry about the fact that they send too much information to other nations for processing and that they rely too heavily on other countries for computer services. Information flow is becoming a big issue not only among the United States and other industrialized nations but also among the developed and the underdeveloped world. UNESCO has become heavily involved.

The 1980 MacBride Commission recommended an overhaul of tariff structures for international information transmission, which according to the UNESCO-sponsored commission discriminates against the poor and developing nations. And it asked for better access to satellite systems for the developing countries. The MacBride report urged Third World nations to set up their own regional centers to receive and process computer data. One UNESCO agency, the Intergovernmental Bureau of Informatics (IBI) in Rome, is concerned exclusively with data traffic. It is now an independent agency with more than thirty member nations, most of which are in the Third World.

The IBI is undertaking an ambitious program to promote telematics (computer-based ways of processing and transferring information) as the "key to national survival" for Third World countries. Conferences are to be held by IBI for the purpose of discussing transborder data flows and their impact on "the international division of labor and technological concentration." The overriding concern, again, is the unbalanced information flow between developed and developing countries.

Third World nations are increasingly challenging the traditional

Western (mainly United States) dominance in world informatics. In 1979, for example, a group of African states claimed privileged access by any state to information on its national activities held in foreign databanks. Big American computer firms have been blasted by Nigeria and Iraq, among other nations, for their strategy of creating artificial obsolescence of information products to increase sales. With the growing sensitivity of the Third World to informatics and with the prompting and help of UNESCO, the next decade promises to be one of intensified battles in the whole field of global informatics.

A NEW "INFORMATION ORDER" FOR THE WORLD?

In the last century the ordering of global communications tended to be mainly along transatlantic lines. As has been pointed out earlier, the American and European news agencies sliced up the world into their own "preserves," which conformed to the political and economic areas of influence of the day.

When national liberation movements began after World War II to change political realities of the world—at least by making a substantial impact through concerted action in the United Nations—the old structure of domination of information by the American–European axis remained. And it is still basically intact. The Third World, or developing, nations contend that they cannot gain real independence until they are ushered into a more equitable and horizontal communications order.

Such feelings of communication domination by the West, very strongly ingrained in the Third World, has given rise to the concept of a New World Information Order, an idea which would largely eliminate the inequities in communication the world over and would bring the developing nations into the global information-sharing picture as partners rather than as helpless consumers.

The Issues of the Debate

Advocates of a new order for world information claim that, at the present time, the global coverage of foreign news is mainly in the hands of a few organizations, mainly in the United States (the AP, UPI, Reuters, AFP, *New York Times, Washington Post, Los Angeles Times,* CBS, NBC, ABC, *Time* and *Newsweek*). The critics of the existing old order also say that the Western media are too powerful, that their services are spotty and inadequate, that they reflect only Western attitudes and interests, and that they lack accuracy and objectivity.

UNESCO has become deeply involved in the new order debate; it is now committed to transforming the volume and content of international news flow so that the Third World nations will find their news and information more acceptable. Such a new order of communication should also help to break down the biased and unfavorable stereotypes of the developing countries which they see as being propagated by Western journalism.

At its Belgrade meeting in 1980, UNESCO adopted a resolution on the New World Information Order that reflected the belief of the Soviet block and Third World that it is the responsibility of nations to control the flow of news across their borders. The resolution would also define the role of journalists with a view toward licensing them and would move toward an international code of journalistic ethics. The Belgrade meeting and others like it are making one thing very clear: Western media are under attack throughout the world. In fact, many of the basic tenets of Western journalism—even the definition of news—are being challenged by the Third World nations and their supporters.

Western journalism is seen by increasing numbers of critics throughout the world as a tool for imperialism—at least cultural imperialism. Western reportage is considered to be biased and especially unfair to the Third World. In addition, large numbers of developing nations believe that they are well within their rights to use the press in promoting their political and social goals; therefore, they immediately clash head on with the concept of a free press as expressed by Western countries such as the United States.

The Third World nations think the Western version of news is wrong. They want positive news about them transmitted worldwide— not just news about catastrophes and government corruption. They want to break the Western monopoly over the world's news flow and to eliminate the inequity of coverage given different countries; they call for an "equilibriated" flow of world news.

With its tradition of a free press, the West sees the call for a new information order as a danger to press freedom and an invitation for government control of media systems—or at least a rationalization for such control. Seen by the West as a growing threat to journalistic freedom and to the free flow of information generally are all the research programs, seminars, debates, and Third World declarations leading to intergovernmental decisions.

Western journalists admit that there are valid criticisms of Western coverage of the Third World, but they feel that it is important to

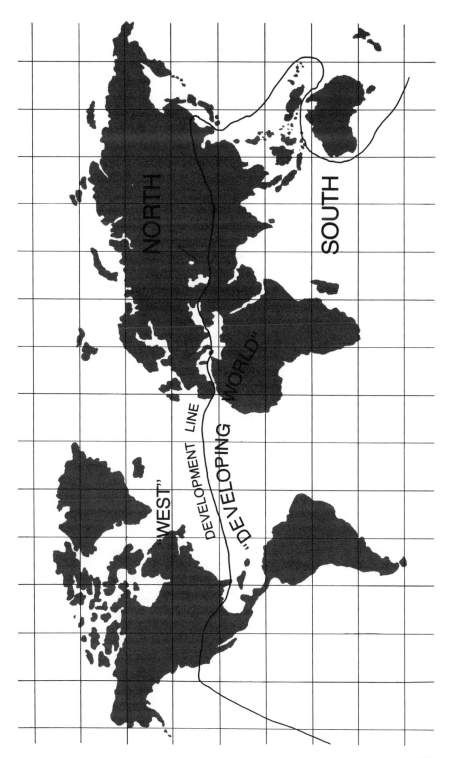

53

keep these criticisms apart from the highly politicized charges often heard at UNESCO and other conferences. And, say the Western journalists, whatever the complaints, government control of the media is no answer.

Participants in the Debate

In this entire international communication debate involving East, West, and the United Nations bureaucracy, it is not easy to keep up with the participants in the contest. Although some Western spokesmen see the whole debate as trivial and not worthy of great effort by Western journalists and communications scholars, it is nevertheless important and involves serious issues which will have important ramifications in the next decade or so. Just what groups are involved in this global debate or ideological communications contest?

Four major groups have been suggested and discussed by Leonard Sussman, executive director of Freedom House in New York City, who keeps up with this ongoing controversy and publishes and speaks regularly on the subject. As Sussman sees it, the participants —with different traditions, motivations and objectives—line up as follows:

Free-Press Advocates. The free-press advocates are led by the United States, the United Kingdom, and West Germany. Such countries accept the basic libertarian position of separation of press and state and believe in an open journalistic dialogue. Nations of this type appear to be a losing group; in 1981 a Freedom House survey showed that only 23 percent of the world's nations have media which can be regarded as free.

Soviet-Bloc and Third World–Marxist Countries. These countries push constantly for UNESCO declarations and global media procedures that would fulfill Lenin's requirement that the media be used for agitation and control of the masses. This group represents only 13 percent of all nations but wields great influence, for it exploits the fears and aspirations of the developing countries of the world.

Nonfree (Non-Marxist) Third World Nations. These countries make up about 40 percent of developing nations. Their main objective is keeping tight control over their citizens and their political and economic systems. About 50 countries around the world consider their communications media as tools to be used by government.

Free and Partly Free Developing Countries. Comprising the important swing bloc in the UNESCO debates, about 25 Third World nations have somewhat independent media (20 percent) and another 36 (30 percent) have partly free media. These are the moderate states (perhaps the only truly nonaligned countries) and cannot be counted on to vote as a bloc. However, it can be said that generally they are more prone to vote with other developing nations than with the free-press advocates of the West.

All in all, the lines appear to be rather well drawn in this global debate. The West is speaking out more forcefully, but appears willing to cooperate in giving technical assistance where needed and in helping in other substantial nonideological ways. At least the West has made its fundamental principles known to the world. In 1981, for example, representatives from more than 20 free press nations met in Talloires, France, and set forth basic principles on which free-press nations will not compromise. For the first time delegates from all parts of the world from large and small nations agreed on basic tenets of journalism.

These free-press principles are clear and precise, unlike many declarations which come from Marxist and Third World conferences: Journalists should not be licensed; no code of ethics or conduct for international communication should be developed; no censorship should be imposed on print or broadcast news, and free access should be allowed the mass media to news events whenever and wherever they occur. At the Talloires conference the delegates also agreed that "the time has come in UNESCO and other inter-governmental bodies to abandon attempts to regulate news content and formulate rules for the press."

This Western free-press perspective is perhaps most vigorously countered by the conferences and pronouncements of the International Organization of Journalists (IOJ), with headquarters in Prague, Czechoslovakia. In harmony with UNESCO, this group, which represents mainly the countries in group 2 of Sussman's typology of participants, is a constant critic of Western journalism, and its critiques are mainly couched in the well-worn Marxist jargon. The IOJ has done much to propagate and systematize the Third World chorus of criticism of Western journalism and to connect it with "imperialistic impulses" which would dominate the cultures and communications systems of the developing countries. The IOJ, of course, is a firm supporter of a New World Information Order.

Having serious reservations about such a new order and speaking for the Western position generally have been such Americans as Elie Abel of Columbia University, William Small of NBC News, and Leonard Marks of the World Press Freedom Committee. Abel, a member of the MacBride Commission, has said that most of the UNESCO–Third World rhetoric is designed to constrict rather than widen the global news flow. Small has pointed out that the New World Information Order would set governmental standards for "truly objective news selection" and establish a system for licensing of journalists.

"That is not in keeping with the Charter of the United Nations," Small has said, "nor is it in keeping with the role of a free press as we in the United States accept and perceive it." Small, like other Western critics of the new world order for communications, believes that it is "an attack on free press principles" and an attempt to help governments manipulate news flow.

Leonard Marks, general counsel of the United States' World Press Freedom Committee, recognizing well the dangers of the new order as suggested by the non-Western group, probably speaks for most Western journalists when he gives his idea of a new information order that would receive his approval:

> I favor a New World Information Order if it will result in a better understanding between people everywhere; if it will remove tensions which lead to war; if it improves the flow of information to and from developing countries; if it is designed to give people access to information about significant events affecting their welfare; if it acknowledges that there is a diversity in contemporary society; and if a New World Information Order is based on a tolerance for differing points of view.

It is not easy to say much more about the New World Information Order, for although thousands of words have been spilled in speeches, studies, conferences, articles, and books about it, such an order remains mystical, fuzzy, and undefined. It has rhetorical significance, of course, in the forums of international ideological debate, but thus far it has little meaning in the real world of journalism.

West's Reluctant Agreement

In late January, 1982, the West reluctantly agreed to support a Third World drive for a New World Information and Communication order but indicated a resolve to watch developments very closely and to keep a tight rein on the purse strings. Such an agreement came out of a UNESCO-sponsored meeting of 35 nations connected to the International Program for the Development of Communications (IPDC).

This week-long meeting in Acapulco, Mexico, was intended to make IPDC a viable, solid organization capable of aiding the underdeveloped nations of Africa, the Middle East, Asia, and Latin America develop their communications systems. The West, generally, conceded the need to help the Third World with their communications development, but only a few (notably France, Canada, and Norway) made monetary contributions to the IPDC general fund, which will be used by UNESCO in communications development.

In 1982 the prize project of UNESCO was the Pan-African News Agency (PANA) designed to serve 50 African nations in Arabic, French, and English when it achieves full operation. Western UNESCO members made it clear at the Acapulco meeting that they will be carefully watching PANA to see that it does not become simply a political instrument and that it is not poorly managed and run. PANA will be controlled by the information ministers of the 50 member states and all its funds will come from government sources.

African and Asian delegates at the Acapulco meeting assured the West that PANA and another regional news agency—the Asia News Network (ANN), which has received a UNESCO grant—will not interfere in any way with other international news operations (e.g., by AP or AFP) in their areas. The United States protested mildly about the Asia News Network with a "reservation" because when the ANN was formed in 1981, its executives suggested that the member states distribute international news through national news monopolies.

Despite Western reservations about such regional agencies and UNESCO aid to them, Western representatives seem to feel they must go along with such projects because almost every nation in the Third World bloc, the so-called Group of 77, solidly supports this kind of assistance. The debate goes on; the conference at Acapulco in 1982 settled nothing. Certain efforts by UNESCO will be started, but the financial base of support is weak and the ideological barriers between East and West (or North and South) have really lost none of their strength.

The MacBride Report

Many of the configurations of the new order are found in the voluminous and turgid MacBride Report (December, 1980). A commission was appointed back in 1976 by UNESCO's director general, Amadou Mahtar M'Bow, to conduct a study of world communications problems; it was to be composed of 16 members and officially was called the International Commission for the Study of Communication Problems. It was soon dubbed the MacBride Commission after its chairman, Sean MacBride, Irish statesman and lawyer and winner of both the Nobel and Lenin Prizes. It was to report to M'Bow in 1980.

The Commission members generally represented the ideological slant of UNESCO; only 6 of the 16 members reflected the Western (press–government separation) press philosophy. The group's report finally came out at the end of 1980 and although there was little concern with it among the general public, it caused considerable controversy in communications conferences and literature. By the end of 1981, however, it was gaining only slight attention.

Most readers consider it overly ambitious, ambiguous, and generally indigestible. It can be interpreted almost any way any reader wants to interpret it; however, most Western readers have felt that it is slanted toward government control of communications. Journalists, the report said, should be free, but at the same time they should promote friendly relations between states, foster cultural identity, support just causes, and do a number of other things. And governments, according to the report, should formulate "comprehensive communications policies" whereby, in short, communication was to become an "instrument for creating awareness of national priorities." Certainly, Western critics could see considerable danger in such policies for the Western brand of press freedom and could foresee a gravitation toward government control of communications.

So after all the rhetoric is in, here in a nutshell is what emerges: The West supports a free press separated from the state, and so do some of the developing countries; along with this they also believe that the press has a right to criticize government action and to air all points of view. The Soviet bloc, on the other hand, asserts that the state is all-powerful and that the press has a responsibility to support government and suppress dissent. Certainly, the New World Information Order is more than this; it includes many other issues; but in the main, all such issues relate to, and are derived from, this basic ideological dichotomy just summarized.

As the reader now proceeds into the more substantive regional overviews of journalism and communications concepts and practices, he will do well to keep in mind that everywhere today—in all the world's regions—there is a concern for the issues subsumed in this New World Information Order, and this concern permeates every aspect of theory and practice of global journalism.

PART 2

THE WORLD'S REGIONS
AND JOURNALISM

1 EUROPE AND THE MIDDLE EAST

PAUL S. UNDERWOOD

EUROPE: NONCOMMUNIST

As far as media are concerned, Europe, like Julius Caesar's Gaul, is divided into three parts—Western, Eastern, and Mediterranean.

In Western Europe, nations enjoy a free, privately owned commercial press and technologically advanced broadcast systems. They have overall more newspapers and more circulation per 1,000 citizens than does any other region of the world. All these states are economically developed. Incomes are relatively high, as are literacy rates, and the bulk of the people look to the media for both information and entertainment.

The Mediterranean area is similar in many way but less developed and less well off. Past dictatorships have meant continuing problems for the media. Literacy rates are lower, and far fewer newspapers are circulated per 1,000 persons than among their northern neighbors.

The third part of Europe—the East—is ruled by communist regimes, which have imposed a media system so different from the rest of the continent that it must be considered separately.

60

All Western European nations have democratic governments and the media are essentially free. Newspapers for the most part are capitalistic ventures that must make money to survive. As in the United States, their income is from circulation and advertising. Many are more politically partisan than are most American papers and some are actually supported by political parties. Except in France and West Germany, papers outside the capital or other big cities tend to be small and relatively unimportant.

The structure of broadcast is somewhat more diverse and, in most countries, its operations are considerably more controlled than is print. In many, broadcast has always been a state monopoly.

Both print and broadcast are going through a period of considerable change. The number of newspapers is falling, even though readership totals are rising. The formation of press groups or chains has become commonplace, as in the United States. The West German press lord, Axel Springer, now controls more than a third of that country's total daily circulation. The Bonnier group in Sweden is responsible for a fifth of the daily circulation there, and a relative newcomer, Robert Hersant, controls about 20 percent in France.

Western Europe has a number of the world's most prestigious papers: *The Times* and *The Guardian* of London, *Le Monde* of Paris, the *Frankfurter Allgemeine* of West Germany, *Corriere della Sera* and *La Stampa* of Italy, the *Neue Zürcher Zeitung* of Switzerland, *Berlinske Tidende* of Denmark—to mention only a few. Yet serious papers such as these seem to be losing ground overall to both sensational tabloids and to what are called boulevard papers—light-entertainment and gossip-oriented publications.

Tabloids such as London's *Daily Mirror* and West Germany's *Bild Zeitung* have been the circulation leaders for some time, but now the boulevard papers seem to be improving their positions, too—and, most ominously for the future, particularly among younger members of the population. Like newspapers everywhere, the West European press has been squeezed by inflation, higher costs, and lower purchasing power. And union resistance to new lower-cost electronic technology has been strong in several countries, particularly in Britain and West Germany.

West Europe is home to two of the great international news agencies, France's Agence France-Presse and Britain's Reuters. It also boasts the largest number of long-established and highly developed national news agencies, several of which play significant roles beyond their country's borders. West Germany's Deutsche Presse Agentur (DPA) and Italy's ANSA, for example, are better described as regional rather than national agencies. These national agencies—and all West European states except tiny Andorra, Luxembourg,

Monaco, and Liechtenstein have their own—are all set up as mass-media cooperatives.

Broadcast has shown a steady growth over the years, both in numbers of receivers and in programming. Cable operations are expanding. Some authorities fear, in fact, that the region as a whole is fast approaching the saturation point as far as radio and TV are concerned.

Changes that have occurred in broadcast have involved structure more than economics or audience shifts. Decentralization of administration and programming with more input from the general public, an increase in the degree of dependence on advertising to meet costs, and the appearance of local, some of it private, broadcasting are among trends that have become evident in recent years. The introduction of direct transnational TV broadcasting, which is on the way, will undoubtedly bring still further changes.

In the Mediterranean states—Spain, Portugal, Italy, Greece, and Turkey—broadcasting is generally more important than is print. Overall, newspaper circulations are quite low. Even in Italy, the number of newspapers per 1,000 persons is only about a fifth of the figure for Sweden or Britain, and the vast majority of these sales are in the industrialized northern third of the country. The Spanish figure has risen in recent years to about the same level as Italy's but the other states still trail far behind. Portugal's, for instance, is only about 56 papers per 1,000.

Poverty and illiteracy are serious problems throughout the Mediterranean region, particularly in the countryside. Except in northern Italy, newspapers tend to be city-bound, with little if any circulation outside their place of production. Illiteracy is not a problem as far as broadcast is concerned, nor are bad roads or poor communication facilities, which explains the predominance of radio and TV in these countries.

Except in Italy, where media freedoms are on a par with states to the north, both press and broadcast in the Mediterranean countries are hampered by restrictions not characteristic of the rest of Europe. In the case of Spain and Portugal, some of these are leftovers from past dictatorships that have not yet been removed. In Greece and Turkey they reflect the political instability that has afflicted both nations.

Print Media

Most West European countries have at least one internationally ranked prestige paper, as well as a number of more popular publications. However, in some (Belgium is an example), any division into popular and prestige is not easy, because all the papers attempt to offer comprehensive news coverage that includes serious as well as light material.

If for no other reason than language, Americans are more likely to have some knowledge of the British press than any of the others. Britain has one of the world's highest readership figures, about 575 copies per 1,000 persons. (The United States figure is about 340.) Almost 90 percent of all adult Britons buy at least one morning daily. The newspaper scene is dominated by nine London-based papers that are distributed throughout the entire country on the day of publication. These make up Britain's so-called national press.

Some of the nine are among the best papers in the world; whereas some, the sensational tabloids, deserve to be ranked among the worst, even though from a technical standpoint they are extremely well edited and put together.

The quality papers include two that are on almost everyone's list of great newspapers of the world—*The Times* and *The Guardian. The Times,* which in the past has often seemed to be the voice of Britain* itself, sells about 294,000 copies a day. *The Guardian,* which is also independent but liberal-leaning, is larger, with a circulation of more than 400,000. The *Daily Telegraph,* independent but conservative-minded, is the largest of the serious papers, boasting a circulation of more than 1,500,000. The *Financial Times,* Britain's equivalent of *The Wall Street Journal,* sells about 180,000 copies a day.

The popular national press includes: *The Daily Express,* 2,400,000; *The Daily Mail,* 1,900,000; *The Daily Mirror,* 2,778,000; and *The Sun,* 3,900,000. *The Sun,* the *Mirror,* and *The Daily Mail* are tabloids. The others are broadsheet size.

London also has a communist paper, *The Morning Star,* which has a circulation of about 35,000. Until recently it had two evening papers, *The Evening News* and *The Evening Standard,* which circulated only within greater London. Each sold fewer than 500,000 copies a day and have now been combined into a single publication.

A fair number of provincial dailies have been able to maintain themselves against the competition of the London-based national press. Best known among these are *The Yorkshire Post* of Leeds, with a circulation of about 100,000: *The Scotsman* of Edinburgh, 96,000; *The Evening Times* of Glasgow, 223,000; *The Liverpool Echo,* 149,000; *The Birmingham Evening Mail,* 348,000; and the *Manchester Evening News,* 347,000.

Britain does not have any weekly news magazines like *Time*

---

* Circulation figures given in this chapter and in those which follow are rough approximations and are rounded. They do give a general idea of readership.

and *Newsweek*. British readers have never taken to that type of publication. However, the country does have several highly influential weekly papers and journals of opinion. The most important of the papers are *The Observer*, with a circulation of 1,116,000, and the *Sunday Times*, 1,400,000.

The *Sunday Times* is not a Sunday edition of *The Times* but a separate publication. However, several of London's dailies do publish Sunday editions, including the *Express*, the *Daily Telegraph*, and the *Mirror*. The circulation of the *Sunday Express* is about 3,240,000; the *Sunday Mirror* claims more than 3,800,000, but the *Sunday Telegraph*'s is only about 850,000.

Largest of all, however, is a sensational scandal sheet called *The News of the World*, which sells about 4,708,000 copies.

Among the important journals are: *The Economist*, which is also widely circulated in the United States, 165,000; *The New Statesman and Nation* which, despite its circulation of only about 40,000, is widely quoted because it tends to reflect views of an influential segment of the Labor Party; *The Spectator*, also a political review but which leans toward the Conservatives; and *Punch*, the famous humor weekly, selling about 85,000 copies.

A wide variety of special-interest publications deal with science, education, gardening, the theater, and women's affairs, among other topics. The largest of these is a television guide called *TV Times*, with a circulation of nearly 3,500,000 copies.

The economics of the publishing industry have fostered the growth of large groups, or chains, of papers. Most of these also publish magazines and journals. One of the newest of the groups has been formed by Rupert Murdoch, the Australian entrepreneur who owns *The New York Post*. He controls London's *Sun* and *The News of the World* and has recently acquired *The Times*.

Some of the other large groupings are the following:

Associated Newspaper Group, which controls *The Daily Mail*, as well as 12 provincial evening and one morning paper and several weeklies, including one with national distribution.

Express Newspapers controls the *Daily Express* as well as its Sunday sister and at least one provincial paper.

Mirror Group Newspapers publishes the *Daily Mirror*, two national Sunday papers, a sports publication, and several provincial papers.

United Newspaper Publications operates nine provincial dailies, one biweekly, and 30 provincial weeklies. It also publishes *Punch* as well as five other magazines.

The Thomson Organisation, which owns papers in the United States and Canada as well as Britain, puts the others to shame as far as size is concerned. It publishes at least 55 daily and weekly papers in various parts of Britain as well as 45 different magazines.

The situation in France differs from that in Britain in several important respects. In France the provincial press is strong, prosperous and growing. The big Parisian papers do not have to the same degree the national distribution enjoyed by their British counterparts. The regular circulation areas of most do not extend much beyond the outskirts of the capital.

Nevertheless, Paris still has eight major newspapers, even though its population is only a quarter of that of New York. Apparently all but one of them—*Le Monde* is the exception—have been losing money. Even *Le Monde*'s financial future appears shaky.

The economic pressures that have led to closings, consolidations, and formation of chains throughout the Western world came late to France but seem now to be at full force. Their effects have already become evident with the formation of the Hersant chain, and it is widely believed that several of the Parisian dailies will become victims in the not-too-distant future.

One exception is the English-language *International Herald Tribune*, whose owners include *The New York Times* and *The Washington Post*. It circulates throughout all of Europe, selling more than 120,000 copies daily.

Among the others, *Le Monde* is unique in both style and organization. It is determinedly serious, almost professorial in tone. Tabloid size, with no pictures, no comics, no entertainment features, it is, self-avowedly, a paper for intellectuals. Yet despite all this, its circulation of 550,000 is the largest of all the Parisian dailies.

It has no owners in the normal sense of the word. Instead, it is a kind of public trust, set up at the end of World War II by a group of journalists who had been in the French resistance. Forty percent of the company's stock (this is voting stock that cannot be sold) is held by an outside advisory board that is supposed to represent a collective national wisdom. Businessmen and politicians are barred automatically from membership in this body.

Another 40 percent of the stock is divided among the editors and writers, according to rank and seniority. The remainder is split up among the administrative staff, the editor-in-chief, and the chief financial officer. Editors are chosen by the staff. Nevertheless, they have the same decision-making authority as do editors anywhere. News is not selected on the basis of a collective vote.

From the standpoint of prestige, the chief competitor of *Le Monde*, which usually takes a left-of-center stance on political matters, is the conservative *Le Figaro*. It sells about 330,000 copies daily, but there are questions about whether or not its sale to Hersant will affect its standing. Several of its most prominent writers and editors have already left the paper.

Le Figaro is not second in terms of circulation, however. That place goes to *France-Soir*, in which Hersant also holds a controlling interest. It sells just over 500,000 copies.

Of the remaining dailies, only the right-wing morninger, *L'Aurore*, 220,000; the French Communist party's organ, *L'Humanité*, 150,000; and the sensationalist *Le Parisian Libéré*, 438,000; are of much importance. The others are little more than forums for the opinions and prejudices of their owners, who range politically from the far right to the far left. *L'Humanité* is one of the two major Communist papers in Western Europe. The other is the Italian party's *Unitá*.

Also unlike Britain, France has four news magazines in addition to several Sunday papers. The best known of the news magazines are *L' Express* and *Le Nouvel Observateur*. The Sunday papers, which are a relatively new feature on the Paris scene, include: *France-Dimanche*, 736,000; *L' Humanité Dimanche*, 360,000; and *Le Journal du Dimanche*, 360,000. These have proved to be so popular that even *Le Figaro* and *Le Monde* have started Sunday editions.

Paris's famous satirical paper, *Le Canard Enchainé*, is also a weekly, with a circulation of about 500,000.

The French provincial press, as was noted previously, is prospering, with some papers even matching the Parisian dailies in circulation. *Ouest-France*, published in Rennes, sells 640,000 copies a day; *Le Progrés* of Lyon, 436,000; *Le Dauphine Libéré* of Grenoble, 362,000; *La Voix* of Lille, 389,000; and *Sud-Ouest* of Bordeaux, 383,000.

A great variety of other periodicals are published in Paris, ranging in subject matter from economics and finance through history, geography, art, literature, and fashions to politics and women's affairs. Oddly enough, among the largest is the *Selection du Reader's Digest*, the French language edition of the United States magazine, which sells more than a million copies a month. The widely known illustrated weekly *Paris-Match* sells 643,000. Along with some of the other large-circulation illustrated magazines, it has lost standing in recent years, apparently because of the competition of television. Some of the old established women's magazines have also been experiencing trouble, apparently as a result of a failure to adapt to changes in French society.

West Germany appears to have a great many papers, but this appearance is somewhat deceptive. The country's 500-plus dailies are actually published by only about 120 different enterprises. Many print papers for several towns that are identical except for different titles and different front pages. If one counts weeklies as well as dailies, only about 400 different publishers produce the nation's 1,200 papers.

Still, compared with some other West European states, the West Germans have a good many papers, some of high quality which are distributed nationally.

Generally given top rank is the *Frankfurter Allgemeine Zeitung*, the heir to a long, proud newspaper tradition. The original *Frankfurter Zeitung*, which was established in that city after having been moved from a variety of other places, was considered one of the best of Europe's papers. It was closed by the Nazis during the Hitler period. The new version was founded in 1949 and has a circulation of about 300,000.

Almost as highly regarded is the *Süddeutsche Zeitung* of Munich, which looks much more like an American paper than the traditionalist *Allgemeine* with its formal, balanced makeup and German Gothic typeface. The *Süddeutsche Zeitung*'s circulation is about 315,000.

Axel Springer publishes one quality paper, *Die Welt*, 230,000, as well as the sensationalist *Bild Zeitung*, which boasts a circulation of nearly 5 million, the largest in Western Europe. Both these papers are published in Hamburg, but the *Bild Zeitung* also has satellite printing operations in eight other cities.

Two other well-regarded and often-quoted papers are the *Frankfurter Rundschau*, 183,000, and *Handelsblatt*, the country's only national business and financial paper. It is published in Düsseldorf and has a circulation of about 81,000.

Besides the *Bild Zeitung*, the largest of the popular papers are the *Westdeutsche Allgemeine* of Essen, 620,00; the Hannoverische *Allgemeine Zeitung* of Hannover, 470,000; the *Rheinische Post* of Düsseldorf, 400,000; the *Hamburger Abendblatt*, 278,000; the *Hamburger Morgenpost*, 236,000; the *BZ (Berliner Zeitung)* of West Berlin, 323,000; and the *Augsburger Allgemeine Zeitung* of Augsburg, 316,000.

West Germany has one internationally known news magazine, *Der Spiegel*, which sells about 1,100,000 copies, and several influential weekly papers, including *Die Zeit*, 360,000; *Bild am Sonntag*, 2,600,000; and *Welt am Sonntag*, 340,000, Two illustrated weekly magazines, *Stern* and *Quick*, have circulations of about 1,600,000 and 1,300,000, respectively. Far and away the largest weekly publication is a radio and television review called *Hörzu*, with 4,300,000 copies.

With respect to the Scandinavian countries, Sweden has one of the freest press systems in the world. Among other things, journalists have the right to protect their sources and the law actually forbids editors to disclose names under any circumstances.

To fight the common trend toward consolidations and chains, Sweden has instituted a subsidy system financed by a tax on advertising. Under it, any newspaper with less than 40 percent penetration of the households in its market area is eligible for a subsidy from the fund.

Still, as was noted previously, the Bonnier group controls more than 20 percent of the national circulation and owns the nation's largest periodical publishing company. It owns two Stockholm papers, *Dagens Nyheter* (408,000) and *Expressen* (532,000), which are generally considered the country's best. *Dagens Nyheter* is a regular-sized morninger and *Expressen* is an afternoon tabloid. Both are politically liberal and are distributed nationally.

The third large Stockholm paper, *Aftonbladet* (423,000) is also a tabloid and is also distributed nationally. It represents the Social Democractic point of view. The major conservative organ is *Svenska Dagbladet*, (186,000). All the major papers have Sunday editions. As a result, there are no influential weeklies. Except for two tabloids with some regional influence, one in Gothenburg and the other in Malmo, the rest of the papers are small and of only local interest. However, these are the ones the subsidy plan is particularly aimed at. Like all Swedish papers, they represent political points of view, and the maintenance of a diversity of such views is the purpose of the plan.

The press situation in Denmark is similar to that in Sweden, although Denmark has done nothing to slow press concentration. As a result, two groups control a large part of the national circulation. The largest is led by the *Berlingske Tidende*. It is the biggest and most prestigious of the dailies, with a circulation of 127,000 on weekdays and 246,000 on Sundays.

It also publishes *B.T.*, a Conservative daily which hits the streets at noon in Copenhagen, as well as a number of local papers and other periodicals. Overall, it controls about 25 percent of the nation's total circulation. Its chief rival is the politically Liberal *Politiken*, with a circulation of 140,000 on weekdays and 205,000 on Sundays. *Politiken* also publishes a largely advertising and marketing daily called *Ekstra Bladet*, which sells 238,000 copies on weekdays, and several provincial dailies.

Other important papers include *Aktuelt* (60,000 daily, 131,000 Sunday). It is the flagship of a group of three Social Democratic papers that are owned and subsidized by the trade unions. The only other Danish daily that is owned directly by a political party is the communist *Land og Folk* (14,500 weekdays, 21,000 Saturdays).

Neighboring Norway has 160 newspapers, including 72 dailies, but most of them are very small. The largest outside the capital city of Oslo is the *Bergens Tidende* of Bergen, with about 85,000 circulation.

By far the largest in the country is Oslo's *Aftenposten*, which publishes both morning (224,000) and evening (159,600) editions. Politically it is independent conservative. Two other independent papers, *Verdens Gang* and *Dagbladet*, with circulations of 170,000 and 125,000, respectively, also circulate nationally, as does the principal organ of the Labor Party, *Arbeiderbladet* (60,000). The Labor press, which includes several provincial publications as well as *Arbeiderbladet*, is subsidized by the party and the nation's trade union federation.

A state fund was set up in 1972 to help newspapers in dealing with cash flow and credit problems.

In Finland, too, the capital city of Helsinki is the country's major press center, although several provincial towns have dailies with sizable circulations. Overall, 12 of the nation's dailies are printed in Swedish, the nation's second language. The Finnish press is also highly political, although most of the Conservative and middle-of-the-road papers are independently owned. Left wing publications are party owned or controlled by the trade unions or other social organizations.

The largest and most respected Finnish daily is the independent *Helsingen Sanomat* (377,000 weekdays, 435,000 Sundays). Another Helsinki independent, *Uusi Suomi* (82,000 weekdays, 84,000 Sundays) is also highly regarded. Other popular papers include *Ilta Sanomat* (122,600), *Hufvudstadsbladet* (61,000 weekdays, 64,000 Sundays) and the independent *Turun Sanomat* of Turku-Abo (132,000).

Of the avowedly party papers, the most important are: *Aamulehti*, the organ of the National Coalition Party (130,000 weekdays), which is published in the university city of Tampere; *Suomen Sosialidemokraatti* (43,000), the chief organ of the Social Democratic Party, and *Kansan Uutiset* (55,000), of the Finnish Communist party.

Belgium is like Finland in at least two respects: it is a two-language country, and daily papers tend to have political leanings whether owned by political parties or not. Belgium's two languages are French and Flemish. Flemish predominates in the north and French in the south. This split has caused serious conflicts and has resulted in a kind of enforced balance between the two, particularly in broadcasting. Nevertheless, the two largest papers are both printed in Flemish or Dutch. They are *De Standaard Nieuwsblatt De Gentenaar* (333,000) and *Het Laatste Nieuws* (308,000), both published in Brussels. The largest French-language Brussels daily is *Le Soir* (233,000). Two Dutch-language papers published in other cities are ranked fourth and fifth. They are *Het Volk* of Ghent (200,000) and *Gazet Van Antwerpen* of Antwerp (188,000).

Papers in the Netherlands also tend to be strongly political. However, the largest is Amsterdam's *De Telegraf* (575,000), which is solidly independent and nonparty. Another in the same category is *De Courant Nieuws Van den Dag* (136,000), also of Amsterdam. Other important dailies include *Het Pàrool* (163,000), which lists itself as independent but usually supports the Labor Party, and *De Volkskrant* (233,000), the nation's principal Catholic paper. Both of the latter, along with *De Telegraaf*, are circulated nationally.

Switzerland boasts two papers that are uniformly listed among the best in the world, although neither has a large circulation, even by Swiss standards: the *Neue Zürcher Zeitung* (115,000), which is printed in German, and the *Journal de Geneve*, in French (19,000). On the whole, the Swiss press is political, opinion-orientated, and relatively decentralized, with well-regarded papers in major centers throughout the country. The largest, however, are Zurich's *Tagesanzeiger*, with a circulation of 260,000, and *Blick*, also of Zurich, with a circulation of 272,000.

The Austrian press scene is dominated by two Vienna tabloids: *Kurier*, which sells about 630,000 copies on weekdays and Sundays, and the *Neue Kronen Zeitung*, with up to 950,000 on weekdays and 1,370,000 on Sundays. Generally regarded as the country's best, however, are Vienna's *Die Presse* (60,000 weekdays and 73,000 Saturdays) and Salzburg's *Salzburger Nachrichten* (56,000 weekdays, 88,000 Saturdays).

As far as the Mediterranean countries are concerned, Italy may not have as impressive readership statistics as its northern neighbors but it can boast some of Europe's top newspapers. Milan's *Corriere della Sera* (750,000); Turin's *La Stampa* (403,000) and its evening edition, called *Stampa Sera* (142,000); and Rome's *Il Tempo* (243,000) and *Il Giorno* (287,000) will stand comparison with any. Several of these, including *Corriere della Sera*, *La Stampa*, and *Il Giono*, are controlled by large industrial firms.

Still, newspapers in Italy take a back seat to the many weekly illustrated papers and magazines that are the real mass media of the country. There are more than 400 nondaily papers, many with sales higher than even the biggest of the dailies. Many of these tend toward the sensational in presentation.

The most popular include *Domenica de Corriere* of Milan (800,000), *Epoca*, also of Milan, (370,000), *Espresso* of Rome (175,000), *L'Europeo* of Milan (250,000), *Gente* of Milan (700,000), and *Oggi* (750,000), another Milan product.

None of the other Mediterranean countries—Spain, Portugal,

Greece, or Turkey—has a truly national paper, either, although some of the larger Turkish dailies are printed simultaneously in Istanbul, Ankara, and Izmir.

The quality of the Spanish press has improved markedly since the death of former dictator Gen. Francisco Franco and the liberalization of the government. In fact, *El Pais* of Madrid (180,000 weekdays, 290,000 Sundays) and Barcelona's *La Vanguardia* (276,000 weekdays and Sundays) are widely considered to be up to the standards of quality papers elsewhere on the continent.

The government has closed some of the 30 papers—all money losers—it inherited from the Franco regime, and still has a number it would like to get rid of but so far has not been able to. They can't simply be closed up because the employees are civil servants and jobs would have to be found for them somewhere else. None has a circulation of more than 10,000, but they take advertising away from the independents.

The Spanish, like the Italians, are big readers of magazines. One of their most popular is *Cambio*, a weekly news magazine modeled on *Time*. Although recently founded, it has become one of the county's major success stories. It is only one of a flood of new periodicals, many of which, in the words of London's *Economist*, "cover current affairs while uncovering girls."

Portugal also has the problem of what to do about newspapers the government does not want. It acquired them at the time of the establishment of the republic in 1975 when it nationalized banks and insurance companies that previously controlled the publishing houses. There are other privately owned independent papers, however. The largest is *Journal de Noticias* (80,000), which is published in Oporto. The largest in Lisbon, the capital, is *O Diario* (55,000).

Greece has 26 dailies, all but six of which are published in Athens. Although few have direct party ties, most have definite party leanings. Sensational and heavily partisan presentations are characterisic. The biggest and one of the best is *Ta Nea*, which politically stands left of center, and sells about 190,000 copies daily. Others include *Eleftherotypia* (135,000), *To Vima* (40,000), and Helen Vlachos' *Kathimerini* (40,000).

The most serious and influential Turkish papers are *Milleyet* (329,000) and *Cumhuriyet* (240,675.).

Broadcasting

Broadcasting is highly developed throughout all of Europe and in several countries is the predominant mass media for information as well as entertainment. Statistics suggest that even in the poorer countries, practically every household has at least a radio and most also have access to a TV set. Education and public service programming have traditionally played a larger role in Europe than in the United States. Considerable emphasis has also been placed on cultural programming, including classical music and drama.

News is a programming feature in all countries, although the number of hours devoted to it varies considerably. As for TV, all European countries have at least one major newscast during the evening hours. Generally, as in the United States, news is more frequently broadcast on radio.

All European states except Iceland, Luxembourg, Andorra, and Monaco also operate foreign broadcast services in a variety of languages. Exchanges of both radio and TV programs are common, either on a bilateral basis or through cooperate organizations such as the European Broadcasting Union (EBU), which maintains both radio and TV networks linking all the western European services. A similar organization, the International Radio and Television Organization (OIRT), links the countries of the Soviet bloc.

The EBU's TV network is known as Eurovision, while the OIRT's is called Intervision. Both function as program exchange centers through which member systems can obtain news as well as entertainment materials from others on the network. The two systems have a common link in Vienna and have been exchanging TV news material since 1965. EBU is also connected via satellite with North American broadcast organizations and with several Middle East states.

Western European broadcasting is in a period of extreme change, reflecting what has been described as a general crisis for both radio and television in that part of the world. The crisis had its roots in the very beginning of the industry when most of the European governments decided against permitting private commercial radio, opting instead for centralized monopolies responsible for programming and production.

There were variations in the form of these monopolies. Some countries, such as Britain, Belgium, Sweden, and Norway, set up more or less autonomous public corporations, answerable to the government or parliament for budgets and such matters to operate their systems. In other countries—France, for example—broadcasting became a function of the central government, administered by civil servants. In Portugal and Spain, private commercial companies ran the services. The Netherlands developed a unique system under which programming became the responsibility of private independent broadcasting societies whose efforts were coordinated by a public corporation. Everywhere governments owned and were responsible for the equipment: transmitters, land lines, and the like. Advertising was taboo. Most systems were financed from money raised by assessing owners of receivers an annual fee. In France a limited amount of private broadcasting was tolerated until World War II, but only in tiny Andorra, Luxembourg, and Monaco was it encouraged.

When television came along, it too was organized on the same basis, usually simply by putting it under the already existing authority. Programming tended to be restricted by political interests and by a general philosphy, evident in the British Broadcasting Corporation from the start, that the services should be concerned primarily with raising cultural standards.

A crisis first surfaced in the 1950s when the public began to realize that the effect of these public monopolies was to drastically limit their choices in programming. Illegal pirate radio stations became popular, as did the programming broadcast by large commercial stations that had developed in Luxembourg and Andorra, mainly with French money.

In response to criticism, the British government in 1954 set up a second broadcast service, the Independent Television Authority, alongside the BBC. It was authorized to operate on a commercial basis but still under rules laid down by Parliament. Later renamed the Independent Broadcast Authority (IBA), it was also empowered to set up and operate local commercial radio stations.

Similar pressures led to the decentralization of broadcast services in other countries, most notably, probably, the reorganization of France's Office de Radiodiffusion-Television (ORTF) and Italy's Radiotelevisione Italiana (IRA) in 1975. In the latter country, a Supreme Court decision in 1976 which held that the official broadcast monopoly did not cover FM radio or cable TV has resulted in the mushroom growth of private local radio and cable operations, with sponsors as diverse as the Catholic Church, industrial concerns, and political parties. However, most of these operations survive by means of advertising revenue.

A similar ruling in France has led to the rebirth of private radio, which like the Italian version is commercial, supported by advertising revenue. Even the official services in some countries have let down the bars. Official figures show that as much as 60 percent of the funds available to France's TV Channel 1 comes from advertising. Only the BBC and a few others are still holding out.

Even West German broadcasting, which has been somewhat decentralized from the start, is feeling pressure for the introduction of private commercial operations.

The West German system, set up under occupation oversight after World War II, put control of broadcasting in the hands of the Länder (states). The broadcast authority in each Länder is responsible for all radio and TV services within its territory. Most provide three complementary radio and two TV channels.

During the prime-time hours, all turn over one TV channel to a national network program, the contents of which are a matter of negotiation between the various authority bodies. In addition, there is still another national channel, the Zweites Deutsches Fernsehen (ZDF), which was established by interstate agreement.

As for radio, there is no common policy with regard to advertising. Some states permit it; some do not. For television, however, there are rules agreed on by all the states. Under these rules, TV advertising is limited to 20 minutes a day. No ads may be aired after 8 P.M. or on Sundays.

All European broadcasting systems have similar rules limiting the amount of advertising and the time that can be devoted to it. In some, advertising must be fitted into specific blocks of time—6:00 to 6:30 P.M., for example. Others set aside 10- or 15-minute blocks at various times of the day. All ban any tie-in between ads and programming.

In West Germany, political differences between the conservative south and the more leftist north have been a threat to the stability of the system. Recently, the Christian Democrats went on record as favoring the introduction of commercial operations. Money problems have also added to the pressure for change. Although the West German TV operations are among the most prosperous in the world, the income from license fees is tending to stabilize as the nation reaches the saturation point, but costs are rising at a record rate at the same time.

For all the western European nations, it is becoming clear that it is virtually impossible to carry on a strictly national broadcasting policy given the increasing availability of a variety of outside programming as a result of technological advances. In countries such as Belgium and the Netherlands, TV audiences already can choose from as many as ten foreign services, and when direct-to-home broadcasting via satellite becomes a reality, the same range of choice will be available to everyone.

Government—Press Relations

Europe is the home of the libertarian press and all national constitutions guarantee freedom of the press. As a whole, European newspapers are among the freest in the world. Nevertheless, the degree of freedom varies considerably from country to country. In all, the media are restricted by laws against libel, treason, disclosure of military secrets and the like, similar to laws in the United States. Most, however—Britain, Belgium, and Switzerland are the exceptions— also have other laws specifically governing the press. Some of these laws, such as Sweden's Freedom of the Press Act, truly enlarge the area of press rights. But others give the authorities the right to restrict press operations under certain circumstances.

In several countries, including France, Austria, Finland, and West Germany, authorities have the power to ban the sale or actually seize offending publications. In West Germany, the printing of what could be deemed untrue or distorted allegations against the army could be subject to such a ban. In the early 1960s, the German news magazine *Der Spiegel* was subjected to extensive impoundment and seizure as a result of an allegedly treasonous article.

In France, laws prohibit the publication of any judicial, governmental, or military information not expressly cleared for publication. This eliminates, for all practical purposes, any chance of investigative reporting of government scandals or wrongdoing. Furthermore, the truth of charges made cannot be used as a defense by the press in such cases.

Even Britain restricts press activities to a degree unknown in the United States, mainly through extremely strict libel laws, the contempt powers of the courts and the Official Secrets Act. The latter prohibits the publication of any information which authorities have declared secret. Editors are informed of prohibited subjects by what are called "D-notices."

British courts limit the publication of any material concerning cases before them to material they have approved. Publication of any unauthorized information can bring a contempt citation and a jail sentence for offending editors.

The British government also has the power to prevent newspaper owners from investing in the private television companies that contract for the rights to do the programming on the independent commercial service. Under another law aimed at limiting the further growth of chains, official approval must be given to the sale of any paper with a circulation of more than 500,000 copies.

Several countries including France, West Germany, and Denmark, have right-of-reply laws that give any person who feels that statements concerning them are false or misleading the right to insist on the publication of a counterstatement.

On the plus side—from the press standpoint—laws of most of the Scandinavian countries provide for unrestricted access to all public documents and records, except those involving trade or military secrets. These same countries, along with most of the West German Länder (states), also give journalists the legal right to protect their sources. The one exception is Norway, but Norwegian journalists point out that no penalties have been assessed for years against news people who have refused to disclose sources.

Direct controls such as precensorship or licensing requirements have been problems in Portugal, Spain, Greece, and Turkey during the post-World War II years. Franco in Spain, Salazar in Portugal, the "colonels" in Greece, and various military juntas in Turkey kept a tight grip on the press during their days in power. Even under civilian regimes, the Turkish press is hobbled severely. That country's 1961 constitution notes that the press is "free within the limits of the law." The law, however, provides among other things for punishment by forced labor for anyone guilty of promoting communism or criticizing government practices. In recent years, editors have been jailed and important dailies banned for periods of time under these and other provisions.

Even before the military dictatorship from 1967 to 1974, Greece also had a number of restrictive press laws under which the government could seize or completely close papers. In both Greece and Turkey, the fact that newsprint had to be imported and that its allocation was in the hands of the government gave and still gives authorities a strong hand in relations with the press.

The replacement of the dictatorship in Greece by civilian governments has not brought about a repeal of any restrictive laws. Although most Greek papers today appear to be operating relatively freely, they remain vulnerable to official pressure. The authorities also have a big carrot to go along with their stick. Government advertising is a major source of revenue for many papers, and the ability of the central administration to withhold it from critical publication gives officials another potent control weapon.

Spanish editors also have complained of problems resulting from holdovers from the past. They are particularly critical of the courts—both military and civilian—which they say are staffed by people appointed under the Franco dictatorship and who do not look favorably on the more liberal press of today.

Most European governments provide the press with hidden subsidies: relief from some taxes, reduced postal rates, artifically low newsprint prices in some, and the like. There are drawbacks to some of these, however. In Italy, for example, the selling price of newspapers is also controlled by the government as a part of the "basket" of goods by which the cost-of-living index is calculated.

But even individual Italian journalists enjoy privileges that are the envy of those from other lands. They get free travel on trains and planes inside the country as well as some control, through their journalists' union, over ownership changes. French journalists have the right to resign with full severance pay if they feel they cannot work for a new employer whose political or social views differ from theirs.

In several countries, probably the most important government involvement in press affairs today concerns efforts to maintain diversity of political viewpoints by preventing the closing of papers and the growth of chains. Rising costs and stationary, if not declining, revenues have thinned the numbers considerably. Subsidy arrangements have already been put into effect in Sweden, Norway, Finland, and Austria and have been discussed in other countries.

Although all European states are more interventionist with respect to the media than the American media are accustomed to, the French government is particularly involved. It controls most of the broadcasting in the country. It is a major advertiser through its nationalized corporations, such as Air France, Renault, the national railway system, and others. In addition, it holds a controlling interest in France's largest advertising agency as well as some control—the exact amount is a matter of dispute—over Agence France-Presse.

News Agencies

AFP, the country's largest news agency, is the odd man out among the majors. It is neither an arm of the government, like the Soviet TASS agency, nor is it owned by participating media organizations, like Reuters, the Associated Press, or even United Press International.

It is run by an administrative council. Three of the fifteen members of the council are appointed by the government. This arrangement was approved by Parliament in 1957, when it also decided that there should be a higher council to check on operations. This eight-man higher council includes four media representatives, one member of Parliament who is automatically chairman, and one magistrate from the Supreme Court of Appeal. There is also a financial commission which includes an accountant appointed by the minister of finance and two members of a government accounts court. Add to this the fact that payments from the state-run broadcasting systems make up 60 percent of AFP's yearly budget and the reasoning behind charges of state control over the agency becomes clear.

AFP operates as a national agency as well as worldwide. Although French papers can subscribe to other agencies, only the larger ones do because of the cost involved. The same situation is true in most of the other European countries. Only West Germany constitutes a large enough market for the internationals to attempt to service directly papers throughout the country. In most others, they function primarily as wholesalers, supplying news to the national agency which then distributes it to its various customers.

There are other agencies in France beside AFP but all are small, contributing only a fraction of the total national news flow. Some specialize in specific areas of coverage. This is also true in some other states, although all have one predominant organization that is owned or controlled by the media of that country. The British show a slight variation on the pattern. In Britain, the principal national agency is Press Association, which is actually a subsidiary of Reuters. It is responsible for gathering and distributing news in Britain but Reuters itself relays the news from abroad.

Two smaller agencies play somewhat unusual roles in addition to more customary functions. The Spanish national agency EFE is an important supplier of news to Latin America, competing there, to some extent at least, with the internationals. The Austrian agency APA subscribes to the services of the smaller Communist-bloc countries and enables Western news organizations, through their representatives in Vienna, to use it almost as a kind of monitoring operation for items from those nations.

Journalism Education

Traditionally, journalism in Western Europe was a matter for on-the-job training, not university-level studies. This has changed completely in recent years. By now, most of the Western European nations have journalism programs, either at established universities or at separate institutes. Some are at the undergraduate and some are at the postgraduate level, and a few are nondegree-granting. Several nations also have special centers for mass communication research. Austria has two such institutes, at the Universities of Vienna and Salzburg, that award the Ph.D. degree, but has no regular school of journalism.

The British still rely heavily on traditional training methods, although the University of South Wales does offer a one-year postgraduate course in journalism. Most recruits to the profession, however, go through specialized programs offered by the National Council for the Training of Journalists, an industry organization. One-year pre-entry courses are given at nine technical colleges throughout the country.

Both France and West Germany, but particularly the latter, have a number of journalism schools. The Universities of Lille and Strasbourg in France have strong departments. The Center for the Formation of Journalists in Paris takes foreign as well as French students. There are also journalism programs at the Universities of Bordeaux and Tours, as well as university institutes at Paris, Bordeaux, Dijon, and Toulouse that are involved in communication research.

West Germany is even more richly endowed. Courses in journalism as well as other aspects of communication are available at at least nine universities throughout the country and at other schools or institutes in seven cities. Most of the universities also have mass communication research programs.

Several of the smaller countries also have journalism schools with international reputations. Among these are the Danish School of Journalism at Aarhus and the programs at the University of Tampere in Finland and at the University of Navarre in Spain.

Historical Highlights

Western Europe was the birthplace of the newspaper as we know it. The time was the first part of the seventeenth century. Publications issued on a regular basis began to be seen on the streets of various European cities, first in Germany and then in nearby lands. In 1637, the *Gazette de France* appeared, the first in that country. The 1640s and 1650s saw the establishment of news-books and other publications in Britain, a process that culminated in the founding of the Oxford (later London) *Gazette* in the 1660s. The first newspaper in Italy dates back to 1645.

It still took a long time for these early examples to develop into publications that united a variety of types of information: comment, advertising, and entertainment as well as news. This did not happen until the latter part of the eighteenth century when within the space of 17 years, three papers emerged that would become models in the field—the Swiss *Neue Zürcher Zeitung* in 1780, *The Times* of London in 1788, and Germany's *Allgemeine Zeitung* in 1797.

Except in Britain, where John Walters had it comparatively easy in his struggle to build up the *Times*, controls and censorship were still the order of the day. Johann Cotta had to move his *Allgemeine Zeitung* several times before he found a relatively safe haven in Frankfurt. As a result of the restrictions, modern newspapers did not emerge in most European countries until after the revolutionary wave that swept the continent in 1848. The ideas and the ideals behind this movement provided much of the shape of the contemporary European press—its freedom as well as its attachment to party or cause.

These newspapers were written primarily for the politically minded and were not designed to attract large audiences, even though the number of potential readers was increasing steadily as a result of the spread of education. As a result, the 1870s and 1880s witnessed the development of a new kind of paper, one that featured entertainment and sensation with the aim of attracting the largest

possible audience. Audience size was essential to this mass press because it had to be financed largely through advertising.

Men such as Alfred Harmsworth in Britain; Rudolf Mosse,
Leopold Ullstein, and August Scherl in Germany; and Moise-Polydore
Millaud in France built huge press empires and fortunes out of the
profits of such publications. Some of the older papers survived, adapt-
ing themselves to new conditions, but many disappeared.

Despite World War I and the great depression, the first part of
the twentieth century was a period of considerable expansion for most
of the European press. Circulations reached new highs. But in Italy,
the Mussolini regime forced the press into a new totalitarian pattern,
an example to be followed in the 1930s by the Nazis in Germany.

World War II put an end to many of the older titles throughout
Europe, both east and west. Some survived and others were replaced
by new foundations. In eastern Europe, communists came to power
and with them came a whole different press philosophy as well as a
new type of paper.

In the west, the postwar years brought at first relative prosperity. But harder times—inflation, increasing competition for advertising and rising costs—once more thinned the ranks of European
newspapers.

A Look to the Future

Most predictions about the future are not bright. However, some publishers have demonstrated that not only survival but even economic
health is possible for papers that can rationalize their operations and
cut per-unit costs.

The papers in greatest danger appear to be the classic "informational" publications such as *Le Monde* and *The Times* of London.
Most of the popular papers, and even some of the quality ones,
belong to groups or other large-scale enterprises that can withstand
financial shocks. But the example of *The Times* demonstrates that
even this is not necessarily real protection.

The Times has now been sold to Rupert Murdoch because neither
the trust that controlled it earlier nor the huge Thomson organization
that next took it over could continue to sustain the losses involved.

Le Monde's profits have been slipping and unless this trend can
somehow be reversed, its prospects do not appear hopeful. But it is not
alone. The increasing popularity of the boulevard papers poses a continuing threat to most of the serious papers. If this means, as it
appears, that the oncoming generation will buy entertainment rather
than information, sooner or later the boulevard papers will also be
out of business.

As far as broadcasting is concerned, the pressures for change that have been apparent in most countries have led some observers to predict a general shift to a great deal more local, and probably commercial, radio and TV operations in the near future. Dependence on advertising almost certainly will increase. Even under present conditions, a ban on advertising makes little sense, since big corporations can find carriers that can broadcast their ads from one country into many others.

The national systems are not expected to disappear. But increasingly they will have to consider audiences beyond their own borders. All are dependent on foreign programs to fill their air time now, and such interlinking will increase. The effect could be a virtually all-Western European network.

EUROPE: COMMUNIST

Of all the various media systems in the world, the one that presents the sharpest contrast to the United States is that of the Soviet Union and its Eastern European allies.

The differences between them range all the way from basic organization to purposes and goals. Instead of developing in response to a market, the Soviet system is a completely planned structure imposed on a market. Instead of having as its principal purpose the furnishing of information about current events, the essential duty of the Soviet media is to build support for the ruling Communist Party and government—political persuasion, in other words.

There is no private ownership of media. Broadcasting is a state function and all newspapers are published by the Communist Party, the government, or subordinate organizations such as trade unions, youth organizations, sports clubs, factories or collective farms, and professional or special-interest associations.

The media structure in the Soviet Union is more complex than that in the other Soviet bloc nations if for no other reason than sheer size. The Soviet Union is the largest country in the world (8,600,000 square miles) while its allies are comparable to single states of the United States. There are other differences that result from historical and cultural factors. Nevertheless, the similarities far outweigh the differences.

Print Media: USSR

The Soviet Union alone produces about 8,000 newspapers—including 640 dailies—in 58 of the various languages spoken within its borders.

It also counts about 6,000 journals and other periodicals, some of which are published in newspaper format.

There are two principal types of newspapers: those that are published on a geographical basis and those that cater to the interests of specialized audiences.

The geographically based general press includes nationally distributed "all-Union" dailies as well as regional and local papers. The all-Union dailies are the most important, of course. They include *Pravda*, the voice of the Communist Party leadership, and *Izvestia*, which serves a similar role for the government.

The regional papers are published in the administrative capitals of the various republics that constitute the Union, as well as in the more important provincial centers. Each republic has its own version of *Pravda* and *Izvestia*, which speaks for the party and government of that area.

The local press is made up of both district and city papers, as well as a large number of periodicals published by factories, collective farms and the like. The latter come in a variety of sizes and frequencies of publication. Some are nothing more than handwritten "wall" newspapers.

The second type of paper—those catering to the interests of specialized audiences—include some of the major dailies, such as *Trud*, the organ of the national trade union leadership, and *Krasnaya Zvezda* (Red Star), the organ of the USSR Ministry of Defense, as well as a wide variety of journals, some of which are more influential than many of the dailies.

Although all propagandize for the party and government, each sector of the press has its special role. The major Moscow dailies that make up the all-Union (national) press carry the messages of the central authorities. They publish the party and government line and generally serve as patterns, as well as principal sources of material, for all newspapers of similar type on the republic, provincial and local levels.

The provincial papers recast this material in regional terms and discuss regional economic and political problems. The local press has the role of translating party directives into guidelines for daily life.

Most of the specialized-audience periodicals are published for specific occupational groups or segments of society, such as women or youth. Their aim is to increase the reader's concern with his or her everyday activity and to push the party's view of how that concern should be translated into action. Generally speaking, these periodicals are not relied on as much for news as for commentary and guidance.

The government administers both the press and broadcasting

through state committees that operate under the Council of Ministers, the government's top executive body. However, each sector of the media is ultimately responsible to and is controlled by the Communist Party. The party exercises this control through its Agitation and Propaganda (Agitprop) sections that exist on each of the various levels of the party organization.

At the top of the pyramid is the USSR Central Committee's Agitprop staff, which directly oversees the all-Union papers and journals. Corresponding units on each of the lower levels (republic, regional, local) supervise the press in their areas. The Agitprop sections at each level not only keep tabs on the papers under their immediate control but also review and criticize those on the next lower level. In addition, the party must approve any editor before he can assume his job.

This elaborate mechanism is only part of the entire Soviet control system, which has two fundamental responsibilities: to see that what the party wants published gets published and, at the same time, to make certain that anything the party considers unfavorable to its interests is kept out of the media. Controversy is tightly controlled.

Conformity to party policy is also enforced by a number of state censorship agencies, usually referred to as GLAVLIT. This is an acronym for the Russian name of the most important of these: the Chief Administration for the Preservation of State Secrets in the Press.

Although almost all-pervasive—only official party publications escape its watch—Glavlit apparently is not as important a control factor as is the strict discipline the party exercises over editors. They are briefed regularly on what the party wants and expects. A misstep could mean dismissal, if not worse, so missteps seldom occur.

Almost all the content is planned in advance, some of it weeks ahead of publication. Editors meet in regular monthly, weekly and daily sessions to discuss newspaper themes, content, and format. By the time each issue goes to press it has been ready for at least two days save only a few small holes left unfilled until the day of publication for any last-minute items deemed necessary.

Reporting of what people in the West would consider news—the major events of the day—plays only a small role in the Soviet press. Emphasis is placed on interpreting selected developments in accordance with the party line and on telling the audience how they should respond, in both thought and action. Editors are responsible for selecting events and using them either to illustrate the progress of "socialist construction," or to suggest that the noncommunist world is plagued with so many problems and dangers that all Russians should be happy to be where they are.

Probably more space is given to what Lenin himself once referred to as "production propaganda" than to any other subject area. This includes articles praising a specific worker or a whole factory staff for exemplary work, exhortations for all to work harder and produce more, or progress reports on fulfillment of the current national economic plan.

A great deal of space is devoted to party instructions and warnings, aimed at ensuring desired conduct on the part of officials, workers, managers, etc. Even the most routine aspects of party congresses or of visits by important international visitors receive extensive play, much of it on the front page.

Soviet culture is a priority subject, and the amount of space devoted to general information, including educational articles and reports on such matters as child care, health, household hints, and even beauty care has increased in recent years.

Personalities are played down. The Soviet press never prints stories about the home life of even the most important political figures, let alone entertainers, movie stars, and the like. More attention is paid to entertainment generally than was true a few years ago, but the emphasis placed on particular aspects depends on their contribution to the party's view of political or cultural value.

Negative information about the Soviet Union is ignored, including stories about accidents, plane crashes (unless foreigners or Soviet VIPs are involved), drug problems, epidemics, and the like. Anything that might be construed as suggesting a flaw or a weakness in the system is taboo.

Consumer information—and advertising—is scarce. The party has retreated from its old contention that advertising was nothing but a capitalist trick to dupe the citzenry, but most of what exists is institutional and not much use to the would-be consumer.

An important feature of the Soviet system is the letters-to-the-editor section, which serves as a kind of safety valve for public frustration and, additionally, provides the party with a means of checking on activities and performances of bureaucrats and managers throughout the country.

It is a part of the official doctrine that the media must provide an outlet for complaints from their audiences. *Pravda* claims it receives 30,000 letters a month. *Izvestia* editors have been quoted as saying their total is even higher: 500,000 a year. Many of these are certainly inspired by lower Party functionaries and serve merely to suggest public support for the regime, but some are aimed at exposing improper activities on the part of individuals. The usual targets are lower-level officials or factory supervisors.

All such complaints are said to be investigated thoroughly. *Pravda* has at least 50 employees in its letter department, including reporters who turn the information into stories. Readers are frequently regaled with accounts of how some wrongdoer has been caught with his hand in the till or how some petty bureaucrat, who had lorded over his neighbors, has received his comeuppance. Such incidents are invariably presented as the sins of individuals, never in such a way as to suggest a flaw in the system or an error in policy.

Despite such sometimes titillating items, the Soviet press is overwhelmingly political and to Western eyes exceedingly dull. Nevertheless, circulations, particularly of the all-Union papers, are huge. *Pravda* prints 11 million copies in 44 different cities throughout the country. *Komsomolskaya Pravda*, the national youth paper, circulates 10 million copies, while *Izvestia* claims 8.6 million, the same as *Trud*.

Soviet-Bloc States

This same pattern was established in all the Eastern European countries—East Germany, Poland, Czechoslovakia, Hungary, Romania, Bulgaria, Yugoslavia, and Albania—when Communist regimes came to power there after World War II. By now, some variations have begun to show, but only in Yugoslavia have these gone so far that the system no longer fits the mold. And, of course, Yugoslavia is no longer a part of the Soviet bloc.

Albania, too, has dropped out of the bloc. But the Communist leadership there has remained adamantly Stalinist, and the media there is held tightly to the old pattern.

There is a possibility that the ferment in Poland, which has given rise to the Solidarity union movement, may have a permanent impact on the system there, but it is too early to say for certain. In all the other countries there has been some improvement in the amount and accuracy of news published, as well as in its display; but except in Yugoslavia, the basic structure and the fact of tight detailed party control remain unchanged.

In each of the seven others, including Albania, the organ of the party's Central Committee is the largest paper in the country in terms of circulation and is the authoritative voice of the regime—the local equivalent of *Pravda*. Each of the seven also has its nationally distributed paper for the youth, for the trade unions, for farm workers, and so forth, mirroring the Soviet structure.

The only variations occur in East Germany, Poland and Czechoslovakia, which have no specific government dailies equivalent to *Izvestia*. Instead, these three have papers that ostensibly represent other political parties, parties which have been coopted by the Communists but have been permitted to exist on paper.

The Central Committee organs and their official circulation figures are: Bulgaria, *Rabotnichesko Delo*, 850,000; Czechoslovakia, *Rude Pravo*, 900,000; East Germany, *Neues Deutschland*, 800,000;

Poland, *Trybuna Ludu*, 970,000; Romania, *Scinteia*, 1,300,000; Hungary, *Nepszabadsag*, 810,000; and Albania, *Zeri i Popullit*, 110,000.

Some of these are livelier than *Pravda*, are more Western in appearance, carry ads, and are more apt to carry "hard" news, even on page 1. In *Pravda*, any such items are usually found in the last two pages of the paper, which, as a rule, has only six.

Hungary's *Nepszabadsag* is also different in that it appears in tabloid format. All the others, including *Pravda*, are broadsheet size.

The more Western appearance of some of these papers undoubtedly reflects differences in cultural inheritance: the pre–World War II press in Eastern Europe was influenced primarily by Western Europe. But it also reflects the fact that in order to retain any credibility among readers, who have access to Western broadcasts as well as other sources of news, these papers have had to give attention to events that *Pravda* ignores.

This development is most evident in Hungary and Poland and least in Romania, Bulgaria, and Albania. The latter has only one daily in addition to *Zeri i Popullit*—a government mouthpiece called *Bashkimi*—which claims a circulation of 35,000.

The situation in Yugoslavia is very different. The most important Yugoslav newspaper is Belgrade's *Politika*, which along with several others describes itself as independent, that is, without official links to either party or government. Events have demonstrated that this freedom is not absolute. The party has ousted editors who failed to carry out its edicts and has moved in other ways to demonstrate its continuing authority. Nevertheless, the Yugoslav media scene is very different from that in any other Communist-ruled country.

This situation resulted from a decision by the Yugoslav League of Communists in the 1950s to adopt a unique system of workers' self-management. In essence, this gives the people who work in any particular enterprise, including media, the authority to run the operation with a minimum of interference from central administration.

As a part of this innovation, the party removed itself from the publishing business, gave up subsidizing newspapers, and decreed that all had to function as commercial operations, earning their own way from advertising and circulation. Although still subject to control—the party sees that bounds are not overstepped and its grip tightens or loosens from time to time in response to both internal and external developments—the Yugoslav media are able to give their audiences a more complete and accurate picture of what is happening in the world than is available in any of the Soviet-bloc countries. Papers are larger, cover a much wider variety of topics, and run far more ads. For example, *Politika*, which is a tabloid-size paper, averages 36 to 40 pages an issue on weekdays, including 10 to 15 pages of ads.

An accompanying decentralization policy led to the development of an almost separate media system—broadcast as well as print—in each of the six republics and two autonomous regions into which the country is divided. As a result, although several of the larger papers can be bought in cities throughout the country, Yugoslavia does not have the centralized press structure characteristic of the Soviet-bloc states.

Although the most important, *Politika* is not the largest Yugoslav paper. That honor goes to a popular Belgrade afternooner called *Vecernje Novosti*, which sells 346,000 copies, compared with *Politika*'s 285,000 daily and 320,000 on Sundays. *Politika Ekspres*, an afternoon offshoot of *Politika*, has 260,000.

Major papers in other republics—Belgrade is the capital of Serbia as well as being the national capital—include *Delo* (93,730) in Ljubljana, the capital of Slovenia; *Vjesnik* (86,600) and *Vecernji List* (267,000), in Zagreb, the capital of Croatia; and *Oslobodjenje* (83,380) in Sarajevo, the capital of Bosnia-Herzegovina. Several of these even have their own correspondents abroad.

The case of *Borba*, which in the years immediately after World War II was the nation's most important paper, is illustrative of the changes that have occurred in Yugoslavia.

In 1949, *Borba* was the organ of the party's Central Committee and a mirror image of *Pravda* in almost every respect. It had a circulation of about 650,000 copies. With the institution of the workers' council system and the withdrawal of direct party control of the press, *Borba* lost its privileged position. Throughout the 1950s and 1960s its circulation fell steadily until in the mid-1970s it stood at only about 30,000.

It was finally rescued by the Socialist Alliance, the mass front organization of the Yugoslav party, on the grounds that since it had been the principal paper of the Partisans during the war, it should be kept in some way. It is now the national voice of the Alliance and sells about 50,000 copies daily.

The Yugoslavs also have a number of influential weeklies, including the only truly Western-style news magazine in the Communist world, a publication called *NIN*. *Politika* publishes a handsomely illustrated weekly called *Ilustrovana Politika*, which, in terms of circulation, trails two Zagreb publications: an illustrated magazine called *Arena* and *Vjesnik u Srijedu*, the weekend feature supplement of *Vjesnik*. Other more specialized weeklies include family and children's magazines, publications covering sports and economic affairs as well as two party publications: *Socijalizm*, devoted to Marxist theory, and *Kommunist*, a widely read journal of comment.

Among the bloc nations, only Poland can claim publications that do not fit somehow within the Soviet pattern. In addition to a number of underground publications that have sprung up in recent years, several Roman Catholic periodicals are significant politically. One group of these is not recognized by the Polish hierarchy. This includes the Warsaw daily Slowo Powszechne, and a number of other journals published by an organization known as *PAX*, a pro-Communist self-proclaimed Catholic movement loosely linked to the government.

Of those papers that are approved by the church leadership, the most important is the weekly *Tygodnik Powszechny (Universal Weekly)*, which is published in Krakow under the auspices of a Catholic lay group known as Znak. Although censored, as are all Polish publications, and with a newsprint allocation that limits production to 40,000 copies, *Tygodnik Powszechny* is eagerly sought after because it is thought to be a reflection of the views of the church, which in Poland is a major force in the society.

Another Polish weekly that does not fit the official pattern is Warsaw's *Polityka*. Although an "official" newspaper, it is written and edited to appeal to the nation's intellectual elite. As a result, it is much more sophisticated in approach and more open and outspoken than the dailies, so much so that it is frequently criticized by them. It survives apparently because it represents views held by some members of the party leadership. Early in 1981 its press run was increased from 300,000 to 400,000.

All capital cities in the Soviet bloc have at least one popular daily designed to appeal to the non-Party audience. Most of these enjoy national circulation. None are sensational in the Western sense, however. Sensationalism is taboo in the Communist world. The most important of these popular papers include the following.

USSR, *Sovietskaya Rossia*, 3,230,000; Poland, *Express Wieczorny* (an afternoon tabloid) 500,000 and *Zycie Warszawy*, 360,000; east Germany, *Berliner Zeitung*, 400,000 and *Berliner am Abend*, 192,367; Czechoslovakia, *Vecerni Praha*, 120,000; Hungary, *Esti Herlap*, 251,00 and *Magyar Nemzet* (an old title resurrected as a paper for intellectuals) 127,000; Romania, *Informatia Bucharestiului*, 200,000, and *Romania Libera*, 300,000; Bulgaria, *Otechestven Front*, 280,000 and *Vecherni Novini*,125,000.

Otechestven Front and *Romania Libera* are roughly equivalent to Moscow's *Izvestia*, although the first is published by the Fatherland Front, the mass "front" organization of the Bulgarian party, while *Romania Libera* is put out by the party rather than the government. Hungary's government paper *Magyar Hirlap* is a relatively new foundation with a circulation of only about 50,000.

The bloc's trade union papers are generally second in importance only to the main party and government organs. In addition to the Soviet Union's *Trud*, these include the following: Bulgaria, *Trud* (cq)

250,000; Czechoslovakia, *Prace*, 317,000; East Germany, *Tribune*, 400,000; Poland, *Glos Pracy*, 160,000; Romania, *Munca*, 320,000; and Hungary, *Nepsava*, 302,000.

Generally of more or less the same rank are the papers aimed at the youth, equivalents of the Soviet's *Komsomolskaya Pravda*. These include: Bulgaria, *Narodna Mladozh*, 250,000; Czechoslovakia, *Mlada Fronta*, 239,000; East Germany, *Junge Welt*, 1,060,000; Poland, *Szander Mlodych*, 235,000; Romania, *Scinteia Tineretului*, 200,000; and Hungary, *Magyar Ifjusag*, 293,000. The latter is a weekly, not a daily.

All Soviet-bloc states also have papers planned for people working in agriculture. In Hungary and Romania these are weeklies, but the others are dailies. The Soviet's *Selskaya Zhign* is, of course, the largest, with 8.5 million copies. The other two of significance are Czechoslovakia's *Zemedelske Noviny*, with 342,000, and East Germany's *Bauern Echo*, with 90,000.

None of the papers published by the captive Party organizations in the three countries without *Izvestia* equivalents are of particular importance except two in Czechoslovakia. These are the old Socialist Party's *Svobodno Slovo*, with a circulation of 228,000, and *Lidove Demokracie,* with 217,000. It is ostensibly the organ of the People's (Catholic) Party.

All seven bloc members have papers devoted to sports, a subject the main papers pay little if any attention to. All also have papers published by the armed forces. Of these, Moscow's *Krasnaya Zvesda* (*Red Star*) with a circulation of 2.4 million is far and away the most important.

None have news magazines in the style of *Time* or *Newsweek*, but all publish a number of weekly newspapers, journals, and illustrated magazines for a variety of different audiences. In most of the countries, the largest of these in terms of circulation are for children. For example, Moscow's *Pionerskaya Pravda*, which comes out twice weekly, distributes 11 million copies. The next largest group, again in terms of circulation, are women's magazines and illustrated reviews. Radio and television journals are popular as are the satirical weeklies that are a feature of the bloc. The best known of these is Moscow's *Krokodil*, but each of the other countries has its own version.

Circulation is not necessarily a reflection of significance, however. Some of the more important of the papers and journals deal with such matters as economics, international affairs and culture. While these may not attract the same size audiences—Moscow's *Literaturnaya Gazeta* with a circulation of 2.6 million is undoubtedly the largest—they are much more apt to be studied carefully both at home and abroad.

Nevertheless, the circulation of all magazines increased enormously in the Soviet Union during the 1960s and 1970s. This was true of both the established publications and a variety of new ones that were started during those years. Among the more interesting new ones are *Inostrahnaya Literature* (Foreign Literature), which prints translations of Western novels and short stories; *Noviye Tovary* (New Products), which reports on new consumer items both at home and abroad; *Za Rubezhom (From Abroad)*, which carries translations of articles from the foreign press; and *Sluzhba Byta (Everyday Services)*, which reports on consumer services.

However popular, these publications, like the newspapers, are intensely serious. Their aim is not to provide the reader with an escape from the daily grind but rather to heighten the reader's concern with his or her everyday activity.

To Western eyes, these and most other Soviet publications look odd. Many of the important journals are printed in newspaper broadsheet form on ordinary newsprint. There are almost no slick-paper periodicals except *Soviet Life*, which is published for foreign audiences and is not distributed in the Soviet Union itself.

Newspapers have relatively few pages. A *Christian Science Monitor* correspondent in 1978 described *Pravda* as follows:

> For three kopecks (4½ cents), 10.7 million readers receive six
> grey sheets of type a day (except Monday, when they receive
> four sheets—and pay only two kopecks, or almost three
> cents). There is no advertising, no crime, no comics, no travel
> tips, no crossword, no personality columns, no law court
> report, no inside gossip from the Kremlin, no late bulletins,
> no list of international sports results. There is also no
> pessimism, no despair, no problem that cannot be solved.

Except for the fact that *Pravda* has increased its circulation slightly, the description still fits. And incidentally, *Pravda* has more pages than any other Soviet daily. Most of them print only four.

As the *Monitor* correspondent suggested, the content presents even more of a contrast with the west. Paul Lendvai has compared the stories published in the October 1, 1979, issues of *Pravda* and the *International Herald Tribune*, published in Paris.

The main story in the *Herald Tribune* that day was a report of an appeal issued by Pope John Paul II for peace in Northern Ireland. Other front-page stories concerned a purge of Iran's armed forces, talks between the United States and Mexico concerning compensation for an oil spill in the Gulf of Mexico, an agreement between the United States and West Germany to support the dollar, a Chinese accusation of Soviet encroachment along their common border, and an interview with a Soviet specialist on United States–Soviet relations. Inside were reports of the killing of students in the Central African Republic, a story about President Carter's concern over Soviet troops in Cuba, a think piece on Senator Kennedy's political plans, and the story of the execution of a deposed African dictator.

In *Pravda*, however, the main news item was a story about the completion of harvest work on a state farm in Central Asia. Two full columns on the front page were devoted to an editorial calling for improved political and economic work. The page also featured a lengthy interview with the Soviet Minister of Power about construction of a new power plant, another story quoting the leader of Austria's small Communist party about the importance to Austria of trade with the Soviet Union, an account of the situation in the Central African Republic, the text of a brief telegram sent by Soviet officials to Chinese leaders on the thirtieth anniversary of the founding of the Chinese People's Republic, and a story about the imminent arrival of Greek Premier Karamanlis that included some biographical material. Three brief domestic news items and two photographs, one showing three outstanding workers at an Odessa oil refinery and the other the interior of a ball-bearing factory, completed the page.

Inside were a number of long articles. Two of them, one written by the chief engineer of an iron foundry and the other by a bookkeeper at a state farm, concerned a campaign to further political indoctrination and the application of Lenin's teaching. Another reported on the situation at a state farm near Novgorod and still another on intermeshing of science and production in the city of Volvograd. A critical assessment of management problems, a cultural feature, an article asserting continued Soviet desire to be friends with China were followed by a piece criticizing Western writers for paying attention to what was described as anti-Soviet propaganda.

Three short reports about activities of Communist parties in Vietnam, Japan and Switzerland, an item about Brezhnev receiving a Socialist International delegation, and a picture of a female worker in a factory in Mongolia made up the rest of the first four pages.

Page five, which is the main foreign news page, had two stories on mass demonstrations staged in Newark and Philadelphia against what was described as racial and political repression. Another story reported a deterioration in Canada's economic situation. A third asserted that United States capital was taking over the Australian economy. A story from Britain accused the London government of violating human rights by not permitting the unification of families that had some members still living in Africa or Asia. Meanwhile, items from Cuba, East Germany, Bulgaria, Cambodia, and Afghanistan reported only "good news."

Page six, the last page, which is where *Pravda* puts such things as the TV and radio listings and the weather report, also had a long feature on a museum in Vladivostok, a report on an international chess tournament, and a long account of Soviet performances at the world water-skiing championships in Canada.

Except possibly in Poland and Hungary, the content of most of the major dailies in the other bloc nations would not have differed significantly from that of *Pravda* on that day. But even in Poland and Hungary, newspapers generally present more information about current events, some of it even on page one, and still provide a limited and highly subjective view of the world. It has been estimated that overall only about 10 to 15 percent of the items in Soviet-bloc papers deal with the current day's events.

Only one of the events reported by the *Herald Tribune* appeared in *Pravda*—the Central African Republic story. But even here, *Pravda* devoted a good part of its account not to the situation itself but to reporting criticisms by the French communist newspaper *L'Humanité* of Paris's decision to send paratroopers to help keep order.

Despite its comparatively limited news hole, *Pravda* claims it has 40,000 correspondents. Whether or not this figure is close to the mark, it is a fact that the paper, like all Soviet newspapers, relies to a considerable extent on nonprofessional volunteer journalists. The idea follows from one of the basic tenets of the Soviet press: that it must maintain active and continuous ties with the mass of the people generally. As long ago as 1918, *Pravda* organized a corps of "rabselkor," or worker-peasant correspondents, throughout the country. Other papers followed suit.

As the press grew, so did the number of rabselkor. As a result, even today many of the stories in any Soviet newspaper are written by such nonjournalists, who may be party or government employees, factory or state farm workers, or others, as evidenced by the Lendvai study. It has been asserted that the importance of the rabselkor has declined somewhat in recent years with the increasing professionalism of Soviet journalism, but they still play a significant role in Soviet publishing.

Pravda is the oldest Soviet newspaper, having been founded in 1912 by V. I. Lenin, the father of the Bolshevik Revolution. Originally published in St. Petersburg, now Leningrad, it was moved to Moscow along with the government following the success of the October 1917 revolution. *Izvestia* dates from the year of the revolution, as does a much smaller Moscow daily called *Gudok* (Whistle), the organ of the Ministry of Communications and the Rail Transport Workers Union. All the others were established later.

Since under Soviet theory the party must actively influence and lead public opinion, it has consistently put a high priority on development of the media. As a result, the number of newspapers and other periodicals has shown a steady increase over the years.

Although some newspapers in the smaller bloc nations bear older titles, all were organized in their present form after the Communist takeover in those countries following World War II.

Throughout the bloc, major newspapers are parts of huge publishing enterprises which are responsible for most of the periodicals available to the reader. *Pravda* reportedly makes more money from the other publications it puts out than it does from its newspaper operations.

In the Soviet Union, all told there are nearly 240 various publishing houses, both national and regional. *Pravda* publishes all types of party materials—books, magazines, and journals—in addition to newspapers. Another house concentrates on science, another on fiction, and so on. The regional houses publish materials designed specifically for those particular areas.

None of these houses are privately owned. While they may operate under the auspices of the party, the trade union organization, government agencies, or such bodies as the Writers' Union, all, in fact, are responsible to the State Committee for Publishing, Printing and Bookselling, which must approve all publications. This structure has led some observers to argue that, in truth, the government is the only publisher.

The circulation of newspapers and magazines as well as the sale of books is also controlled by central authority. No newspaper or magazine handles its own distribution. All this is in the hands of a separate organization which oversees the circulation of all printed materials.

Publishing and circulation are equally concentrated in the other bloc countries. In East Germany, for example, a party-operated enterprise, known as Zentrag, controls the publishing of about 94 percent of the nation's daily press circulation. It also handles the export and import of all books and has a monopoly of advertising and publicity in the country. It operates two of the nation's largest paper mills and runs more than 100 publishing enterprises. Circulation in East Germany is handled by the Post Office, which also operates all news stands from which publications may be sold.

The Polish equivalent of Zentrag is RSW Prasa-Ruch, which supervises the publication of 95 percent of the country's daily press circulation. It is also responsible for the production of more than half the nation's magazines and journals. Furthermore, it handles the distribution of all printed materials in the country—newspapers, magazines, and books—as well as the export and import of books.

In each of the bloc nations the capital city is far and away the most important publishing center, although several have important regional centers. In Czechoslovakia, where Slovak regionalism has been an important political issue, Bratislava, the Slovak capital, runs a fairly close second to Prague. In Poland, the ancient city of Krakow is significant. East Germany has Leipzig, Dresden, and Karl-Marx Stadt. Each of these three cities has a daily paper with a circulation larger than that of any of the East Berlin dailies except *Neues Deutschland* and the *Berliner Zeitung*. However, like all the others, these run only six to eight pages an issue.

In this, too, the Yugoslavs are different. Because of decentralization, each of the republics has its own individual publishing operations in its capital. Belgrade and Zagreb would certainly rank at the top but cannot claim exclusivity.

In the orthodox Communist view, newspapers are the most important medium. They are the main forum for presenting material to the general population and for relaying information to the party's rank-and-file members. Radio and television officially rank second but are closing the gap simply because of their efficiency in reaching the mass of the people quickly.

An indication of the shift in emphasis and the larger place given broadcasting is the fact that the Soviet news agency TASS, which in the past sent important news to the newspapers first, now will sometimes let the radio and television services know about certain developments before it notifies the papers. This seems to be particularly true when the developments involve situations that are likely to be picked up by foreign broadcasters. The idea appears to be simply to alert the Russian services.

Broadcasting

Broadcasting is a state monopoly in every Soviet-bloc nation. In the Soviet Union, it is controlled by the State Committee for Radio and Television, an arm of the Council of Ministers, the nation's top executive body. Except for differences in names and titles, the setup is the same in all of Moscow's allies.

In each, the bulk of the programming is provided by a central service in the capital city, be it Moscow, Warsaw, East Berlin, Prague, Budapest, Bucharest, or Sofia. Regional services originate some programming of their own, particularly in the Soviet Union, where the sheer size of the country and the great number of different languages dictates greater diversity. Nevertheless, all have at least a limited amount of regional or local service.

The Soviet Union employs 67 different languages and dialects in its regional operations.

In the past, most Soviet broadcasting was by means of wired systems, transmitting a single program. There were several reasons for this: wide areas of the country were not yet electrified so normal radio receivers could not be used and inexpensive versions of such receivers were in short supply. But it is clear that the regime also was happy with the system because it gave the authorities complete control over what the people could listen to.

All this has changed in recent years with the development of the transistor, the spread of electrification, and an explosive expansion of all aspects of broadcasting. The growth has presented the Soviet leadership with new problems. A vast increase in the number of normal radio receivers has enabled more people to listen to foreign broadcasts that present a world view different from the official Moscow line.

The initial response of all bloc nations was to try to jam the frequencies used by Western broadcasters to prevent their citizens from listening. This was stopped for most services in 1963 but resumed again with the 1968 Soviet invasion of Czechoslovakia. At the same time, Moscow began investing in the development of more wired systems which would handle only the official programs.

As far as the Soviet Union is concerned, both efforts continue. Moscow and some of its allies jam Western broadcasts fairly regularly. However, several others have all but given up and millions of East Germans, Czechs, and Hungarians not only receive Western radio broadcasts more or less freely but also West German and Austrian TV. In fact, at least one Hungarian paper, published at Gyor, near the frontier, even publishes the daily schedule of the Austrian TV service. And a Czech joke has it that so many TV antennas in one section of Bratislava are tuned to receive Vienna that the area is known locally as "the Vienna woods."

As far as Soviet-bloc broadcasting operations are concerned, the same guiding principles that have been laid down for the print media also apply to radio and television. These general rules are supplemented for all media by a continuous stream of directives and briefings from government and party officials as to specifics.

News broadcasts are tailored to serve the purposes of the regime. One study of the Soviet broadcast services asserts that the most important quality of a Soviet newscast is "purposefulness" and it goes on to quote a directive which explained:

> A durable political impression should be made, one item
> standing out and remaining in the listener's memory to
> stimulate action. The principle underlying this characteristic
> is "a newscast is not a mirror but a magnifying glass."

All newscasts are supposed to deal with up-to-date events, but these events are carefully selected and must always take second place to the coverage of party matters. The most routine aspects of party congresses are covered in detail, even though this may mean that quite important developments go unmentioned for days.

This is not unique to broadcast. Soviet-bloc papers do virtually the same thing, devoting page after page to texts of even the most routine speeches. And Westerners getting their first look at *Pravda* or *Izvestia* are usually bemused by front-page items that are nothing more than lists of names of dignitaries attending a Kremlin function. The papers may not have any inside gossip from the Kremlin but they do run Kremlin social notes.

The forms of Soviet news broadcasting are quite standardized. In addition to the newscasts themselves, which are made up of both reports and comments on the selected events, programming includes surveys of press comments, interviews, and "international surveys" that deal mainly with the press of other communist countries or leftist voices in the Third World.

All news is presented in a manner designed to illustrate the correctness of Soviet policy or the "imperialistic, war-mongering" tendencies of the West. Revolutionary movements in other parts of the world are played up, as are activities of Communists or Communist sympathizers in the West.

Radio Moscow, which is the central programming and transmitting authority, transmits eight main programs daily for listeners within the Soviet Union on long, medium, short, and FM bands. These programs total more than 1,000 hours a week. On the average, about 55 percent of the total broadcast time is devoted to music, 16 percent to news, 12 percent to sociopolitical discussions, 9 percent to literature and drama, and about 7 percent to children's programs.

In addition, the Soviet Union is one of the world's major international broadcasters. Programs are transmitted in 64 foreign languages and beamed to almost all parts of the world. The other bloc nations are also heavily involved in this kind of effort. Taken together, they are usually ranked about fourth in the world in terms of hours of external broadcasting, behind the Soviet Union, United States, and China. Oddly enough, tiny Albania by itself ranks among the top ten, thanks to the gift some years ago by China of some quite powerful transmitting equipment.

All aspects of broadcasting in the Soviet Union have grown tremendously during the past 20 years, but television has almost literally exploded. In 1960, the Russians counted only about five million TV sets in the whole country. By 1975, this figure had skyrocketed to 55 million and estimates now place it at better than 70 million, closing in on the one-to-a-household goal. Programs are relayed by microwave and by satellites that can cover most of that vast country.

The number of channels available to the viewer varies from place to place. The central TV service in Moscow programs six channels. However, people in Leningrad have only three and most other major cities only two. One of the Moscow channels broadcasts in color. This began as a regular operation in 1967. Several other cities also have color, and current plans call for the early opening of color TV stations in all capital cities of the various republics in the Union, as well as in other major provincial cities.

The color channel is on the air for about 20 hours a day. The others operate for shorter periods of time—one is on the air 12 hours a day, another for six, and still another for only four. One channel operates only on weekends.

General subject matter also varies from channel to channel. One is devoted exclusively to instructional broadcasting, both for regular school classes and for adult education. Another programs material considered of only regional interest. A third carries primarily entertainment features, including films, variety shows, and plays. Children's programs are emphasized on most channels, particularly during the late afternoon. There are no ads.

The Russians do have quiz and game shows, crime series, and serials that have a soap-opera touch. But all these are very different kinds of shows from what might be thought of as their equivalents in the United States. There is no sex and no violence, and crime never pays. Virtue is always rewarded. Everything is designed to promote what the party considers proper thought and action.

News is broadcast several times a day on radio. The main TV newscast, called *Vremya (Time)* comes on at 9 P.M. It lasts a half hour and is repeated at 8 o'clock the following morning.

Regardless of what might be going on, the broadcast almost always follows the same pattern, beginning with government announcements and other official news. Next comes other domestic items, usually economic in nature, then regional reports, and last, international news. A weather report and a few minutes devoted to sports closes out the half hour.

To illustrate how even TV news is used as a vehicle of political instruction or persuasion, the Landvai study mentioned previously listed all the items, except sports and weather, contained in the Vremya cast on April 14, 1974, in the order in which they were shown. They were:

The Central Committee issued its annual 68 slogans for the May 1 celebrations which are published in all papers on the front page.

It was announced that on April 21, Lenin's birthday, a "subotnik" (a no-pay work day) will be staged. Workers and farmers in the whole country will work free of charge on this day.

A film about a textile plant in Kirgizia (Central Asia) was shown that stressed ever faster and better production; an outstanding female laborer who overfulfilled her norm was interviewed.

Leningrad—Brezhnev sent greetings to a scientific conference discussing the "new socialist man." A speaker quoted Lenin's words about the quality of labor. Pensioned miner talked about plan fulfillment.

Film about an oil refinery with reference to cooperation with East Germany in this branch of industry was shown.

Reports were given from the world of labor: a car plant in the Urals increased production, more vegetables were harvested in Azerbaijan, with a film about new methods showing women harvesting cabbages.

The first Bulgarian cosmonaut and a Soviet colleague received decorations.

Moscow—a report was given about a conference on science day, with an academician talking about science in the service of industry, agriculture and the Communist party.

Tiflis (the capital of Soviet Georgia)—meeting of the Communist Youth Union in Lenin Square.

Vienna—United States-Soviet talks about satellites.

Sofia—Bulgarian President Todor Zhivkov received unionists and spoke with them about disarmament.

Hanoi—Vietnamese note is handed over to the Chinese. New accusations against Peking leadership.

Damascus—Protest meeting against Egyptian-Israeli peace treaty.

Beirut—Palestinians protest against Sadat's "capitulation line."

Teheran—Premier Bazargan predicted further successes in the reconstruction of Iran.

Islamabad—According to a report by *The New York Times*, American citizens are involved in a "counter-revolutionary" conspiracy against the Afghan government under Premier Taraki.

Rome—Film about the election campaign that asserts the "conservative bourgeoisie and the monopolies" place their hopes on anticommunist propaganda.

Nicaragua—Opposition to the Somoza regime increases; successes of guerrillas reported.

Kampala—Uganda's capital calm as new Premier Lule sworn in. Western agencies report that Idi Amin still has some support in parts of the country.

Addis Ababa—Ethiopia recognizes Lule's government in Uganda.

Stockholm—Protest demonstration against unemployment with film that portrays this as a typical crisis system in a capitalist country.

New Delhi—Chinese "bands" stir up unrest on India's borders.

Moscow—Opening night performance of ballet "My Vietnam" in the Kremlin's Congress Palace.

The main evening newscasts of the TV services in the other bloc countries that night would have been somewhat livelier, with pretty faces, more sophisticated graphics, and even more items that would be considered news in the West. Nevertheless, overall they still presented essentially the same world view—steady progress by happy citizens living in peace in their part of the world.

News Agencies

Television is popular, but in the official scheme of things the most important news organization in the Soviet Union may actually be the news agency TASS. The name is an acroynm for Telegraph Agency of the Soviet Union. It is the voice of the government and the screen through which most of the news reaching the Soviet people is filtered.

A 1935 decree declared TASS to be the "central organ of information" for the country. It is not the nation's only agency, however. Individual republics have their own agencies, responsible for the collection and distribution of information within their specific areas. But these, in reality, are nothing more than subsidiaries of TASS. The 1935 decree also declared that TASS "exercises direction and control over the work of the telegraphic agencies of the Union Republics and gives them concrete orders for the collection and distribution of information."

TASS was also granted exclusive rights in the distribution of domestic information from one republic agency to another as well as the distribution of foreign and all-Union news within the country and the distribution of information about the Soviet Union in foreign countries.

In 1961, this monopoly was broken in part when a new agency, the Agentstvo Pechati Novesti, commonly known simply as Novesti, was organized. It gathers and distributes feature material both at home and abroad and functions as a kind of official publicity agency for the government. For example, foreign news organizations are expected to work through Novesti in carrying out any special assignments in the Soviet Union.

But TASS is still very much king of the hill, retaining all other aspects of its monopoly position. Its importance is underlined by the fact that it is attached directly to the Council of Ministers. Its director-general and four deputies are appointed by that body.

The agency has correspondents throughout the Soviet Union and about 200 stationed abroad. It subscribes to or exchanges news with the national news agencies of more than 50 countries as well as all the major international agencies, including AP, UPI, Reuters, and Agence France-Presse.

At home it lists about 10,000 subscribers to its news and photo services, radio, and TV operations as well as newspapers and periodicals. Each subscriber pays a mutually agreed-on fee for the services supplied and TASS officials say the agency is self-supporting.

Materials received by TASS can be transmitted directly to the central press in Moscow and to the offices of the central broadcasting services. Reports are sent by wire, or even by mail in the case of nonurgent information, to subscribers throughout the country.

Not everything the agency receives is selected for publication, even though some of it may be essential information for policy-makers. To make certain that people who need to know are informed about matters kept from the general public, TASS issues daily four different bulletins for party and government leaders as well as for selected media personnel.

Each is distributed to people on certain security classification levels, the specific level of which is indicated by the color of the cover. Thus, the first, or lowest, classification, is called the violet TASS. Materials in this are relatively unrestricted and could even appear in print if a responsible editor so decided.

The second level, the "white" TASS, is confidential—for information and reference only. It is much more detailed and goes only to trusted functionaries of the party and government and to chief editors. Next is the "red" Tass, which is even more confidential, so much so that "secret" is stamped on its cover and it is delivered by an armed guard. It may contain what is referred to as "dangerous" news.

The fourth and most exclusive of all these bulletins is distributed only to very top level people. Known simply as the "Special Bulletin," it contains material the regime wants to keep as secret as possible, as well as information about anti-Soviet activities, abroad as well as at home.

Each of the other bloc nations boasts a national news agency that in essence is a smaller version of TASS, performing virtually the same functions on a lesser scale. These are referred to generally by their logotypes: Bulgaria, BTA; Czechoslovakia, CTK; East Germany, ADN; Hungary MTI; Poland, PAP—although the Romanian agency uses the name Agerpress.

Three of these states also have an equivalent to Novosti. In Bulgaria it is called the Sofia Press Agency. Czechoslovakia's version is known as Pragopress and Poland's as Interpress. Poland also has another small agency, the Agencja Robotnicza (AP) as well as a Central Photographic Agency, associated with Interpress.

The two Communist-ruled but nonbloc states—Albania and Yugoslavia—also have national agencies. Albania's ATA is a miniature version of TASS, but Yugoslavia's Tanjug is quite different.

Like other enterprises in that country, it operates on a commercial basis, selling its services to a variety of customers. Among these is the Yugoslav government, payments from which amount to about half the agency's annual income.

Tanjug no longer has a monopoly on the distribution of news within the country. Newspapers can, and do, subscribe to others. For instance, the Belgrade newspaper *Politika* takes *The New York Times* service.

Tanjug has a number of correspondents stationed throughout the world, including places in the Third World that are largely ignored by the big international agencies. It also functions as the relay center for the so-called Non-Aligned News Pool, to which a number of Arab and Third World nations belong.

Government—Press Relations

In the Soviet bloc, the media are literally arms of the party and government—"our trusted transmission belt," as Khrushchev once described them. They are the engines of the system of restriction and persuasion by which the state controls the citizen's access to information and through which it pumps the information it wants them to believe.

Long before the Bolshevik Revolution, Lenin laid down the basic principles under which the press has functioned:

A periodical is a political utterance, a political enterprise.

Objectivity is objectionable since "a periodical without tendentiousness is a ridiculous, absurd, scandalous and harmful thing."

A paper is not merely a collective propagandist and collective agitator, it is also a collective organizer.

This last dictim is repeated over and over again in Soviet literature on the media, so it is worth examining more carefully. The idea behind the word "collective" stems from the purely ideological notion—which bears no relation to the facts—that the press is owned by the people. Both it and the people are held to be working toward a common goal: the building of communism. Therefore, the press and the people cannot be divided into producers and consumers but form a "dynamic collective."

The words "propaganda" and "agitation" also have special meanings in the Soviet context. Broadly speaking, propaganda involves the analysis and discussion of Marxist theory among a relatively small elite, primarily Communist Party members. Agitation, on the other hand, is designed to motivate the masses by taking one idea and hammering it home to large groups of people.

The third function in the Lenin dictum—collective organizer—means that through its agitation and propaganda work, the media "organize" society to actively struggle for realization of the party's plan and help to create a new "socialist consciousness" among the people.

Soviet ideologists hold that the mass media can never, under any circumstances, be politically neutral. They are always instruments of a class whose interests they promote. Therefore, the diversity of opinion western media boast about they see as a sham, a false front, behind which there is little if any questioning of the system itself.

For their part, the Soviet leadership make no pretense of objectivity or neutrality. Instead, they deliberately shape all forms of communication to further their own goals. As a result, even though the constitutions of all Communist nations supposedly guarantee freedom of thought and of the media, there is no free flow of ideas in the Soviet Union or any other Communist-ruled state. There are limits even in Yugoslavia. The reason is that such a flow probably would lead to the formation of opposition groups, endangering the Communist Party's monopoly over societal action.

The controls are backed by laws that appear to be in direct contravention of the various constitutions. For example, all 14 Soviet republics have laws that make free political communication illegal.

They bar "agitation or propaganda for purposes of weakening Soviet power," the spreading of "slanderous fabrications which defame the Soviet political and social system" and other similar acts.

The party is the sole arbiter of what constitutes a violation of any of these restrictions, since it also controls both the police and the court system. A citizen accused of such behavior is practically without legal protection.

Under this system, the media is simply a tool of the regime. The leadership can establish or abolish any periodical or broadcast operation at will. Such enterprises don't have to make money, although many do, including apparently all the larger newspapers. Those that do not make money for one reason or another are subsidized, because their continued existence has been deemed vital to realization of the regime's aims.

As was indicated earlier, those that do make money depend on returns from circulation or profits from other ventures. Advertising exists but it is not much of a factor in the economics of the media in any Soviet-bloc country, although it has been growing in some, particularly Hungary and Poland. Nevertheless, only in maverick Yugoslavia has it become a significant factor in media profit statements.

How tight and detailed the controls on the media are was evidenced by the Polish government's instructions to the press of that country on the occasion of the visit of Pope John Paul II to his homeland in 1979. Ten pages of instructions were issued (later published in the West). Among other things, most newspapers were told that on the first day of the visit, they were to print a picture of the Pope, an item reporting his arrival, a profile of the man, and a commentary. The commentary was prepared by the national news agency PAP. Nothing more was to appear.

The official party newspapers were even more limited. They were told to publish only an item about the arrival, a biographical sketch of the Pope, and the PAP commentary. No photographs.

All information printed concerning any aspect of the visit had to come from PAP. Although some papers, particularly the Catholic press, were permitted to publish their own commentaries, everything had to be cleared first with censorship. Even headlines and other details were prescribed. All photographs taken during the visit had to be approved before they could be published. After the visit was over, certain illustrated magazines were told they could publish pictures but four was the limit.

There was nothing unusual in this. The same kind of detailed orders are issued on a regular basis in all the Soviet bloc countries— a complete list of do's and don'ts.

Journalism Education

All the bloc nations have journalism programs at at least one university. The Soviet Union lists 22 institutions of higher learning that provide some kind of training. The largest and most prestigious of these is Moscow State University which has a five-year program that resembles in many respects those offered at United States universities. The biggest difference is that Soviet students are required to take courses in Marxism-Leninism, which is the principal reason the course takes five instead of four years to complete.

Poland and Hungary offer only post-graduate journalism training, with two centers each for such work. Two Czech institutions, Charles University in Prague and Comenius University in Bratislava, offer four-year undergraduate programs, as does Sofia University in Bulgaria. The top school in East Germany is the Institute for Journalism at Leipzig University, although the East German journalists' union also operates a school in East Berlin. Romania's sole journalism program is offered at the Stefan Gheorgiu Institute in Bucharest, which is also a center for training party and government functionaries.

The Soviet Union, East Germany, Hungary, and Czechoslovakia also operate training programs of varying durations for journalists from developing countries.

As for the nonbloc states, Albania has never indicated that any of its educational institutions offer such training, but Yugoslavia has a number of programs, the best known of which is at the University of Ljubljana.

The Future

There are some signs of change in the Soviet bloc. The media in some of the smaller nations, those more exposed to the West, have become somewhat more open. But the degree of change should not be exaggerated. The party still exercises tight control. Hungary and Romania may have abolished formal censorship, but editors are still held responsible for seeing that only what the party wants is published.

Some journalists, even in the Soviet Union, have urged that greater emphasis be placed on factual reporting instead of commentary, but there is little sign that they are being heeded. Nevertheless, some scholars believe that important changes have been taking place and are continuing to take place.

They point out that with the spread of television, people can share personal reactions with each other in the privacy of their own homes instead of having to conceal reactions at public gatherings, as was true in the past, and that this can make an enormous difference in the Soviet audience.

A number of authorities agree with Soviet dissident Roy Medvedev who argues that the new technologies of communication will force changes in the society and therefore the media. He argues that foreign radio broadcasts have already had an effect. And when TV broadcasts via satellites are added, it will be impossible for the authorities to keep the lid on the spread of information and ideas.

THE MIDDLE EAST AND NORTH AFRICA

The 20 nations lying along this huge arc from the Indian Ocean along the southern shore of the Mediterranean Sea to the Atlantic Ocean are a hetrogeneous lot—traditional kingdoms, revolutionary regimes, and parliamentary democracies all share uneasy borders. Their media are equally diverse; however, all but two share a common language, cultural heritage, history, and religion.

These ties link the Arab states of Algeria, Bahrain, Egypt, Iraq, Jordan, Kuwait, Lebanon, Libya, Morocco, Oman, Qatar, Saudi Arabia, Sudan, Syria, Tunisia, United Arab Emirates, Yemen Arab Republic, and the Yemen People's Democratic Republic. The odd men out in the area are Israel and Iran.

The most obvious differences between these two and the Arab states involve language and religion. The Arabs and the Israelis are both Semitic peoples but the Israelis follow Judaism and their official language is Hebrew. The Arabs are Moslem and all regard Arabic as their mother tongue. The Iranians, on the other hand, are an Aryan people who speak Persian. They are Moslem but follow the creed of a minority sect of Islam, the Shia. Most Arabs accept the more orthodox Sunni faith.

Despite differences in societies and governments, all Arab media have certain common features. Iran shares some of these, too; but Israel is quite different. Its media's closest relatives are in Europe rather than elsewhere in the area.

The majority of the founders of the state of Israel came from Europe, and they built up newspapers on the general pattern of those in their former homelands. The structure of broadcast was also adapted from European practice.

Foreign influences helped shape the media in the other countries as well, and some of the differences among the Arab states can be traced to those influences. But overall, indigenous forces in each have been the primary shapers of the media structure and operations.

In Israel, the European heritage, the highest literacy rate in the Middle East, a democratic government, relative prosperity, and a heavily urbanized population have contributed to the establishment of the most vigorous press in the area. Radio is also important as a communication link, but TV, with only one black-and-white channel, is somewhat of a stepchild.

Among the Arab states radio and television are as a rule under the direct control and supervision of the government. Only a few exceptions are to be found. With respect to newspapers, no capsule description is adequate.

In his book on the Arab press, William A. Rugh divides the 18 countries into three groups, which he labels the Loyalist Press, the Mobilization Press, and the Diverse Press. Although imprecise, because no country fits neatly into its assigned slot, these categorizations help point up the relations between the media and the society it represents—particularly with respect to its politics.

According to the classification, the Mobilization Press includes the media of Algeria, Egypt, Iraq, Libya, the People's Democratic Republic of Yemen (South Yemen), the Sudan, and Syria. All these are ruled by leftist or revolutionary regimes that tend to use the press as a tool to push their goals.

In the Loyalist Press category, Rugh placed the media of the small oil states of Bahrain, Qatar, and the United Arab Emirates, as well as those of Jordan, Saudi Arabia, and Tunisia. With the exception of the latter, these countries are ruled by traditional authorities —kings, princes, or emirs, for the most part—who have been able to maintain their positions despite the rapid political and economic change characteristic of the area. Tunisia won its independence from France in 1956 and a single party has monopolized political power since, but it has followed a moderate line.

In the Loyalist Press countries, radio and television are government monopolies, as they are in the Mobilization Press group. Most newspapers, however, are privately owned. Nonetheless, they all support the ruling regime and its policies. This unanimity is due both to a concurrence of views and to various indirect controls by which these governments can exert influence.

In the three Diverse Press countries (Lebanon, Morocco, and Kuwait) newspapers are also privately owned, but they also represent various points of view and enjoy much greater freedom of expression. In Lebanon, which had the freest press of all the Arab countries until the civil strife and Syrian occupation of the 1970s, even the television service is privately owned.

This listing omits two other states—Oman and the Yemen Arab Republic—because their media are so new and relatively unimportant that it is still difficult to place them properly. Neither had daily newspapers or television until the 1970s.

Despite their differences, the people of the Arab states are linked by strong cultural and psychological ties. The fact of their common language, history, culture, and faith engenders a sense of common destiny and strong pan-Arab feelings.

Although newspapers have a fairly long history in some of the Arab countries, appearing in both Iraq and Egypt in the early nineteenth century, the media did not become an important societal force until relatively recently, particularly since the development of radio and television.

In that part of the world, newspapers are and always have been a medium for the elite. Lebanon, which has a higher literacy rate and more papers than any of the others, is the only Arab country to surpass the UNESCO suggested minimum of 100 copies of daily newspapers per 1,000 persons.

Radio is the real mass medium. Everywhere, people have access to a variety of programming from their own national as well as foreign services. Television is coming fast. In fact, the spread of all telecommunications in the past 30 years has been remarkable. Television, for example, was nonexistent in the area until the late 1950s, but now every Arab country, even the poorest, has its own system, and many even have satellite ground stations to receive international transmissions.

The four without this particular status symbol—Oman, the Sudan, and the two Yemens—are among the poorest in an area where the range between the haves and have-nots is enormous. The per capita income in the Yemen Arab Republic is a mere $300 a year, while in the almost neighboring oil-producing United Arab Emirates it is more that $22,000, the highest in the world.

Print Media

The most significant newspapers in the Middle East are published in Israel, Egypt, and Lebanon. *Ha'aretz, Davar*, and *Ma'ariv* of Tel Aviv; *Al Ahram*, *Al-Gomhouriya* and *Al-Akhbar* of Cairo; *Al-Nahar* and *Al-Anwar* of Beirut are read and quoted in capitals throughout the Western world. The area is also home to several foreign-language dailies, the best known of which is probably *The Jerusalem Post* which is printed in English and is one of the few Israeli papers published in Jerusalem rather than Tel Aviv.

By far the largest in terms of circulation are the big Egyptian dailies. The most popular is *Al-Akhbar*, which claims 695,000 readers, considerably more than the somewhat staid *Al-Ahram*, which is generally considered the most authoritative. It sells about 400,000 copies daily, the same as the figure for *Al-Gomhouriya*. The latter is known more for its political commentaries than for its news coverage, which in the other two is extensive.

The largest in Israel is the independent *Yedioth Aharonoth*, with a daily circulation of about 180,000. This goes up to 280,000 on Fridays, which is the day Israeli papers publish weekend editions, since the Jewish sabbath is Saturday.

This small country of less than 4 million people is home to about 400 newspapers and magazines. Most of these are published in Hebrew, but others appear in English, French, Polish, Romanian, Yiddish, Hungarian, German, and Arabic. Total daily circulation amounts to about 210 copies per 1,000 inhabitants.

Because of the size of the country, it is a national press, that is, the main papers are sold throughout the entire country. Most are privately owned, although all but a few are linked to political parties. religious organizations, or other public bodies. In some cases, they are subsidized by their sponsors since income from advertising and circulation is not sufficient to maintain all of them in economic health.

Although not the largest, top rank among the dailies is generally given to the independent *Ha'aretz* (55,000 daily, 75,000 weekends) and *Davar*, the organ of the *Histadrut*, the trade union organization (50,000). Both are morningers. *Yedioth Aharonoth* and *Ma'ariv*, the second largest, are both afternooners. *Ma'ariv*, which is also independent, sells about 147,000 weekdays and 245,000 on Fridays.

Two dailies are published in Arabic, *Al-Anba* and *Al Quda*. Both are based in Jerusalem. Neither is large in terms of circulation, selling fewer than 10,000 copies each.

There are a number of weeklies and other periodicals. Most of these are published in Tel Aviv, although some are printed in Jerusalem and a few in Haifa. Probably the most important of these, certainly from an international viewpoint, is the weekly *International Jerusalem Post*, which distributes 55,000 copies to 90 different countries.

In Lebanon, civil war and Syrian occupation hampered press operations during most of the 1970s and the early 1980s. Some newspapers disappeared, particularly after 1977 when the government imposed censorship; but enough others appeared on the scene to maintain the characteristic diversity of views.

An-Anwar and *Al-Nahar* not only are most respected of the dailies but they have the largest circulations. Most Lebanese papers reputedly have ties to foreign as well as internal political interests, but these two are generally considered truly independent. *Al-Nahar* claims around 85,000 and *An-Anwar* about 75,000 circulation. Both are distributed abroad as well as inside the country. The English-language *Daily Star* (19,000) and two French-language dailies, *L'Orient-Le Jour* (21,000) and *Le Soir* (16,000), also circulate abroad.

Although nice to have, such international circulation is not so important to Lenanese dailies as it is to Lebanese magazines. Most of the country's leading weeklies are sold throughout the Arab world and, for some, foreign sales are larger than domestic ones. For example, two-thirds of the 45,000-copy run of the illustrated news magazine *Al-Jamhour* goes to foreign markets.

These markets are almost as important for some of the others, for instance, the feature magazine *Achabaka* (126,000) and the review *Al-Ousbau al-Arabi*, or *Arab Week* (125,000). The daily *An-Anwar's* Sunday supplement, which emphasizes cultural and social affairs, sells 90,000 copies, a figure matched by at least two other weeklies, *Al-Moharrer* and *Assayed*.

A similar situation exists with the Egyptian print media. Among the newspapers, only *Al-Ahram* and *Al-Akhbar* circulate widely outside the nation's borders, but several weeklies as well as other periodicals have large foreign markets. In some cases these amount to as much as a third of total sales. Important Egyptian weeklies include *Akhbar al-Yom*, which sells more than a million copies every Saturday, the illustrated news magazine *Al-Mussawar* (162,000), *Rose al Youssef* ((35,000), and *Akhersa'a* (134,000).

Other than these, few Arab publications enjoy much circulation outside their home countries. One major exception is a monthly magazine published by the Kuwaiti Ministry of Information called *Al Arabi*. More than 80 percent of its 250,000 copies are distributed elsewhere in the Arab world.

Locally important dailies appear in most of the other Arab states, but only one has a circulation exceeding 100,000. It is *Moudjahid* of Algiers (130,000). Few others exceed 50,000. Those that do include Kuwait's *Al-Qabas* (60,000) and *Al-Watan* (55,000), Iraq's *Al-Thawra* (70,000), and Saudi Arabia's *Al-Medina al-Munawara* (60,000). The latter paper is published in Jeddah, the country's principal Red Sea port.

The circulation of the two principal papers in Khartoum, the capital of the Sudan, is listed as "between 50,000 and 60,000." Tunisia is somewhat unusual in that its capital, Tunis, boasts four major papers, all of which circulate between 40,000 and 50,000 copies daily.

In the area as a whole, only Iran can come close to rivaling the circulation figures of the big Egyptian dailies. Tehran's largest, known as *Kayhan*, sells about 350,000 copies. At the present time, it is little more than a mouthpiece for the revolutionary government. Its closest rival, *Ettela'at*, has a press run of about 220,000.

Broadcasting

Broadcasting presents a somewhat simpler picture. With few exceptions, radio and television in the Arab world are government-controlled and -operated monopolies. They are also monopolies in Israel, but operations there are under the control of the Israeli Broadcasting Authority (IBA), an autonomous public body set up in 1965 along the lines of Britain's BBC.

The IBA airs five different radio programs for both domestic and foreign listeners and directs the nation's one black-and-white TV channel. An Israeli Army station also broadcasts one medium-wave program for the general public.

In the Arab world, the only exceptions to the government-monopoly structure exist in Lebanon and in Dubai, one of the United Arab Emirates. In the latter, private commercial radio and TV coexist with government services. The situation in Lebanon is unusual in that the government controls the official radio but the two separate TV services are and always have been privately owned. A variety of clandestine radio stations representing various factions in the civil war are also on the air from time to time.

The predominance of government control does not mean an absence of advertising. The majority of the broadcasting services rely on advertising for part of their income. In some, this is supplemented by a tax on receivers. In others, the costs are paid by the government.

The importance of broadcasting throughout most of the Middle East is a result of a combination of factors: the low literacy rates in many countries, the importance placed in Arab societies on traditional patterns of oral communication, and the deliberate fostering of the role of telecommunications by various governments.

Egypt has the largest and most far reaching broadcast operation in the area. Cairo Radio airs 197 hours of programming daily, using eight different languages in its home service and 30 in its foreign services, making it one of the major international broadcasters in the world. The national television service operates two channels that reach most of the country's populated areas. Virtually all this has been built up since the 1952 revolution.

Programming varies considerably from country to country. As one might expect, it tends to be more political in the Mobilization, or revolutionary, countries. These governments use broadcasting actively in their efforts to gain popular support for policies and programs. The general philosophy is exemplified by an official Libyan statement which defined the objectives of that country's broadcasting operations as follows:

> To embody the Arab revolutionary objectives of freedom,
> socialism and unity and to permeate such objectives in the
> minds of the people ... to bind the Arab struggle for
> liberation of the occupied territories with the cause of
> liberation and freedom in the Third World.

Not all programming is political, even in the most revolutionary countries. Entertainment is a major component on both radio and TV, but particularly the latter. Much of this is imported from the other Arab countries, or from Europe and even the United States. As a general rule, the less revolutionary the regime, the more imported programming can be seen. However, almost all governments screen imports carefully to guard against violation of social, religious, or political taboos.

There is a surprising amount of cross-border TV viewing as well as radio listening throughout the area. TV broadcasts in the Persian Gulf area can be received in various neighboring states. Many Jordanians are able to watch Israeli TV, and vice versa. When climatic conditions are favourable, people living along the North African coast can pick up European TV services, particularly Italian programs. Libyans living in the eastern part of that country can also watch Egyptian TV. In fact, Libyan sources report a booming business in trading video tapes of programs picked up from such outside services.

The Arab states are linked in the Arab Broadcasting Union, which has exchange arrangements—exchanges are made via satellite—with both Eurovision, Western Europe's TV net, and Intervision, the Communist equivalent. Israel is also associated with Eurovision.

Government–Press Relations

Arab newspapers have always been highly political. Most of the earliest, in fact, began as official government organs. Others emerged during struggles against colonial domination, serving as voices for liberation movements. But given the widespread poverty and illiteracy, few survived long without outside help. Those that did were subsidized by governments, political parties, or wealthy individuals with political interests.

Some sources assert that as a whole the Arab press today is less of a partisan press than it used to be and that newspapers are paying more attention to conveying information than to simply propagandizing. This is probably true in some countries, not only in the diverse press category but also in several of the mobilization press countries —Egypt and Tunisia particularly. But even in these, political matters are dominant.

There is, as was suggested earlier, no one pattern for government–press relations. In some countries the press is simply an arm of the government. In Libya, for example, the only daily newspaper, one called *Fajr al Jadid* (*New Dawn*), is published by the nation's Ministry of Information. Of the two weeklies, one is published by Colonel

Qaddafi's revolutionary council and the other by the women's revolutionary committee in Tripoli, the capital.

On the other hand, the Lebanese press, at least until current civil strife, was generally considered fairly free even by Western standards. The government held, and sometimes exercised, the power to shut down papers violating specific rules and to ban the import of foreign publications. The restrictions did not seem to inhibit the newsmen to any great degree, however.

The other Arab states fall somewhere between these two extremes, but in all of them the government, either directly or through ruling parties, has a great deal more influence, if not direct authority, over the press than is common in the Western world.

In Egypt, newspapers are owned by the government and controlled by a Higher Press Council. In Iraq, private newspapers are illegal. All existing ones are published by the ruling party or allied organizations. The Iraqi Ministry of Information controls all advertising and distribution. Much the same situation pertains in Algeria, where the ruling party owns all the significant papers. In Syria and Jordan, publishers must obtain licenses from the government. Journalists themselves must be licensed by the government in the United Arab Emirates.

Private ownership of newspapers exists in Tunisia, Jordan, Saudi Arabia, Bahrain, Qatar, Morocco, Kuwait, and the United Arab Emirates as well as in Lebanon and Israel.

Revolutionary Iran also allows private ownership of periodicals. On paper, the press there has more freedom than it did under the Shah. Nevertheless, Iranian editors must be very careful about what they print. Under the 1979 revolutionary constitution, all periodicals are required to obtain publishing licenses from the government. Some which survived that hurdle—many did not—subsequently ran into trouble and lost their licenses for varying periods of time.

Some Iranian papers have occasionally published articles reflecting disapproval of government policies without suffering retribution, but apparently the line between what is tolerated and what is not is unclear, except on one point. The constitution makes it a criminal offense to print anything that could be construed as insulting to the country's religious leaders.

In Israel, censorship is a fact of life for the media, given the continuing hostility of her Arab neighbors. Critics have charged that the press–party connections also limit freedom of comment. Nevertheless, newspapers, and even broadcasting, are relatively free and vigorous voices in Israeli society.

News Agencies

Every country in the area has its own national news service. In all but Israel, these are government agencies, usually an arm of the nation's Ministry of Information. In 17 of the Arab states—Lebanon is the exception—the agencies have a monopoly on the distribution of domestic news; and in eight countries—Algeria, Iraq, Libya, Oman, Sudan, Tunisia, and the two Yemens—they also have a monopoly of the acquisition and distribution of foreign news. Individual publications in these eight are barred from subscribing directly to any foreign agency.

In the other nine—Bahrain, Egypt, Jordan, Morocco, Kuwait, Qatar, Saudi Arabia, Syria, and the United Arab Emirates—agencies function as the authoritative voice of the government but newspapers are free to obtain foreign news from other sources.

Although Lebanon's news agency is a government office, it has no monopoly of any kind. It not only faces competition from foreign agencies with direct access to the press but also has domestic commercial competitors. Almost its only advantage is that it is the voice of the government.

Only one of the 18 Arab news agencies has international significance: Egypt's Middle East News Agency (MENA). With correspondents throughout the area and in major world capitals, it has become one of the top-ranking regional agencies. Its services, transmitted in English and French as well as Arabic, come close to blanketing the area. It also relays copy for a number of foreign agencies, Western as well as Arab, over its teleprinter network.

The situation in Israel, as one might expect, is quite different. There are two agencies: the News Agency of the Associated Israeli Press, known as ITIM, and the Israel News Agency (ITA). The first, a cooperative organization owned by the nation's press, is the important one. ITA exists mainly to transmit stories received from the old Jewish Telegraph Agency services in New York and London.

Philosphical Considerations

Most Arab governments are more or less authoritarian; and if their press systems were to be classified according to one widely used set of categories, they would have to be labeled authoritarian. The Israeli press, on the other hand, would fall into the libertarian category. Not all fit comfortably into any such generalizations, however. In more peaceful times, an argument certainly could be made that Lebanon, as well as Israel, should be classed as libertarian. Some of the other states seem to be moving toward a more libertarian approach.

It should be kept in mind that a desire to control information reaching the general public is not the only reason for the predominant role of governments in the media systems of the Arab countries. In the past, media growth was blocked as much by the lack of an adequate economic base and the general illiteracy as by government authority. Most newspapers that survived any length of time were able to do so only because they were subsidized in one way or another.

In many of the Arab states, the government represented almost the only source of capital needed for the development of the media, particularly broadcast. Even today, advertising revenues and mass circulation sales, with few exceptions, are relatively low compared with the Western world. Overall, nongovernmental commercial advertising is still not an important source of income for newspapers.

Ruling regimes in the Mobilization states deliberately use the media to help advance their interests and causes. The attitude of other governments varies from careful supervision, particularly in times of crisis, to relative tolerance. It is worth noting that the proportion of party-affiliated newspapers in the area has fallen in recent years, accompanied by an increase in emphasis on the information role of the press.

Education for Journalists

As a general rule, journalism as a profession has not been highly regarded in the Middle East. In the past, formal training did not exist; participants learned by doing. Pay was low; most journalists held down a second job in order to make ends meet. Talented individuals tended to use newspaper work as a stepping stone to careers in politics, government, or literature.

This is changing slowly and there is now a severe shortage of competent, trained personnel. Efforts are being made in several countries to deal with this problem. Students have been sent abroad. Specialized training programs have been established at home.

Schools or departments of journalism have been set up at the university level in a number of countries. Faculties often include individuals who have received higher degrees from European and American universities. Egypt has been one of the leaders in this development; the program at the University of Cairo is probably the best known in the area. Other schools or departments have been established in Iran, Tunisia, Algeria, Iraq, Saudi Arabia, Libya, and Lebanon. In Israel, the Hebrew University offers a two-year graduate-level program.

Historical Highlights

Throughout most of the Middle East and North Africa, the history of the indigenous press is limited to the twentieth century. As suggested earlier, the first newspapers were established by governments, which in most cases represented colonial powers. A few published by private individuals appeared before 1900, but only in Lebanon, Egypt, and Morocco. Of all those now publishing in the Arab states, only three— all Egyptian—were in existence before World War I. A few others predate World War II, but most have been established only since 1960.

Few journalists have become widely known and, in most cases, those that have are famous for other reasons. For example, President Habib Bourguiba of Tunisia is remembered as the George Washington of that country, not as a man who spent years writing for and editing newspapers.

Muhammad Hassanein Haykal, the former editor of Cairo's *Al-Ahram*, is probably the most widely read journalist in the Arab world today, but he gained his reputation because it was generally believed that he reflected the views of Cairo at a time when Gamel Abdel Nasser was the most important leader in the Arab world.

Look to the Future

The Middle East is an area of great stress and vast uncertainties. Predictions are dangerous. Yet currents in the area suggest that as audiences become more educated and more sophisticated and as the media continue to develop, the press—at least in some countries—will move in the direction of greater diversity.

Given the enormous problems of economic development compounded by the political strife seemingly endemic to the area, even the most independent-minded newsmen find it difficult to resist the pressures for national unity and limitations on their freedom. But in a more stable environment, increasing professionalism will lead journalists to seek more independence from government controls.

This is already evident in Egypt. Regimes may fight back. But economic development and increasing wealth tend to bring new political factions and alignments into being. Such a development could lead to greater scope and more freedom for the press.

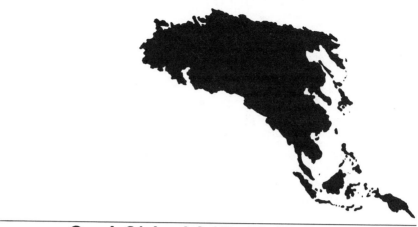

2 ASIA AND THE PACIFIC

JOHN LUTER
JIM RICHSTAD

The Asia and Pacific region covers more than a third of the earth's surface and contains nearly 60 percent of all its inhabitants. It stretches east from the western borders of Afghanistan to the most distant islands of the South Pacific, and north from New Zealand to the far reaches of China and Japan. As defined here, it does not include the Asian portions of the Soviet Union (or Hawaii, a United States state). But it embraces more than 40 nations and major dependencies, so different from one another that it is impossible to describe the region in general terms.

China, with more than one billion inhabitants, and India, with some 700 million, are the world's two most populous countries; together they contain more people than the whole of Africa, Europe, and North America combined. Yet among the countless islands scattered across the South Pacific lie some of the smallest of all nations, including the phosphate-rich Republic of Nauru, an eight square mile atoll with a population of 8,000, and Tuvalu, a nation of nine tiny islands inhabited by fewer than 7,500 people.

The region is home to hundreds of different ethnic groups who speak a vast variety of languages and dialects (more than 700 in Papua New Guinea alone) and whose attitudes are influenced by differing cultures, religions, and political ideologies. Australia and Japan boast the world's highest rates of literacy (99 percent); yet in parts of the region less than a third of the population is literate. A few of the nations have long histories of self-rule, but most are former colonies that have gained independence since World War II.

Much of the past half century has been marked by conflict—by wars, revolutions, military coups, and other struggles for power which have left a residue of hostility that continues to threaten political stability. China and Korea are now divided countries; an exile regime seeks to return to power in Kampuchea (formerly Cambodia), and Afghan rebels have continued to resist the Soviet forces that occupied their country to bolster its puppet government.

Governments differ greatly in form, as well as in the degrees of freedom they allow. The largest Asian nation, the People's Republic of China, is a Communist state, as are North Korea, Vietnam, Kampuchea, Laos, Mongolia, and (for all practical purposes) Afghanistan. Burma, which has sought relative isolation from outside influences, practices its own unique form of socialism. Hong Kong is a British crown colony; Macao is a colony of Portugal; and Thailand, Nepal, and the South Pacific island nation of Tonga are hereditary kingdoms. Democracy has taken firm root in Japan; it continues to flourish in Australia, New Zealand, and India (where liberties denied during the 1975 to 1977 "national emergency" have been restored); and it also appears to be succeeding in a few other Asian and Pacific countries. Democracies, however, are far outnumbered by authoritarian regimes, including some in nations that have retained the trappings of democracy. Such major nations as Indonesia, Pakistan, and Thailand are under military rule; and in many other parts of the region, governments that are troubled by internal disorder or are distrustful of certain of their neighbors have imposed tight controls, which have often included periods of martial law.

The region is diverse economically as well. Most Asian and Pacific nations belong to the developing world, and in some, poverty is rampant and famine is a recurring threat. Asia is the home of some of the world's fastest growing economies, however, with high growth rates in trade; and its economic potential is enormous. Japan ranks third among the world's industrial powers and is a leader in foreign trade. Australia, South Korea, Taiwan, Hong Kong, Malaysia, and Singapore also have economies that are prosperous and expanding, although far smaller than Japan's.

The media of Asia and the Pacific reflect the complex character of this vast region. Japan has a highly developed media system, which employs the latest in modern technology and reaches into almost every home and virtually every facet of national life. Substantial media systems also exist elsewhere in the region—notably in Australia, India, the People's Republic of China, Taiwan, and South Korea. Throughout much of Asia and the Pacific, however, the media suffer from a lack of modern equipment, adequately trained personnel, and sufficient financial support. In many countries, their problems are compounded by diversity of cultures and languages, low incomes, illiteracy, geographical barriers, and political controls.

The region's newspapers range in size from the giant national dailies of Japan to the struggling, rudimentary journals found in many parts of South and Southeast Asia and in some of the territories and new island nations of the South Pacific. The larger, more affluent papers generally are well printed, attractive, and serious in content and tone. With few exceptions, they devote more attention to world news than do most United States newspapers.

Throughout much of the region, however, the press is generally underdeveloped. There are countless small papers—some only mimeographed sheets—particularly in the outlying areas of South and Southeast Asia. For the most part, these papers, many of which are weeklies and some that have only a few hundred subscribers, are crudely produced and struggling for survival.

Daily papers are concentrated in the major urban centers, with few published in the smaller provincial towns. Some are notable for their quality and influence and are prospering. In many countries, however, even the more substantial dailies tend to have few pages (sometimes no more than eight or twelve) and circulations that are small in relation to the population. Advertising revenues also tend to be modest, or even nonexistent; and some papers are supported by subsidies—from individuals, governments, or political parties.

Newspaper circulations in South and Southeast Asia and many parts of the South Pacific are limited by the multiplicity of languages and dialects, as well as by illiteracy. India alone has newspapers in as many as 20 languages.

English and Chinese are the region's most common tongues, and newspapers in these languages are found in many countries. Chinese language papers—apart from those published in the People's Republic and Taiwan—are the most numerous, particularly in Southeast Asia, where they have significant influence and account for a large share of the total newspaper circulation. In India, Singapore, Malaysia, and a few other places once part of the British empire, the most solidly entrenched and prestigious papers still are English-language publications, which like the newspapers of Australia and New Zealand closely resemble British papers in makeup and style. American influence on the region's press is less pronounced, although it is clearly apparent in the Philippines and also in Guam, where the only daily is owned by the Gannett Company, the largest United States newspaper chain. The two English-language dailies that circulate over the widest areas of Asia, however, are special editions of two American newspapers: the *Asian Wall Street Journal* and the Asia edition of the Paris-based *International Herald Tribune*, both with headquarters in Hong Kong.

Some publishers of major dailies also produce separate Sunday papers that attract substantial numbers of readers; and many publish magazines as well. In general, however, the region is not noted for its magazines. It has a wide range of special-interest magazines and some of more general interest, including several local news magazines, but circulations tend to be modest in relation to the populations.

Many peoples of Asia and the Pacific look primarily to newspapers for news and (in some countries) guidance. However, the broadcast media are of growing importance.

Broadcasting is mainly in government hands, operated either by government departments or, in an increasing number of nations, by government supervised public corporations. In some countries, however, private ownership of broadcast stations is allowed; and in a few, including Japan, private stations compete vigorously with the national broadcast organization. Government broadcast stations generally are financed in part by license fees on receiving sets, but the great majority also accept commercials, from which they derive much of their revenue.

In many parts of the region, radio remains the principal broadcast medium and in a few countries it is the only one. It is the universal medium in most of the Pacific Island nations and territories, and it is also particularly important in developing Asian countries with large rural populations. In some places, it provides the only means of rapid and effective contact with all the populated areas.

Receiving sets are still spread thinly in some countries, particularly in the more remote areas and in areas where incomes are low. However, the development of relatively inexpensive battery-operated transistor sets has greatly increased the size of radio audiences. Where governments in developing countries have encouraged the local manufacture, assembly, or importation of such sets, many people now are able to afford them.

Television is also growing in importance. In Japan, Australia, and other places where living standards are high, TV reaches virtually all the population. A few developing countries, however, have yet to begin television broadcasting for financial reasons. In the case of Fiji, it is out of concern for TV's potentially harmful effects on local cultures. In other of the less affluent countries, TV is usually limited to the major urban centers, and most TV receivers are black-and-white models. Color television has been introduced in most countries but it cannot be expected to reach large audiences for many years, except in the few nations where it already is widespread. However, the use of videocassette players is growing greatly in some areas where broadcast television has not been introduced or is of limited service.

NEWSPAPERS

The region's major publishing centers are Hong Kong, Tokyo, Beijing, New Delhi, Sydney, and Singapore.

Hong Kong, densely populated but tiny in area, is more notable for the number and variety of its publications than for their size. About 60 Chinese-language newspapers, most of them entertainment-oriented but together reflecting every conceivable shade of Chinese political opinion, compete for readers among the colony's Chinese residents, who account for 98.5 percent of the population of more than 5 million. The most popular by far is the 600,000-circulation *Oriental Daily News*. Among its major rivals, the most important is the *Sing Pao Daily News*, with a circulation of 250,000. The largest and most respected of the several English-language dailies is the *South China Morning Post*, which has a circulation of only 65,000 but is widely read by the colony's elite, including many prominent Chinese.

Hong Kong's importance as a publishing capital, however, derives mainly from its central location and excellent transportation facilities, advantages that (along with the colony's "free" environment) have made it the principal production and distribution point for newspapers and magazines that circulate in both the northern and southern parts of the region. Its printing plants produce more than 100 magazines, as well as two newspapers with area-wide circulations: the *Asian Wall Street Journal* (which also prints a facsimile edition in Singapore) and the Asia edition of the *International Herald Tribune*. Some of the magazines are primarily for the local market, and nearly half the total are trade and technical publications which generally have small circulations. Hong Kong, however, is the main base for numerous magazines of regional reach and importance.

Tokyo is the principal publishing center for Japan's national newspaper companies, which dominate the world's most highly developed press system. This island nation of approximately 117 million people, which has Asia's highest living standards and literacy rate (99 percent), leads all nations in the per-capita circulation of daily papers.

The larger Japanese papers publish both morning and evening editions, which are edited to provide continuity. The morning and evening editions usually are sold to subscribers as sets. If the two editions are counted separately, the nation's total daily newspaper circulation approaches 65 million, second only to that of the Soviet Union and slightly ahead of the total for United States dailies.

Five national newspapers together account for more than half the copies sold. The largest are the *Yomiuri Shimbun, Asahi Shimbun*, and *Mainichi Shimbun.* ("Shimbun" means newspaper.) All three publish morning and evening editions at plants in Tokyo and four regional centers, and issue separate editions for various localities—far more editions than newspapers in any other country. *Asahi*, for example, produces 18 major editions in the morning and 10 in the afternoon, as well as 105 other editions that vary with the locality they serve.

Asahi and *Yomiuri* have the largest daily circulations in the world, larger even than the Soviet Union's *Pravda*. The *Asahi Shimbun* (literally the Rising Sun Newspaper), founded more than a century ago in Osaka, is regarded as the most influential among the big three. Serious in tone and somber in makeup, it is particularly appealing to the nation's intellectuals, but it also has a mass circulation: approximately 7.5 million in the morning and slightly above 4.5 million in the afternoon.

Until the past few years, *Asahi* led the world in circulation. But it has lost this distinction to its arch rival, the *Yomiuri Shimbun* (the Read and Sell Newspaper), which circulates more than 8 million copies of its morning editions and nearly 5 million in the afternoon. *Yomiuri*, like *Asahi*, carries serious political and financial stories, but it has a livelier makeup, uses larger pictures, and devotes more attention to human-interest stories—features that have attracted a growing number of readers.

The *Mainichi Shimbun* (the Daily Newspaper), once *Asahi's* closest competitor, has limped behind both its rivals in recent years, burdened by a heavy debt load that required financial reorganization of the company in 1977. *Mainichi* remains influential, however, and its total morning and evening circulation of approximately 7 million is more than three times that of the largest United States daily.

Smaller than the big three but also important are two other national dailies: the *Sankei Shimbun* and the *Nihon Keizai Shimbun*, each with a combined circulation of about 3 million. The *Nihon Keizai*, often referred to as Japan's equivalent of the *Wall Street Journal*, is the nation's most influential business newspaper. Published at plants in Tokyo and three regional centers, it is regarded as essential reading by most Japanese business executives. Japan also has about 120 other daily newspapers—regional and local dailies of general interest and nearly a dozen sports papers, some of which are published at several locations and have wide readership. Among the regional or bloc papers that compete with the national dailies for readers and influence, the most notable is the *Chunichi Shimbun*, which covers the densely populated Chubu district of central Japan and heads a group of five dailies that includes two sports papers and the 1.5-million-circulation *Tokyo Shimbun*. The *Chunichi* papers together have a circulation of more than 4 million, and the *Chunichi*, like the national newspapers, maintains an extensive network of foreign as well as domestic bureaus. Other substantial regional dailies are the *Hokkaido Shimbun*, published at four plants on the northern island of Hokkaido, and the *Nishi Nippon Shimbun*, which serves the southern island of Kyushu.

More than 90 percent of Japan's newspaper circulation is home-delivered to subscribers by a small army of more than 400,000 distribution agents and school-age carriers.

Japan's newspapers also have unusually large staffs of reporters, editors, and technical personnel by Western standards. *Asahi*, for example, has nearly 10,000 such employees, in five major Japanese cities, 23 overseas offices, and about 280 domestic news bureaus. For use in its news-gathering operations, *Asahi* maintains some 125 automobiles, 82 motorcycles, 53 radio-equipped jeeps, 13 vans equipped for radio-photo transmission, 3 jet airplanes, and 4 helicopters.

Almost all Japanese papers, including the small dailies, are well edited and serious in tone, and economic news receives a high priority. The national papers devote nearly a third of their news space to national and international news, and even the strictly local papers generally feature such news on their front pages.

The major newspapers are fiercely competitive. They wage constant promotional campaigns to woo readers and advertisers, and sponsor many cultural, sports, and community activities to enhance their visibility and prestige. In addition to daily newspapers, many of the larger companies also produce a substantial number of other periodicals, including weekly papers, magazines, and annuals; and operate a wide range of nonpublishing enterprises.

Each of the three big national dailies issues a daily English-language edition, but these contain fewer pages than the parent papers (which average about 24 pages) and are published more for prestige than for profit. None attracts as many readers as the independent *Japan Times*, which has a circulation of less than 50,000 but is regarded as the leading English-language paper.

The region's single most influential newspaper is the Beijing-based *Renmin Ribao*, or the *People's Daily*, the principal official organ of the People's Republic of China. Mainland China's press system—which now includes 382 newspapers with a combined circulation of more than 70 million—was patterned after that of the Soviet Union. All elements of the press, as well as the broadcast media, are controlled strictly by the Communist Party, and their primary function is to guide the nation's more than 1 billion people so that their thoughts and actions will conform to the party's policies and goals. Newspapers in particular serve to communicate official policies and goals to the masses, to stimulate national pride and loyalty, and to mobilize public support for the government's political, economic, social, and cultural objectives. As a subsidiary function, they also receive feedback from the public in the form of letters from readers, many of which are passed along (with names of the writers withheld if they wish) to party organizations and administrators for their information and possible investigation of alleged misconduct.

The *People's Daily*, founded in 1948—a year before the Communists took over China—at the revolution's headquarters in Hebei province (where the party's Central Committee located after moving from Yenan) but published now from a well-equipped plant in Beijing, is the pacesetter for this press system. Operated under the jurisdiction of China's Central Politburo, it is the official paper for both the Communist Party and the government, and its influence filters down to even the most remote villages. Its circulation is only about 5 million, but copies circulate throughout the country and set policy for other papers, which reprint its most important editorials and official declarations. The *People's Daily* also sets the policy tone for the broadcast media in China.

The paper's daily eight-page issues provide a heavy diet of reading matter, including articles that although significant are frequently lengthy and uninviting in style. The *People's Daily* carries no comics, sports, or entertainment news or divergent political opinions, and it leaves the printing of local news to the many provincial and municipal dailies and other smaller journals. However, it frequently devotes some of its limited space to readers' letters, of which it receives some half million a year.

The *People's Daily* is not the largest daily in the People's Republic. That distinction now belongs to the *Reference News* (*Tsan Kao Hsiao Hsi*), a restricted circulation paper that resulted from a suggestion by the late Chou En-lai, who, it is said, wished to "open the eyes of the people a bit more" to news not filtered through China's own press system. The *Reference News*, published by the official Xinhua (New China) News Agency, reprints stories by various international wire services and newspapers. Its circulation, limited at first to party and government officials of a certain rank, has been expanded gradually in recent years to lower-ranking cadres and students and is now about 10 million copies daily.

A comparable, but much more confidential publication, is *Reference Materials* (*Tsan Kao Tse Liao*), sometimes referred to as *Ta Tsan Kao*, or "Big Reference." *Reference Materials*, issued in morning and evening editions, is designed only for the information of relatively high-ranking Communist cadres. It contains many more articles about Hong Kong and Taiwan (which government and press in the People's Republic refer to as "the breakaway province"), and often prints reports critical of the Communists.

Other major central-level or national papers, among a total of 36, are the *Guangming Ribao* (Brightness Daily), which focuses on cultural, educational, and scientific matters; the *Liberation Army Daily*, which is circulated to military units and state institutions (with no individual subscriptions permitted); the *Worker's Daily*, which serves as the mouthpiece of the National Workers' Union; the *China Youth Daily*, published by the Chinese Communist Youth League; and the new *Chinese Peasant Daily*, introduced in 1980.

Newsprint is in short supply, and total newspaper circulation in the People's Republic is small in relation to the population. But newspapers are regarded as the most important communications medium, so there are many local dailies, as well as hundreds of weeklies, to provide readers throughout the vast area with news and information that officials wish them to receive. Each province and major municipality has at least one daily of its own, and the more developed areas have more, all supervised by local party committees.

Most of China's dailies, particularly the larger ones, are attractive in design and typography. They are influenced strongly by the *People's Daily*, however, and offer little variety. Many local-level papers carry sports news, poems, and political cartoons, in addition to declarations by local party officials, letters from readers, and other materials in line with the general thrust of the nation's press. All of China's papers, however, avoid publishing criticism of government policies, reports of illness among national leaders, and discussion of politically sensitive issues. They also ignore police and court news unless—as in the case of the Gang of Four trial, which received extensive coverage—the case is seen to be teaching a political or moral lesson.

Since the downfall of the Gang of Four, there have been gradual changes in the Chinese press, which reflect the new regime's emphasis on efforts to develop the economy and improve living standards and an increased interest in developments in the world at large. In line with the government's efforts to build a consumer economy (while continuing to emphasize the evils of personal greed), a growing number of China's newspapers and magazines (as well as broadcast outlets) now accept advertising, including ads for foreign products, which have been allowed since early 1979. The *People's Daily*, without ads for many years before 1977, now devotes one-sixteenth of its space to ads, which occupy as much as one-eighth of such important local papers as the *Beijing Daily* and the *Guangming Daily*.

Some major newspapers also have broadened their content, giving more attention to world news; and papers generally have been encouraged to criticize the daily workings of government (although not its structure or goals). The *People's Daily* in 1980 gradually removed photographs of government leaders from its front pages, and even carried articles criticizing the former use of such pictures, which tended to glorify the leaders as heroes. In 1980, for example, it also conducted an 8-month investigation of an offshore oil-rig accident and published articles blaming the government oil ministry for the tragedy—an accusation then unprecedented in China's Communist press.

The new trend toward liberalization and a broader world outlook is reflected in the *China Daily*, China's first English-language newspaper since the establishment of the People's Republic, which began publication in mid-1981 after nearly two years of planning and trial runs.

A significant new paper despite a planned circulation of only 50,000 at the end of the first year (which it achieved in less than six months), the *China Daily* is designed to appeal to foreigners, although its readers include many high-ranking Chinese. Offering a more lively writing style and a less limited view of the world than is usually found in China's newspapers, the *China Daily* is circulated in China's major urban centers, and is also published in Hong Kong. The paper's eight-page editions give prominent play to foreign news and also carry reports on major foreign sports events and stock-market summaries and a bridge column and crossword puzzle. Its domestic stories, many of them from the New China News Agency or condensed from other Chinese publications, present a positive image of the new China, with emphasis on its economic and social progress and goals. However, the paper is remarkably free of ideological exhortations and blatant propaganda.

South Asia's principal publishing center is New Delhi, although such other major Indian cities as Bombay, Calcutta, and Madras also are important publishing points.

To serve its large population and many language groups, India produces some 800 daily newspapers—about one-third of all the dailies in Asia and more than any other country except the United

States. It also has about 19,000 nondaily papers, magazines, and other periodicals. The vast majority of Indian newspapers have circulations of less than 15,000. But there are many substantial dailies with wide readership and influence.

As a group, the English-language dailies, which resemble British newspapers in makeup and range of content, are the most solidly entrenched and prestigious. Owned in most cases by large business houses that control a chain of other publications, they receive a major share of the advertising and reach readers throughout the country as well as abroad.

The largest of the English-language dailies is the Bombay-based *Indian Express*, which is published also in New Delhi and eight other cities and has a circulation of nearly 600,000. Serious in content and tone, the *Express* frequently engages in investigative reporting and has tended to be critical of the Gandhi government.

However, the *Indian Express* is usually considered less influential than the rival *Times of India*, a well-balanced and serious daily that often over the years has reflected government policy. Published in Bombay and New Delhi, the *Times* has a circulation only slightly smaller than that of the *Express*. Also ranking high in prestige among India's English-language dailies are the *Hindu* of Madras (circulation 340,000), which frequently has been compared to Britain's *Guardian*; and the *Statesman* of Calcutta and New Delhi, which tends to be progressive in opinion. The *Statesman* has less than half the circulation of the *Express* or the *Times*, but it maintains high standards and has a considerable following among intellectuals and well-placed bureaucrats. Another important paper is New Delhi's *Hindustan Times*.

Newspapers in Hindi, India's official language, are more numerous than those in English and together reach more readers. The most important of the Hindi dailies is the Delhi-based *Navbharat Times*, with a circulation of approximately 425,000. India's largest circulation daily, however, is a paper in the Malayalan language, the *Malayala Manorama*, which is published in the densely populated state of Kerala (where the literacy rate is much higher than the national average) and has a circulation of well over a half million.

Sydney is the main publishing center in Australia, whose press is influential also in some of the territories and new island nations of the South Pacific. Melbourne is also important, but Sydney is one of the region's most competitive newspaper cities and the home of Australia's two nationally circulated dailies—the influential *Australian* and the *Australian Financial Review*. It is also the principal publishing point for the nation's extensive magazine industry.

Most of Australia's major metropolitan newspapers are owned by a few large corporations, including John Fairfax and Sons Ltd., the

Herald and Weekly Times Ltd., and Rupert Murdoch's News Ltd. In addition to newspapers, all three companies publish magazines and books and control or own broadcast stations, record companies, and newsprint mills. The *Herald* and *Weekly Times* company is based in Melbourne, but the other two—Fairfax and Sons and News Ltd.— are centered mainly in Sydney, as is the Australian Consolidated Press, another major company, which publishes some of the most popular magazines, including the widely read *Australian Women's Weekly* (circulation 880,000).

The two most distinguished dailies are the *Sydney Morning Herald* and *The Age*—serious papers noted for their authoritative reporting, penetrating analyses, and interesting features. Fairfax and Sons owns the *Sydney Morning Herald* and a partnership formed by the Fairfax group and David Syme and Company Ltd. holds a controlling interest in the Melbourne-based Age.

The *Sydney Morning Herald*, founded more than a century and a half ago, is the broader of the two in its appeal and has a slightly larger circulation (about 275,000). Dignified in its appearance and approach to news, it devotes considerable attention to business and economics, keeps a watchful eye on government, and carries well-written reports from correspondents based in major foreign capitals. But it also caters to popular tastes by carrying a wide range of local news, including police and court stories.

The Age, which has grown dramatically in recent years to a circulation approaching 250,000, is the most serious of Australia's dailies and probably provides the best all-around news coverage of the country and of public issues. Politically liberal but somewhat more conservative in its social attitudes, it has a strong following among the nation's opinion leaders.

Neither *Age* nor the *Sydney Morning Herald*, however, is as large in circulation as some competing newspapers that are less serious in content and tone. Melbourne's newspaper scene is dominated by the Herald and Weekly Times group, which owns the well-edited evening *Herald* (circulation nearly 400,000) and the less-restrained *Sun News-Pictorial*, which sells more than 600,000 copies. The company also publishes two substantial weekly papers: the *Weekly Times* and (in partnership with David Syme and Company Ltd.) the *Sunday Press*.

In Sydney, the largest circulation dailies are two sensational afternoon tabloids: the *Daily Mirror* (358,000) and the Fairfax company's *Sun* (348,000). Rupert Murdoch's *Daily Telegraph* also leads the *Sydney Morning Herald*. Among Sunday papers, however, the Fairfax-owned *Sun-Herald*, with a circulation of nearly 700,000, holds an edge over the *Sunday Telegraph*.

New Zealand is often considered along with Australia, although the two nations are 1,000 miles apart and considerably different in their characteristics. New Zealand, more isolated and more pastoral, has only minor importance in the region's overall publishing picture. Its press system, however, includes more than two dozen daily newspapers and three nationally circulated weekly papers. The largest of the dailies is the well-edited morning *New Zealand Herald* (circulation 239,000), published in Auckland. Other notable dailies, although much smaller than the *Herald*, are the evening *Auckland Star*, Wellington's morning *Dominion* and *Evening Post*, and two papers published in the southern city of Christchurch: the morning *Press* and the evening *Christchurch Star*.

Singapore is of growing importance as a publishing center. This is due largely to its political stability and location, which makes it a desirable production point for publications distributed also to other parts of Southeast Asia. But Singapore itself has Southeast Asia's highest newspaper circulation rate (about 210 copies per 1,000 inhabitants).

The dominant publishing company for generations has been the Straits Times Press, Ltd., founded in 1834 and now the owner of seven newspapers which together reach approximately 75 percent of the nation's adult population. Its principal paper is the well-edited, establishment-oriented *Straits Times*, which is airlifted also to Bangkok, Hong Kong, and Jakarta, and is the largest English-language daily in Southeast Asia (circulation approximately 220,000).

The company also issues a range of other publications, including the afternoon *New Nation*, which has almost as many readers; Sunday editions of both the *Times* and the *Nation*; the *Business Times*, Singapore's only business daily; and two Malay-language papers, the daily *Berita Harian* and the weekend *Berita Minggu*, each read by more than 60 percent of the nation's adult Malays.

The largest among some half-dozen major Chinese-language papers is the *Sin Chew Jit Poh* (circulation of 112,500 daily and slightly more on Sunday). It has several close rivals, however, including the enterprising *Nanyang Siang Pau*, which in 1981 began publishing a slimmed-down eight-page special edition (about one-fourth the size of the Singapore edition) in San Francisco, for distribution also in the large overseas Chinese communities in Los Angeles, New York, Toronto, and Vancouver. Another notable competitor, although slightly smaller, is the *Shin Min Daily News*. In 1982, the *Sin Chew Jit Poh* and the *Nanyang Siang Pau* were preparing—with encouragement from the government and financial backing from several local banks—to challenge the *Straits Times* company's local monopoly of Singapore's English-language newspaper market by publishing a new daily called the *Monitor*.

Other publishing centers include Kuala Lumpur, Taipei, Seoul, and Manila.

Kuala Lumpur is the main publishing point in multicultural Malaysia, where the publishing industry resembles that of Singapore, with which Malaysia was linked politically from 1963 until they agreed to separate in 1965. Malaysian publications, which appear in seven languages (as compared with three in Singapore), generally are more numerous than those in Singapore but tend to have smaller circulations.

The major publishing company is the New Straits Times Press, Ltd., now separate from the Singapore company and owned 80 percent by Malaysians. Affluent and influential, it produces the *New Straits Times*, which is much like the Singapore paper and is Malaysia's dominant English-language daily, with a circulation approaching 200,000. The company's other publications include the English-language *New Sunday Times, Business Times, Malay Mail,* and *Sunday Mail*, and two Malay-language papers, the morning *Berita Harian* and the *Sunday Berita Minggu*.

Singapore's leading Chinese-language publications also have Malaysian offshoots now mainly owned by Malaysian interests. The largest and probably the most influential is the *Nanyang Siang Pau Malaysia*, with a circulation of about 120,000; but the *Sin Chew Jit Poh Malaysia* and the *Shin Min Daily News* also have substantial readership.

Although the *New Straits Times* is by far the largest English-language paper, there are several relatively small English language dailies in Kuala Lumpur, including the morning *Star* (circulation 85,000), and others in Sabah and Sarawak, the nation's two states in East Malaysia. Among newspapers in other languages, Chinese papers are the most numerous, but there are also dailies in Malay, Tamil and Kadazan. The leading Malay-language daily is the morning *Utusan Malaysia*, which has a circulation of about 155,000, compared with slightly more than 120,000 for the New Straits Times company's *Berita Harian*.

Taiwan has a thriving publishing industry. Its printing plants, mostly located in Taipei, turn out an estimated 1,600 periodicals a year in Chinese and Western languages, and there are approximately 31 daily newspapers, including two in English. In Taipei, approximately 75 percent of the people subscribe to at least one newspaper.

Newspaper publishing is dominated by three Taipei-based dailies —the *United Daily News*, the *China Times*, and the *Central Daily*

News, all with circulations of more than 600,000. The *Central Daily News*, which also issues a special edition for the northern areas, is the official newspaper, published by the Nationalist Party. The other two major dailies are privately owned and fiercely competitive, although carefully tuned to government policy.

Both the *United Daily News*, which has held a narrow edge in circulation and perhaps in stature, and the rival *China Times* are attractive papers; both also produce other publications.

The *United Daily News* owns the *Economic Daily News*, the *Free-China Weekly*, several notable magazines (including the *China Tribune* and *Sinorama*), and a news agency specializing in economic and financial news. Since 1978, it has also published a family-oriented sister newspaper, *Min Sheng Pao* (People's Livelihood). The *China Times'* satellite newspapers and magazines include a commercial daily and a feature-filled weekly, both launched in 1978 to compete with United Daily News publications.

Seoul and Manila have lost some of their former prominence as publishing centers, as a result of government reorganization of the news media in South Korea and the Philippines.

Seoul remains important as the capital of South Korea's publishing industry, although the regime of President Chun Doo Hwan, who assumed power following the assassination of President Park Chung Hee in 1979, has forced the consolidation of news agencies and of some newspapers, reducing their number both in Seoul and in the provinces. The government has also imposed new laws that have changed ownership structures and placed the press securely under the government's thumb. However, Korean newspapers continue to be privately owned; and (within the limits allowed by the government) they still have extensive influence.

The nation's press, like that of Japan, is dominated by a few highly competitive national dailies. All are published in Seoul, where newspaper readership is greater than the total for all other parts of the country; and all devote much of their space to political and economic news, which frequently is colored by opinion.

The most prestigious of the national papers is the afternoon *Dong-A Ilbo*, which also has the largest circulation (more than 1 million) and publishes several popular magazines. Founded in 1920, the *Dong-A Ilbo* chafed under the Japanese rule; and frequently since Korea regained its independence, it has been at odds with the country's authoritarian rulers—calling for more democratic government and the restoration of civil rights and guarantees of greater individual and press freedom. As a result, it has been a major target of repression by a succession of Korean regimes, which from time to time have sent armed troops into the newsroom, jailed *Dong-A Ilbo* editors and reporters, forced the firing of others, and brought pressures on the paper's advertisers (which, at one point in the 1970s, led to withdrawal of nearly 98 percent of its ads). Though now forced to be docile, *Dong-A Ilbo* has earned wide popular support and respect for its independent and often courageous stands.

Other major national dailies include the prestigious and long-established *Chosun Ilbo*, the *Joong-ang Daily News* (which claims to have the largest circulation, although circulation figures are hard to ascertain with certainty), and the *Hankok Ilbo*. None of the three has been as noted for its independence as has the *Dong-A Ilbo*, but all are important newspapers, which (like the *Dong-A Ilbo*) maintain foreign bureaus, issue several subsidiary publications, and have a large following. The Korean press also includes two English-language dailies with substantial circulations—the government-owned *Korea Herald* and the *Korea Times* (published by the *Hankok Ilbo*).

The major newspapers in the Philippines—where English-language publications are dominant—are published in Manila. Since the declaration in 1972 of martial law, under which almost all existing papers (with the notable exception of the *Daily Express*) were closed and replaced by papers under new ownership closely linked to President Marcos, the country has had no truly independent newspapers. Manila's best-known premartial law papers (as well as some papers in the provinces) have failed to reappear. The most notable casualty has been the *Manila Times*, previously the nation's most popular daily, which was owned by a family known to be critical of the Marcos regime.

Manila's most important papers now are owned largely by friends or relatives of the President. The three major English language dailies (morning papers with combined circulation of more than 600,000) are the *Bulletin Today*, the *Philippine Daily Express* and the *Times Journal*. The largest and most influential is the *Bulletin Today* (circulation approximately 282,000), owned by a former Marcos aide.

The Daily Express (circulation 194,000) is owned by an influential businessman who is a close friend of the President, and the *Times Journal* (circulation 170,000) by a diplomat who is a brother of Mrs. Marcos. The Daily Express is regarded as the mouthpiece of government policy, but the other papers also hew closely to the official line. Sister publications of the *Times Journal* include the *People's Journal*, a bi-lingual morning tabloid (English and Filipino) introduced in 1979 and edited to appeal to popular, escapist tastes.

Elsewhere in Asia, the press is generally underdeveloped. The vast majority of newspapers suffer from a lack of modern equipment, adequate financial resources, and sufficient numbers of well-trained personnel. Many of the larger dailies, however, are important within the country they serve.

In Pakistan, nearly 100 dailies have survived a confrontation with the military regime of President Zia-ul Haq, who since 1978 has banned many newspapers and other periodicals. Most of the papers have very small circulations, however, and the country's rural population (about three-quarters of the total of some 90 million) generally lacks access to dailies, which circulate almost entirely in cities of more than 50,000 inhabitants.

The country's 12 English-language dailies account for only about 150,000 of the estimated total daily newspaper sales of 900,000 copies, and they are losing ground to papers published in Urdu (the national language) and the major regional languages (Baluchi, Pushto, Sindhi, Gujarati, and Punjabi). As a group, however, the English-language papers are still regarded generally as the most influential. Two of the largest, the 50,000-circulation *Pakistan Times* (published in Lahore and Rawalpindi) and the 35,000-circulation *Morning News* (published in Karachi), are owned by the National Press Trust (NPT), a government-created statutory body founded in 1946 to guide public opinion toward support of government policies. The NPT, whose chairman is appointed by the nation's president, also owns two of the nation's top five Urdu newspapers (the important 150,000-circulation *Mashriq* and the 50,000-circulation *Imroze*) and two weekly magazines. Among the less official English-language dailies (which nevertheless support government policy) the most important is *Dawn*, which migrated from Delhi after the creation of Pakistan. The only other one of consequence is the *Sun* (32,000), which, like *Dawn*, is published in Karachi.

Papers in the Urdu language, which are the most numerous and account for the major share of the total circulation, depend on handwritten copy prepared by calligraphers. Using special ink and lead-pointed pens, the calligraphers slowly and painstakingly transcribe material provided by the editorial and advertising staffs onto thin "butter" paper, with the sheets then being proofread, pasted onto newspaper-size sheets, and sent to the back shop for plate-making. An Urdu paper of 10 pages requires at least 50 calligraphers, who receive pay comparable to that of reporters and editors. An Urdu keyboard that would have eliminated the need for this slow and costly transcribing was developed in the late 1960s, but Pakistan newspapers have not adopted it because their readers consider the calligraphers' script more decorative and easier to read.

The major daily among the Urdu newspapers, which have been growing in influence as well as readership, is the *Daily Jang*, a 200,000-circulation morning paper produced in Karachi and Rawalpindi. The only other dailies with more than 100,000 circulation are the *Daily Mashriq* (150,000) published in four cities (Lahore, Karachi, Peshawar, and Quetta) and the *Nawa-i-waqt* (145,000), issued in Lahore and Rawalpindi. Although owned by the NPT, the *Daily Mashriq* carries a great deal of light news and enjoys considerable credibility. A popular feature in its eight- to twelve-page issues is a special magazine section (two pages on most days and six pages in the Friday weekend issues) which helps compensate for the scarcity of domestic political news. The magazine section is devoted largely to articles related to national affairs, but it also frequently contains material translated from *Time, Newsweek,* and other English-language publications.

In Indonesia, also under military rule, the press is more vigorous. The government has made clear to editors that they should guide rather than reflect society and help achieve national goals rather than agitate for change. But newspapers do criticize the government, although it is risky to do so.

The Indonesian press faces a multitude of special problems, apart from government controls and shortages of trained staff and equipment. Advertising is scarce, newsprint is costly, and geographical and cultural barriers are formidable. The nation stretches over some 3,000 islands, and its estimated 155 million people include about 50 ethnic groups speaking more than 200 languages and dialects.

Despite its difficulties, the Indonesian press has grown impressively in size and quality in recent years. The country now has more than 40 daily newspapers, with a combined circulation of well over 2 million. More than two-thirds of them have been established since the downfall of Sukarno in the mid-1960s, and many have a strong political flavor.

The two largest and most influential dailies, both published in Jakarta, are *Kompas*, a Catholic paper with 275,000 circulation, and *Sinar Harapan*, a Protestant paper with 200,000 circulation. Other important Jakarta papers, smaller in circulation, are *Merdeka, Berita Buana, Poskota*, and the official *Suara Karya*.

Newspapers in Thailand have also improved in printing quality and physical appearance, but they are allowed very little freedom by the country's military regime, which has closed many papers and remains acutely sensitive to criticism. As a result, caution is the watchword among the nation's publishers and editors, some of whom have close ties with the government.

Daily newspapers appear in three languages: Thai, Chinese, and English. Thai-language papers are the most numerous, together having the greatest circulation and the most influence with the masses. Next in total circulation are the papers that serve the Chinese community, which accounts for about 10 percent of Thailand's population of nearly 50 million.

By far the largest of the Thai dailies is the morning *Thai Rath*, less noted for serious news content than for its neat appearance, splashy graphics, and often sensational tone. Most other Thai-language papers in Bangkok as well as in the provinces tend to follow the style of the *Thai Rath*, which devotes much of its space to gossip columns, sports, entertainment news and features, and women's pages, and sells some 800,000 copies daily.

Among the serious Thai-language papers, the leaders are Bangkok's liberal *Matichon* and the more conservative *Siam Rath*, which have much smaller circulations than the *Thai Rath*. Even the more serious papers, however, carry little hard news and often devote as much as half their space to articles of opinion. The foreign-news content is rarely more than 5 percent.

The leading Chinese-language dailies are the *Sin Sian Yit Pao* and *Sirinakorn*, both morning papers with more than 50,000 circulation. The morning *Universal* is smaller, but it is also distributed in Hong Kong and Taiwan.

Among the three English-language dailies (which are influential with the elite), the most comprehensive and important is the 35,000-circulation *Bangkok Post*, owned by the London-based Thomson organization. The others, which have fewer readers, are the *Bangkok World*, owned by a group of American investors, and the *Nation Review*.

In several of the smaller South Asian nations—Bangladesh, Sri Lanka, and Nepal—prospects for the press have brightened. Change has been notable particularly in Sri Lanka, where newspapers and other publications have grown spectacularly since 1977 under the government of President J. R. Jayawardene, who has allowed them freedoms denied by previous regimes. In 1979 alone the circulations of Sri Lanka's leading newspapers increased by more than 30 percent and would have grown more but for restrictions on the import of newsprint.

Sri Lanka newspapers appear in three languages: Sinhala (the official language), Tamil, and English. Papers in Sinhalese and Tamil are the most numerous, and those in Sinhalese tend to have the largest circulations and the greatest influence.

The industry is dominated by three major publishing houses, each of which produces daily and weekly newspapers and several magazines. The most solidly entrenched is the state-owned Associated Newspapers of Ceylon, Ltd., popularly known as the "Lake House" group, which owns the largest Sinhala-language daily (*Dinamina*,

132,000) and weekly (*Silumina*, 352,000), as well as the largest and most prestigious of several English-language dailies (the morning *Ceylon Daily News*, 87,000). It also publishes an English-language Sunday paper (the *Observer Magazine*, 85,000) and small afternoon papers in English and Sinhalese and daily and Sunday papers in Tamil. Its closest rival is the new Independent Newspapers Inc. (the "Sun group," established in 1961), which owns English and Sinhalese papers of secondary importance. Its Sinhalese papers include the daily *Dawasa* (117,000) and three Sunday papers, of which the 300,000-circulation *Rivirasa* is the most important. It also publishes two English-language papers, the daily *Sun* (56,000) and the *Weekend* (69,000). A third major publishing house is the state-owned Times of Ceylon, Ltd. (the Times Group), which publishes the English-language *Ceylon Daily Mirror* (29,000) and *Sunday Times* (65,000) and two substantial Sinhalese papers, the daily *Lankadipa* (67,000) and the weekly *Sri Lankadipa* (87,000). Sri Lanka also has a number of small newspapers, including politically oriented papers opposed to the present government. The Communist Party of Sri Lanka, for example, publishes several dailies and weeklies, but its largest daily, the Sinhala-language *Aththa*, has a circulation of only 40,000.

Newspapers in Nepal also grew and became more vigorous when controls in effect for nearly two decades were lifted in 1979. By 1982, however, a government less favorable to press freedom was back in control. Expansion in any case has been limited by poor technical facilities and the shortage of newsprint, and only two of the nation's 25 dailies have circulations of more than 5,000. The two most important papers are the Nepali-language *Gorkhapatra* (circulation 35,000) and its sister English-language daily, the *Rising Nepal* (circulation 20,000).

In Bangladesh, four years of martial law ended in 1979, but the nation's undernourished press, which reaches far fewer people than the government-controlled broadcast stations, has continued to be handicapped by government restrictions and the rising cost of newsprint. The most important of the daily newspapers is Dacca's morning Bengali-language *Ittefaq*, whose circulation of 190,000 is almost as great as that of the nation's other 19 dailies combined. There are seven English language dailies, but most have circulations of 5,000 or less. The largest and most influential is the *Bangladesh Observer* (55,000), which for all practical purposes is government-operated, as are its closest English competitor the *Bangladesh Times* and the *Dainik Bangla*, perhaps the second most important of the Bengali dailies.

Socialist Burma, with some 35 million people and a 60 percent rate of literacy, has a meager press system. There are only nine daily newspapers, with a combined circulation of well under a million. Eight are published in the capital of Rangoon (including one English-language paper, the 20,000 circulation *Working People's Daily*) and one in Mandalay. All are government-owned; and although they compete for circulation and try to outdo one another in producing other periodicals, they have little individual character. Produced on outmoded equipment and by small staffs, the papers have been hampered also by the lack of political and press freedom, and by the rising cost of newsprint, all of which must be imported.

With the notable exception of the People's Republic of China, the press in the Communist countries of Asia is of little consequence. Newspapers in North Korea and Vietnam are few in number, and they are primarily propaganda organs, filled with carefully selected and officially prescribed news and frequently virulent attacks on the United States and other nations that the regimes regard as unfriendly. In Afghanistan, Kampuchea, and Laos, the press has never been of much importance and it has virtually disappeared in recent years. Laos, where private publishing ceased early in 1975, has only two small dailies: *Sieng Pasason* (Voice of the People), the mouthpiece of the ruling Laos People's Revolutionary Party, and *Vientiana Mai* (Victory of Vientiane), also operated by the regime. And in Kampuchea, where the government closed all periodicals in 1975 immediately after the defeat of the Lon Nol regime, the only publication in 1980 reportedly was a monthly issued by the country's new rulers.

Weekly Newspapers

Asia's weekly newspapers may be divided roughly into three main groups: large general-interest weekend papers published in the major urban centers; smaller urban weeklies published for minority-language or special-interest audiences and supported in some cases by political parties; and the many thousands of weekly papers that serve readers in the less populous provincial towns and villages.

Newspapers in the first group are generally published by large companies that also operate important dailies, and some are only Sunday editions of the dailies, although edited by separate staffs. In countries where British influence on the press remains strong, however, weekend newspapers often have names that distinguish them clearly from dailies published by the same company. In Australia, for example, the company that publishes the daily *Melbourne Herald* produces two substantial Sunday papers: the *Sun News Pictorial* and the *Weekly Times*. In Sri Lanka, the important Sinhala-language Sunday papers *Rivirasa* and *Silumina*, each with a circulation of more than 300,000, are issued by publishing combines that put out dailies under different names.

Many of the major weekend papers in former British territories—particularly in Australia, New Zealand, India, Malaysia, Singapore, and Sri Lanka—tend to resemble British Sunday papers. Well edited and fatter than the dailies, they generally contain a wide range of features and circulate nationally as well as in the cities in which they are published.

Small weeklies are numerous in most Asian nations, and especially in developing countries with large rural populations. India alone reportedly has nearly 19,000 papers of less than daily frequency. Most weeklies (and papers that appear less frequently), however, have circulations of only a few hundred to a few thousand copies; and except in countries where they are government-owned or supported, they must struggle to survive. Most of India's small papers, for example, are crudely printed publications whose existence is uncertain from one issue to the next. Many appear only when their editors can get official advertising or subsidies from political parties or other special-interest groups, and some are said to exist only in the hope of obtaining newsprint quotas for resale to larger newspapers.

Some governments, however, are supporting the development of weekly newspapers to serve provincial and rural areas. The most notable effort is underway in Indonesia, where the government has made the theme Koran Masuk Desa (Newspapers for Villagers) an important item in its third 5-year development program, which began in April, 1979. In line with the program, the official Indonesian Press Council in 1980 limited daily newspapers to 12 pages and to 30 percent advertising content. This regulation, designed to make more advertising and newsprint available to weeklies, has tended to reduce the size and affluence of the two leading Jakarta newspapers— Kompas and Sinar Harapan—and the nation's three leading provincial dailies: the Suara Merdeka of Semarang, the Surabaya Post, and the Pikiran Rakyat of Bandung. By mid-1981, 20 regional papers— aided by government subsidies to help cover printing and distribution costs—were selling some 150,000 copies weekly of special four-page rural editions, written in simple language and designed to help change rural Indonesians from a nonreading to a reading society.

The government in the Philippines has also encouraged the development of provincial papers. Although Manila remains the dominant publishing center, with well over half the total number of publications, there now are about 65 weekly tabloids in outlying communities. Most have circulations ranging from 1,000 to 3,000, but they tend to have greater audience penetration than the dailies, whose subscription costs are too high for most wage earners.

The Pacific Islands

The press situation in the Pacific Islands differs so greatly from that in Asia that it should be considered separately.

The Pacific Islands press is a new press, a pioneering press, a press of developing countries with a strong overlay of Western press models and standards. It is a press seeking its own identity as the Pacific Islands shed the final vestiges of colonialism and seek their own road to development. There is a rich diversity, from the monthly *Miscellany*, published in tiny, isolated Pitcairn Island, to the highly competitive and modern Western style daily press of Suva, Fiji. Although the *Fiji Times* has passed the 100-year mark, more than half the newspapers have been started within the past 20 years, and only a handful go back before 1950.

The Pacific Islands still bear the fading stamp of their colonial past, and this is reflected in the press systems that have emerged in the different areas of the Pacific—the British model in much of the South Pacific, the French model in French Polynesia (Tahiti) and New Caledonia, and the American model in Guam, American Samoa, and the recently formed political entities of Micronesia.

The Pacific Islands represent three major overlapping intermixed cultural groups—Melanesia, Micronesia, and Polynesia. Papua New Guinea, with some 3 million people, is the central nation of Melanesia, which extends through the Solomons to Fiji. Fiji is a major interface among the regions, exhibiting strong Melanesian and Polynesian political and cultural forms. Polynesia includes Tahiti, Samoa, New Zealand, Tonga, and numerous smaller island groups. There are also strong cultural links between Polynesia and Micronesia, which comprises such island groups as the Carolines, Marianas, Marshalls, Tuvalu, Kiribati, and smaller islands.

In some areas, such as Guam and New Zealand, Western influence was so strong that indigenous culture and populations had difficulty surviving in any form, while in most of the other parts of the Pacific, large indigenous populations survived to the time of independence. Examples are Papua New Guinea, Fiji, and Western Samoa, three of the most influential countries in the Pacific.

Pacific Island journalists face the classic problems of the press and broadcasting services in developing countries, including lack of equipment and trained personnel, inadequate access to regional and international news, small advertising bases, low pay and prestige, and government restrictions.

In addition, there are some special concerns related more directly if not uniquely to the Pacific Islands. These include geographic isolation, small and scattered populations, and the persistence of strong colonial structures that affect news operations.

In a 1976 study of the flow of news in the Pacific Islands press systems, data showed that the traditional colonial-based flow patterns still prevailed, after most of the countries were politically independent, and that

- There were one-way imbalances in the flow of news from the metropolitan countries to the Pacific Islands.
- There was little flow of news among the Pacific Islands.
- There was even less flow between the colonially based blocs of countries in the "American," "British," and "French" Pacifics.
- There were indications of intra-Pacific news flows through the PEACESAT satellite system and through the exchange of newspapers among editors.

The first complete census of the press in the Pacific Islands, published in 1973, reported a pattern that has changed little over the years. In all, 63 publications were listed, with 12 dailies, 19 weeklies, and the rest less than weekly, including 11 monthlies. The numbers constantly fluctuate, given the uncertainty of the publishing business, but have generally increased.

Weeklies remain the predominant form of newspaper publication in the Pacific, with English as the most widely used language, and many publish in varying mixes of English and indigenous languages. Most of the publications are printed by offset, with several mimeographed or cyclostyled, and a few letterpress. The format is tabloid or smaller, with an average of 16 to 24 pages, although the metropolitan papers are often much larger.

Ownership of the press in 1973 showed 41 privately owned and 22 government-owned publications. The trend has been toward more private and less government ownership. Several areas, including Tonga, the Cook Islands, and Niue, are served primarily by government-owned publications (as well as official broadcast services). The Solomons in 1982, however, was seeking to turn over its government *News Drum* to private operations, to go with the private weekly *Toktok*.

In American Samoa, the government publishes a 5-day-a-week newssheet alongside two private papers, the *Samoa News* and *Pago Pago Times*. In Western Samoa, an independent country of about 155,000 people, six privately owned weeklies compete, and the government publishes an official paper, *Savali*. There is no daily newspaper in the country. The established paper, *The Samoa Times*, founded in 1967, competes vigorously with such papers as the *South Seas Star, Observer, Samoana, Advertiser*, and others. Western Samoa's capital of Apia (population about 33,000) may be the liveliest newspaper town for its size in the world. The newspaper scene there is never the same; it has a pioneering feel to it.

Fiji remains the busiest publications center in the Pacific Islands, with a wide variety of daily, weekly, and other publications, in English, Fijian, and Hindustani. More than a dozen publications reach widely across Fiji's competitive publishing business. Papua New Guinea, despite its much larger population, lags behind Fiji; but more and more publications are beginning to appear. Tahiti and New Caledonia produce daily newspapers in French, and receive international news from Agence France-Presse.

In Suva, there is a classic competitive battle between the long-established *Fiji Times*, the grandfather of the Pacific press, and the *Fiji Sun*, established in 1974, with New Zealand, Hong Kong and United States owners. They are close in circulation: about 25,000 and are trying to outdo each other in coverage of rural news. Both publish in English.

In Papua New Guinea, the *Post-Courier* is the national daily newspaper for a population approaching 3 million, and it is published in English (there are more than 700 languages and distinct dialects in Papua New Guinea, and English, Pidgin, and Motu are the more "universal" means of communication). Circulation of the *Post-Courier* is over 25,000 daily. Ownership control is with the *Melbourne Herald* group in Australia, as it is for the *Fiji Times*. The *Nivgini News* is a 5-day-a-week (Tuesday to Saturday) newspaper published in English.

A substantial competitive publishing group—the Word Publishing Company—has grown out of Christian organizations in Papua New Guinea. Five churches own the company, which grew from the Wantok Publications, founded in 1969. The *Wantok* weekly, published in Pidgin, served as the base for further publications. The group since 1980 has published the weekly *Times* of Papua New Guinea, which has a circulation of more than 10,000 and focuses on in-depth political, economic, and cultural reporting. The company, which also publishes sports periodicals and magazines, opened its first bookstore in 1981.

Exchange of news among the Pacific press occurs through the exchange of newspapers, by listening to such services as Radio New Zealand's "Pacific Link," and the Regional News Exchange over the PEACESAT system. Plans for implementation of a Pacific news service were under discussion in 1982, with several plans offered.

Other major newspapers in the Pacific include the *Tohi Tala Niue* (Niue); the *Nauru Bulletin*; the *Norfolk Islander*; the *News Bulletin* and *Pago Pago Times* (American Samoa); *News Drum* and *Toktok* (Solomons); *News Sheet* (Tuvalu); *Cook Island News; Le Depeche de Tahiti* (French Polynesia); *Atoll Pioneer* (Kiribati); *Pacific Daily*

News (Guam); *Marianas Variety* (Commonwealth of the Northern Marianas); *Ko e Kalonikali Tonga* and *Tonga Chronicle* (Tonga). In the new political entity of the Federated States of Micronesia, the *Ponape Sun* and *Truk Chronicle* were started in 1979, and the *Micronesian Independent* is published in the Marshall Islands.

NEWS MAGAZINES

The most widely read newsmagazines in Asia and the Pacific are the regional editions of the leading American newsweeklies, *Time* and *Newsweek*. *Time* publishes several special regional editions, with a combined circulation of nearly 700,000, while *Newsweek's* comparable editions have a total circulation of about 400,000. *Business Week* and *Fortune* also publish special Asian editions, as do numerous American and some British magazines that are not primarily news-oriented. The *National Geographic*, for example, has a Pacific edition with 335,000 circulation.

Several Asian nations also have newsmagazines of their own, generally modeled after *Time* and *Newsweek*. One of the most important is *India Today*, a political news fortnightly established in 1974, which has become so popular among upper-class and upper-middle-class English-language readers that several comparable publications have appeared. Other major newsweeklies include *Asiaweek*, published in Hong Kong and partly owned by *Reader's Digest*, which circulates through many ASEAN countries; Japan's *Shukan Asahi* and *Shukan Sankei*; and Australia's *The Bulletin*. The important Indonesian newsmagazine *Tempo* was closed in 1982 by the government, which was displeased with its election coverage.

There are also some substantial news and picture weeklies. The English-language *Illustrated Weekly of India*, founded in 1880, has grown in recent years to become the largest-circulation all-India magazine. A notable newcomer in Japan is *Focus*, a 64-page *Time*-size pictorial news weekly, which began publication in October 1981, with 300,000 circulation.

Rapid growth of the region's economies has led in recent years to the appearance of many new business news magazines (as well as business and financial dailies and trade and technical publications) and to the expansion of older business periodicals. The business and financial news magazine with the widest influence in Asia is the 35-year-old British-owned *Far Eastern Economic Review*, published in Hong Kong, which maintains correspondents in many major Asian capitals and is respected for its authoritative and objective coverage. Some other business magazines, although less wide-ranging, have larger circulations and greater importance within the countries where they are published. One of the largest is Japan's fortnightly *Nikkei Business* (circulation 155,000), a joint venture of New York's McGraw-Hill Inc. and a Japanese publishing firm.

Other Publications

By far the largest circulation magazine of any type in the region is the monthly *Reader's Digest,* which publishes special English-language editions in Hong Kong and Australia and editions in four Asian languages: Chinese, Japanese, Hindi, and Korean. The region generally is not noted for its indigenous magazines, but they are growing rapidly in number and importance in some countries; and a few trends and individual publications are noteworthy.

Among the many periodicals issued by Asian governments, one of the best known abroad is the *Peking Review,* a political and theoretical magazine on Chinese and world affairs, which is published in at least a half-dozen foreign languages (Arabic, English, French, German, Japanese, and Spanish). Newspapers that circulate widely in the region, in addition to the *Asian Wall Street Journal* and the Asia edition of the *International Herald Tribune,* include *Asia Magazine,* a feature-filled supplement printed in Hong Kong and distributed with some major Asian newspapers.

A notable trend has been the recent appearance in Japan of new leisure magazines. The growing number of leisure periodicals is attributed in part to a magazine sales boom in 1979, when nearly 200 new magazines appeared and total magazine sales increased by more than 11 percent. Another factor is said to be the changing attitudes of middle-aged and younger Japanese, who reportedly are showing more interest than past generations in entertainment and family life. A substantial new publication that reflects the trend is *BOX,* which began publication in 1980 with a press run of 400,000 copies and provides reports on health care, housing, personal investments, men's fashion, and leisure activities.

Magazines are also growing rapidly in India. English-language periodicals have made some of the greatest gains; but magazines in major Indian languages—including Hindi, Gujarati, Tamil, Malayalam, Bengali, Marathi, Telugu, and Kannada—are also flourishing and expanding. Some 60 such magazines (with prices ranging from 6 to 45 cents) now have circulations of more than 100,000, and several monthlies sell about a half million copies.

Women's magazines are of major importance in some areas, including Australia, Japan, Taiwan, Hong Kong, and the Philippines. In Australia, where sports and trade and technical periodicals abound, the most popular magazine is the *Australian Women's Week-*

ly, which has a circulation of nearly 900,000. One of Taiwan's most widely read magazines is *The Woman*, a high-quality monthly that advocates family planning and a higher status for women. To mark its ninth anniversary in 1977, it put out a 248-page issue, the bulkiest magazine yet published in Taiwan.

Hong Kong's many magazines include some widely circulated Chinese- and English-language fashion publications, and women's magazines account for an important share of the magazine market in the Philippines. As a group, however, the most widely read publications in the Philippines are comics magazines. Started in 1947 to help people forget the Japanese occupation and now often used to promote nationalism and the government's social programs, the "komiks," mostly in the Filipino language, now sell more than 2 million copies weekly and have an estimated readership of 16 million, including many adults.

BROADCASTING

In broadcasting, as well as in the print media, the region is one of vast differences. Japan has one of the world's most technologically advanced and most pervasive broadcast systems. Its national broadcasting system, the NHK (Nippon Hoso Kyokai), is the world's largest broadcast organization, and a competing commercial system composed of some 120 privately owned companies is virtually equal to it in scale, strength, and impact. NHK's overseas service, Radio Japan, airs programs to foreign audiences in 23 languages; and NHK and the commercial companies saturate the domestic airwaves with a wide variety of radio and television programs. License fees on radio receiving sets were abolished in 1968, but the number of radios has been estimated at 60 million. It may be greater.

Television in Japan is even more important as a communications medium. Nearly 11,000 NHK and commercial TV transmitters blanket the country, offering viewers in even the remote areas a choice of several channels. Nearly every Japanese family owns at least one TV set, and among some 30 million officially registered sets in 1981, more than 26 million were color models.

In contrast, some countries in the region have not entered the television age. In 1982, television broadcasting had yet to begin in Kampuchea, Laos, Nepal, the tiny Portuguese colony of Macao, or most of the small island nations and territories scattered across the South Pacific.

Despite the great diversity within the region, however, some general observations may be made.

- Broadcasting in Asia and the Pacific is mainly national, controlled by government departments or, in a gradually increasing number of countries, by government-created public corporations. Privately owned broadcast stations are allowed in some nations, but they operate under much closer government supervision than do the print media.
- Most national broadcast operations are supported in part by license fees on TV sets (radio license fees having been eliminated in many countries, often because they were too difficult to collect). Many national stations, however, carry commercials, which account for much of their revenue.
- Radio and television operations throughout much of the region have been handicapped severely by the shortage of trained staff. This problem is gradually easing. Numerous training programs have been established, and in many countries standards of professionalism in radio and TV now approach those in the print media. There is still great need, however, for training news, technical, and managerial personnel—to improve the quality of existing services and provide adequate staffing for their expansion.
- High production costs and the shortage of production skills have led broadcasters in many developing countries to use a high percentage of imported programs, particularly to fill television time, even though such programs are often unrelated to local cultures and values. As staffs have become better trained, however, the dependence on imported programs has decreased. This trend is particularly strong in some Asian countries, where radio and TV organizations are encouraging the work of local writers and performers in an effort to build up their own sources of program material.
- Governments in many Asian and Pacific countries have been slow to recognize the potential of broadcasting as a tool for education and development. In broadcasting's early years, some governments tended to regard it primarily as an entertainment service, and to give it a low priority in allocation of their limited funds. This attitude has been changing. Governments and broadcasters have gradually realized that radio and television can be used effectively to raise the levels of education and literacy, teach technical skills and more efficient farming methods, arouse public interest in development projects, further national unity, and do many other things that serve the national and public interest.

Most nations now operate educational broadcasting services (although such systems vary greatly in extent, quality, and degree of success), and some have given broadcasting an increasing role in the development effort. Some other nations, however, do not yet seem to fully understand broadcasting's potential, and there it continues to be regarded lightly and to receive meager financial support.

- News programs are regarded as important in almost all countries of the region. Where television exists, newscasts are often presented in prime time and tend to draw as large audiences as do the entertainment programs. In a few nations (notably Japan, Australia, and New Zealand), broadcasters determine the content of the news programs on the basis of professional standards. In some nations and territories, however, news is supplied by official sources; and in the remainder, government guidelines or controls restrict the broadcasting of certain types of news.

- TV news programs in most countries tend to be lacking in showmanship. There are very few show-type news programs comparable to those in the United States, where the personality of the newscaster is important. News programs often consist of a series of short items read by a newscaster.

- Technical facilities for domestic TV news operations have improved greatly in recent years. Electronic news gathering (ENG) equipment has been introduced in most countries and news studios gradually have been modernized. Almost all broadcasting organizations, however, still lack news vans for on-scene pickups and microwave networks for the transmission of visual materials from remote places. As a result, the visuals for domestic stories are generally ENG-recorded scenes from big-city areas. With exceptions (Japan and Australia in particular) broadcasting organizations have no resident correspondents of their own abroad, depending on Visnews and other foreign agencies for visual materials to accompany their international news reports. In some places, these materials are transmitted by satellite; but in most cases, they are air shipped to the stations.

Generalizations do not apply to Japan, where broadcasting is almost entirely free from government controls and is far more advanced in every respect than it is in any other Asian or Pacific country.

The Japanese system is also distinctive in its division into two almost equal parts, government and commercial.

The NHK, a special government-created corporation, accepts no advertising. It derives its revenue from the fees paid by owners of TV sets, who contract to receive its services. In addition to its external service (Radio Japan), NHK operates two medium-wave radio networks, an FM radio network, two national TV networks (general and educational), and high-power experimental UHF stations in Tokyo and Osaka. NHK provides an impressive number of educational programs on both radio and television and also offers a wide range of entertainment programs, of which dramas and variety shows are the most popular. For its news broadcasts, which occupy more than a third of the total air time on its principal AM radio and general TV channels, NHK often gathers material in cooperation with the major newspapers, but it also maintains correspondents of its own in Japan and foreign countries and obtains material from domestic and foreign news agencies. It makes frequent use of satellites to bring its viewers telecasts of major foreign news and sports events, and by 1983 it expects to employ a domestic satellite to provide audiences in remote areas with clearer sounds and pictures. Experiments with the CAP-TAIN system (which enables TV set owners to obtain news and other imformation through telephone lines connected with the CAPTAIN center) began in 1979; practical use of the system is scheduled to begin in 1983.

Commercial stations, which are supported entirely by advertising revenues, were first authorized in 1951 by American occupation officials. Originally licensed for only local or regional operations, the privately owned stations have grown greatly in number and become linked into informal networks. The commercial companies together now operate nearly 200 radio stations and more than 4,500 TV transmitters, most of which are UHF. Unlike the NHK, the commercial stations are primarily entertainment-oriented, devoting only a little more than 13 percent of their air time to news.

Television systems elsewhere in the region are far smaller and less developed than they are in Japan. But television has replaced radio as the most influential broadcast medium in Australia, Hong Kong, South Korea, and Taiwan, and it is of major importance also in some other localities, including Singapore, Indonesia, and New Zealand.

Throughout most of Asia and the Pacific, however, radio remains the principal broadcast medium, and in some places, it is more important than newspapers. Radio's advantages are obvious. It is far less expensive than is television to install and operate; it requires fewer well-trained personnel; and radio receivers—particularly simple transistors—are within the means of vast numbers of people who cannot afford the much more costly TV sets. Radio is also particularly well suited to the communication needs of nations and territories spread over vast areas (such as China), those composed of many scattered islands (such as Indonesia, the Philippines, and many nations and dependencies in the South Pacific), and those (including Afghanistan and Nepal) where the mountainous terrain is a formidable obstacle to the development of television. Furthermore, radio is better able than any other medium to overcome the barriers imposed by often extensive illiteracy and by the region's multitude of languages and cultures.

There are no reliable recent figures for the number of radio receivers in the region, because some governments no longer require the licensing of radio sets or attempt to count them. China alone has more than 150 million, and the total for the region is probably several times greater. In many of the less-developed parts of the region, however, radio receivers are still thinly spread. Although the development of inexpensive battery-operated transistor sets has greatly increased the size of radio audiences, even these simple sets are beyond the means of many. In Bangladesh, for example, a survey in 1976 indicated that two-thirds of the rural population either had no radios or felt unable to afford the batteries to keep their sets in working order.

Radio listening is nevertheless widespread throughout the region. Some governments have made radio programs more available to rural masses by establishing, or encouraging the creation of, community listening centers; and a few of the Communist countries in particular have done even more to extend radio's reach. In China, wired broadcast units and loudspeakers in countless communes, factories, and mines enable radio programs to be heard throughout much of the nation. North Korea and Vietnam have also extensive wired broadcast systems.

China's Central People's Broadcasting Station in Beijing operates four domestic services—two devoted to news, policies, and culture; one to music, literature, and art; and a fourth for the nation's 53 ethnic minorities, who account for only about 6 percent of the population but are spread over nearly 60 percent of the land area. Stations at the provincial, municipal, and local levels are required to transmit news, commentaries, and other important policy programs relayed from the central station. In addition, they produce programs to meet the needs of the party and government units at various levels.

China also broadcasts in numerous languages to audiences in other countries. Its Radio Peking has more than 40 powerful transmitters scattered across the country and ranks with Britain's BBC, the Voice of America, and Radio Moscow as one of the four major international broadcasters in the world. Other notable external broadcasting services in the region besides those in China and Japan include stations operated by North Korea and South Korea (which wage an unceasing propaganda battle), Taiwan (where the principal target is mainland China), Vietnam, Australia, India, Indonesia, Malaysia, and Pakistan.

Television is growing rapidly in many parts of the region. But throughout most of South and Southeast Asia, it is still in the early stages of development, reaching only a small portion of the population. Some governments—Indonesia, India, and Pakistan among them—have taken steps to make television more widely available through such means as the construction of provincial relay stations, the use of satellites to beam programs to earth-receiving stations in the provinces, and the establishment of community viewing centers in rural villages. Indonesia, for example, began in 1976 to transmit programs via a domestic satellite, Palapa, which now sends TV broadcasts over wide areas of the country. India has experimented with the use of a satellite system to provide educational television to 2,400 remote rural villages clustered around five centers; and was developing its own domestic satellite system (Insat) in the early 1980s. Pakistan, which originates TV programs from well-equipped studios in Lahore, Karachi, and Rawalpindi, has built new rebroadcast stations, including three located at altitudes of over 8,000 feet in areas of permanent snow, and set up community viewing centers in many rural areas. Even Bangladesh has built several new transmitting centers linked to the main studio complex in Dacca, and the government is planning a new television channel (its second).

The most impressive recent growth has occurred in China, where television broadcasting began in 1958 (with the Beijing Television Station), as part of the Great Leap Forward. In 1978, China was reported to have fewer than 1.5 million television receivers; but by 1982, the number had grown to an estimated 10 million; and TV programs were said to be reaching nearly one-third of the population. With local production of TV sets increasing rapidly and the prices falling, it was predicted that as many as 33 million TV receivers would be in operation by 1985.

Although most of the TV sets are small black-and-white models, China introduced color telecasting in the early 1970s. China Central Television (CCTV), the national TV service, now operates two color channels, and coaxial cables and microwave links carry the programs to nearly 40 provincial and local stations and to viewers in most areas of the country. Beijing TV is now a local station, providing a third channel in the capital city. Planning was well underway in 1982 for a domestic satellite system, using Intelsat transponders at the start, to extend television's reach further.

Television in China, like radio and the print media, is directly supervised by the Chinese Communist Party's Central Committee and is used to promote party and government policies. Television is administered by the Central Broadcasting Administration, with provincial TV stations directed by provincial broadcasting authorities and the Central TV station in Beijing. Unlike the TV systems in other Communist countries of Asia, however, TV stations in China now carry a limited number of commercials, and there are other differences as well.

China's television still suffers from outmoded technology, short broadcast hours, and generally dull programs. But there are continuing efforts toward better and more interesting programming. Since the end of the Cultural Revolution, China, once one of the most closed societies to foreign television programs, has been televising some carefully selected foreign films. It has also broadened the content of news programs—which are regarded as important and as attracting wide audiences. There is very little direct broadcasting of domestic events, most of which are videotaped and delayed in presentation. Since 1980, however, CCTV has been receiving world news by satellite from two Western agencies, Visnews and UPITN, whose visual materials are aired with local commentary and are usually edited to eliminate stories of brutality and crime and such frivolous events as beauty contests.

In most countries, however, television viewing is limited largely to the major urban centers, and even there, audiences tend to be small. Where incomes are low, as they are throughout most of the region, television sets are a costly luxury. In all of Asia and the Pacific outside of Japan, the total number of TV sets is only slightly greater than the approximately 30 million in Japan alone. China now has the next largest number; Australia and South Korea have more than 5 million; and Taiwan has more than 3 million. As of 1980, however, no other country in the region reported as many as a million TV receivers, and most counted far fewer.

Almost all countries with TV facilities have begun—some only within the past several years—to provide telecasts in color. But outside Japan and a few other places where living standards are high, black-and-white sets greatly outnumber color models. Although some countries manufacture (or in some cases assemble) black-and-white sets, color receivers generally must be imported. China, for example, produces many small, relatively inexpensive black-and-white sets but imports most of its color sets from Japan. In some parts of the region, imports are restricted; and in some others, customs duties add to the already high prices of color receivers. Color sets in any case are so costly, even in relation to incomes of the middle class, that color TV viewing in most Asian countries is unlikely to become widespread for many years.

Broadcasting is a government monopoly in all the Communist nations of Asia, all countries of South Asia, and almost all the small island nations and territories in the South Pacific. It is also under direct government administration in Malaysia, Singapore, South Korea and socialist Burma. Until 1981, South Korea had a mixed system. A number of privately owned commercial radio and TV networks and stations, first allowed in 1961, competed with the radio and TV networks of the government-operated Korean Broadcasting Service (KBS). Private stations were closely supervised by the government, and like the KBS, they devoted nearly half their programming to news, cultural enlightenment, and service information. They nevertheless attracted a considerable share of the broadcast audience.

In 1981, however, President Chun Doo Hwan completed a sweeping reorganization of the media. One of the private radio stations was limited to evangelical broadcasts, and the other private broadcast outlets were merged into the government's KBS.

Burma's broadcasting system is one of the least developed in the region. The government radio carries no advertising and all programs originate from a single center in Rangoon. There are no repeater transmitters or provincial stations, presumably because Burma feels unable to afford a radio network and also considers provincial stations too vulnerable to attack and takeover by dissident political groups outside the capital. Burmese radio devotes considerable time to music, but programming is generally highly ideological in content and designed to reinforce messages carried in the government-owned print media. Television, introduced only recently, is also government-run and follows much the same pattern.

Elsewhere the patterns vary. Thailand has a fairly extensive broadcasting system, funded by government grants and advertising revenues. All branches of it are officially controlled, although unofficial and unregistered pirate stations traditionally have operated openly. The official stations are required to broadcast news programs prepared by the government's Public Relations Department (PRD) and are expected to promote national policies. Administration, however, is divided among many government agencies and departments, including the PRD, army, navy, air force, police department, agriculture and foreign affairs ministries, education ministry, and the official university bureau. Some municipalities also have radio stations but employ military personnel as program directors. The largest broadcast organization is the Thai Television Company Ltd., which operates radio stations as well as two of the five major television channels. The PRD holds a 55 percent interest in the company, and the remaining 45 percent is split among the army, navy, air force, and police department and the state tobacco monopoly, sugar organization, liquor factory, and lottery bureau. The PRD also administers the external radio services and owns the Thai Television Channel 3, which is operated by the Bangkok Entertainment Company Ltd., a private commercial enterprise.

The largest number of domestic radio stations, however, are under the administrative control of the Thai army, whose Royal Thai Army Television Company also operates two of Bangkok's main television channels—one in color and the other in black and white.

Television reception is limited largely to the major urban areas, but many among Thailand's population of almost 50 million, listen to radio programs, particularly to Thai country-western music and talk shows.

The Philippines is the only nation in the region in which broadcasting is dominated by privately owned companies. Under martial law imposed in September 1972, however, almost all existing radio and TV stations (as well as newspapers) were closed, and the entire ownership structure of the broadcasting system was revamped, to eliminate control by powerful families regarded as unfriendly to the regime of President Ferdinand Marcos. Martial law was lifted in 1981, but until that time broadcasting was regulated strictly by an official broadcasting board, whose first head was a pro-Marcos newspaper columnist. The board was under the government's public information department.

Private ownership still predominates, although about 19 of the more than 200 radio stations and some of the more important television stations are operated by the government. Ownership, as it was before martial law, is mainly in the hands of a small number of companies, 10 of which own a majority of the radio stations. However, almost all private broadcasting companies are now controlled by interests friendly to President Marcos. The most important is the Kanlaon Broadcasting Corporation, owned by Roberto Benedicto, the Marcos supporter who owns the *Daily Express*. Of Manila's five TV channels, one—the Maharlika System's Channel 4—is owned by the government and run by its National Media Production Center.

Taiwan's more than 110 radio stations are owned by the ruling Kuomintang party, private enterprises, or various government agencies. The Kuomintang stations make up the largest combine (BBC), which operates four island-wide domestic networks (including one primarily educational and one FM), which broadcast in Mandarin and in the Amoy dialect. The KMT also has two overseas services—one (the Voice of Free China) for overseas audiences generally and the other (Central Broadcasting Station) directed at the Chinese mainland. In Taiwan's television industry, the ownership pattern is complex. Capital for one of the three island-wide television networks (Taiwan Television Enterprises) came in part from the Taiwan Provincial Government (49 percent) and local private interests (11 percent), with the remaining 40 percent supplied by four Japanese private firms. A second TV network (China Television Company) was established by the Kuomintang's BBC, which supplied 50 percent of the capital but shares ownership with a financing group formed by 28 private radio companies (28 percent) and a group of private citizens who had applied for a TV license (22 percent). The third network (China Television Service) originally was a joint venture of the Ministries of Education and Defense, but the ministries in 1972 invited private investment to increase the station's capital and now hold only a 49 percent interest.

Australia, Hong Kong, and Indonesia have dual ownership systems, resembling those in Japan and Britain, in which privately owned stations compete with government broadcast operations.

In Australia, where some 15 million people inhabit a land mass nearly as large as the continental United States, broadcasting is more highly developed than in any nation of the region except Japan. The major broadcast organization is the government-created Australian Broadcasting Commission (ABC). It operates domestic radio and television networks and the external radio service, Radio Australia, which has a reputation for objectivity and is among the most widely listened to international services. The ABC accepts no advertising, depending for its support on annual appropriations from the parliament. The owners of radio and TV sets pay annual license fees, but the fee income goes into the government's general fund and is not earmarked for broadcasting.

Privately owned stations, on the other hand, are supported entirely by advertising revenues. Commercial broadcasting has existed in Australia since 1924, years before the establishment of the government system, and about 120 commercial radio stations and some 50 commercial TV stations now compete with the ABC. A government control board, whose authority over ABC is limited to technical matters, regulates commercial programming rather rigidly. The ownership structure of private broadcasting is also controlled by regulations that forbid any one company to own more than eight radio stations (only four may be metropolitan stations or in any one state and only one in any state may be a metropolitan station) or more than two television stations. These rules have prevented the formation of commercial networks. There are frequent program exchanges, however, and most of the leading private TV stations (as well as some radio stations and smaller rural TV stations) have ties with local newspapers.

TV reception of at least one channel is available in almost all areas; in addition to TV sets, Australians own more than 10 million radio receivers. The ABC is particularly noted for its news, public affairs, and cultural programming, although it offers light entertainment (including rock music) as well. It also provides facilities for an extensive educational service to schools, the vast majority of which have classroom radio and TV receivers. ABC also has noteworthy access and ethnic program services. The commercial stations are primarily entertainment-oriented, as they are in most countries where private broadcasting exists, and private TV stations (which use many syndicated American and British programs) attract the largest share of the viewing audience.

In Hong Kong, where more than a million radio sets were in operation when radio license fees were abolished in 1967, Radio Hong Kong is the official government station, responsible to the colony's director of broadcasting. Adless and supported by license fees on TV sets, Radio Hong Kong operates Chinese- and English-language radio services and presents balanced programming, with some emphasis on information and public affairs. It also maintains a television unit that produces programs for airing by two privately owned TV stations.

Commercial broadcasting in Hong Kong began in 1959, when a privately owned radio station was licensed. Commercial radio now offers two services in Chinese (one providing such popular programs as serial dramas and Mandarin song requests, and the other offering educational programs and other high-quality fare), plus an English service on which pop music attracts the largest audiences. Except possibly within China, it is the world's largest producer of Cantonese-language programs. It employs staff writers, producers, actors, and storytellers, and exports some of its programs to Radio Singapore, Radio Malaysia, and the Voice of Chinatown in San Francisco.

Hong Kong also has two commercial TV broadcasting companies: Rediffusion (Hong Kong) Limited, a locally controlled subsidiary of Britain's Rediffusion International, and Television Broadcasts, Ltd. (HKTVB), also controlled by local investors. From 1957 to 1967, the only television in the colony was a cable service offered by Rediffusion, which still monopolizes the cable market, providing a variety of wired TV and audio services in both English and Chinese to subscribers. In 1967, however, HKTVB was given an exclusive five-year license for over-the-air telecasts, offered on two channels: Jade (Chinese) and Pearl (English). Since the early 1970s, the Rediffusion station (RTV) has competed with HKTVB by providing wireless TV services in Chinese and English.

The commercial stations are subject to strict government regulation. TV stations, for example, have been required to limit advertising to 10 percent of program time and to transmit school programs free of charge if requested. Commercial radio's license also limits commercials and specifies that its only newscasts are to be those supplied by government information services—a provision that has not been strictly enforced due to increasing official confidence in the station's responsibility.

In Indonesia, a nation of 155 million people divided into many different ethnic and language groups and spread over nearly 3,000 inhabited islands, privately owned radio stations are allowed but television is a government monopoly. Televisi Republik Indonesia (TVRI), the official network, follows policies laid down by the Ministry of Information and is expected to contribute to "building a modern, just and prosperous society." Television's reach is greatly restricted, not only by the high cost of receiving sets but also by such factors as Indonesia's geographical spread and often mountainous terrain and by the absence of electricity in rural areas. TVRI, however, has transmitters in Jakarta and some major regional centers and a substantial number of relay stations. Its operations are financed largely by license fees on sets and government subsidies. It had accepted limited advertising, but the government in 1981 banned TV commercials.

Radio, on the other hand, has many different voices. The major organization is Radio Republik Indonesia (RRI), the official network, which has transmitters on all the major islands. But there are also some 100 Radio Derah (regional-government) stations, set up by provincial administrations, which usually relay RRI news but otherwise do their own programming. In addition, amateur and commercial transmitters operate with government licenses, granted on approval from governors of the areas in which the stations are located. Some of the non-RRI stations are owned by commercial interests and others by universities and government agencies. The Indonesian air force, for example, operates a commercial station in Jakarta. The so-called amateur stations first appeared in 1966 after the overthrow of Sukarno and they have since declined in number. They are allowed only limited power; many are one-person, one-room operations. However, among the amateur stations—about half said to be run by Christian groups—a few are more professional than the competing RRI stations.

A dual system also exists in Macao, a Portugese colony perched on a peninsula at the mouth of China's Pearl River. A six-square-mile enclave whose population of 250,000 is 97 percent Chinese, Macao has both a government-run AM and FM radio station and a privately owned station (Radio Villa Verde), which is supported mainly by advertising revenues from nearby Hong Kong. Programming concentrates on music and entertainment, heavily emphasizing sports (including dog racing results, which draw the largest audiences).

In three other countries—Malaysia, Singapore, and New Zealand —broadcasting is virtually a state monopoly, but other operations are allowed. In Malaysia, where most families own radio sets but few have TV receivers, a private company, Rediffusion Malaysia, provides radio programs (including commercials) over two wired or closed circuit channels (mainly in Chinese) to subscribers who pay a monthly fee. Rediffusion has transmitters in Kuala Lumpur and several other cities, but its coverage is limited to a small part of West Malaysia. With these exceptions, however, broadcasting is handled by the official Radio-Television Malaysia (RTM), headed by a director-general of broadcasting who is responsible to the Ministry of Information. RTM is supported largely by license fees on radio and TV receivers. It also carries advertising on both radio and TV; but on the national radio network and one of the two TV channels, commercials must be only in the national language (Bahasa Malaysia), and RTM is forbidden to accept some types of advertising, including those for political or religious meetings, funeral establishments, food with pork content (offensive to Muslims), or TV commercials that show males with hair lengths the government regards as excessive.

As headquarters for RTM, the government has constructed Southeast Asia's largest centralized radio-TV complex, a modern $19 million facility at Angkasapuri (Space City), near downtown Kuala Lumpur, and an extensive network of regional production centers and transmitters, linked by microwave. RTM broadcasts on both radio and TV in four languages (Bahasa Malaysia, English, Chinese, and Tamil), and many programs are related to national development, although music accounts for the largest share of broadcast time on radio. Foreign short-wave broadcasts attract substantial audiences, and set owners in the southern part of Malaysia also have a choice of radio and TV programs from neighboring Singapore. RTM programs, however, reach almost all parts of the country, including Sabah and Sarawak, which are separated from West Malaysia by the South China Sea; and educational programs are received in about two-thirds of the nation's primary and secondary schools.

In Singapore, broadcasting is conducted almost entirely through the government-owned Singapore Broadcasting Corporation (SBC), administered by the broadcasting department of the Ministry of Culture. SBC, formed from Radio Television Singapore in a 1980 reorganization, is funded through license fees on sets and advertising.

Rediffusion (Singapore) Ltd., a government-financed but privately owned cable company with ties to Rediffusion operations in Hong Kong and Malaysia, operates 10 recording studios and two wired networks, over which it provides programs—mostly entertainment-oriented—in Malay, English, and Chinese dialects to subscribers who pay a monthly fee. In addition, the Singapore Ministry of Defense operates a radio service designed for ANZUK (Australian, New Zealand, and United Kingdom) forces stationed in the former British colony; and the British Broadcasting Corporation maintains a relay station (moved to Singapore in 1975 after being ousted from Malaysia) for broadcasts of its world service.

All other broadcasting, however, is handled by the Singapore Broadcasting Corporation, which airs programs in the nation's four main languages (Malay, English, Mandarin, and Tamil), plus at least a half dozen Chinese dialects. The Chinese radio network often features art songs, while English, Malay, and Tamil networks devote the largest share of time to popular variety programs. Public affairs programs are usually presented in prime time, and racial tolerance and national unity are frequent themes in SBC programming. The SBC also is used to promote such campaigns as "Keep Singapore Clean" and "Save Water."

New Zealand's broadcasting structure has changed frequently as new governments have come to power. A reorganization in 1975 created three separate public corporations—one for radio and one each for two television channels. All three are supervised by a Broadcasting Council of New Zealand, which (among its responsibilities) allocates TV set license fees, receives news gathered by the radio corporation (Radio New Zealand), and makes news available to the two television services (TV-1 and TV-2). Programming on the public stations tends to be entertainment-oriented; and TV-2 in particular has used many American situation comedies, but local TV production is increasing. Both radio and TV accept advertising. TV, however, carries commercials only on certain days of the week, and on fewer nights.

Privately owned radio stations have competed with the government radio-TV system since 1967, when two pirate stations began broadcasting from ships outside New Zealand's territorial waters. The government at first tried to check them; but in 1970, it bowed to popular opinion and allowed two—including Radio Hauraki, the most successful of the pirate stations—to operate in the Auckland area. By 1980 there were nine privately owned stations, seven of which were supported entirely by advertising. Government directives, however, have forbidden them to form a network (to ensure that they serve local needs), and have limited newspaper investment in private radio stations to 30 percent.

Among the South Asian nations (where broadcasting is a government monopoly), four—India, Pakistan, Sri Lanka, and Bangladesh—have introduced television, but even in these countries, radio is by far the most important broadcast medium.

The major broadcast organization is All-India Radio (AIR), which has the status of a government department and is supported mainly by license fees. AIR also obtains revenue from sales of program journals and related publications; and since 1967, it has operated a growing commercial service. In addition to spot advertisements, sponsored shows are accepted for broadcast, but only if they are entertainment-oriented; and AIR retains the right to censor or edit the content of any sponsored program.

Television has been slow to develop in India. Thirteen years passed between the establishment of the first TV station in 1959 (in Delhi) and the opening of the second (in Bombay); and although TV broadcasting has expanded considerably since, it is limited almost entirely to urban areas, and only about one person in a thousand owns a TV set.

Radio operations, however, are extensive. AIR is one of the largest radio systems in Asia, with 84 stations broadcasting for a total of about 700 hours a day. It devotes well over half of domestic transmission time to music (in two styles—Carnatic and Hindustani —each with many subdivisions), but it also provides a steady stream of news. The domestic service central unit in Delhi originates nearly a hundred news bulletins a day in about 18 languages, while regional stations together produce an even larger number, in as many major languages and more than 30 tribal dialects. AIR also has an external services division, which broadcasts in about two dozen languages.

Pakistan's television system, more developed than that of India, covers a large part of the country, but few of its people can afford to own TV sets. Fewer than a half million receivers were in operation in 1980. The nation's TV networks are operated by the Pakistan Television Corporation Ltd. (PTC), a public-limited company established in the 1960s with the help of foreign capital. Japan's Nippon Electric Company and England's Thomson Television International Limited are major shareholders, but the Pakistan government holds the controlling interest, and foreign investors are to be repaid from PTC profits until the company is entirely Pakistan-owned.

Radio broadcasting is handled by the Broadcasting Corporation of Pakistan (BCP), a statutory corporation which, like the TV corporation, is under the direct control of the Ministry of Information and Broadcasting. Both radio and TV are funded in part by license fees on receivers, but they also carry commercials and (because advertising revenues are often meager) receive government subsidies.

In Pakistan's multilingual, largely rural society, radio is an extremely important medium. To most Pakistanis, even radio sets are a luxury, but the nation had an estimated 2 million radio receivers in 1980, and the government has encouraged community listening.

All broadcasting serves the regime. Broadcasting not only reflects official views but is used extensively to mobilize support for government leaders and policies and to propagate the Muslim faith. The nationwide radio network broadcasts religious programs every morning and afternoon in which recitations from the Koran are followed by talks and discussions to relate Koranic teachings to problems of everyday life. Programming is also designed to reach the nation's many language groups and to further national unity. Most programs from Karachi are in Urdu, the national language; but many of those originating in other cities are in various regional languages. The BCP uses as many as two dozen languages in its domestic news broadcasts.

Broadcasting in Bangladesh, as in Pakistan, is handled by two official organizations, both supported by license fees, advertising, and government subsidies. Radio Bangladesh—by far the more important, because the nation has few TV receivers—broadcasts (mainly in Bengali) from headquarters in the capital at Dacca and a half dozen regional stations, and also operates a modest external radio service. Television, limited largely to Dacca, is run by the Bangladesh Television Corporation, in which Japan's Nippon Electric Corporation holds a minority interest. Both radio and TV offer a mix of news, information, and entertainment programs, along with a substantial number of guidance shows designed to mold public opinion.

In Sri Lanka, where an estimated 45 percent of the population listens to radio daily, broadcasting is conducted by the Sri Lanka Broadcasting Corporation, a semiautonomous public corporation created by the government. Radio programming is divided into three language services—Sinhalese, Tamil, and English—each aired over commercial as well as noncommercial channels. The SLBC, which is supported by license fees and ad revenues, also operates a separate educational service in all three languages.

Construction of a $40 million television network, donated by the Japanese government, was completed in 1979, but its reach was limited to the Colombo area, with development of a national system to follow. A private agency originally was to have been responsible for TV broadcasting, but Sri Lanka President J. R. Jayawardene nationalized it soon after April 1979, when ceremonies held to inaugurate the TV system were marred by technical problems that delayed its actual operation.

The Pacific Islands

With regard to broadcasting, as well as the press, the situation in the Pacific Islands differs markedly from that in Asia, and deserves separate consideration.

The development of broadcasting in the Pacific is a relatively recent phenomenon, strongly influenced by the colonial experience. While this is changing with more years of independence, and more awareness of particular Pacific Island broadcasting needs, the stamp of the British Broadcasting Corporation (BBC) on the Fiji Broadcasting Commission, for example, is deep and long-lasting. Similarly, the pervasive influence of American private commercial broadcasting is having a profound impact on Micronesia and American Samoa. Virtually every political entity in the South Pacific has its own national broadcast service—from Radio Sunshine in 3,000-population Niue, for example, to the broadcast system of Papua New Guinea, the most elaborate in the Pacific Islands.

Radio is the universal medium in the Pacific. It can reach hundreds of miles across the ocean, to the "outer islands" of the main centers. It serves as the only real-time link for many islanders. The problems in radio include low-power transmitters, lack of training for personnel, difficulties in keeping equipment operating efficiently, lower salary schedules, lack of sufficient funding from government, and government interference or control. Yet despite these many difficulties, radio is showing progress. It is an integral part of the communities it serves, providing what is often the only timely news of the region and world.

Pacific Islands radio services started in Fiji with ZJV, a private station, in 1935, and more than half of the services date since 1960. Except in the areas influenced by the United States, most services are public. Western Samoa and the then British Solomon Islands began services in the post-1945 period. A commercial operation in Papua New Guinea was interrupted by the war in 1943, and the Australian Broadcasting Commission initiated a service in 1946, primarily for the small European population. In 1962, the Papua New Guinea Service was established, and the two services were combined under the National Broadcasting Commission in 1973, two years before independence.

Papua New Guinea has the most extensive national broadcast service in the Pacific Islands countries, with 12 national stations, 20 provincial stations, and 4 relay stations. Broadcasts are in English and in Pidgin, Hiri Motu, and 30 other vernacular languages.

National radio services operate in the Cook Islands, Fiji, Kiribati, Nauru, Vanuatu, Niue, Papua New Guinea, Western Samoa, Tuvalu, the Solomons, and Tonga. French Polynesia (Tahiti) and New Caledonia operate France Region 3 services. Commercial and private services operate in American Samoa, Guam, and Saipan; and a private station competes with the Cook Islands government service. District stations in the Trust Territory of the Pacific Islands (Micronesia)—Ponape, Truk, Palau, Yap, Marshall Island, and

Kosrae—are shifting their status as the Trust Territory government fades out in place of new political entities. Community services are operated in the Australian territories of Norfolk Island and Lord Howe Island, and United States armed forces stations operate on Guam, Johnston, Midway, and Wake islands.

Papua New Guinea was moving toward a commercial radio service in 1982, with the idea of offering people both commercial and noncommercial services.

Television is highly developed in several parts of the Pacific, and poised for introduction in a few others. The quiet development of video cassette systems in such places as Papua New Guinea, Fiji, and the Cooks offers an interesting phenomenon, especially when serious consideration is being given in Fiji for taking that path to television—rather than open broadcasting. And for the many small places in the Pacific, the video cassette approach—backed by a yet-to-be-developed regional distribution system and local production units—may be the only way for television to have a chance. The issue was particularly intense in Fiji during 1981 and the "for now" position of the government is to hold off broadcast television and to consider a library system and production centers for video cassettes.

Television was introduced in Guam in the mid-1950s; in New Caledonia, Tahiti, and American Samoa in the mid-1960s; in Micronesia in the early 1970s; and in Easter Island in the mid-1970s. Western Samoa has long received the extensive television broadcasts of American shows from American Samoa, and has more television sets than does American Samoa itself. Cable television systems have pervaded the main centers in Micronesia, and have been proposed in such places as Tonga and Niue.

Although both Fiji and Papua New Guinea, the largest population centers in the Pacific, had decided against introducing broadcast television, the pressures and outside influences are now strong toward television. First, the extensive development of video cassette systems in both countries has gone largely unchecked, although a video cassette player and tapes represent a substantial capital investment in developing countries. In Fiji there are continuing efforts for open-broadcast television, and also proposals for direct-broadcast satellite television. In Papua New Guinea, the Australia Domestic Satellite System (Aussat) has plans in the early 1990s for television transponders for PNG, and PNG decided in 1981 that TV would be introduced as a pilot project in 1983. Technically, most of the major population centers in the Pacific are already linked to the Intelsat system, and could, at a cost now beyond most of the countries, tune into international television.

An important development in both press and radio over the past decade has been the "localization" of the media—the gradual replacement of expatriate experts by nationals. Tonga provides an example in both broadcasting and newspapers. At the start of the 1970s, both were being run by expatriates; but well before the start of the 1980s both systems were run by Tongans, with Tongan staffs. In places such as Papua New Guinea and Fiji, there are strict laws limiting use of expatriates in positions that could be filled by nationals, and this has had a dramatic, if not complete, effect on localization of the media in both countries.

Multilingualism is a matter of great concern to several broadcasting services. In Papua New Guinea, the service must deal with hundreds of languages, and broadcasts programs in 33 languages. In Fiji, trilingualism prevails, with English, Fijian, and Hindustani mixed through the two broadcasting channels. In Tonga, broadcast time over one channel is split between Tongan (75 percent) and English, mainly overseas news reports. Western Samoa recently started a second channel, and in late 1980 doubled its broadcast coverage area to include 80 percent of the Samoan population. Vanuatu, with one channel, practices trilingualism with English, French, and Pidgin. All the broadcast services rely for international news on overseas news broadcasts of such foreign services as the Voice of America, the British Broadcasting Corporation, Radio New Zealand, and the Australia Broadcasting Commission. English is commonly heard over the South Pacific airwaves, as is French in French Polynesia and New Caledonia.

GOVERNMENT–PRESS RELATIONS

The broadcast media in Asia and the Pacific, as almost everywhere else in the world, enjoy less freedom than the print media. Where nongovernment radio and television stations exist, their operations are regulated carefully by the respective governments, and the contents of news and public affairs programs in particular are generally subject to official guidelines and controls. Employees of state-operated stations are usually expected to exercise self-control. But news programs in many areas—including Bangladesh, Hong Kong, Indonesia, and Sri Lanka—are subject to prebroadcast checking by authorities, and in South Korea military censorship has been imposed.

Supervision of the print media is less strict and in a few parts of the region they enjoy a large measure of freedom. The press in Australia is among the freest from government restrictions in the world, and that of New Zealand is almost as free. The Australian Broadcasting Commission, which controls a major share of the country's radio and TV operations, is relatively autonomous, but it must seek funding each year from the parliament and thus is subject to varying political pressures. The ABC, though, has an enviable reputation for objectivity in its news programming.

In Japan, where laws to control the press would be unconstitutional, the press is also free, but it does not exercise its freedom fully. It is motivated in part by concern for what it regards as the national interest. For more than a decade, for example, the Japanese press has tended to avoid criticism of the People's Republic of China, in support of the Japanese government's efforts to improve relations between the two countries. When China in the late 1960s indicated a willingness to admit Japanese correspondents on permanent assignment in exchange for the right to station its own correspondents in Tokyo, the Japanese media also agreed to withdraw their reporters from Taiwan—an agreement they justified on the ground that coverage of China was of greater importance.

There are also a few other self-imposed limitations. The imperial family is regarded as above criticism, for example, and the larger newspapers in particular generally avoid overtly partisan attitudes, so as not to offend any significant segment of the public. Furthermore, many newspaper companies, most of which are joint stock companies owned largely by people within the organization, operate with relatively small amounts of capital, a factor that makes them vulnerable to the influence of business and financial interests.

In practice, the print media in Hong Kong enjoy considerable freedom. The colony has a number of restrictive laws, including a Control of Publications Ordinance, which limits who can start a newspaper and what may be written. Publishers must have a printing license issued by the police, pay a yearly registration fee and post a cash deposit (about US$2,000) to ensure their ability to pay any fines or damages that may be assessed. There is also an Objectionable Publications Ordinance, passed in 1975 to control pornography, which is so vague in wording that some journalists fear it could be used to suppress almost any type of material the government considered objectionable. Except in rare emergencies, however, the authorities have allowed the print media free rein.

In India, the print media have regained freedom after being repressed severely during the "national emergency" imposed by Prime Minister Indira Gandhi in June 1975. Precensorship of all mass media (as well as reports by foreign correspondents) was imposed for a time; the nation's four leading news agencies were merged into one (called Samachar) under government control; the licenses of more than 2,600 newspapers were canceled by district magistrates, more than 750 journalists had their accreditation withdrawn, and some whom the Gandhi regime regarded as hostile were jailed. Some magazines were also shut down; and *Seminar*, a prestigious monthly of intellectual opinion, closed voluntarily rather than comply with a government order that all copies be submitted for censorship before publication. One of the principal targets of repression was the *Indian Express*, the nation's largest English-language newspaper. Its editor was jailed and the *Express* was almost squeezed out of existence because of its criticism of Mrs. Gandhi's methods.

Government guidelines and restrictive new laws were issued to bring the press under control; and for nearly two years, newspapers, magazines, and the government-operated All India Radio (then often referred to as "All Indira Radio") operated under pressure that forced them to toe the government line. However, public reaction to excesses of the emergency rule, including the crackdown on the press, led to Mrs. Gandhi's defeat in the March 1977 elections. Press freedom was restored under the new government, and the four news agencies that had been combined into Samachar resumed separate operations. Mrs. Gandhi returned to power in January 1980, but as of early 1982, the press remained free—although its freedom is somewhat fragile.

Elsewhere in Asia, press freedom in a Western sense is rare.

In the Communist nations, where all media are owned by the state, all media personnel are government employees; and almost all news is supplied by official sources. Newspapers and other print publications are under the jurisdiction of the government, or (in the case of regional or local publications) of party committees at different levels. In China, for example, the *People's Daily*, the official government and party newspaper, operates directly under the supervision of the Central Politburo. Day-to-day operations are directed by an editorial committee, headed by the editor in chief, which also makes routine decisions regarding its policies and personnel. Important Party or government statements are published immediately, but other major news that is regarded as potentially sensitive customarily is submitted to high Party officials for review and approval and frequently is slow in appearing in print. International news is provided by the official Xinhua (New China) News Agency, which receives the services of international news agencies and passes along what it considers suitable for public consumption. The official news agency is also the source of most of the national news that appears in the *People's Daily* and other papers.

Other national-level newspapers in China are under different command systems, although all are supervised by the party's Central Committee. The culture and science-oriented *Kwang Ming Daily*, for example, is controlled by the Party's Department of Propaganda; the *Liberation Army Daily* by the General Political Department of the Ministry of Defense; the *Workers' Daily* by the National Workers

Union; and the *China Youth Daily* by the Chinese Communist Youth League. Regional, municipal, and local papers are supervised by Party committees at the appropriate levels.

In socialist Burma, the system is slightly different, but control is equally tight. The government operates all the newspapers, which vary little in content, and (because Burma's meager media system is aimed primarily at an elite audience) limits circulation by rationing newsprint.

In other Asian countries, most newspapers and magazines are privately owned but subject to various types of restrictions and controls. Except for Thailand (where a military regime resumed power in 1976), these remaining Asian nations have achieved (or regained) independence only since World War II. All have taken steps to ensure that the press will contribute to national development and unity and not oppose the government or its leaders, although such steps have not been entirely successful.

Methods of regulation and the strictness with which controls are enforced vary greatly; they have often changed as political winds have shifted. Generally, however, the developing nations of Asia tend to regard press freedom as a luxury they cannot afford. At one time or another within the past decade, almost all have jailed some dissident journalists, banned publications they considered subversive, and applied pressure or adopted new regulations to bring other recalcitrant publications into line.

Current regimes that have been the most severe in their repression of the press are those in Pakistan, the Philippines, and South Korea.

The press in Pakistan, subject to censorship and other controls by a succession of authoritarian regimes, has been treated with particular harshness by the military government of the current president General Zia ul-Haq. Cracking down on the press soon after he seized power, General Zia in 1978 banned opposition newspapers and other periodicals and jailed hundreds of journalists. Some were publicly flogged, and General Zia threatened to hang several he regarded as troublemakers. Strikes and protest meetings eventually led to a lifting of the ban on the large-circulation Urdu daily *Musawaat* (which had been owned by former premier Zulfikar Ali Bhutto, who was later executed), and world protests ended the flogging practices. The administration imposed new restrictions on the media, however, and established a puppet union, forcing many journalists to join and dismissing some who refused to obey. Reflecting the government's decision to follow a strict Islamic code of conduct, the radio network was ordered to broadcast all the Islamic calls for prayers; female TV announcers were required to cover their heads; and TV was forbidden to show dancing (because some mullahs consider it part of Hindu rather than Muslim culture).

The press in the Philippines was once among the freest in the world and notable for its often vigorous political partisanship. In September 1972, however, President Marcos imposed martial law and closed all the nation's news media except for a few (such as the *Daily Express* and Kanlaon Broadcasting's radio and TV stations) owned by his family or friends. The government contended that the news media had been infiltrated by Communist propagandists and had been guilty of distortions, speculation, and criticism that were weakening the society. An apparent major aim, however, was to end domination of the nation's media by a few powerful families known to be critical of the Marcos regime. Their media properties were confiscated and turned over to new owners. As a result, all important newspapers in the Philippines (as well as most broadcasting stations) are now owned by close associates, relatives, or other staunch supporters of the president.

To solidify his control of the news media, Marcos created two media councils—one to supervise the print media and the other to control broadcasting. Both councils are stacked with his trusted friends and have the power to deny licenses to media that fail to observe government-imposed guidelines and standards. The Philippine Council for Print Media, for example, is composed of the publishers of the nation's five leading newspapers, and no paper may be published without its approval. Controls have been relaxed gradually, and martial law was lifted in 1981. The press now carries some reports of official corruption or incompetence, but criticism of the president and his family, government policies, and the military is forbidden. Conscious of the power of President Marcos, with or without martial law, the press remains cautious, and unflattering stories are greatly outnumbered by those that reflect credit on the Marcos regime.

In South Korea, where the press has long been subject to official pressures and controls, the government completed a sweeping reorganization of the media in 1981. All broadcasting was placed under direct government administration; newspapers were consolidated to reduce their number both in Seoul and in the provinces; and the nation's privately operated news agencies were merged into a single state-run agency (Yunhap), established as a joint venture among all newspapers, broadcast organizations, and previously existing news agencies. News is subject to military censorship, and new mass-media legislation approved by Korea's docile legislative assembly has restricted the freedom of the media further. The new laws forbid editors to publish articles encouraging violation of the law, give the government the right to deny access to information if it would obstruct official performance or damage public or private interests, bar foreign investment in any mass medium, and limit all individuals and organizations to no more than 50 percent ownership of any mass-media company. They also deny journalists who violate national security laws the right to practice journalism until at least three years after completion of their jail terms.

In Taiwan, under martial law for more than three decades, pre-censorship has been lifted and controls are less sweeping. All publications must have government-issued licenses, however; and laws forbid the press to attack the government policy of recovering the Chinese mainland, support the Taiwan independence movement, publish "demoralizing" articles, or provide assistance to Communist propaganda. Within such limits, the news media at times have been allowed considerable freedom, but the regime has occasionally dealt harshly with dissidents. In 1979, following a riot in the provincial city of Kaohsiung, the government banned three non-Nationalist political magazines—*Formosa, The Eighties,* and *Spring Wind*—and arrested the publisher and editor and some other staff members of *Formosa* on charges of sedition. Two progovernment periodicals (*Patriotism* and *News*) were also banned in 1979 for failure to register with the authorities.

All Southeast Asian nations have imposed licensing requirements and other regulations designed to control the press. In Singapore legislation within the past decade has restricted the ownership of publishing companies by breaking up individual and family control and forcing the companies to become public corporations. All newspaper directors must now be Singaporeans, management shares (as opposed to ordinary investment shares) in publishing enterprises cannot be held by foreigners without the explicit permission of the Minister of Culture, and no shareholder may own more than 3 percent of any newspaper. The authorities may also ban publications they consider undesirable (as they have in some instances) and conduct searches without warrants for those that have been outlawed. Early in 1982, the government placed a retired internal security officer from the Ministry of Defense in the office of the *Straits Times* as a censor, although it did not acknowledge publicly that it was imposing censorship.

Neighboring Malaysia (whose publications are not allowed to circulate in Singapore without permission from Singapore's Ministry of Culture) has adopted comparable regulations, including one that gives the government authority to deny a license to any publication not owned by Malaysians. As a result, the New Straits Times company, an offshoot of Singapore's Straits Times publishing house, is now an entirely separate company, 80 percent owned by the Malaysian state trading company Pernas. Majority control of all Malay-language papers is held either by Pernas or by the United Malays National Organization (UMNO), a political group in the national front coalition; and in response to government pressure, the Chinese-language papers since 1972 have sold a majority of their shares to local interests.

Other press-control measures in Malaysia include a provision that a newspaper's publishing license may be withdrawn if it distorts incidents related to public order or stirs communal hostility, and a ban on press discussion of four sensitive government policies—those dealing with the national language, citizenship, the special rights for Malays, and the special roles of Malay royalty.

In Indonesia, the current press law, promulgated during the post-Sukarno liberal period, bars censorship. But it requires local ownership of the media and stipulates that the press cannot use materials that violate the national ideology (Pancasila). After a few years during which the press enjoyed considerable freedom, government supervision became more strict. Between 1973 and 1976, more than 20 newspapers lost their printing permits; the important daily *Sinar Harapan* was suspended temporarily; and some journalists were arrested, denied permission to travel, or barred from newspaper work. Since 1976, the government again has tended to tolerate press criticism, but Indonesia editors recognize the limitations on their freedom and are generally careful to avoid a confrontation with the authorities.

Thailand's press enjoyed almost unlimited freedom during a three-year period that ended abruptly with a military coup in October 1976. The country's new military junta promptly imposed press censorship, closed a dozen Thai- and Chinese-language publications as being too leftist, suspended the English-language newspaper *Voice of the Nation* (which reappeared a month later as the *Nation Review*), and detained some journalists, including the editor and publisher of the weekly magazine *Chaturat*. The junta also issued editorial guidelines which (along with many other provisions) banned materials giving damaging impressions about the government and sensational stories that would "create public alarm over the destiny of the country." Some relaxation has taken place since, but the Thai press remains subject to tight official control. Three newspapers lost their licenses in January 1979 for "sensationalized stories" about the situation in Kampuchea; and in November 1979, the revocation of publication and editor's licenses forced 57 other Thai dailies to close.

Prospects for press freedom have improved in the past few years in the South Asian nations of Sri Lanka and Bangladesh, as well as India. Gains have been slight in Bangladesh, where three of the larger newspapers (the *Bangladesh Observer, Bangladesh Times,* and *Dianik Bangla*) as well as broadcasting stations remain under government control. The press, however, has been subject to fewer restrictions since martial law ended in 1979. Greater change has occurred in Sri Lanka, where a new government replaced a repressive socialist regime in 1977. With many controls now eased or lifted, new publications have appeared, and all the leading newspapers have made large gains in circulation. Among the three principal newspaper groups, two—the Lake House and the Times groups—are state-owned; and the third—the Sun group—is strongly progovernment. But there is an opposition press composed largely of small-circulation newspapers—many of them tabloids—which have limited resources and influence. In the absence of an impartial press, however, this provides an outlet for opposition news and views.

Press freedom, however, has suffered setbacks in Afghanistan (where it was almost nonexistent even before the Soviet occupation) and Pakistan; and restrictive laws remain in force in almost all parts of South Asia. Some are so broad as to allow almost any official interpretation, such as the press law in Nepal, which forbids the publication of materials detrimental to the national interest, peace, law and order, and the power of the king.

Like most other countries in the region, all South Asian nations in which print media are privately owned require publishers to obtain government licenses, which may be revoked at will. Governments are also able to exert pressure through their control of newsprint and official advertising. In most South Asian countries, the government is the principal advertiser, and many newspapers depend heavily on official advertising, which the authorities may place in papers they favor and withhold from those which they find displeasing.

In the Pacific, relations between the government and the press are mixed—sometimes abrasive, sometimes comfortable. Behind much of the conflict is the concern by Pacific Islands leaders that the press should be a constructive force in the new countries of the Pacific and not adopt a hostile confrontation mode from the Western press. One expatriate observer in Fiji has noted that "press freedom is not yet a great issue in the region simply because the press already is mostly free" and much of the rest of it is government-owned or -managed. There is nothing remotely resembling the kind of press suppression or control seen in many Asian countries.

NEWS AGENCIES

The development of regional and national news agencies in Asia and the Pacific carries much of the hope for increasing the quality and quantity of news flow in those areas, and righting the imbalances in news flow and communication resources intensely examined over the past decade in UNESCO and elsewhere.

Great changes in news agency service have occurred in Asia since the end of World War II and the ending of colonialism in the postwar period. Where once Reuters dominated most of Asia, there is now wide competition. The other big international agencies—the Associated Press, Agence France-Presse, and United Press International—are now commonly available (with Reuters) and used by many nations, increasingly in cooperation with a national news-agency. The emergence of two international television news agencies—Visnews and UPITN—has also expanded the news sources available in Asia.

Equally significiant, if not more so, is the growth of national and particularly regional news agencies in Asia, and the serious beginnings of a movement to implement news agency service in the Pacific Islands. Perhaps the most promising event was the birth in late 1981 of the Asia-Pacific News Network (ANN).

ANN, sponsored by the Organization of Asia-Pacific News Agencies (OANA), encompasses a wide range of countries, news systems, ideologies, and economic systems. Whether this diverse mixture can produce a truly sound regional news agency for Asia and the Pacific is an open question, to be answered after ANN is fully operational for a few years.

Virtually every country in Asia has a national news agency, and some have two or more. Only Singapore and the Maldives in Asia were listed by a UNESCO report as not having news agencies of their own. Many of the agencies are government-run or -sponsored, with others under private operation. In some countries, such as Bangladesh and Indonesia, there are both government and private news agencies. In most parts of Asia, even the private operations face a degree of direct or indirect government control or influence. Singapore, Hong Kong, Tokyo, and Manila are central points for the international news agencies operations in Asia, while ANN headquarters are in Kuala Lumpur with the Malaysian national agency Bernama. New Delhi is a key center for the Press Agencies Pool of the Non-Aligned Countries. Inter Press Service, a Third-World oriented international agency, operates its regional service out of Colombo.

Despite the number and geographic coverage of the national, regional, and international agencies, there continue to be many problems in getting an adequate news file for Asia and between Asia and the rest of the world. An important news agency study in 1977 found that the developing countries in Asia were receiving a more than adequate *quantitative* coverage of other developing countries, but raised questions about the *qualitative* coverage.

The news-flow problems in Asia and the Pacific have been well identified, and in most cases there has been marked improvement in the past few years. A UNESCO report on news agencies says the "small circulation of most newspapers, difficulties in teletype transmission of characters, multilingualism and inadequacy of telecommunications facilities continue to hamper agency development at home and exchanges within the area and with the rest of the world."

In addition, the role of governments in the operation of news agencies is a major factor in the abilities of the agencies to cover fully at an international standard the news of their own countries and to provide a news file to the media of their own countries. News agencies often receive a low priority from their governments, with resulting low pay scales and inadequate equipment and facilities. Government controls often inhibit professional standards. Much of the difficulty in the Non-Aligned Pool, for example, is that it is too highly oriented toward government policy statements and handouts rather than the news of both the good and bad events in the member countries. Not all government control on news agencies, as on newspaper, radio, and television, is done simply to suppress criticism and maintain the government in power. There are broader concerns involved with national development, cultural integrity, and stability, drawn together under the concept of development journalism. The difficulty Westerners have of understanding this concept is illustrated by an Associated Press official's comment that the developing countries wanted his organization to report the building of a dam but did not want coverage if the dam collapsed, or if there was widespread corruption or faulty construction.

One of the key characteristics of regional and national news agencies in Asia is constant change: reorganization, new technology, new exchanges, and new agencies. The government of India, for example, insisted one year on consolidating the four main news agencies of that country into one agency and then, after a change of governments, the one agency was broken up into what it was before— four private agencies. In South Korea, the government in 1981 merged seven news agencies into one. In other agencies, the structure may remain the same, but the process of news gathering and dissemination may undergo great changes, as in the case of the Xinhua News Agency in China.

Asia is also served by a variety of supplementary news agencies, and by such global forces as the Non-Aligned Pool and the Inter Press Service. Although the latter two services are international in character, they provide important sources of developing country news to Asian news media. Within Asia, such examples of regional services range from the veteran Depthnews in the Philippines to the Asia-World Feature Agency, a 1981 newcomer, in Hong Kong.

There is a strong movement in Asia and the Pacific to reduce the costs of news transmission, with a low-cost Press Bulletin Service (PBS). Sri Lanka has led the Asian nations by establishing in 1979 a concessionary tariff for sending news and visuals via satellite. Sri Lanka's overseas telecommunication service in 1981 extended the special at-cost rate for three years and raised it from US$180 a month to US$200.

Training for news-agency personnel has been taken in hand within Asia, at such institutions as the Indian Institute of Mass Communication, and through such international efforts as those at the Thompson Foundation training center in Britain. There is likely to be a continuing and expanding need for news agency training for many years, before the agencies have the numbers of trained news professionals needed for adequate service.

Regional News Agencies

The establishment of the Asia-Pacific News Network (ANN) at the end of 1981 is one of the more important recent developments in news agencies in Asia and the Pacific, and it is a strong sign of the growing diversity of news-agency service, particularly to meet the special needs of the developing countries.

Although it will take a few years to determine if ANN is going to be a significant factor in news flow and exchange, it has a broadly based membership and solid home base.

Representatives of 23 news-agencies met in Malaysia in late 1981 to form the new regional agency, a long-time goal of UNESCO. Seven news agencies from Communist countries—Xinhua (China), Tass (Soviet Union), Vietnam News Agency, Korean Central News Agency (North Korea), Khaosan Pathet Lao (Laos), Bakhtar (Afghanistan), Montsame (Mongolia)—were admitted to membership, raising the question of how ideology and politics affect news operations. The task of keeping ANN on a professional course fell to Encik Ahmad Mustapha Hassan, new president of OANA and head of the Malaysian agency Bernama, and the ANN executive board.

ANN was to be fully operational in 1982, using an already adequate telecommunications infrastructure. Initially, five news centers—Tokyo, Manila, Jakarta, New Delhi, and Moscow—were to be established, with each member agency transmitting short bulletins daily.

OANA itself has been in existence for more than 20 years but for much of that it was generally ineffective, caught in the political cross-winds of the China–Taiwan issue as well as being hampered by a general lack of adequate telecommunications and professional staffs for timely news service.

Regional television news exchanges have a shorter history, not getting underway until the mid-1970s. The Asia-Pacific Broadcasting Union, in cooperation with other broadcasting unions and organizations, organized a news exchange program using air-freight and satellite, but most of the international news used by television services in Asia still comes from the two main international visual news agencies Visnews and UPITN. Japan and Australia are the two main customers for the satellite news service by the international agencies, and their preferences influence the whole package of news for Asia and the Pacific. Hong Kong is a regional point for the Visnews from London and the United States. Except for those in Japan and Australia, Asian and Pacific television services do not collect their own international news to any extent.

Asian news agencies have for years exchanged news bilaterally on a regional basis, but it is only in the past decade that the technical means of exchange have made these arrangements productive. With increased technical transmission capabilities in Asia and the Pacific, there is little reason for the national news agencies not to receive the kinds of news they want from where they want it in Asia. In the Pacific, the expansion of satellite earth stations has been phenomenal over the past few years. Virtually all political units—even those as small as Nauru and Niue—now have satellite links with each other and the rest of the world. It is clear that the problem of news exchange on a regional basis in Asia and the Pacific is technically solved—but there is much more involved than technical problems in news flow, as has been noted about the Asia and Pacific press in general.

Other efforts at regional news in Asia include the short-lived but highly professional Asian News Service in the early 1970s, and the Depthnews features and background service from the Press Foundation of Asia. Depthnews in late 1981 restructured its operations, under noted Indonesian journalist Mochtar Lubis, in an effort to overcome financial problems and make the service more relevant to Asian needs for news about development.

Another regional grouping, within a strong political and economic context, was formed by the 1980 exchange agreements among the ASEAN (Association of South East Asian Nations) agencies of Indonesia (Antara), Malaysia, (Bernama), and the Philippines (Philippines News Agency). The Thai News Agency was to join in later, and all were to use a special press bulletin service for lower-cost transmissions. The Indonesia Palapa satellite system was expected in 1982 to link all the ASEAN countries and Papua New Guinea.

The Big Four have regional services for Asia and can increasingly tailor news to Asian interests through improved satellite and computer-distribution patterns. The international agencies also provide specialized regional services to Asia, such as the Reuters Monitor Service for business and price information on stock-exchange matters.

Although regional and national news agencies in Asia are gaining in strength and professional abilities, they are still dwarfed by the Big Four agencies. The Associated Press, the largest, which operated on a total budget of some $170 million in 1981, is heavily employing the latest in satellite and computer services. It has an almost instantaneous global network for news and pictures. The exchange rate of news between Asia and the West reflects this stronger position, with AP sending from New York and average of 90,000 words daily to Asia and taking in about 19,000 words daily from Asia. Asia and Australia have about 17 percent of the news-agency correspondents, compared with 34 percent stationed in the United States and 28 percent in Europe.

National News Agencies

The predominant national news agency in Asia is Kyodo of Japan, with Xinhua of China and the Press Trust of India moving ahead strongly. Kyodo and Xinhua are the only non-Western agencies that are approaching self-sufficiency in international news coverage. Here is a quick look at these and other key national news agencies in Asia, and a look at what's to come in Pacific Island news service.

Kyodo is one of the two major news agencies in Japan—the other being the business-oriented Jiji Press. Privately owned Kyodo and Jiji were formed in 1945 after the demise of the Domei agency. Kyodo, in its report to the MacBride Commission, reported it had 47 offices in Japan and bureaus in 37 countries. It employs about 1,900 persons, about 600 of whom are journalists. The agency issues about 220,000 characters in Japanese and 35,000 words in English daily. It lists as subscribers 33 national agencies, 40 foreign news agencies, 64 Japanese newspapers, 59 commercial television and radio stations, and 14 nonmember newspapers (Kyodo is a cooperative). Jiji lists 62 offices in Japan and 31 abroad and has exchange agreements with Reuters, UPI, and AFP. It produces a domestic file of about 400,000 Japanese characters a day, 12,000 words for overseas Chinese use and 30,000 English words for national and foreign distribution.

Kyodo is the largest noninternational news agency in the world, with revenues exceeding those of Agence France-Press; and along with China's Xinhua, it is nearly self-sufficient in gathering world news. Despite its news-coverage strength, however, Kyodo is unlikely to emerge as an international news agency on the scale of the Big Four, for language and other reasons.

Xinhua (or the New China News Agency), which celebrated its fiftieth birthday in November 1981, is the official state-owned news agency of the Chinese government. Established as the Red China News Agency, it changed its name to Xinhua in 1936. It is the only news-agency source for printed international news in China and is the main supplier of news to all publications and broadcast services. In all, it monitors an inflow of about 1.5 million words in international news a day. Xinhua employs about 5,200 persons, 80 percent of whom are in its central offices in Beijing and the others in the rest of China and overseas, in addition to thousands of stringers or part-time correspondents. Internationally, it has some 170 resident correspondents abroad in more than 40 countries, with the main bureaus in Hong Kong (about 100), Tokyo, Geneva, London, Paris, and the United Nations in New York. It subscribes to the Big Four, Kyodo, and other agencies and has teleprinter service agreements with 41 news agencies and newspapers outside China. It offers Chinese, English, and Russian services worldwide, and also transmits in Spanish, Arabic, and French for an international file of about 7,500 words a day to Hong Kong, hardly a fourth of what the Big Four agencies provide. Its total daily file in six languages is 350,000 words. Xinhua gives a high proportion—88 percent in a 1977 study—of its news file to events in the Third World, with half of the stories of Asian happenings. Much of the news file is about China or events in China. It provides up to 50,000 words a day of domestic and world news to China's national media.

India has a diverse national news agency system, including four main agencies and several other important and specialized agencies, and then even more specialized agencies to serve a combined daily and weekly circulation of 40 million. The strongest and most international agency is the privately owned Press Trust of India—which has been called the backbone of daily journalism in India. It was established in 1947 and operates as a nonprofit company.

PTI's main rival is the United News of India (UNI), established in 1961 and sponsored by eight major newspapers. UNI has some 75 bureaus in India and stringers in 200 towns and cities. It has arrangements with several foreign news agencies, including the Associated Press, for its world news file, and it monitors international broadcasts for additional world news. Since 1978 it has received its AP file by satellite. In 1980, UNI has some 400 subscribers and revenues of about $2 million.

The two other main news agencies, which concentrate on vernacular languages of Hindi and several others, are the Hindustan Samachar with 30 bureaus and Samachar Bharathl with 20 bureaus. Both operate on annual revenues of less than $500,000 each.

All four agencies were combined under government pressure in 1976 into a single agency, Samachar. After a change in governments in 1977, the four agencies were restored to their former positions in April 1978 with government grants in aid totaling over $2 million in 1978 to 1981.

PTI has correspondents at the United Nations headquarters, London, Moscow, Colombo, Beijing, Kathmandu, and Dacca, with plans for expanding to such places as Islamabad, Kuala Lumpur, and Nairobi. In addition, stringers file copy from many countries around the world. PTI revenues were at $3 million in 1980, with 400 subscribers. There are 87 offices in India, 40,000 kilometers of teleprinter lines, and a staff of nearly 1,200. Its biggest customer is All India Radio, which gives the Indian government an easy method of exerting pressure on PTI.

PTI's long-term development plan calls for increased satellite links, expanding rural coverage, increasing overseas coverage, and creating more bureaus and additional news exchanges.

Other National Agencies

Diversity is a dominant theme in Asian media and news agency services, as indicated by the variety in national agencies. Some of the important Asian-Pacific agencies after Kyodo, Xinhua, and PTI include the Australian Associated Press, Bernama, and Antara.

The Australian Associated Press (AAP) is a national agency that takes in the major international news services and distributes them and Australian news to the media in Australia. It is the leading source of international news for the Australian press, television, and radio. AAP, a newspaper cooperative, is a partner in the Reuters news agency and in the Visnews visual agency. Its headquarters is Sydney, and it is linked to the rest of the world through the COMPAC cable system and the international satellite system. AAP correspondents cover Western Europe, particularly London, and Asia, although not in great numbers.

AAP has access to the major agencies—Reuters, AP, AFP—and more than 2 million words of world news flow into it each week, from which 10 to 15 percent is sent along to members in Australia (UPI withdrew from AAP arrangements in the late 1970s and distributes directly to Australian media). AAP also supplies international news to three regional agencies within Australia.

For many years AAP has supplied news service to Fiji and Papua–

New Guinea; and in the past few years it has expanded its satellite news service to such remote places in the Pacific as Nauru.

Antara, the Indonesia national news agency, is administratively under the Ministry of Information. It has 440 workers, including 160 journalists, and 27 national bureaus in Japan and West Germany. Correspondents are in Hong Kong, Kuala Lumpur, Cairo, and Rangoon. Antara has agreements with the major news agencies (except AP), including Kyodo and the West German agency Deutsche-Presse Agentu (DPA) and 20 or so other agencies. Part of the ASEAN computerized news exchange network through satellite, it is also a member of the Organization of Asia-Pacific News Agencies, International Islamic News Agency, and the Non-Aligned News Pool. The agency, founded in 1937, moved in 1981 to a modern new building in Jakarta. Antara, for years the headquarters of OANA, is an active member of the Confederation of ASEAN Journalists. The AP world file is taken in Indonesia by KNI, a private agency owned by newspapers.

Bernama, the Malaysian national news agency that began operations in 1968, is one of the fruits of the UNESCO-sponsored push for development of national news agencies. Under the Ministry of Information, it provides three news services—general news (domestic), economic news and features, and foreign news. The agency in its 1978 report to UNESCO listed 104 editorial/journalist personnel and a similar number of technical/administrative workers. There are some 400 stringers, or part-time journalists, throughout the country. Eighty percent of Bernama's income comes from the government radio and television services and other government subscribers.

Bernama (Pertubohan Berita Nasional Malaysia) has agreements with 20 other national news agencies, and sole distribution rights in Malaysia for AFP (AP, UPI, and Reuters sell directly to customers in Malaysia). It is a member of the Non-Aligned News Pool, the Islamic News Agency, OANA, and the ASEAN news exchange.

Under its long-term plan, Bernama hopes to expand its national, regional and international coverage and improve and modernize its services, including a photo service. Training is a major priority.

There remain a number of national news agencies throughout Asia and the Pacific, with the main ones for each country being the New Zealand Press Association; Bakhtar (Afghanistan); Bangladesh Sangbad Sangstha (BSS, Bangladesh); Khao San Pathet Lao (KPL, Laos); Vietnam News Agency (VNA); Korean Central News Agency (North Korea); Montsame (Mongolia); Rashtriya Sambad Samity (RSS, Nepal); Philippine News Agency; Press Trust of Ceylon (Sri Lanka); Central News Agency (Taiwan); Thai News Agency (Thailand); Pakistan Press International (PPI); Yunhap News Agency (South Korea).

The Yunhap News Agency in South Korea is the result of a merger in January 1981 of all existing news agencies into a joint venture with newspapers and broadcasters. The move was part of tightening controls on all news media in South Korea under a new mass-media law, following the 1979 assassination of President Park Chung Hee. Previously, South Korea had such highly regarded and privately owned news agencies as the Orient Press and Hapdong News Agency, as well as an agency specializing in economic reports. Three smaller agencies specialized in local economic affairs. All news agencies were merged under the mass-media law.

Continuing efforts were under way in 1982 to establish a news service for the Pacific Islands. The Australian Associated Press, AP, and UPI at a 1980 meeting in Honolulu expressed interest and support for some kind of service, and proposals have been made through the government of Papua New Guinea, the University of the South Pacific, the Asia-Pacific Broadcasting Union, and others. The Pacific Islands is the largest geographical area of the world without its own regional service, although Reuters and AAP supply news to the Commonwealth parts of the Pacific, AFP supplies Tahiti and New Caledonia, and UPI and AP provide service for the American territories. The Micronesian News Service, a government-operated agency in the Trust Territory of the Pacific Islands, was phased out in 1981 as the Trust Territory political structure was being dismantled. Since 1974, the Regional News Exchange has been operated weekly under the sponsorship of the South Pacific Commission, using the PEACESAT satellite system. This has been the only Pacific-wide news exchange, although its use in the mass media has been limited, and its potential far from reached.

PRESS PHILOSOPHIES

Press philosophies in Asia and the Pacific vary widely, ranging from the classic "four theories of the press" to the still-emerging concept of development journalism. The four theories of the press—Soviet Communist, authoritarian, libertarian, and social responsibility—are all found in the region. The new element is the concept of development journalism. This is a distinct theory of the press, although it clearly encompasses aspects of the other four theories.

Dramatic changes in press philosophy in Asia have occurred over the past decade as part of broader political changes. In the Philippines, for example, the declaration of martial law in 1972 turned overnight what had been the freest, most libertarian press in Asia into a press under authoritarian control. The pattern continued into the 1980s. In India, perhaps the most noted example of a change in press systems, the government imposed a clear authoritarian philosophy during the "emergency" period in the mid-1970s, when it clamped down hard on the press and imprisoned journalists. With a change in government, however, the Indian press reverted to what is generally considered a free-press philosophy in the Western tradition, with control in private business hands. Thailand, which for a brief period in the 1970s had a press philosophy based on full freedom, is another country where dramatic shifts have occurred with changes in government.

The most stable liberal democratic press systems are found in Japan, Australia, New Zealand, India, and some Pacific Island countries, including Fiji and Papua New Guinea. These countries have a philosophy that tends to follow the social responsibility theory. This theory is based on private ownership of the media and an open society. The press has the task of informing the public of events of importance to them and assumes the obligation of being responsible to the society (not government). This approach is based on the political philosophy that the people are the ultimate decision makers and that the role of the press is to provide them with news and commentary important to them.

The other clearest group of press systems comes under the heading of Communist philosophy. Countries in Asia representing this approach include China, which is developing a distinct pattern of its own, and the more Soviet-style countries of Afghanistan, Kampuchea, Laos, Vietnam, and North Korea. Under this system, the role of the press is made clear: to support and promote the government and Communist Party policies among the people and to respond to external threats. The press is owned and operated by the state and is an integral part of the government or party system. Therefore, it does not serve in the Western tradition as a watchdog on government, except in well-defined and nonideological areas.

China offers a clear look at how the press operates under this approach, and also how political changes within China are producing new directions for the press, although it remains within the fundamental ideological framework of communism. While the press in China, from the *People's Daily* on down, is the organ of the Central Committee of the Communist Party of China, there has been a shift in directions since the downfall of the Gang of Four and the end of the Cultural Revolution. Until after the Cultural Revolution, the task of the press was to carry out the class struggle between the proletariat and the bourgeois. The "barrel of a gun and . . . the barrel of a pen" were both important to Mao Tse-tung, reflecting the importance put on the press in its four functions: propagate policies, educate the masses, organize the masses, and mobilize the masses.

After the Cultural Revolution, the class-struggle focus was deemphasized. The main task of the press now is to work toward the party-decreed national policy of "four modernizations" in politics, economics, and culture to developing the socialist economy. While the shift from a class struggle to a positive support for the modernizations has resulted in an obvious change in the content and tone of the Chinese press, the overall mantle of communism has been maintained. But a remarkably different press has emerged from this change in political direction and press philosophy. There has been an increase in the amount of news and features in the press (*People's Daily* has expanded from four to eight pages, for example), as well as an attempt at a brighter, more interesting style of news writing and presentation. Other trends have included the expansion of journalism education at the university level; increased discussion of professional journalism concerns at forums and within publication staffs; increased exchange of scholars and journalists; efforts at more objective and accurate news reporting; growing attention to substantive information, news, and entertainment (with fewer of the long political statements); and expansion of content to include literature and art, science, sports, economic affairs, cartoons, and so forth.

Some of the changes seem to be a move toward westernization of the press, but this is denied by some observers who contend that the form should not be confused with the essence of the changes.

The philosophical base of the Chinese Communist press remains as it was, but within that framework there has been a growing pragmatic approach—emphasizing developmental concerns rather than ideology—which has led to a press that is more understandable to Westerners. The basic control of the media by the Chinese Communist Party has even been questioned by some officials who say the media should have a more autonomous role and be under the people and not the party. China has served as a model to some other third-world countries, and its experience with the press could have significant influence.

The other major press philosophy in Asia and the Pacific is more difficult to classify—it is really a new and not fully defined press theory, which mixes authoritarian with libertarian and social-responsibility principles. The new form is classified as development journalism, which generally means that the role of the press is to support national interests for economic and social development and to support such objectives as national unity and stability and cultural integrity. Within this broad concept, there are many different ways to practice development journalism.

One positive way, advocated by some journalists, is to find ways of making stories about such subjects as commodity pricing and farming interesting and understandable to the readers, and to focus on the developmental aspects of the news. This approach does not mean an uncritical stance toward development programs, but it does mean getting at the heart of them in people's terms. Under this approach to development journalism, its advocates say, the press itself and individual journalists would carry the responsibility, without government pressure or control.

Another approach, advocated by many political leaders, is that the press act in positive ways to promote national and governmental policies and programs of development. While not entirely giving up a critical stance, journalism would be handled with caution and sensitivity to the needs of often unstable and fragile developing countries. The Prime Minister of Fiji, Ratu Mara, put it this way a few years ago: "If criticism is not based on *constructive* comment then we perhaps should begin to question its place in a developing society. A major 'function' of the press is to increase integration and consensus in society, to bridge social gaps, to provide people with views and factual commentary on current events." Ratu Mara, like many other Asia and Pacific leaders, urges the press to assume a responsible role in the development of society. "All we ask of the press is that in our efforts to stabilize the country, point it in the right direction, and develop a truly multi-racial community, the media present a balanced view of our progress."

A third general approach to development journalism, one feared and fought in the Western nations, is that the press will serve the government in its policies, good or bad, and do nothing to offend the government in the name of national security and development, cultural integrity, and so forth. This is really an authoritarian philosophy of the press, displayed in the modern dress of development journalism. Telling the difference between the different approaches to development journalism is not always easy, and such journalism may shift from one form to another, depending on how stressful the political situation is at any given time.

Press philosophies, as can be readily seen, are part of the broader social, political, and cultural context of the various societies—they could not and do not lead separate lives.

JOURNALISM EDUCATION AND TRAINING

Journalism education and training in Asia and the Pacific are very much in the development stage, with the final shape, at least in education, not yet clear. The 1970s was a period of rapid growth and increasing stability for both journalism and mass communication education and training. While the predominant models for both activi-

ties came from the West—Britain and the United States primarily—
the 1970s saw much questioning of Western models and method-
ologies, and the seeking of more appropriate, or Asian, models.

Whether in fact there is an Asian model of journalism education
and training, there is no doubt that the needs for such education vary
greatly among the countries in Asia and the Pacific, and offer in
many cases sharp contrast to the needs of Western countries.

Development concerns greatly influence the curriculum in education and training institutions in Asia, and a whole new field of spe-
cialty—development journalism—has firmly established itself across
Asia.

Although great advances have been made in the past decade or
so, there are still many persistent needs in journalism education:
textbooks and related materials in vernacular languages, and, increasingly, specialized texts; in-service seminars and courses for
faculty; institutional encouragement and funding for research; updated and standardized curriculums; more and upgraded publication
programs within institutions; opportunities for advanced degree work
both within and outside Asia; improvement of teaching standards;
broader curriculum reform to meet the needs of the emerging information societies; development of more and better information and
documentation centers in the region.

Several principles persist in discussion of journalism education:
Journalism departments should as a primary task prepare their
students for professional mass-media careers and, to an increasing
extent, produce basic and advanced research relevant to the needs of
the country.

Lecturing remains a traditional method of teaching journalism
and communication in Asian universities, with a carryover of formal-
ity between student and teacher. Although indigenous textbooks are
becoming more common, much material is still imported from the
West.

The numbers and kinds of journalism education and training
institutions vary widely across Asia and the Pacific, with four authorized journalism programs in China with its 1 billion people and
about 30 in India, the next largest country. One of the most obvious
differences among the journalism departments is the split between
theoretical and practical approaches. In Japan, for example, the
emphasis is almost entirely on the theoretical study of mass communication and journalism, while in such places as Hong Kong, it is
on media production and journalism skills. In most countries, there is
a mix of the two approaches.

In Japan, with highly competitive entrance requirements for the
major newspapers, the journalism departments do not teach the skills

of writing, editing, and production, but focus on theoretical studies and on research concerns. Keio University, for example, has an Institute of Journalism that focuses on the theory of mass-media management, and an active communication research program in other parts of the university. The University of Tokyo also has a theoretically oriented Institute of Journalism. On the practical level, Nippon Hoso Kyokai (NHK), the national broadcasting service, offers a wide range of practical training in its Training Institute, both for its staff and persons from other Asian countries. South Korea, in another model, offers theoretical studies at Seoul National University in the Department of Communication, and has a research institute. Yonsei University has some practical training and theoretical courses, with a communication and journalism department and an interdisciplinary research unit in communication. Sogang University's journalism education is more on the theoretical level. There is a strong tradition in Korea of master's studies by working journalists.

China has undergone a rapid expansion of its mass media and particularly of its publications in English since the Cultural Revolution ended in 1976. The major journalism education schools include People's University in Beijing; Fudan University (the oldest of the schools, established in 1929) in Shanghai; Chi Nan University in Canton; and Amoy University of Fukien. Other universities, such as Yunan, Shagtun, Kwangsi, Kianhgsi, Nanking Normal, Heilongjiang, Wuhan, Zhengzhou, Xiaman, Jiangxi, and the Institute of International Politics offer journalism courses but are not accredited by the Ministry of Education. The four-year curriculum is generally in three parts: political theories (e.g., Marxism-Leninism); literature, history, and languages; and professional skills courses. The trend has been toward more vocational level training in journalism and less political training. Course titles are similar to those found in American universities, but the content may differ. Internships on newspapers are part of the requirements. The Journalism Institute of the Academy of Social Science in Beijing offers graduate study in journalism. It is in the *People's Daily* compound, training journalists for the *People's Daily*, the Xinhua News Agency, the *China Daily*, and other news organizations. Beijing Broadcast Institute focuses on electronic technology, broadcast journalism, and foreign languages.

Fudan University's journalism department has the largest number of and most diversified offerings, and Chi Nan University is open to overseas Chinese. Facilities and textbooks and other materials are serious problems in the journalism departments, partly as the result of the earlier political turmoil, including the closure of the departments.

In Taiwan, National Chengchi University is the oldest (1954) and most prestigious journalism department and the only one to offer a master's program. Fu-Jen Catholic University puts emphasis on advertising and photojournalism. Chinese Culture University offers journalism, and the World College of Journalism, with enrollment in the thousands, is one of the largest in the world. The curriculum at Chengchi has been shifting over the past several years from a basic skills approach to a skills and theory and methodology approach.

Hong Kong has two major journalism programs—at the Chinese University of Hong Kong, which emphasizes print media and has a communication research center; and at Hong Kong Baptist College, an early starter in broadcast and film education.

Thailand has three strong and different journalism and mass communication programs, and they have been working since 1981 toward a consortium to rationalize curriculum and develop joint research projects. The most extensive program, including journalism, public information and relations, and broadcasting, is offered in the Faculty of Communication Arts at Chulalongkorn University in Bangkok. Thammasat University's Department of Journalism and Mass Communication has developed a strong program in film as well as journalism, and Chiangmai University's Department of Mass Communication has an emphasis on rural journalism and communication. Many of the senior faculty members in Thailand, as at many other Asian journalism and communication departments, have advanced degrees from foreign universities, particularly in the United States and Europe.

The Institute of Mass Communications at the University of the Philippines offers training and research in journalism and mass communication, with research focusing on such developmental communication areas as population communications. Bachelor and masters degrees are offered in journalism, broadcasting, and communication. The Department of Agricultural Communication in the College of Agriculture at the University of the Philippines focuses on development communication and rural change. The School of Journalism and Communication at Silliman University emphasizes the community press in its educational and research programs.

India has the most extensive development of journalism departments in Asia, and one of the most noted training institutions, the Indian Institute of Mass Communication. The first continuous journalism education program began in 1941 at Panjab University, in Lahore (now Pakistan), and has since moved to Chandigard. In the 1940s and 1950s, programs began at the universities of Calcutta, Madras, Mysore, Nagpur, and Osmania. Programs began later in universities in Poona, Gujarat, Gauhati, Raipur, Ludhiana, and Kolhapur, with many other universities offering shorter courses. Many other private colleges and universities and nonuniversity (particularly government) training and educational institutions complete the picture. Lectures on theory and practical assignments in reporting and editing are a common pattern. Several universities offer postgraduate programs.

Journalism and communication education in Malaysia is offered through the Mass Communication program at the University Sains Malaysia in Penang and the School of Mass Communication at the Mara Institute of Technology in Kuala Lumpur. Both offer advertising, journalism, broadcasting, and public relations. Kuala Lumpur is also the home of the Asia-Pacific Broadcasting Institute (AIBD), the regional broadcast training center.

Indonesia, Pakistan, and Sri Lanka also have journalism and mass communication education and research programs at the university degree level. Singapore discontinued formal university journalism education in 1980, although there is a communication course at the National University of Singapore and the *Straits Times* conducts a training program. Burma began a journalism education program at the university level in the late 1970s, and Nepal's Tribhuwan University in Kathmandu offers a two-year course in journalism.

Journalism training and education at the university level has grown in recent years in Australia and New Zealand, with 15 institutions in Australia now offering courses. There are several training programs by professional organizations and at such educational institutions as the Wellington Polytechnic, which also provides basic journalism training for Pacific Islanders.

In the Pacific Islands, activity was increasing in early 1982 to develop a communication program at the University of the South Pacific (USP) in Fiji, with students helping to operate a proposed Pacific news agency. There is a certificate journalism course at the University of Papua New Guinea and a communication program at the University of Guam. Two-year colleges in American Samoa, Ponape, and Saipan provide some journalism/communication/information coursework. A regional journalism course in 1981–1982 utilizing the USPNet satellite extension service at USP drew more than 100 students from several countries. The Pacific Island News Association in Suva serves as a coordinator when appropriate for in-region training programs and assists in arranging external training and education programs. Plans were underway in mid-1982 for a meeting of the educational institutions in the Pacific to develop a five-year plan for journalism and communication education and training.

Several regional institutions provide training, seminars, and workshops and conduct other activities related to journalism and communication education. These include the Asian Mass Communication Research and Information Center in Singapore, the Indian Institute of Mass Communication in New Delhi, the Asia-Pacific Institute for Broadcasting Development in Kuala Lumpur, and the Press Foundation of Asia in Manila and elsewhere. Many national programs, especially in broadcasting, are conducted in various parts of Asia and the Pacific. The Australian Broadcasting Commission and Nippon Hoso Kyokai are two strong national organizations that also provide regional training. A regional broadcast training center in Western Samoa, sponsored by the United Nations Development Program in the 1970s, has become a national center. Hawaii, although a state of the United States, plays a special role in journalism education and training in Asia through the University of Hawaii Journalism and Communication departments and the Communication Institute of the East-West Center.

HISTORY

The print media in Asia have ancient roots. Paper was invented in China early in the second century. Woodblock printing began in 593, and well before the beginning of the tenth century, woodblocks were used to print classical essays that reported happenings in the imperial court. In 1038, a Chinese named Pi Sheng developed movable typefaces made of clay; and printing with movable metal type is said to have begun in Korea in 1234, more than 200 years before Johann Gutenberg introduced that art to Europe.

Print media developed slowly, however. Asia and the Pacific remained largely isolated from the rest of the world, and newspapers in the modern sense did not begin to appear until the seventeenth century. A publication called *Memorie des Nouvelles* was issued in Indonesia as early as 1616, but it was essentially a newsletter for the employees of the Dutch East India Company, and it was not followed by a paper of more general interest until 1744. Elsewhere in the region, newspaper publishing began much later. The first newspaper in India, and one of the first English-language papers anywhere in Asia or the Pacific, was the *Bengal Gazette,* a small four-page news sheet that began publication in Calcutta in 1780. Issued by James Augustus Hicky, an Englishman who had come to India as an employee of the British East India Company, the Gazette contained foreign and local news items, a full page of advertising, and a poet's corner. It lasted until 1782, when its criticisms of government and East Indian Company officials led the authorities to ban it and confiscate Hicky's printing equipment.

The first newspapers in almost all parts of the region were published by Westerners—in most cases by colonial authorities, Christian missionaries, or trading companies. As a result, most of the early papers were in the language of the Western nation that dominated the area in which they were issued. Papers in native Asian languages were generally slower to appear.

This was not the case in China. The first modern newspaper in China, although founded by a British missionary, was (despite its name) the Chinese-language *Eastern Western Monthly Magazine*, published in 1833 in Canton. The first newspapers in Afghanistan and Burma—and in Korea, which did not have one until 1883—also were in the native language. The pioneering paper in Thailand, however, was the monthly English-language *Bangkok Recorder*, put out in 1844 by an American missionary; and in Japan, the twice weekly English-language *Nagasaki Shipping List and Advertiser* began publication six months before the Tokugawa Shogunate began issuing the first Japanese-language paper (a translation of a Dutch-language paper from Indonesia) in January, 1862.

A few present-day publications in the region have long histories. One of the oldest major papers is Singapore's *Straits Times*, the dominant paper in its area for well over a century. Founded in 1834 and a daily since 1858, the *Straits Times* shares a common heritage with Malaysia's *New Straits Times*, which became a separate company in 1972, 20 percent of which is now owned by the Singapore company and 80 percent by Malaysians. Other important long-established newspapers—some of them older than the *Straits Times*—include four respected Australian dailies and half dozen of India's influential English-language dailies. The *Sydney Morning Herald*, founded in 1831, is the oldest of the Australian papers, followed by the *Melbourne Herald* (1840), the *Age* (1854), and Sydney's *Daily Telegraph* (1879). In India, the influential *Times of India* traces its history to 1838, the *Statesman* to 1875, and the *Hindu* to 1878. Smaller Indian dailies a century or more old are the *Bombay Samachar* (1822), the *Amrita Bazar Patrika* (1868), and the *Tribune* (1881). Among Japan's three giant dailies, two (*Asahi* and *Yomiuri*) were founded in the 1870s and the third (*Mainichi*) is the successor to a paper established in the same decade.

In general, however, the press of Asia is relatively young, and that of the Pacific is even younger (although the *Fiji Times* dates from 1869). The print media have been transformed almost beyond recognition in the past half century—by an assertive new nationalism as former colonies have sought and gained their independence, by long periods of war, by revolutions and coups that have brought new regimes to power, and by lingering political turmoil and tension that have led many governments to impose tight controls on the press and to suppress publications they considered too critical. Many well-known publications have disappeared, and vast numbers of new newspapers and other periodicals have emerged—some now well entrenched and many others small and struggling to survive. The proliferation of new publications has been due only in part to shifting political tides. It may be explained also by the economic development that is apparent in much of the region, and growing populations, rising rates of literacy, and increased attention to education. In some countries—among them Afghanistan, Vietnam, Pakistan, the Philippines, and South Korea—the press has suffered setbacks within the past decade. Overall, however, the region's press is expanding and growing also in strength and quality.

There are few towering figures in the history of the Asian and Pacific media, due largely to the media's comparative youth, the many changes they have experienced, and the tight official controls that have existed—and continue to exist—in many parts of the region.

Some editors and publishers have come to be celebrated within their own contries for their role as pioneers, for leadership in seeking press freedom and other reforms or for their courageous resistance to oppressive regimes.

One highly respected figure from India's past, for example, is Raja Ram Mohan Roy, an early nineteenth-century fighter for press freedom and social reform, who founded a number of important newspapers and magazines and has sometimes been called the father of modern India.

A few publishers also have become noted for their business acumen. One was the late Aw Boon Haw, Hong Kong's "Tiger Balm King," who established a successful chain of Chinese-language newspapers in Southeast Asia (including the important *Sin Chew Jit Poh*, now published in Singapore and Malaysia as well as in Hong Kong). Another is Australian Rupert Murdoch, who has expanded his newspaper holdings in Australia into a publishing empire that includes major papers in England and the United States.

For the most part, however, the region has not been noted for outstanding media personalities, and to the extent that personal journalism existed, that age has passed. Where newspapers are privately owned, they generally are joint stock companies, better known as institutions than for the individual who heads them.

In many nations that once were colonies of Western powers, newspapers reflect the influences of the colonial past. In South Asia and many parts of Southeast Asia, for example, newspapers generally resemble British papers in makeup and style, as they do also in Australia and New Zealand. Similarly, American influence is apparent in newspapers in the Philippines, and Dutch influence in the style of Indonesian papers. In such former British colonies as India, Malaysia, and Singapore, English-language papers as a group remain the most influential, despite the growth of papers in indigenous languages. And, particularly in India, Singapore, Malaysia, and Sri Lanka, major publishing houses founded in colonial times continue to flourish, although ownership has generally been diversified and now is held by citizens of the respective countries.

The Japanese press system, dominated by a few massive national newspapers, owes its present structure largely to measures imposed by the Japanese military in the 1930s. To conserve supplies and make control of the press easier, the military forced newspapers to merge, reducing their number from 1,200 dailies and 7,700 weeklies and fortnightlies in the early 1930s to only 55 in 1943. South Korea, in turn, has a press system structured much like that of Japan, which occupied Korea from 1910 until the end of World War II.

In broadcasting, Japan was among Asia's pioneers. The first United States radio broadcasts, from station KDKA in Pittsburgh in 1920, captured the interest of Japanese technicians and business concerns, and by 1922 experimental stations were in operation. Some 55 companies soon sought broadcasting licenses. The government, however, opposed proliferation of the new medium. It urged the applicants to get together and establish one radio station in each of three major cities—Tokyo, Osaka, and Nagoya. The three privately owned (although adless) stations began operating in 1925; but in 1926, the government ordered them to consolidate into a single officially controlled network, the genesis of Japan's powerful NHK and the nation's public broadcasting system.

Japan's competing commercial broadcasting system began in 1951 by order of American occupation authorities, who feared that if allowed to monopolize broadcasting, the NHK might become overly bureaucratic and subject to control by antidemocratic elements. Licenses were originally issued for 17 privately owned commercial radio stations. Private stations grew rapidly in number, however, and after NHK introduced television in 1953, commercial TV stations quickly appeared. Competition since has stimulated both NHK and the commercial broadcasters to expand and modernize their facilities and to diversify programming to attract larger audiences.

Experimental radio stations were also set up as early as 1922 in Australia, China, Indonesia, and the Philippines, and in a few localities licensed stations began broadcasting in 1924 or 1925. In most parts of the region, however, broadcasting tended to develop slowly.

Radio broadcasting systems in many nations of the region were established by the colonial powers. After World War II, as former colonies gained independence, the existing services were taken over and developed by the new governments. In some cases, foreign governments and commercial firms have contributed equipment and technical assistance. Rates of development have varied greatly, however. In some nations, progress has been limited by inadequate resources or lack of political stability; and in some, official attitudes have been an even more important factor. Where broadcasting has been regarded mainly as an entertainment service, its expansion and modernization have lagged. Where its potential contribution to the national development effort has been recognized, progress often has been impressive.

3 AFRICA

L. JOHN MARTIN

At a United States exhibition in the Soviet Union several years ago, young American tour guides were eagerly quizzed by Russian visitors. What was life like in the United States? What kinds of homes did Americans live in? What did they eat? "How many loaves of bread does the average American worker eat each week?" asked one suspicious visitor. "One or two," said the guide. "Ah," exclaimed the inquisitor, "just as I thought. The poor, oppressed American worker! The average Russian worker eats eight or nine loaves," he informed the guide proudly.

Many analysts of the world's press use the same kind of logic in dealing with daily newspaper statistics. Some comparative data are given in the table.

The African continent obviously has the smallest number of dailies in terms of its total population—only 0.387 daily newspapers per 1 million people. This means that on the average, there are more than 2½ million people living on the continent for each daily newspaper that is published there. One is inclined to compare this with

Daily Newspapers by Continent*

	Number of Dailies	Popu- lation, in millions	Dailies per million popu- lation	Popu- lation per Daily
Africa	171	442	0.387	2,583,979
Asia	2,706	2,461	1.100	909,091
North America	2,244	359	6.251	159,974
South America	716	233	3.073	325,415
Europe	2,541	480	5.294	188,893
Oceania	117	221	5.294	188,893

* The figures for the number of daily newspapers are taken from the Encyclopedia Britannica *Book of the Year, 1981*; the population figures are from
Information Please Almanac, 1981. Since no daily newspaper or population
figures for Africa are accurate, the ones given are presented merely for
purposes of comparison.

some 160,000 living in North America for each daily published on
that continent. The easy conclusion one might draw is that Africans
have a long way to go before they catch up with the West.

It has been suggested that daily newspapers are a good indicator of
development. Daily newspaper reading in the so-called developed
countries tends to be high, as measured by circulation figures per
1,000 population. In fact, there appears to be a high correlation between per-capita income and the number of daily newspapers read in
a country, as many researchers such as Wilbur Schramm, Daniel
Lerner, Raymond Nixon, and Bradley Greenberg have shown. (Incidentally, accurate circulation figures are even more difficult to come
by than are figures on the number of daily newspapers, and even
estimates are highly suspect.)

Another more reasonable way of looking at these figures is that
people in Africa more commonly get their information and entertainment from sources other than their daily newspaper. Even if they
were to develop economically much beyond their present standards,
newspapers would not play the same role they play in the Western
world. This probably reflects more accurately the media situation in
Africa. There is reason to believe that mass communication on the
African continent will develop along different lines from those of the
Western world.

There are many reasons why the press developed the way it did
in the Western world. Commerce, science, and technology, Western

Map courtesy of *Africa Report.*

political systems, and social interactions all require the kind of daily report on the details of individual and organizational activities that the Western press has come to provide and that Western publics have become used to and have come to expect of their press. People want their unadulterated facts and both mass media and the wire services have been molded by the expectations of the public.

A variety of factors have created a totally different kind of press system in Africa. How people use and are able to use printed media as well as their needs and expectations are very different in Africa from what they were in the West at the same stage of development.

For one thing, Africa has still not emerged from its tribal disjuncture at a time when it is technologically far ahead of where the West was when it was similarly tribalized. Most tribes in Africa are both culturally and linguistically diverse. Estimates of the number of discrete languages and dialects in Africa range from 800 to 2,000, and between 80 and 95 percent of these have no written form or literature. It has been estimated that Cameroon, with just over 8 million people, has tribes speaking 100 different languages; that Nigeria, with a population of close to 80 million, has as many as 250 discriminable languages and dialects; and that Gabon, with only 637,000 people, can identify 10 discrete languages.

Producing printed media, especially daily newspapers, for populations often as small as half a million is economically not a viable proposition. Furthermore, since most of the languages have no written form, the problem is moot. Then why not provide printed media in some lingua franca such as English, French, or Portuguese?

Actually, these are the very languages in which most African dailies are published, with the addition of Afrikaans in South Africa. A few dailies are published in such widely spoken African languages as Swahili in the East and Hausa in the West. But they have limited audiences. However, literacy is not very high either in the European lingua francas or in any of the African languages. And it has been estimated that fewer than 10 percent of Africans even speak a European language. Literacy ranges from a low of 5 to 10 percent in Ethiopia, Upper Volta, Mali, and Senegal to (again estimated) 60 to 70 percent in the Cameroon, Lesotho, the Seychelle Islands, and Mauritius. This is excluding South Africa, of course, where the literacy of whites is as high as 98 percent; of coloreds, 85 to 90 percent; and of blacks, 50 to 60 percent. The modal range for all of sub-Saharan Africa is approximately 25 to 30 percent.

Literacy is increasing. But so is agitation for national, non-European languages, and there is much controversy about which tribal language should be raised to national language status. Often the rulers belong to a tribe that is not the dominant group in the country, yet they wish to impose their particular language as the lingua franca. Tribal fragmentation and jealousies have led African journalist Frank Barton to predict that "Even if national pride wins the day and 'national' languages become the pattern of the media, it is highly unlikely that English, French and Portuguese will ever totally disappear from the press."

Apart from the proliferation of languages and low literacy, both of which control the number and size of newspapers, Africa's colonial past has played an important role in the kind of press that has evolved on the continent. During the colonial period—that is, until the 1960s—the majority of newspapers that existed in Africa were owned, written, edited, and read by European settlers and by a very few foreign educated blacks. This press carried two types of content: some "home" news (although most of this news was gleaned by white settlers from home newspapers that arrived by sea mail or, after the mid-1930s, was obtained from radio broadcasts), and social and official local news about the white population's social affairs, promotions, arrivals, and departures. Judging from most of these local newspapers, one would suppose that blacks barely existed except insofar as they impacted on the white population.

The few irregularly appearing African-owned and -run newspapers had a totally different mission and content. They were organs of revolution and dissent. Their goal was African independence. Many African leaders began their political careers as journalists or newspaper owners. Prior to independence, Julius Nyerere, president of Tanzania, edited *Sauti ya TANU*, an organ of what is now the only authorized party in the country. Jomo Kenyatta (formerly Johnstone Kamau), first president of Kenya, started the Kikuyu-language monthly, *Muiguithania* in the late 1920s. Hastings Banda of Malawi, Nnamdi Azikiwe of Nigeria, and Ghana's Kwame Nkrumah were all newspaper proprietors before independence and became presidents of their countries. In French-speaking Africa, President Felix Houphouët-Boigny of the Ivory Coast was editor of *Afrique Noire* before independence; and President Leopold Sedar-Senghor of Senegal was editor and publisher of *La Condition Humaine* in Dakar in the fifties. Finally, both President Mobutu Sese Seko and the late Premier Patrice Lumumba of what is now Zaire were editors of Congolese newspapers.

Africans have never had an information press. Theirs has always been an opinion press. Advocacy journalism comes naturally to them. To the extent that they feel a need for hard news, that need is satisfied by the minimal coverage of the mass media, especially of radio. Soft news, i.e., human-interest news or what Schramm has called immediate-reward news, is equally well transmitted through the folk media—such as the "bush telegraph" or drum; the "grapevine," or word-of-mouth and gossip; town criers and drummers; traditional dances; plays, and songs.

Timeliness here, as in most African intercourse, is of secondary importance. Neither the interest nor the usefulness of a story diminishes with time. Accuracy is a frill and often a detriment, since events that are used as object lessons to make or to illustrate a point lose their didactic potency if they must conform to fact in all their details. Objectivity is seen as a red herring with which Western media attempt to arrogate truth to their viewpoint. Importance and size, other Western criteria of newsworthiness, are relative. Only proximity holds the kind of importance it has in the West, except more so. African media are highly parochial in their interests.

The need for printed media in Africa, such as have evolved in the West, might have been greater had African social, economic, and political institutions developed along with its technology. But the former were held back by Africa's colonial vassalage while it fell heir to modern technology upon gaining its independence. It moved directly into an electronic age with its communication, storage, and retrieval facilities. To expect Africa to take the long, hard road of printed media to achieve modernization is like asking a child to do long division or extract square roots manually just for the exercise, when the answer lies at its fingertip on a cheap calculator. Thus Africa has traveled a different path and comparisons with areas that have taken the long route to achieve communication sufficiency are futile and spurious. In the course of their development, African printed media may yet draw closer to Western media than they are at present. But this is not essential. To judge their stage of development by how closely they resemble the Western ideal in numbers, size, frequency, readership, or content is a meaningless exercise.

PRINT MEDIA

Of the 46 separate states or political entities in sub-Saharan Africa, eight had no daily newspaper whatsoever at the start of 1982. These are mostly small countries with populations of around half a million or less, but they include Guinea in West Africa, with 5¼ million people, and Lesotho, a state surrounded by South Africa, with a population of 1.3 million. Ironically, 70 percent of the population in Lesotho is literate, which is the highest reported literacy rate in black Africa. Guinea, too, reports a relatively high literacy of 48 percent, with 15 to 25 percent literate in the French language. This is another indication that the reading of daily newspapers is an acquired habit rather than a need that necessarily comes with education and development.

True, per-capita income as late as 1977 in both these countries was below $500 a year. But then so was that of Kenya, Ghana, Zambia, and Zimbabwe, all of which have relatively well developed daily newspaper systems. Furthermore, in the three countries of sub-Saharan Africa that are listed by the World Bank as having annual per-capita incomes in the highest range (for sub-Saharan Africa) of $500 to $1,000 (excluding South Africa, of course), two—Nigeria and the Ivory Coast—have newspapers with circulations of over 50,000, while the third—the Congo—has only a mimeographed daily bulletin, according to the United States press officer in Brazzaville.

Nine additional African countries have only bulletin-type dailies. These are often mimeographed and occasionally, as in Botswana, circulated free. All are government-owned and are generally produced by the state-run press agencies, which get their news from one or more international wire services, principally Agence France-Presse, Reuters, or the Associated Press. The international news in the bulletins is meagerly supplemented by local news written by government press officers in the major towns. Thus 17 countries, representing close to 40 percent of the states in sub-Saharan Africa and roughly 36 million people, have apart from radio and, in a few cases, television no more than a bulletin to keep them abreast of daily events in the world and in their countries. They are listed in the following table.

Country	Population, in Thousands	Literacy, Percent	Dailies
Botswana	764	35	Bulletin
Burundi	4,192	25	Bulletin
Cape Verde	328	30	None
Central African Rep.	2,284	18	Bulletin
Chad	4,528	15	Bulletin
Comoros	359	n.a.	None
Congo	1,508	40	Bulletin
Djibouti	386	n.a.	None
Gambia	585	12	None
Guinea	5,275	48	None
Guinea-Bissau	638	10	None
Lesotho	1,305	70	None
Liberia	1,788	18	Bulletin
Mauritania	1,474	23	Bulletin
Niger	5,346	14	Bulletin
Rwanda	4,955	25	Bulletin
Sao Tome and Principe	82	n.a.	None

Even where such bulletins are circulated, they seldom go to more than 2,000 individuals and offices. The main exceptions are the Botswana *Daily News*, which is produced by the Department of Information and Broadcasting in English (12,500 copies) and Setswana (6,000 copies) and is given away free, and Niger's mimeographed *Le Sahel*, published by the government Information Service and circulated to some 3,000 to 5,000 people.

A plurality of 21 countries on the continent have one or more minor dailies with circulations ranging from 5 to 50 thousand. Most of these countries have only a single daily; but they include two countries with relatively well developed newspaper systems. They are Mauritius, an island state off the East coast of Africa with a population of less than 1 million, but with as many as 12 dailies by some counts (ICA says only half of these are true dailies); and Madagascar, the world's fourth largest island, West of Mauritius, with a population of over 8 million and with 12 to 17 dailies, depending on when and how they are counted. The 21 countries are given in the following table.

Country	Population, in Thousands	Literacy, Percent	Dailies	Ownership
Angola	6,543	12	1	Government
Benin	3,379	20	1	Government
Cameroon	8,323	60	1	Government/ party
Equatorial Guinea	244	20	2	n.a.
Ethiopia	31,780	7	2	Government
Gabon	637	40	1	Government
Madagascar	8,349	40	12–17	Government/ private
Malawi	5,862	40	1	Private
Mali	6,464	5	1	Government
Mauritius	941	60	6–12	Private
Mozambique	10,030	15	2	Government
Namibia	909	35	3	Private
Senegal	5,532	10	1	Government
Seychelles	64	58	2	Government/ party
Sierra Leone	3,309	15	1	Government
Somalia	3,474	10	1*	Government
Swaziland	541	54	1	Private
Togo	2,544	30	1	Government
Uganda	13,225	25	1	Government
Upper Volta	6,661	7	1*	Private
Zaire	28,090	35	4	Government

* Government press agency also publishes daily bulletin.

Private ownership of daily newspapers is unrelated to literacy. In the six or seven countries that have privately owned dailies among these 21, the literacy rate ranges from 7 percent in Upper Volta (close to the lowest in Africa) to 60 percent in Mauritius, which is close to the top literacy rate in black Africa.

Eight countries in sub-Saharan Africa have major dailies, defined as a daily with a circulation of over 50,000. They range from the Ivory Coast with a single daily to South Africa, which has 12 major dailies and 11 minor ones. The countries are listed in the table.

Country	Population, in Thousands	Literacy, Percent	Dailies	Ownership
Ghana	11,742	30	2	Government
Ivory Coast	7,761	25	1	Government/party
Kenya	15,778	35	3	Private
Nigeria	77,100	25	15	Government/private
South Africa	27,799	98*	23	Private
Tanzania	17,364	20	2	Government/party
Zambia	5,649	35	2	Government/party
Zimbabwe	7,254	30	2	Government

* This is white literacy. Colored literacy is 85 to 90 percent and black literacy is 50 to 60 percent.

In all of sub-Saharan Africa, only Nigeria and South Africa have more than three major dailies. (The minor dailies of Madagascar and Mauritius have been noted above.) South Africa's newspapers are privately owned, as are three of Nigeria's 15 dailies. The federal government of Nigeria owns 60 percent of the shares of the major publishing house, the Daily Times Group, and 100 percent of several other dailies, while a number of state governments own daily newspapers with circulations of over 50,000 in Nigeria. Kenya's privately owned dailies should also be mentioned for their unusually high quality.

The distribution of daily newspapers in sub-Saharan Africa provides a good index of the use being made of the printed media as a whole in the area. One might think of the African continent as divisible into 10 groups of countries, one being the North African or Arab tier, which is discussed elsewhere in this book. In terms of the development of and dependence on printed media, South Africa, which is the only country in Africa that remains completely dominated by its white settlers, clearly stands alone as having a press that is most similar to that of the Western world.

By weighting each of the countries according to its dependence on daily newspapers, English-oriented East Africa, comprising Kenya, Mauritius, Seychelles, Tanzania, and Uganda, comes immediately after South Africa. It is followed by English-oriented West Africa with Gambia, Ghana, Nigeria, and Sierra Leone. Next come seven political entities in Southern Africa: Botswana, Lesotho, Malawi, Namibia, Swaziland, Zambia, and Zimbabwe. The 17 states that were once French colonies and are mostly in West Africa fall below the median in daily newspaper dependency. They are Benin, Cameroon, Central African Republic, Chad, Comoros (East Africa), Congo, Djibouti (East Africa), Gabon, Guinea, Ivory Coast, Madagascar (East Africa), Mali, Mauritania, Niger, Senegal, Togo, and Upper Volta. The former Belgian colonies of Burundi, Rwanda, and Zaire follow closely. Then come former Spanish African Equatorial Guinea and the former Portuguese African colonies of Angola, Cape Verde, Guinea–Bissau, Mozambique, Sao Tome, and Principe. Significantly, the two African countries that never were colonies—Ethiopia and Liberia—are the ones that have the lowest printed news media dependency on the continent. Somalia is in about the same category. This former Italian colony that merged with former British Somalia has a meager press system. Its one small government-owned newspaper, *October Star*, is published in Somali and Arabic. There is also an English-language daily bulletin published by the government.

A closer examination of these groups shows not only decreasing dependence on the printed media but increasing tendency toward advocacy and didactic journalism. Thus, on the whole, Anglophone Africa shows more developed daily newspaper systems than does Francophone Africa, and Iberophone Africa has the weakest press system. This should in no way be interpreted as a qualitative judgment of the cultural, social, political, or economic development of these countries. It is merely an indication of differences in the traditions, habits, and needs of the peoples involved.

Daily Newspapers

South Africa. The South African daily press is owned and edited by whites, who make up about 16 percent of the population. Although there are four legally distinct ethnic groups in the country (the other three being black, 72 percent; colored, i.e., Malay and mixed parentage, 9 percent; and Indian, 3 percent), and at least 16 languages spoken, the 23 daily newspapers in the country are published in only two languages: English (15) and Afrikaans (8), the official languages of South Africa.

While the ratio of whites whose mother tongue is Afrikaans to those with English as their mother tongue is six to four, three times as many English newspapers are sold as Afrikaans. This is both because the other ethnic groups tend to read the English rather than the Afrikaans press, and because almost half of the Afrikaners themselves do not read dailies, preferring weeklies. However, among the

Afrikaners who do read dailies, almost a third read English dailies, while only 5 percent of English speakers read an Afrikaans daily, according to a 1968 survey. In the largest South African city of Johannesburg, which has two morning and evening English-language dailies, there are twice as many nonwhite as white readers. Johannesburg also has two morning and one evening Afrikaans dailies whose readership is almost exclusively white. However, one-third of the readers of Cape Town's Afrikaans paper, *Die Burger*, are colored.

South Africa can boast of having had the first English-language newspaper in sub-Saharan Africa. It appeared in Cape Town in 1800, roughly 150 years after the Dutch first settled there. The *Capetown Gazette and African Advertiser*, as it was called, had news in both English and Dutch. The first Afrikaans newspaper was *Di Patriot* in 1875. There was an all-Dutch newspaper, *De Zuid-Afrikaan*, published in 1830, but by 1875, the Society of True Afrikaaners had been launched, and the need was felt for a political organ that was distinctly African rather than European Dutch. The two major English-language newspaper chains in South Africa began with the *Cape Argus* in 1857 and the *Cape Times* in 1876.

Today the newspaper with the highest circulation in South Africa, and indeed one of the highest in all of sub-Saharan Africa, is *The Star* of Johannesburg, an evening paper with a circulation that has hovered just under 200,000 for the past 20 years or more. According to a study by C. A. Giffard, the circulations of evening newspapers have been dropping since the advent of TV in South Africa in 1976, while morning dailies have increased slightly. He speculates that this is because people have substituted evening TV watching for newspaper reading.

The Star belongs to the Argus Group, the largest newspaper publishing company in Africa, with holdings not only in South Africa but also in several other Southern African states. It, like a majority of English speakers, supports the opposition United Party. *The Star*'s major competition is the *Rand Daily Mail*, a morning paper that belongs to the second major chain in South Africa, the South African Associated Newspapers, Ltd., which, with other morning papers, formed a loose alliance known as the South African Morning Newspapers. *The Star* is a conservative, serious, quality daily directed mainly at the more affluent white reader, while the *Rand Daily Mail* is more liberal and reflects the views of the Progressive Party, which opposes the National Party in power. Its goal is to achieve interracial communication.

To counteract the liberal tendencies of the English-language press, an Afrikaner industrialist, Louis Luyt, with, it is said, the secret help of the government's Department of Information, launched in 1976 an English-language broadsheet in Johannesburg called *The Citizen*, which has drawn some readers from other English-language papers, principally *The Star*. The fourth English-language daily, *The Sowetan*, began publishing in January 1981. It is aimed specifically at blacks, although it is owned by whites. It carries a large amount of crime, sex, and society news, and it steers clear of politics. It replaced *The Post*, which was banned by the government and which, in turn, replaced *The World* in 1978, when that publication was closed down. This change in name has enabled the Argus Printing and Publishing Company, which owned all three papers, to continue to serve the mass market of blacks.

The Afrikaans press is solidly behind the ruling National Party. It is more knowledgeable about government policies than the English-language press and focuses more on domestic than on foreign news. It has practiced advocacy journalism from the start, viewing newspapers as instruments of political influence. Leading Afrikaans papers are the ultraconservative *Die Transvaler* (owned by Perskor), the unofficial organ of the National Party; and its chief competitor in the morning field, *Die Beeld*, owned by Nasionale Pers and published in Johannesburg. *Die Vaderland*, an evening paper, is the third Afrikaans newspaper in Johannesburg; it is also owned by Perskor. Perskor owns two small Afrikaans dailies in Pretoria; and Nasionale Pers owns a major Afrikaans paper in Cape Town and smaller papers in Bloemfontein and Port Elizabeth. Besides *The Star* and *The Sowetan* in Johannesburg, Argus owns the *Cape Argus*, a major evening paper in Cape Town and the first newspaper in the Argus empire, and newspapers in Durban, Bloemfontein, and Kimberley. South African Associated Newspapers, Ltd., owns the morning paper in Cape Town, two papers in Port Elizabeth, and a morning paper in Durban. The three remaining dailies (including *The Citizen*) are independently owned.

East Africa. Moving on to black Africa, there is no doubt that next to South Africa, Kenya has a newspaper system that is most similar to that of the West. Its three daily newspapers are widely read, privately owned, and by Third-World standards uncensored. Of the three formerly British-administered territories of Uganda, Kenya, and Tanzania—which at one time had plans to form a federation upon attaining their independence—only Kenya developed along capitalist lines. Uganda came under military rule and Tanzania is strongly socialist. Mauritius and the Seychelle islands on the East coast of Africa, both formerly British, also have capitalist economies, and the former has a well-developed private press system. The two daily newspapers in the Seychelles are run by the government and by the Seychelles Farmers' Association, respectively, and have very small circulations.

Newspapers have been published in Mauritius since 1773, when the French-language weekly *Annonces* first appeared. Mauritius, which along with the Seychelles, was seized from France by the British in 1810 and ceded to Britain by the Treaty of Paris in 1814, also has the second oldest continuously published French-language daily in the world—*Le Cernéen*—founded in 1832. Today it also has pages in English, as do at least five other dailies on the island. In addition, there are three Chinese-language newspapers.

Britain acquired most of its East African territories in the late nineteenth and early twentieth centuries and the first news publication was a mimeographed missionary quarterly that appeared in 1897. The first newspaper, the *East Africa and Uganda Mail*, was published at Mombasa, Kenya, in 1899. In 1902, an Indian railway contractor, A. M. Jeevanjee, founded the weekly *African Standard, Mombasa Times and Uganda Argus*, which became the daily *East African Standard* in 1910, when it moved from Mombasa to Nairobi, the new capital. It became the leading newspaper in East Africa, when it bought out its main competition in 1923. In 1977 it became a tabloid. The same company that published the *Standard* published an English-language daily in Kampala, Uganda, from 1955 to 1972 called the *Uganda Argus*, and another daily in Dar-es-Salaam, Tanzania, called the *Tanganyika Standard*, which lasted from 1930 to 1972. It was nationalized in 1969 and merged with the *Nationalist* to become the *Daily News* in 1972.

In 1959, the Aga Khan, leader of the Ismailis, a Muslim sect, established East African Newspapers (later Nation Newspapers), Ltd., which founded a Swahili daily, *Taifa Leo*, and an English-language paper, *Daily Nation*. (He also established a Swahili weekly and a Sunday paper.) All these papers are tabloids and have rapidly developed into influential publications in Nairobi and throughout East Africa. The *Daily Nation* now has two or three times the circulation of *The Standard*, and people attribute its popularity to its sprightly content and layout and the fact that it has a more liberal tone than *The Standard*. As in the rest of East Africa, the daily press is an urban and elite institution. Outside the cities, people are largely ignored by the printed media, especially if they are not literate in English or, to a lesser extent, in Swahili.

West Africa (Anglophone). In terms of dependence on and use of printed media, the former British colonies of West Africa, taken as a whole, come after East Africa. Although after South Africa, Nigeria has the largest number of daily newspapers, it also has the largest population in Africa (close to 80 million). Despite fairly large circulations, this places Nigeria somewhat lower than many other countries in newspapers per 1,000 of population. Anglophone West African newspapers are also less news-oriented and more didactic and polemical in their content. This is due to their origins. Unlike East Africa, where an English-language press catered mostly to white settlers and practically ignored black Africans, in British West Africa an English-language press developed quite early as a local medium. It united the African elite, for whom English became a lingua franca; it gave them outlets to vent their grievances against the colonial power and a means for fanning nationalist aspirations and building political support. "We are not clambering (sic.) for immediate independence. But it should always be borne in mind that the present order of things will not last for ever," wrote the *Lagos Times and Gold Coast Advertiser* on March 9, 1881.

The first newspaper in black Africa was published in Freetown, Sierra Leone, in 1801. It was the *Royal Gazette and Sierra Leone Advertiser*. Very soon thereafter, a handwritten newspaper appeared in Accra, the Gold Coast (now Ghana). It was called *The Royal Gold Coast Gazette and Commercial Intelligencer* and was published from 1822 to 1825. The first African editor in the Gold Coast was Charles Bannerman, who founded the *Accra Herald* in 1858. The following year, *Iwe Irohin*, a church-related biweekly, appeared as the first African-language paper on the continent. The Rev. Henry Townsend, a missionary, had developed an alphabet for Yoruba and taught it to some 3,000 Nigerians.

For a few weeks, Accra had a daily in 1895 called the *Daily Express*. The first successful daily in West Africa was the *Lagos Daily News*, which appeared in 1925, published by Victor Bababunmi but taken over by the better-known Herbert Macaulay and Dr. J. A. Caulcrick in 1928 as a political party paper. In less than a year, the Lagos Chamber of Commerce raised money to start a competing paper, the *Daily Times*, which despite several metamorphoses is still being published, now owned by the Nigerian government with the largest circulation in black Africa. But it suffered a setback in 1937, when an American-educated journalist, Nnamdi Azikiwe, who later became Nigeria's president, started a new daily, the *West African Pilot*. This was a hard-hitting political newspaper, which attracted many African readers. After World War II, Cecil King, who owned the London *Daily Mirror*, bought the *Daily Times* and turned it into a popular, somewhat sensationalistic tabloid, similar to his *Daily Mirror* but minus the sex. Although the federal government has owned 60 percent of the *Daily Times* since 1975, the paper still attracts 28 percent of the readership in its circulation area, according to two separate 1980 surveys.

Today only the *National Concord*, with about half the circulation of the *Daily Times* and around 18 percent of readers in the area where it is sold, and *The Punch*, with a slightly lower circulation than the *National Concord* and read by about 10 percent of newspaper readers, are privately owned in Lagos. A third daily in Ibadan, the *Nigerian Tribune*, is also privately owned and has an 8 percent readership. All other dailies in Nigeria are owned either by the federal government or one of the state governments.

In 1950, the Mirror Group that had bought the Lagos *Daily Times* founded the *Daily Graphic* in Accra. It easily outsold the *Evening News*, one of several newspapers being published in Accra, edited by another United States–educated journalist and politician, a Ghanaian by the name of Kwame Nkrumah, who also became president of his country. In 1958, the year after Ghana was established as an independent state, the *Ghanaian Times* was founded with public funds. It and the *Daily Graphic*, now also government-operated, remain the only dailies currently appearing in Ghana. A third daily was purchased by the London *Daily Mirror's* Cecil King in West Africa in 1952. It was the *Daily Mail* of Freetown, Sierra Leone; but he sold it to the government in 1965 because it turned out to be a poor economic investment.

Southern Africa. Skipping back to Southern Africa, we find a group of seven countries that were colonized from the South and controlled either by South Africa or by Britain. One of them—Namibia—is still a South African mandate. This group has a somewhat lower dependence on printed media, but includes two countries that have major newspaper systems, albeit owned by the government or the ruling party.

Until they achieved their independence as black African states—Zambia in 1964 and Zimbabwe in 1980—both countries had a series of newspapers produced by and for white mining interests. They were known as Northern and Southern Rhodesia, respectively, and were colonized through the aggressive entrepreneurship of British empire builder Cecil John Rhodes. In 1891, the Argus Company that owns the *Cape Argus*, produced for the miners the handwritten *Mashonaland and Zambesian Times*, which became the *Rhodesia Herald* in 1892. In 1894, the same company started the *Bulawayo Chronicle*. These two newspapers are still being published; but in 1981, the government of Zimbabwe set up the Mass Media Trust with a $5 million endowment to purchase the two newspapers, which are now run under government supervision.

Zambia, too, has two major daily newspapers. The *Zambia Daily Mail* was purchased by the government in 1965 from its coowners,

David Astor, editor of London's *Sunday Observer*, and Alexander Scott, a Scottish doctor turned journalist. They had started it as the weekly *African Mail* in 1960 and renamed it the *Central African Mail* in 1962; in 1967 the government called it the *Zambia Mail* when it went semiweekly; and in 1970 it became a daily. The other daily, the *Times of Zambia*, was founded as the *Zambia Times* in Kitwe, a town in copper mining territory, in 1962 by Hans Heinrich, a South African. He soon found he was losing money on the paper and sold it, along with other properties, to Lonrho, a British firm formerly called the London and Rhodesian Mining and Land Company, which owns newspapers throughout East and Southern Africa.

Close by, in Ndola, the Argus Company owned the *Northern News*, a newspaper aimed at the European mining community. It had attractive makeup, plenty of advertising, and, what European readers wanted, foreign news. But the Argus Company wanted to get out of Zambia and consolidate in South Africa. So it sold the *Northern News* to Lonrho, which closed down the *Zambia Times* in Kitwe and renamed the Ndola daily *The Times of Zambia*. Lonrho appointed Richard Hall, a white Rhodesian civil servant and later a very successful editor of the *Mail*, as editor of the *Times*. Hall strongly believed in Africanization of newspapers and had soon trained an African editor in chief and a staff of reporters and copy editors to take over. In 1975, the *Times* was nationalized and its editing came under the control of the United National Independence Party, the ruling party in Zambia. Its editorial offices were later moved to Lusaka, the capital.

Malawi (formerly Nyasaland) and Swaziland, a kingdom in the northern corner of South Africa, each have a small daily newspaper, poorly edited though balanced in coverage. Namibia, a former German colony known as South-West Africa, is a South African mandate seeking independence. It has three small dailies, one each in English, German, and Afrikaans. All these papers are privately owned, except that Malawi's *Daily Times* was sold as a semiweekly to its president for life, Hastings Kamuzu Banda, in 1972 by Canadian and British press tycoon Roy Thomson, who had bought the *Nyasaland Times* in 1962. It had been founded in 1895 in Blantyre by a Scot who named it the *Central African Planter*, a few years later renamed the *Central African Times* and finally *Nyasaland Times*.

The paper must carry a picture of Malawi's president (and its owner) every day, preferably on the front page—a practice that is common in authoritarian states throughout the Third World. Another rule is that the speeches of the head of state may not be edited or cut. The *Swaziland Times*, which was founded in 1897 as a weekly, owned, edited, and read by Europeans, was bought by the Argus Company in the late sixties. When Swaziland became independent in 1968, it continued to be owned and edited by whites. In 1975, the Argus Company sold it to a Scotsman, who turned it into a daily in 1978.

Francophone Africa. "Fourteen independent states were to emerge from France's African Empire. But between them they could hardly muster a Press worth the name," writes African journalist Frank Barton. France treated its overseas dependencies as an extension of the mother country. Selectively, it educated those Africans who could absorb the education and culture of France and become "black Frenchmen"—évolués is the name given to this elite group. They spoke French with distinction, while the English spoken by most Africans in British territories was poor in quality. However, only the elite were privileged to speak French, while in the British colonies English was taught down to the lowest levels of society.

France did not encourage newspaper or magazine publication in Africa, and until the mid-thirties, only French citizens were permitted to publish them. Several of these, intended for French settlers, appeared in Dakar, Senegal, in the late nineteenth century. Among them were *Le Reveil du Sénégalais* in 1885 and *L'Union Africaine* in 1896. In 1907, the French Socialist Party published *L'A.O.F.*, a weekly, in Dakar. In the twenties, some nationalistic papers, such as *La Voix du Dahomey, Le Phare du Dahomey,* and *Le Cri Nègre*, appeared briefly in what is now Benin. During the thirties, France admitted the Senegalese to full French citizenship, and when parliamentary elections were held, political candidates started a number of papers that closed down immediately after the elections. But some survived for several years, including *L'Ouest Africain* and *Le Journal de Dakar*. In 1935, the Ivory Coast produced its first anticolonial paper, *Éclaireur de la Côte d'Ivoire*, which was also the first French African newspaper owned and operated by Africans.

At about the same time, Charles de Breteuil, a Frenchman who had some journalist friends and also knew the French colonial minister Paul Reynaud, was encouraged to go traveling in Africa. He saw a market for newspapers in several of the colonies, especially among the French settlers, and he began publishing a weekly in Senegal in 1933. *Paris-Dakar* became a daily in 1935, changing its name to *Dakar-Matin.* In 1970, the government assumed 65 percent of the shares, with de Breteuil and a French state publishing enterprise, Société Nouvelles d'Editions Industrielle (SNEI), owning the rest. Its name was changed once again to *Le Soleil du Sénégal*. In the Ivory Coast, de Breteuil established *France-Afrique* in 1938, which became *Abidjan-Matin* in 1954. When the Ivory Coast gained its independence in 1960, de Breteuil formed a partnership with SNEI to continue

Abidjan-Matin. In December 1964 it was renamed *Fraternité-Matin* and taken over by the government. It was placed under the control of the ruling party and received technical and editorial aid from de Breteuil and the French government. By the end of the seventies, only the head printer was French. *Fraternité-Matin* is the only major daily in Francophone Africa.

Another newspaper started by de Breteuil was *La Presse de Guinée* of Conakry, Guinea. He started it in 1954 and it folded in 1958, when Guinea became independent, rejecting the new French constitution. Guinea became a Marxist state and today has no daily newspaper. In 1955, de Breteuil founded *La Presse du Cameroun* in Douala, the largest city in the Cameroon. This was closed in 1974 when the government decided that its sole daily should be published in the capital, Yaounde. It owns 70 percent of the shares in the newspaper, which it named *Cameroun Tribune*. One day a week the paper is published in English. De Breteuil and SNEI own 30 percent of the stock.

As for the rest of Francophone West Africa, the government owns the only daily in Benin, *Ehuzu*, formerly known as *Daho-Express*. In Libreville, Gabon, the government has been publishing a small daily tabloid, *L'Union*, since 1975; and in Bamako, Mali, there is a government-controlled daily called *L'Essor—La Voix du Peuple*. The Togo government has published a small daily in Lome, *La Nouvelle Marché*, formerly *Togo Presse*, since 1962. It is in French, with pages in Ewe and Kabie. Upper Volta is the only former French possession in sub-Saharan Africa still to have a wholly privately owned daily. It is *L'Observateur* of Ouagadougou, which was founded in 1973 by a local publishing firm, Société Nationale d'Edition et de la Presse. There also is a daily news bulletin distributed by the Ministry of Information.

In East Africa, only Madagascar among Francophone countries has a developed press, and while circulations are small, the newspapers are numerous. They include the privately owned *Madagascar-Matin*, the largest of the dailies on the island, published in both French and Malagasy, and the government-owned daily *Atrika*, founded in 1977. There are several other small privately owned dailies in both French and Malagasy.

Belgian Africa. The only country in the former Belgian colonies of Africa with a press worthy of note is Zaire, formerly Belgian Congo. Neither Rwanda nor Burundi have more than daily news bulletins. The earliest publications in the colony that was to become Zaire were produced by Belgian newspapers mainly for Belgian settlers. The first on record was *Le Journal du Katanga*, which started in

1911 as a weekly and became a daily in 1919. It was succeeded in 1930 by *L'Echo du Katanga*. Other dailies were *L'Essor du Congo* (1922), *L'Informateur* (1934), *Les Nouvelles* (1934), and *Centre Afrique* (1948), which had been a monthly and became a weekly in 1931.

Catholic missionaries were the first to bring out newspapers intended for Africans as well as Europeans. Among the first was *Courrier d'Afrique* (1930), the only daily in Kinshasa before 1962, and *La Croix du Congo* (1936), which was taken over by Africans in 1958 and renamed *Horizons*. Because of its revolutionary tone, it was closed down by the government the following year. In 1956, *L'Avenir Colonial Belge*, a daily for Belgian settlers founded in 1930 in Leopoldville, produced a weekly supplement with an all-Congolese staff and called it *Les Actualités Africaines*. It invited African intellectuals to contribute letters and articles. Its first editor was Mobutu Sese Seko, later to become president of Zaire. It survived as a daily until 1960, when it became a weekly, renamed *Nkumu* in 1972. A second daily, published by Africans in 1957, a couple of years prior to a Belgian decree permitting Africans to own newspapers, also survived for several years. It was *Présence Congolaise*, renamed *Epanza* in 1972, by which time it had become a weekly.

All dailies today are government owned and have small circulations. A 1974 survey shows that a third of the population of Kinshasa, the capital, are regular newspaper readers, while 42 percent never see a newspaper. The dailies in Kinshasa today are *Salongo*, formerly *L'Avenir Colonial Belge*, which in 1962 became *Le Progrès* and was given an African name in 1972, along with all other Congolese papers. It is a morning paper, while *Elima* (formerly *Courrier d'Afrique* mentioned above) is an evening paper. In the provinces, two small dailies are published. One is *Boyoma* (formerly *Le Renouveau*) of Kisangani, the other is *Mwanga* (formerly *La Dépêche*) of Lubumbashi. All dailies are in French.

Iberophone Africa. Of the five former Portuguese African colonies, only Angola and Mozambique have minor daily newspaper systems. Equatorial Guinea, which formerly belonged to Spain, has two small newspapers—*Ebano*, published in the capital, Malabo (formerly Santa Isabel), and *Poto Poto*, published in Bata on the mainland in Rio Muni.

Both Angola and Mozambique, upon gaining their independence from what had been a conservative Portuguese regime, adopted Marxist governments in 1974. Of the two, Angola has had less of a press history. Before independence, it had a morning daily founded in 1923 —*A Provincia de Angola*—which was nationalized and renamed *O*

Jornal de Angola in 1976. An evening paper, *Diario de Luanda*, later *Diario da Republica*, has been closed by the government.

Mozambique has had a long press history. Its earliest recorded publication was the *Lourenço Marques Guardian*, founded in 1905 by the large British community in Mozambique's capital. In 1956, it was purchased by the Roman Catholic church and renamed *Diario*, publishing in both English and Portuguese. Much of the preindependence history of the press of Mozambique centers on a conflict that existed between the conservative Roman Catholic Archbishop of Lourenço Marques, called Maputo since independence, and the liberal, pro-African Bishop of Beira, the second port of Mozambique. In 1918, *Noticias da Beira* was started as a biweekly English and Portuguese publication by the Archbishop. In 1932, the Bishop supported the publication by local Africans of a weekly, *A Voz Africana*. In 1950, the Bishop founded a daily in Beira, *Diario de Moçambique*, upon which the Archbishop's biweekly was raised to daily status. Meanwhile, a conservative retired Portuguese army officer, Manuel Simoes Vaz, founded a Portuguese-language newspaper in Lourenço Marques called *Noticias* in 1926. It became the official spokesman for the Portuguese in 1933 and was taken over by the Marxist government as its main publication in 1975. All other dailies folded that year, except *Noticias da Beira*, which continued as the country's second daily.

Independent Africa. Ethiopia and Liberia, which have never been colonies of a Western power, as has the rest of Africa, cannot boast of well-developed press systems. Liberia, in fact, has reverted to a mimeographed daily bulletin published by the Ministry of Information since its military coup in 1980. It did have newspapers in the past, starting in 1826 with the *Liberia Herald*, a four-page monthly, published off and on until 1862. Liberia had no daily newspaper until 1946, when the *Daily Listener* was founded by a Liberian politician, Charles Cecil Dennis. It folded in 1973. Roy Thomson of Britain published the *Liberian Star* as a daily in the sixties (it had been founded as a weekly in 1939), but abandoned it in 1968. It was revived in 1969, toeing the government line, since it recognized that "the order of the day was 'survivalism not journalism'," as a former assistant editor, Rufus Darpoh, put it. The *Liberian Star* was closed down before President William R. Tolbert, Jr., was deposed in the military coup. A few weekly and semiweekly publications still appear in Monrovia, and by mid-1982, Head of State Samuel Doe had begun to revive other elements of the press.

Until the overthrow of Emperor Haile Selassie, Ethiopia had a fairly large number of small dailies, in both the capital, Addis Ababa, and in Asmara, capital of the former Italian colony of Eritrea,

annexed to Ethiopia by the United Nations in 1952. All were published by the government to extol the emperor and his government.
As in many other authoritarian states, Ethiopian news dealt
mostly with what the emperor and his ministers did and said rather
than with the people whom it affected. Among the dailies were the
Ethiopian Herald in English (founded in 1941) and *Addis Zemen* in
Amharic (founded in 1974). There also was a French daily in Addis, a
Tigrinya daily in Asmara, and two Italian dailies in Asmara. When
the emperor was deposed in a bloodless Marxist coup, some of these
dailies ceased publication, leaving two Amharic dailies.

Weekly Newspapers

South Africa. Five Sunday papers of national importance are
published in South Africa, four with main offices in Johannesburg.
But the *Sunday Times*, for example, which has the highest Sunday circulation in Africa—close to half a million—is printed simultaneously
in Cape Town and Durban and distributed throughout southern Africa. While the *Sunday Times* is an English-language paper belonging
to the liberal South African Associated Newspapers group, its Afrikaans counterpart is *Rapport* with a circulation that is almost as
high. It is the only Afrikaans Sunday newspaper, and it supports the
government as all other Afrikaans papers do. The *Sunday Express* is
another English-language Johannesburg paper belonging to the
SAAN group. Its circulation is much lower than that of the *Sunday
Times* and it is more conservative. The *Sunday Post* belongs to the
Argus group. It is a tabloid intended for nonwhites and has special
editions for Africans, colored and Indians. One Sunday paper, the
Sunday Tribune, is published in Durban.

There are at least 40 other weekly or semiweekly publications in
South Africa catering to all interests. Notable among these for their
influence, though not for their circulation, are *To the Point* and the
Financial Mail. Several Afrikaans weeklies are published on Fridays.
Indian Opinion, founded by Mahatma Gandhi in 1903 and still being
edited and published by relatives, is a weekly addressed to Gujerati-
speaking Indians in South Africa. Another weekly for Indians, *The
Leader*, is in English. Both are published in Durban. Other weeklies
are published in Zulu, Xhosa and Yiddish. Surveys show that education and age are factors in weekly readership in South Africa.
Weeklies are read by people in the higher-education and lower-age
brackets.

East Africa. Kenya, once again, has the most lively weekly publications in this English-speaking black African area. The *Sunday*

Nation, 70 percent of which is owned by the Aga Khan's Nation Newspapers, has a circulation of more than 100,000. Like the *Daily Nation*, it is a tabloid and is modeled after the London *Daily Mirror*. In 1977 a Harvard educated Kenyan, Hilary Ng'weno, started a competing Sunday paper, *The Nairobi Times*. A broadsheet, it is patterned after the more serious *London Observer* and has a low circulation. A third Sunday publication is in Swahili and is also owned by the Nation Newspapers. It is called *Taifa Weekly* and has a circulation of over 50,000. Two other Kenyan weeklies should be mentioned. The *Weekly Review*, published by Ng'weno, was founded in 1975 as a serious journal of political analysis, similar to the London *Economist*. Its circulation is said to be rising steadily, although it is still low. A popular weekly launched by Ng'weno in 1976, called *Picture Post*, failed. The *Voice of Africa* is a propaganda weekly that is believed to be supported by the Libyan government.

Tanzania has two Sunday newspapers. The *Sunday News* is in English and is owned by the government, while the ruling (Revolutionary) party-owned *Mzalendo* is in Swahili. In addition, there are five weeklies and one biweekly published in English and Swahili in Dar-es-Salaam and Zanzibar. Uganda has four weekly publications, all in Kampala, its capital. Three are in English and one is in Luganda. The small island of Mauritius boasts of nine weekly or biweekly publications, including *Weekend*, which advertises itself as having the largest circulation in the Indian Ocean.

West Africa (Anglophone). There are 11 Sunday newspapers in Nigeria and more than a score of other weeklies. Like its daily counterpart, the government-controlled *Sunday Times* has the highest readership. Among other Sunday newspapers with high readership are *Sunday Punch, Sunday Sketch, Sunday Tribune* and *Sunday Observer*. The weekly magazine insert in the *Sunday Times, Lagos Weekend*, also is popular. Another weekly publication of the Daily Times Company, *Times International*, is a magazine of international news commentary, but is not regarded as a very strong publication. Nigeria's weekly periodicals generally cater to most interest groups and are widely read by literate elements of the population. In a 1980 survey, 54 percent of a cross-section of the population said they had read a newspaper or magazine. Even in rural areas, the proportion of readers was as high as 35 percent.

On the other hand, because of newsprint shortages and lack of transportation, Ghana's periodical press is in disarray at present. But a number of government, private and religious weeklies and biweeklies are published from time to time. The *Daily Graphic* has a weekly supplement called *Mirror* that used to be quite popular, but has a small circulation now. The *Spectator*, weekly supplement of the *Gha-*

naian Times, has been suspended. Other weeklies that have in the past played important roles in Ghanaian journalism but have fallen on bad times include *The Echo*, a right-of-center, intellectual weekly which probably still has the highest circulation of all weeklies; *Palaver-Tribune*, given to exposés and investigative reporting, and *The Pioneer*, whose claim to fame is that it opposed President Nkrumah. The biweekly *Legon Observer* established a reputation for itself as a leading intellectual publication when a group of University of Ghana professors launched it in 1966.

Southern Africa. The seven English-speaking countries north of South Africa have remarkably little in the way of weekly periodicals or newspapers. Zambia has a Sunday paper, the *Sunday Times*, with a relatively large circulation in the neighborhood of 70,000, which easily outdistances the daily press in that country. In Zimbabwe, *The Herald* and *The Chronicle* each has a Sunday paper, the *Sunday Mail* and the *Sunday News*, respectively. The eastern part of the state is served by the *Umtali Post*, founded by the Argus Company in 1893. It has a minuscule circulation. There also is a farmers' weekly and a radio and TV guide.

Francophone Africa. Only five of the 17 countries in the former French colonies have weeklies that should be mentioned in this section. Probably the most noteworthy is *La Semaine Africaine*, founded in 1952 and published by the Archdiocese of Brazzaville, the Congo. It is the only privately owned publication in the country and it is distributed not only in the Congo, but in neighboring Gabon, Chad and the Central African Republic. The Cameroon has two French and two English-language semiweeklies, plus a Sunday paper, the *Weekender*. *La Gazette*, published in Douala, is the largest French weekly and is privately owned. The *Cameroon Times* and the *Cameroon Outlook* are published in English on alternate days. They are printed in Victoria.

The Ivory Coast has no more than five weeklies, among them the Sunday edition of *Fraternité-Matin* in Abidjan. It is called *I.D.* (formerly *Ivoire-Dimanche*) and is printed in color. Its content is heavy on sports and cultural events. Another weekly is the organ of the ruling party, and its editorial director is the president of the Ivory Coast, Felix Houphouet-Boigny. It is called *Fraternité-Hebdo*.

In Senegal, the daily *Le Soleil* has a recently added weekly tabloid supplement, *Zone 2*. It, too, focuses on sports and culture. The Catholic Church supports an illustrated weekly magazine of news and features called *Afrique Nouvelle*, founded in 1947. It is distributed throughout Francophone Africa. Finally, on the east coast, the island of Madagascar supports seven weeklies or biweeklies printed in Malagasy.

Belgian Africa. Only Zaire has weekly publications of any importance, although the government of Burundi publishes two weekly newspapers and a biweekly. Most important of Zairian news weeklies is *Zaire*, published by the government in Kinshasa. It claims readership outside of Zaire. There also are four French weekly newspapers and several vernacular weeklies published in Kinshasa and in the provinces.

Iberophone Africa. None of the countries in this area have any important weekly publications.

Independent Africa. The Ministry of Information of Liberia publishes two semiweekly newspapers, the *New Liberian* and *The Redeemer*, under the overall supervision of a single editor. Six other weeklies in Amharic, Arabic and Oromigna, and five biweeklies in *Focus, Sunday Express, Express Special, Liberian Inaugural* and *Sunday People.*

The Ministry of Information in Addis Ababa, Ethiopia, publishes weeklies in Amharic, Arabic and Oromigna, and five biweeklies in Amharic. None of these is of major importance. The one with the highest circulation is *Ethiopia Today*, an Amharic weekly covering government activities.

Other Publications

The African magazine that probably is the most widely read by Africans is *Drum*. Founded in 1951 by James R. A. Bailey, son of a millionaire mine owner, it was directed at a non-European, English-speaking market, although its first editors were white. Tom Hopkinson, one of these editors, extended its readership into other parts of southern Africa and into Anglophone East and West Africa. *Drum* is a slick, folio-sized monthly, featuring advice columns and personality stories about internationally renowned blacks, general topics of interest to blacks, coloreds and Indians, and such touchy subjects as riots and the need for prison reform.

For many years it served as the training ground for African journalists. During the late sixties and early seventies, *Drum*'s popularity in South Africa declined in the face of the rising popularity of a sister publication. This was the *Post*, a tabloid weekly newspaper focusing on crime and sex. Special editions were published for African, colored and Indian communities in South Africa. In 1965, the monthly

Drum was discontinued in South Africa and made into a supplement to the more popular *Post*; but it was revived as a monthly in 1968 and given its first nonwhite editor the following year. *Drum*'s West African edition was opened in Lagos in 1954 and an East African edition was added in Nairobi two years later.

Other than *Drum*, almost the only magazines published in sub-Saharan Africa that circulate outside their country of origin in any quantity are published in Senegal. One is the French-language *Africa*, founded in 1962 as a political, social and economic review of African affairs. It appears 10 times a year and is sold throughout Francophone Africa. Another is a popular picture monthly intended for urban youth. Brought out in 1952 by de Breteuil, it was, at the time, the only publication in his empire designed strictly for Africans and it was probably his most successful venture. It claims a circulation of over 100,000 throughout Francophone Africa. Other monthly or quarterly publications of importance published in Dakar are *Amina*, a women's magazine; *Ethiopique*, a scholarly journal devoted to African culture; and *Afrique Medicale*, a medical review.

Entente Africaine is published quarterly in the Ivory Coast in French and English. Its aim is to attract foreign investment and tourists from neighboring countries.

In all of the rest of sub-Saharan Africa, only Kenya and Nigeria have internally circulated magazines of importance. *Kenya Yetu* is a Ministry of Information magazine published in Nairobi and widely read throughout Kenya. It is in Swahili. Another is the privately owned humor magazine, *Joe*, that calls itself Africa's entertainment monthly. In Nigeria, Drum Publications also produces a general interest picture monthly for internal distribution called *Trust*, and the Daily Times Publications has a monthly family magazine, *Spear*, which is widely read. *Ophelia* is a cultural magazine of high quality that first appeared in October 1980. There also are several women's magazines. Ghana currently has no magazines worthy of note. In Zambia, the government publishes a number of vernacular magazines but, on the whole, there are no magazines of significance in southern Africa. Other than Senegal and the Ivory Coast, no Francophone African country (including Belgian Africa), and no Iberophone or independent African country has important magazines.

Foreign Publications

One finds, in traveling around Africa, that there is no shortage of reading materials in hotel lobbies and bookstores. In English-speaking countries, the *International Herald-Tribune* is readily available on the day of, or the day after, publication, as are several British newspapers and periodicals such as the London *Times*, the *Daily Tele-graph*, the *Daily Mirror* and the *Economist*. International editions of *Time, Newsweek* and the *Reader's Digest* also are widely read. In French-speaking countries, Paris newspapers and periodicals such as *Le Monde, L'Express* and *Realités* may be purchased.

A crop of political and economic journals published in London and Paris especially for African readers also are commonly found on the newsstands. Oldest among these is the weekly *West Africa*, founded in 1917 and purchased· in 1947 by Cecil King of the London *Daily Mirror*. It is an influential journal of news and opinion about Africa. The monthly *New African* has been available since 1966 and covers business and economic news, while *Africa* is a still more recent pub-lication of economic and political news. Like *New African*, it is a monthly and is published in London.

The two most widely read French journals are *Jeune Afrique* and *Afrique-Asie. Jeune Afrique* is a weekly political journal originally published in Tunis in 1960. Its publishing offices were later moved to Paris. *Afrique-Asie* was founded in 1969 and also is published in Paris. It is a biweekly.

Rural Journalism

Because of the high illiteracy in Africa, efforts have been made by a number of African countries both to raise literacy levels and to pro-vide easy reading materials for new literates. UNESCO sponsored a survey of rural newspapers and newspaper needs in 11 African coun-tries and a team of African journalism educators made suggestions for the establishment of a rural press. Liberia had started to experi-ment with mimeographed rural newspapers in 1963, and Niger ran a similar experiment in 1964. Following the guidelines of the UNESCO consultants, Mali launched a rural newspaper called *Kibaru* in March 1972. It was written in the Bambara language and its purpose was to help readers retain and improve their literacy.

Today, 16 African countries are participating in the experiment. Some, like Burundi, Ghana, Mali and Tanzania, have a single rural newspaper, while others like Liberia and Niger, which have used rural journalism the longest, have 10 to 15 newspapers. Most of the papers appear monthly or less frequently and are either mimeographed or printed on offset presses. Circulations range from 100 to 60,000, but the majority are in the 1,000 to 3,000 range. Many are in local languages, which has posed a dilemma, since some of the languages are spoken in very limited areas. Some are in English or French or in one of the more widely spoken vernaculars, such as Hausa or Swahili. They are all written in simple language, are generally printed in tabloid format, and they concentrate on hygiene, social, cultural and economic problems, in addition to local news. Mostly they are published by government ministries, but in some countries missionary groups help out, as does UNESCO.

In an experiment using such a newspaper in beginning classes of rural schools in Ghana, Neff Smart in 1974 found more reading improvement in the schools that used the paper, *Densu Times*, than in a control group of schools, especially after the second year. And there were several fringe benefits, including increased motivation of those students who read the newspapers and a favorable impact on adults, such as parents and teachers.

BROADCAST MEDIA

Radio

The low literacy rate, coupled with the traditionally high dependence on and respect for oral communication, make radio the ideal medium of mass communication in Africa. Unlike television, which requires expensive equipment beyond the means of most Africans and high voltages to run the equipment, radio transistor sets are both cheap and can run on batteries. This puts them within reach of individuals and communities everywhere in Africa. As a medium for quickly rallying the population or for long-range mass education, radio is without peer. It is no coincidence, therefore, that one of the first things African states did upon gaining their independence was to consolidate their hold on whatever broadcasting facilities may have been left behind by the colonizing power. Furthermore, radio stations in many African states are as closely guarded as the presidential residence because they are among the first targets of insurgents. In fact, Gabon has a second studio and transmitter in the presidential compound for just such an eventuality. It is significant, as Elihu Katz and George Wedell have pointed out, that no African state has decided to do without a radio system, while several are managing quite well with only limited printed media.

There are some negative factors, however. Radio transmission on medium-wave, which is easy to tune in to and is less subject to atmospheric interference than shortwave, limits the reception area geographically both in terms of distance and in terms of terrain. A mountain or other physical barrier, for example, would interfere with reception. In Africa, where many countries cover vast areas and where obstructions abound, this is a problem. In the United States, the problem is overcome in two ways: Every town or urban area has its own stations, and wireless, telephonic and satellite relays make network broadcasts possible. Africa lags behind both economically and technologically. While short-wave is used by many countries to overcome the distance and obstruction dilemma, solar interference due to sunspots curtails such broadcasting, especially in the winter. Hence, coverage is not 100 percent.

Cost is another factor. Producing programs is expensive and, although expenses are occasionally covered by charging a license fee on all sets, fees are hard to collect anywhere, but especially in Africa. Besides, there are, relative to the size of the population, not many set owners to collect fees from. There are many listeners per set or even community sets that bring in little revenue. As for commercials, even if people could afford to advertise in the subsistence economies of most African countries, the governments are reluctant to open up this potent medium to commercial exploitation.

Then there is the problem of the proliferation of languages. Every community wants to be addressed in its own language or dialect, which not only means more hardware, but more programing. And while it is a headache for governments to decide on how much air time to give to each language, it is found to be politically necessary to cater to each major language and culture. This is having a negative effect on education and development, since it is far slower and more expensive to educate a large population in many languages than to mass produce education in a single language. Furthermore, social, political and economic development depend on speedy interaction, and this is slowed down by a multiplicity of cultures. It has been said that the British Broadcasting Corporation is responsible for the evolution and widespread use of the "King's English." The broadcast policies of most African nations support continuing diversity of language and culture.

South Africa was the first African country to introduce radio broadcasting. It had a station operating out of Johannesburg in 1920, with additional stations in Cape Town and Durban soon thereafter. In 1927, the British East African Broadcasting Company, Ltd., began relaying BBC broadcasts to British settlers in much of Africa from a short-wave station in Nairobi, Kenya. It broadcast from 1 to 2 p.m. and from 6 to 8 p.m., daily. In 1930, Imperial and International Communication, Ltd., took over this station and in 1931 the company was renamed Cable and Wireless, Ltd. In return for a monopoly on all international telegraphic traffic and a wireless license fee it collected through the Post Office (with a reduced rate for Africans), it agreed to do all the broadcasting for the colony. At first, broadcasts were in English only. During World War II, Asian and African language programs were added to keep the many colonials who were contributing to the war effort apprised of the progress of the war. Cable and Wireless, Ltd., handled the English and Asian programs, while the Kenya Department of Information prepared programs in Swahili, Kikuyu,

Kikamba, Nandi, Luo, Luhya, Kipsigis and Arabic. Cable and Wireless, Ltd., was replaced by the Kenya Broadcasting Service in 1959 with the help of a grant from the British government.

In southern Africa, a broadcast service relaying the BBC out of Salisbury, Southern Rhodesia (Zimbabwe), to the entire area was started in 1932 to coincide with inauguration of the BBC's Empire Service. A monitoring station was also built in Lagos, Nigeria, that year, also providing wired service over phone lines to Nigerians who could afford it. In 1935, Overseas Rediffusion, Ltd., a private company, was given the franchise for an extensive radio distribution service, which it ran for the Nigerian Post and Telegraph Service, the government department that owned the equipment. Similar wired service was provided in Sierra Leone in 1934 and in Ghana in 1935. In the meantime, the French had inaugurated a wired service in Madagascar in 1931, making their overseas programs available to the island.

The Jesuit Fathers started educational broadcasts in Kinshasa, the Belgian Congo (Zaire), in 1937. One of their two transmitters was taken over by the Belgian government in 1940. Not until 1950 were there any broadcasts for Africans, however. All broadcasts until that year were in French and Flemish for European listeners in Africa. It was World War II that opened up a number of additional African countries to radio. Among the ones that acquired broadcasting facilities during the war, in addition to the Belgian Congo, were Cameroon, the Congo, Ethiopia, Gambia, Mauritius, Senegal, Somalia, and Northern Rhodesia (Zambia). By the end of the war, about 15 African countries had broadcasting facilities.

No African state permits its radio broadcasting to be controlled largely by commercial interests, as they are in the United States, with the state being involved mainly in allocating air waves and licensing the operators. And while a few states like Ghana have constitutional provisions that permit broadcasting by private concerns, so far no applications have been received in Ghana for a license and no one is likely to apply because of the cost and the shortage of foreign exchange. With the exceptions noted below, all African governments own the broadcasting facilities in their territories and in all but six states operate them as well. The six countries that have broadcasting systems operated by "autonomous" public corporations modeled after the BBC are Ghana, Malawi, Mauritius, Nigeria, South Africa, and Zimbabwe. This means that they are supported by public funds but their day-to-day operations are the responsibility of a board of directors appointed by the government or determined by statute. Of course, how much independent judgment this board is permitted to exercise varies from country to country and with the prevailing political climate at any given time.

Besides the government-owned and -operated stations, three countries have given broadcasting privileges to radio stations owned and operated by private religious organizations; three have privately owned commercial radio stations; two permit foreign governments to broadcast from their territory; and four countries allow the South West African People's Organization (SWAPO) of Namibia to broadcast revolutionary programs to Namibia.

In Liberia, station ELWA, which was founded in 1954 by United States church groups, is run by the Sudan Interior Mission. It is non-commercial and broadcasts on short and medium wave to West, Central, and North Africa in English, French, Arabic, and 42 West African languages. The Seychelles are hosts to the Far East Broadcasting Association, which beams religious programs to both India and East Africa in 21 languages. In Swaziland, Trans World Radio, an international evangelical organization which also has transmitters in Monte Carlo, Guam, Sri Lanka, Cyprus, and the Netherlands Antilles, broadcasts to East, Central, and North Africa in English, Afrikaans, Swahili, and other African languages. When Emperor Haile Selassie was still in power, Ethiopia permitted the Lutheran World Federation to run the oldest evangelical broadcasting operation out of Addis Ababa. It was called Radio Voice of the Gospel and was founded in 1941. But the station was nationalized in 1977 by the new government and renamed Radio Voice of Revolutionary Ethiopia.

In Liberia, two iron ore mining companies operate radio stations. The Lamco firm broadcasts on station ELNR in nine African languages and English for its employees, and the Bong Mining Company operates ELCBR for a similar audience. Swazi Radio is a privately owned commercial service in Swaziland that broadcasts to southern Africa in English, Afrikaans, Portuguese, and Indian languages. Gambia has a commercial station, Radio Syd, that broadcasts mainly music. The Voice of America has a relay station in Liberia; and Deutsche Welle, West Germany's overseas broadcasting station, has relay facilities in Rwanda. SWAPO's Voice of Namibia is permitted to broadcast into Namibia on transmitters in the Congo, Angola, Tanzania, and Zambia.

Most radio in Africa is financed through direct government subventions. At least 29 of the 46 countries also allow commercial advertising. But in most African countries, this accounts for a very small proportion of the revenue. In Senegal, for example, it amounts to a mere 10 percent. Even where advertising promises good returns, as in South Africa, only 14 percent of the total expenditures on advertising in that country went to radio in 1977. Fewer than half the countries have license fees; but these must of necessity be low, and they are hard to collect. Many radio sets in African countries go unregistered.

Broadcasting facilities have been increasing in Africa every year.

Thus the number of transmitters in 1955 was 151; in 1960 it was 252, in 1964 it had gone up to 370, and in 1976 it was 428. But these figures are hard to substantiate and should be taken only as a measure of the growth of broadcasting in Africa. One must remember that for every transmitter that is put into operation, hundreds of listeners tune in newly acquired sets.

Because radio is so important to the continent, one finds that even the smaller countries in Africa have extensive radio services, broadcasting many hours in an amazing number of languages. One would expect it of South Africa, of course. It has 16 full-time services broadcasting in 17 languages a total of 2,270 hours per week. Fifteen of these services are domestic and one is an all-night external service called Radio South Africa, which broadcasts to Africa, Europe, and North America.

The Voice of Kenya in Nairobi operates three services: National (in Swahili), General (in English), and Vernacular (in 15 African languages and Hindustani). It also has an educational service for schools and a short-wave service for distant villages. The Federal Radio Corporation of Nigeria which since 1978 has replaced the Nigerian Broadcasting Corporation operates three national networks and an external service known as the Voice of Nigeria, broadcasting to Africa, Europe, the Middle East, and the Americas. In addition, each of the 19 state governments in Nigeria has its own broadcasting corporation and originates its own broadcasts in local languages and English.

Ghana's Domestic Service has an English channel and a vernacular one. The English channel carries commercials, while the vernacular channel broadcasts in six languages. There also is an External Service which broadcasts in English, French, and Hausa. Similarly, Zambia has an English channel, a vernacular channel broadcasting in seven Zambian languages, and an external short-wave channel broadcasting mainly to the South.

In Francophone Africa, Senegal runs two networks, with a parent station in Dakar and four regional stations broadcasting 132 hours a week, mainly in six local languages. The news is carried in French simultaneously on both networks. The Ivory Coast operates three services: National Regional, and International. The broadcasts are mainly French on the national and international network, except for five daily newscasts in English for neighboring countries. The regional network broadcasts in 13 local languages. The Cameroon has a national, a provincial, and an international short-wave service broadcasting in English and French. There are seven provincial stations in as many cities, each broadcasting in French, English, and a variety of local languages. The Voice of Zaire has a powerful 600-kilowatt transmitter covering most of the western area of Central Africa, and two powerful (100-kilowatt) short-wave transmitters that cover all of Zaire. It also has a number of other medium-wave and short-wave transmitters in major towns and in each region, and there is a short-wave transmitter that covers West Africa and Europe. Zaire devotes 62 hours per week to news broadcasts, 41 hours of which are in French and the rest in four vernacular languages. Of its 23 hours a week of educational and cultural programs, 18 are in French; and it also broadcasts 17 hours a week of entertainment. Because of inadequate transportation, phone, and postal facilities, Rwanda uses its radio, which is partly financed by West Germany, as a national bulletin board.

Adult education occupies a large proportion of the time on African radio. Serious programs, including news and current affairs programs plus educational programs on hygiene and social problems, constitute about 40 percent of total program time. Katz and Wedell found that in Tanzania and Senegal about half the programs fell into this category and that even Tanzania's commercial service devoted 40 percent of its programs to information. It may be that cost is an important factor. Many of these serious programs are talk shows that are cheap to produce. Among the most popular programs in Nigeria are request programs. These include a message program, a children's program, a traders' program, and a women's program. Letters are sent to the station from all over the state with messages to loved ones or questions to be discussed by panels of peers. A farmers' program discusses and recommends new farming methods. Talk shows are favored by almost a third of Kenyan radio listeners, next to news, which about three-fourths of the public listed as the program they enjoyed in a 1980 media survey. Significantly, 16 percent said they liked greetings programs, close to the 15 percent who liked popular music.

Despite the importance of radio on the African continent as a medium of education and social integration, it has not been able to penetrate the hinterland in many African countries. Its major audience in the smaller countries is in the urban areas. Nevertheless, it is still the most efficient and effective way to reach large segments of the population from central locations.

Nigeria, which has gone all out to use radio as an educational and political medium, has among the highest listenerships. In a nationwide survey in 1980, 90 percent of the population claimed to have heard radio at some time or other. Significantly, 86 percent in the rural areas said they had listened to radio, and urban listenership was 93 percent. The presence of television in the home does not decrease radio listenership, as another 1980 study showed. In this study, 92 percent of television owners claimed also to listen to radio regularly. In Lagos, the capital, regular listenership of TV owners is 97 percent. These are, of course, elite homes.

However, in Kenya, which is also very active in the use of radio for national development, only 69 percent of a cross section of the population said they had ever listened to radio, according to a 1980 media study. Urban listenership is, of course, higher. In response to the question, "Do you listen to the radio?" 91 percent of the urban population said they did, as against 68 percent of the rural population. Only 42 percent listened in their own home, with 41 percent claiming to own a working radio (35 percent in rural areas). And, lest anyone think that people probably listen in their cars, as they do in the United States, only 0.02 percent said they listened on a car radio. The frequency of regular, e.g., daily or weekly, listening is, of course, much lower in all cases.

Audience data are not readily available in Africa, but in Francophone Africa, studies were done by a reputable French market research organization in 1980 in the Cameroon, Gabon, and Ivory Coast. All available data are from major cities alone. Thus in Yaounde and Douala, two principal cities of the Cameroon, daily radio listenership is 67 percent, with an additional 25 percent claiming to listen several times a week. In Libreville, the capital of Gabon, 62 percent said they listened daily and another 19 percent several times a week. A 1977 study by the same organization showed a similar 80 percent "regular" urban listenership. In Abidjan, capital of the Ivory Coast, daily listenership was 56 percent, with another 25 percent claiming to listen several times a week.

Overall, an estimate of radio-set ownership in Africa in the midseventies puts the figure at less than 7 percent of the population. This might be compared with 27.5 percent in South America or 23 percent in the poorer Central American states. Incidentally, radio-set ownership in the USSR was only 20 percent, according to the same source, while the United Kingdom had 70 percent ownership, France 76.5 percent, and the United States, where most people own an average of two sets, 181 percent. To make radio more readily accessible in Africa, many countries have community speakers in rural areas. These make it possible for large numbers to listen to a single set, but they limit the choice of station. Ghana has 68,000 such loudspeaker boxes. It is currently phasing out the rental of closed-circuit radios in favor of inexpensive preset radios.

Television

Unlike radio, which even poor countries can afford and no African country is without, television often requires outlays that are beyond the means of both the transmitter and the receiver of the service. The government that wants to make use of the medium needs capital equipment, such as transmitters, studios, cameras, and recorders; it must train the personnel; and it also has recurrent and continuing maintenance and production costs. Because film industries are absent in sub-Saharan Africa, there is not much locally produced entertainment material to feed the voracious monster. African countries are forced to go to their former colonizing countries or some other foreign power for entertainment materials (a thing many of them resent) or they must resort to locally produced talk shows, political propaganda extravaganzas, or amateurish educational programs and short broadcasting hours. None of this is an efficient use of costly investments.

Of the 46 discrete political entities in the area, 28, or around 60 percent, had television as of the start of 1982. Other countries are planning to introduce television in the near future. Only one country —Burundi—has positively outlawed the importation or use of TV, although it can be received from neighboring Zaire. Residents of Botswana and Lesotho can and do watch South African TV, and Gambia gets reasonable reception from Senegal. Equatorial Guinea can pick up signals from Nigeria and/or Gabon under favorable conditions, and more than 1,000 TV sets exist in the country. Similarly, people in Mozambique, which, unlike Angola, has no TV, watch it from neighboring states. The only major African country that continues to resist TV is Tanzania. But the islands of Zanzibar and Pemba, which merged with Tanganyika to form Tanzania, installed a color television system in 1973.

All African TV is state-owned and -operated except that Swaziland, which inaugurated its service in 1978, shares equal ownership with a private company under a royal charter, with the understanding that eventually it will acquire full ownership. Some foreign companies have assisted in bringing TV to Africa but in all cases have withdrawn because television was found to be a losing proposition for the foreseeable future. Africa is too poor to support it profitably. Thus, a private British company helped Western Nigeria introduce the first television in sub-Saharan Africa in 1959. In 1976, the Nigerian Television Authority was constituted as the federal body responsible for television production, and it set up a federal station in each of the 19 state capitals. In 1980, Lagos State began a state television broadcasting system of its own, and all the other states are expected to follow suit.

Zambia acquired a commercial system on the copperbelt at Kitwe in 1961, which the state took over in 1966. The year 1963 saw a large surge of interest in television. Four Francophone states inaugurated television broadcasting in that year. They were the Congo, Gabon, the Ivory Coast, and Upper Volta. The three Anglophone states of Kenya, Uganda, and Sierra Leone also introduced television that year. In the following year, both Ethiopia and Liberia, the two sub-Saharan states that never were colonies, started TV broadcasting. That same year, Senegal, with the help of UNESCO, Canada, and France, began experimenting with educational television. Ghana started its system with the help of the Japanese company Sanyo, which wanted the franchise for TV manufacture and sales in the country. South Africa had no television until 1976, when it inaugurated a single channel, broadcasting alternately in English and Afrikaans. National Party leaders had hinted that their longstanding opposition to TV was due to their fear that it would have to depend too much on English-language imports for entertainment shows, slighting the Afrikaans-speaking elements of the population. In January 1982, a second TV channel was introduced for blacks. It broadcasts in Zulu, Xhosa, Sotho, Venda, and Tswana, with heavy emphasis on soap operas and sports.

Like radio, TV is financed through direct government subventions, commercials, and license fees. In addition, some countries, such as Upper Volta and Zambia, receive foreign assistance. Mauritania received a $3 million gift from Iraq to build its color TV transmitter and studios. Some countries, such as Nigeria, also have a stiff (100 percent in Nigeria) excise tax on receivers. As in the case of radio, license fees are hard to collect. In Kenya, for instance, where there were some 50,000 sets in use in 1976, only 3,458 television licenses were issued. (The actual number of sets in use can be estimated from imports and sales.)

A few countries, such as Kenya and Northern and Southern Rhodesia (now Zambia and Zimbabwe), introduced television mostly for their European population before independence. It was considered an expensive toy, and to the present day it is a medium for the elite. Of some 14,000 television sets in Kenya in 1968, 11,000 were said to have been owned by Europeans and Asians, and 500 were community sets. Most of the 70,000 sets in the country today are in Nairobi and Mombasa, where a station was opened in 1970. Less than 10 percent of the population of Kenya lives in these two cities.

Countries that have introduced television since independence emphasize the educational role of TV. Not only is this emphasis politically wise, since the benefit thus supposedly accrues to the masses rather than the elite, but it is economically the most expedient use of the medium. Educational programs are cheaper to produce than many entertainment programs, and they generally satisfy the nationalistic goal of most African countries to do as much as possible of the programming locally.

A typical day's schedule starts around 5 or 6 P.M. and runs for three to five hours. It may have between two and five newscasts of 5 to 15 minutes, at least one of which would include international news. It is likely to have a talk show, a children's educational program, local music and dancing, an adult educational program on health, art, clothing, the theater or books, and possibly a foreign import, such as a film or a network rerun from the United States, Britain, or France. On weekends, and often on weekdays too, there is likely to be a sports event.

Sports is among the favorite television programs of many Africans. In a 1980 Kenya survey, 11 percent said their favorite program was wrestling; 4 percent said it was sports in general and "Football Made in Germany"; 18 percent liked news best; while 6 percent enjoyed the "Six Million Dollar Man" most. In Kenya, as was pointed out, TV reaches a very small segment of the population. Only 3 percent of the public claim to have TV; only 12 percent have ever seen it. Many see it at a friend's home or at a community center.

TV has a larger audience in Nigeria, which, of course, has a higher per-capita income than does Kenya. A 1980 study there found that 68 percent of the public claimed to have seen TV and the urban proportion was as high as 89 percent. In rural Nigeria, 41 percent have seen TV, according to the survey. But only 7 percent of the rural public say they watch it every day, as against 61 percent of the urban public. It should be noted that Nigeria has 33 transmitters, while Kenya has only two, plus two relays. A 1977 study in Libreville, Gabon, found 43 percent who claimed to view TV daily.

Overall, 0.6 percent of the African public owns television sets. This is the same proportion as TV-set ownership in 25 Asian countries, according to a study by Katz and Wedell based on 1975 figures. South American TV-set ownership is about 9 percent and in Central America it is 6 percent. For purposes of comparison, 20 percent of the public owns TV sets in the USSR and 53 percent own sets in the United States and United Kingdom. In France the figure was about 24 percent. TV remains a medium of wealthy countries. The fact that about half of all sub-Saharan African countries (24) belong to Intelsat and can potentially receive foreign programs directly via satellite does not mean that TV will bring African people closer to the rest of the world. Africa's integration in the global village must be preceded by its economic and educational development.

GOVERNMENT—PRESS RELATIONS

The relations between the mass media and government can range all the way from total independence of the two institutions to total control by the government of the mass media. In the former case, mass media are a true Fourth Estate, serving the public in their area of responsibility and competence with no interference from the government. In the latter extreme, mass media are an arm of the government with no purpose other than to further the goals and programs of the government. No country in Africa has a mass media system that may be characterized as pure Fourth Estate. On the other hand, about a third of the countries in sub-Saharan Africa have media that either function as the mouthpiece and organizers of the public to implement government objectives or are permitted absolutely no freedom to operate outside government guidelines.

African countries were rated according to the following criteria:

1 Press free to criticize government, with full protection of the rights of individuals and of the press through an independent judicial system.

2 Varied opinions expressed in the press, but some constraints exist; strong judiciary.

3 Some censorship of the press, criticism discouraged; but some legal recourse; free speech permitted and foreign publications readily available.

4 Press censored, no criticism of the government allowed; but private speech and assembly not inhibited.

5 Press and speech censored and no legal recourse, but media privately owned or, if government-owned no interference with private speech.

6 Strict censorship, only government views available in mass media; military or Communist dictatorship.

Using these criteria, no country in sub-Saharan Africa rates a 1. The countries that rate a 2, in the opinion of this author, are South Africa, Gambia, Nigeria, Mauritius, Botswana, and Lesotho. Until the 1979 coup, Ghana would have been placed in this category; but since the coup, it has rated a 3, along with Kenya, Swaziland, and the following Francophone African countries: Djibouti, Ivory Coast, Senegal, and Upper Volta. Eight countries were given a rating of 4: Malawi, Zambia, Zimbabwe, Sierra Leone, Rwanda, Central African Republic, Gabon, and Mauritania. Another eight countries were rated 5: Uganda, Seychelles, Zaire, Cameroon, Madagascar, Mali, Niger, and Liberia. The 16 countries that were rated lowest for press freedom are: Tanzania, Burundi, Equatorial Guinea, Benin, Chad, Comoros, Congo, Guinea, Togo, Somalia, Ethiopia, and all five of the Portuguese African countries, namely, Angola, Cape Verde, Guinea–Bissau, Mozambique, and Sao Tome and Principe.

Grouping the countries as before, we find that the degree of dependence on the printed media is somewhat, though not wholly, related to an area's press freedom. Thus, South Africa is rated freest, despite the racial policies of the government. One must recognize that approval of the official policies of a government must be divorced from an assessment of the degree of freedom of its press. As stated, South Africa has a rating of 2 on the latter score. Anglophone West Africa, although lower on the printed media dependency scale, is next on the freedom of the press scale, with an average rating of 2.75. The other regions rate as follows, on the average: Southern Africa, 3.17; East Africa, 4.2; Francophone Africa, 4.7; Belgian Africa, 5.0; Independent Africa (Ethiopia/Liberia), 5.5; Iberophone Africa (Portuguese/Spanish), 6.0; and Italian Africa (Somaliland), 6.0.

A 1981 Freedom House survey rates the countries somewhat differently. The difference in rating is due to the fact that Freedom House considers, in addition to factors involving the mass media, other civil liberties, such as the right of political assembly, the detention and even torture of political opponents, freedom of travel, and private ownership of property. While these are valid considerations, they go beyond the scope of our concern, which is: What can the mass media do to and for people? For purposes of comparison, however, here is the Freedom House rating, with P standing for printed media and B for broadcast media.

	Generally Free	Partly Free	Generally Not Free	Civil Liberties*
Angola			PB	7
Benin			PB	6
Botswana	P	B		2
Burundi			PB	6
Cameroon			PB	6
Cape Verde			PB	6
Central African Rep.		PB		5
Chad			PB	6
Comoros				5
Congo			PB	6
Djibouti				4
Equatorial Guinea			PB	6
Ethiopia			PB	7
Gabon			PB	6
Gambia	PB			3
Ghana		PB		3
Guinea			PB	7

	Generally Free	Partly Free	Generally Not Free	Child Liberties*
Guinea-Bissau			PB	6
Ivory Coast		P	B	5
Kenya		P	B	4
Lesotho		PB		5
Liberia			PB	6
Madagascar			PB	6
Malawi			PB	7
Mali			PB	6
Mauritania			PB	6
Mauritius	PB			3
Mozambique			PB	7
Namibia				5
Niger			PB	6
Nigeria	P	B		3
Rwanda				6
Sao Tome and Principe			PB	6
Senegal		PB		4
Seychelles			PB	6
Sierra Leone			PB	5
Somalia			PB	7
South Africa		P	B	6
Swaziland			PB	5
Tanzania			PB	6
Togo			PB	6
Uganda		PB		4
Upper Volta		PB		5
Zaire			PB	6
Zambia		P	B	6
Zimbabwe		P	B	4

* On a scale of 7, with 1 representing the highest and 7 the lowest level of civil rights. See Raymond D. Gastil (ed.), *Freedom in the World: Political Rights and Civil Liberties, 1981*. Westport, CT: Greenwood Press, 1981, pp. 60–63.

South Africa is one of the most controversial countries in the world. It is a white-dominated African state in which whites make up less than 20 percent of the population. It openly discriminates in its laws and practices against nonwhites. Yet its mass media are free to the extent that it is no offense for them to oppose the policy of apartheid. The government's Department of Information itself distributes press comment critical of the government. South Africa has an out-spoken white-owned and -operated English-language press that takes strong stands against government policies and practices. It is read by more people than read the pro–National Party pro-apartheid Afri-kaans press. Yet while the courts are independent and generally fair, the police can easily get an injunction against a newspaper if they wish to stop publication of a story they consider undesirable. And in early 1982, the Steyn Commission of Inquiry into the Media rec-ommended to parliament that journalists be registered and that a press council be formed with powers to suspend a newsman's registration. Broadcasting is a state monopoly and the broadcast media, which, like the Afrikaans press, support the government, get preferential access to government news.

Despite all this, many observers, including Africans, say that the press of South Africa is still the freest in Africa. One must therefore examine the constraints on the press of other African countries. What makes the press of Nigeria, which many regard as the freest in black Africa, less free than that of South Africa? Frank Barton, African director of the International Press Institute and a keen analyst of the African press, refers to the "slap happy junta in Africa's largest na-tion, Nigeria, whose engaging bag of tricks for the media ranges from horse whipping to stripping and head shaving." The chilling effect that such demeaning treatment will have on newsmen and publishers can be imagined. Not that equivalent treatment, especially of blacks, in South Africa is unknown. But the press follows up acts of barbar-ism with vigorous investigative reporting. Not only is there less of such comeback in the relatively free press of countries such as Nigeria, Gambia, Ghana, and Kenya, but self-censorship is much stronger there so that brutal acts are less frequently reported. Never-theless, recently in Nigeria the courts awarded punitive damages to an editor who had been whipped.

In the rest of Africa, one must distinguish between countries that actively use the press to achieve political objectives and ones that tolerate the mass media as an evil necessary for the entertainment and diversion of the public. Kwame Nkrumah was among the first type. "The truly African revolutionary press does not exist merely for the purpose of enriching its proprietors and entertaining its readers," the Ghanaian leader told the Second Conference of African Journal-ists in 1963. "The African press must present and carry forward our revolutionary purpose." Or, speaking of the role of radio, Jean-Jacques Kanda, former Minister of Information in Zaire, said: "In countries where independence is still ceaselessly being brought into question . . . How can we tolerate the radio's becoming an instrument of division, slander or controversy? . . . I am convinced that the radio should always be under public control."

Countries such as Zambia, Zimbabwe, Tanzania, and Sierra Leone are very conscious of the developmental role of the mass media and control them accordingly. On the other hand, Gambia, Mauritius, Swaziland, and even Kenya are more tolerant of private ownership and profit-making on the part of the press. This does not mean that they are disinterested in the educational and socializing potential of the press; but they do not utilize the press single-mindedly with this one role in mind. The fact that the press is being used by the government places the press in a manipulative role, thereby reducing its freedom status. In a truly free country, where the press is the Fourth Estate—an institution of society—people use the press to serve their needs. Using the press offensively makes it a tool of government, whereas defensive use puts the government on the alert against any possible harm the press might do to it. Both types of uses call for government controls.

No country in Africa is without press controls, as we have said. In most countries, the controls include such legal constraints as libel and sedition laws. This kind of constraint naturally exists in even the freest countries of the world. But the laws can be liberal or restrictive. They can define libel and sedition so broadly that criticism of any kind becomes a crime. Dennis L. Wilcox, in a study of the African press, found that about one-fourth of African countries have highly restrictive libel and sedition laws, another fourth have fairly restrictive laws, about 30 percent have not very restrictive laws, while in one-fifth of the countries, the laws have no effect at all in the opinion of journalists, largely because the press is so heavily controlled or is government-operated.

One of the most pervasive and effective forms of press control is outright or majority ownership of printing presses or newspapers by the government. As we have seen, in at least three-fourths of the countries, the government is either the sole or the principal owner of the print media; and in all countries, government owns and operates most radio and television stations. In a few countries, such as Tanzania, Zambia, the Ivory Coast, Cameroon, and the Seychelle Islands, the political party in power also plays a major role in running the print media.

Another form of government control is through the allocation of newsprint. Except for South Africa and Zimbabwe, African countries must import newsprint and must set aside foreign exchange for the purpose. Ghana is so limited in its supply of newsprint at the present time that circulations have been drastically cut back and some publications are not now being printed. Wilcox found that 47 percent of the African countries he studied treated governmental and private publications equally, and in 44 percent of the countries, the problem of equal treatment did not arise because there was no privately owned press. Most of the remaining countries gave preference to government publications.

Censorship is another way that the government intrudes itself in mass communication. There are two types of censorship: prepublication and postpublication. It is hard to say which is the more undesirable. Wilcox found that almost six out of ten African countries had prepublication censorship. This involves submitting galley proofs or page proofs to an official censor, who often has an office in the newspaper building. The censor approves every item that goes into the paper. In the case of three-fourths of these countries, prepublication censorship is implied by the very fact that the newspapers are government-owned. About four in ten countries have no ostensible prepublication censorship. This includes some government-owned publications. Postpublication censorship means that the government can punish an editor and staff for publishing something the government objects to. Such second guessing is very unnerving, because one can never tell what the government will take exception to. Occasionally a newspaper is closed or an issue is seized, or an editor is fired without any reason being given. Wherever there is the threat of postpublication reprisal, self-censorship inevitably results. In such cases, there is a tendency toward overcautiousness on the part of the journalist.

There are other methods that governments have used to control their media and their newsmen, and African countries have tried them all. In his 1975 book, Wilcox says that 44 percent of the 34 countries he studied required that journalists be licensed, and 53 percent required the registration of the print media themselves. Without proper certification, a journalist cannot have access to government news and neither can one who represents a medium that is not registered. Even licensed journalists have a hard time getting access to government information. In almost all African countries, the government gives out the news it wants the press to have. There is no Freedom of Information Act in any African country.

REGIONAL AND NATIONAL NEWS AGENCIES

The idea of a news agency is a very simple and obvious one. If a number of individuals and organizations all need the same kinds of information on a regular basis, it makes sense to gather the information cooperatively. This is what led to the founding of Reuters, the Associated Press, and all the other major and well-known wire services of the world. Newspapers, banks, the stock exchange, and other commercial interests wanted news fast and they found it economically sound to share the cost of collection. The newspapers, and later radio and television stations, that subscribed to a news service seldom had overlapping readerships, and it broadened their feasible coverage immensely to be able to use wire copy. The stationing of correspondents in all the places that need to be covered from time to time is prohibitively expensive if each newspaper and other medium must have its own correspondent on location.

We are restating the obvious just to remind ourselves of the rationale for a news agency. Since the question is one of economizing by sharing expenses, the more participants there are who share in the service, the cheaper it is for each of them. And this is what creates a dilemma for most African countries. As we have seen, most states in sub-Saharan Africa have no more than one or two newspapers, a radio and, possibly, a television station. Furthermore, in most cases they all belong to the same owner—the government. The cost of maintaining a staff of correspondents around the world is beyond the means of most governments. They must therefore buy the service from a major news agency with an international clientele. A national clientele will hardly suffice, because the potential number of subscribers would be too small to provide a broad enough coverage. This leaves the international news agencies—Agence France-Presse, Reuters, the Associated Press, United Press International, and TASS. None of the others can provide worldwide coverage. It boils down to taking the service or doing without international news coverage, or pirating the news from international broadcasts of the BBC, VOA, Radio Moscow, and others.

The dilemma is very real for African nations because most of them feel very strongly that the news carried by the international wire services is biased in selection and presentation. It is especially biased, they feel, against Third-World countries in that the little that is carried about these countries generally deals with conflict and disaster, and is distorted in presentation even on that. They would like the world to see their developmental side. This dissatisfaction has led to much discussion at Third-World conferences and, after the 1973 Non-Aligned Summit conference in Algiers, the Yugoslav news agency Tanjug volunteered to set up a Non-Aligned News Agencies Pool which would provide the kind of news about Third-World countries that these countries wished to see circulated. In January 1975, Tanjug began relaying Third-World news under the code name "Pool," and by the following year there were 40 members. Each member is permitted to submit 500 words each day and Tanjug incorporates the submissions unaltered in its daily file, translated into English, French, and Spanish where necessary. The member countries are asked to exercise self-censorship and to submit items "on the basis of mutual respect." Of the 41 members in 1977, only one country in sub-Saharan Africa—Ghana—was active enough to have submitted materials during eight days randomly drawn from a three-month period in a study by a United States foreign service officer, Edward T. Pinch.

Placement of Pool stories is meager. In the 1977 Pinch study, it was found that only 22 percent of the stories had a high potential for placement in Western media. The rest were too specialized or ideological, i.e., were obvious propaganda. Even when a story has potential for placement, it is unlikely to be used unless the news flow is light or the item has some local relevance. A 1980 study done at the University of North Carolina showed that Third World news was carried mostly by Third World countries, Western news by the West, and Communist-bloc news by the Communist countries.

Many Africans recognize that Western newsmen see things from their own perspective and need to do so, since their clientele demand news from that viewpoint. As one Kenyan publisher, Hilary Ng'weno, put it to an American journalism professor, "If I could have a reporter in London or Washington, I would want him to be a Kenyan with a Kenyan perspective and aiming at a Kenyan audience." Not all journalists necessarily want only positive news published about their country. The editor of an Icelandic newspaper, speaking at the December 1979 Conference on Information and Human Rights in Venice, Italy, said Iceland, like many Third World countries, has to "live with a one-way information traffic." It is interested in what is going on in the world, but cannot expect the world to be interested in Iceland's cod wars with Britain.

> Even if we could join an eventual Third World rulers' conspiracy against the news agencies, the distributed materials would end up in the wastebaskets.... I accept the lack of good news from Iceland in the international press.... But I miss the other side. I miss the bad news....the men in power in my country are extremely sensitive to foreign opinion—their image abroad.

There are other reasons, however, for setting up national news agencies than that of covering world news. One is that a country interested in monitoring all incoming news can use the national news agency as a gatekeeper to sift through all the news and to funnel only desirable news to its mass media. Some media have neither the staff and translating capabilities nor the inclination to winnow all the news and prefer to have it predigested by a national news agency knowledgeable about the country's interests. At the same time, the news agency can serve as a gatekeeper for news leaving the country. In some African states, the international wire services do not maintain a bureau or are not permitted to have one. In such cases, the national news agency serves as the main conduit of news about the country.

Of the 46 sub-Saharan countries in Africa, 31 have national news agencies and 30 of these are government owned and operated. The sole nongovernmental national news agency is that of South Africa—the South African Press Association. Founded in 1938, it was the first national news agency in Africa. It is cooperatively owned by the English and Afrikaans newspapers, much as the Associated Press is media owned in the United States. The agency was started by Reuters in 1912 as the Reuters South African News Agency to serve southern Africa. It was not until 1957 that a black African news agency was founded. This was the Ghana News Agency. President Nkrumah was anxious to develop it into a Pan-African news agency and established a number of bureaus, both in African countries and in London and New York. Its early start gave Ghana an advantage over other national news agencies in terms of the training of its staff and through its reputation as a reliable wire service.

The Pan-African news agency idea was picked up by the Organization of African Unity when Ghana proposed it at the 1963 Algiers conference. The following year, the Union of African News Agencies, comprising the 20 or so African countries that had them at the time, adopted a plan of organization at its Yaounde, Cameroon, conference. The purpose of the agency was to project a "true image" of African countries through the exchange of news. It was felt, however, that many things were lacking for the operation of such an agency, including trained personnel, telecommunication links, political harmony among the participants and, above all, money. Although the members of the Union of African News Agencies agreed at their 1967 conference in Addis Ababa that there was a need for a Pan-African news agency, 10 years were to pass before a secretariat for such an agency was established in Kampala, Uganda. Then, in 1979, the Pan-African News Agency (PANA) was founded and based in Dakar, Senegal, but without any funds. Finally, UNESCO came to the rescue, and in January 1982, it agreed at a conference in Acapulco, Mexico, to allocate $100,000 to get PANA started. The Arab Gulf States said they would contribute the remaining $1.4 million that PANA requested to establish a news and features division, train personnel, and acquire and install telecommunications equipment.

At the present time, government-run national news agencies are in operation in the following countries:

Angola: Angop

Benin: Agence Benin-Presse

Burundi: Agence Burundaise de Presse (ABP)

Cameroon: Société de Presse et d'Edition du Cameroun (IOPECAM)

Central African Republic: Agence Centrafricaine de Presse (ACAP)

Chad: Agence Tchadienne de Presse (ATP)

Congo: Agence Congolaise d'Information (ACI)

Ethiopia: Ethiopia News Agency (ENA)

Gabon: Agence Gabonaise de Presse

Ghana: Ghana News Agency

Guinea: Agence Guinéeane de Presse

Ivory Coast: Agence Ivoirienne de Presse (AIP)

Kenya: Kenya News Agency

Liberia: Liberian News Agency (LINA)

Madagascar: Agence Nationale d'Information "Taratra" (ANTA)

Malawi: Malawi News Agency (MANA)

Mali: Agence Malienne de Presse et Promotion (AMPA)

Mauritania: Agence Mauritanienne de Presse (AMP)

Mozambique: Agencia de Informação de Moçambique (AIM)

Nigeria: News Agency of Nigeria (NAN)

Rwanda: Agence Rwandaise de Presse (ARP)

Senegal: Agence de Presse Sénégalaise

Somalia: Somalia National News Agency (SONNA)

Tanzania: Shihata

Togo: Agence Togolaise de Presse

Uganda: Uganda News Agency

Upper Volta: Agence Voltaique de Presse (AVP)

Zaire: Agence Zaïroise de Presse (AZAP)

Zambia: Zambia News Agency (ZANA)

Zimbabwe: Zimbabwe Inter-African News Agency (ZIANA)

Fifteen countries have no indigenous news agencies. They are: Botswana, Cape Verde, Comoros, Djibouti, Equatorial Guinea, Gambia, Guinea–Bissau, Lesotho, Mauritius, Namibia, Niger, Sao Tome and Principe, Seychelles, Sierra Leone, and Swaziland. In addition, there is a private Protestant news agency and a private Catholic news agency in Zaire.

National news agencies, in turn, subscribe to international and some major national wire services. The national news agencies then compile news bulletins based on the wire service material and either circulate the news directly to private and institutional subscribers or pass it on to the public through local press and broadcasting facilities. In this process, the news agencies exercise judgment about what the public should know, and discard a large proportion of the material they get. Thus, a North Carolina study found in 1980 that Ghana uses only about 10 percent of what it gets from its wire services.

In addition to selling news to national news agencies, the global wire services and some major national news agencies also maintain bureaus in many African countries. The agency that has the largest number of bureaus in Africa is the French Agence France-Presse (AFP). It was the first news agency in the world, founded as Havas in 1835. Two of its employees, Julius Reuter and Bernard Wolff, went off to England and Germany, respectively to start their own agencies. AFP had bureaus in many of its colonies after World War II, and when the colonies gained their independence, AFP helped them establish national news agencies, often by merely changing the name of the local AFP bureau. Similar services were rendered the former British colonies by Reuters. In a few cases, as for example in the Ivory Coast and Malawi, a global agency only sells its service without also maintaining a news gathering bureau in the country. But in most cases, there is a reciprocal arrangement, with the national news agency paying the difference between what it gets for its coverage and the cost of buying the wire service.

While the following table is not all-inclusive, it gives some indication of international and wire service activities in Africa.

Wire Service	*Countries in which News Agencies Maintain Bureaus*
Agence France-Presse (AFP)	Angola, Cameroon, Chad, Congo, Djibouti, Ethiopia, Ghana, Ivory Coast, Kenya, Liberia, Madagascar, Mali, Mauritania, Niger, Nigeria, Senegal, Sierra Leone, South Africa, Togo, Uganda, Upper Volta, Zaire, Zambia, Zimbabwe
Reuters (R)	Cameroon, Chad, Ivory Coast, Kenya, Liberia, Madagascar, Mali, Mozambique, Nigeria, Senegal, Sierra Leone, South Africa, Tanzania, Uganda, Zaire, Zambia, Zimbabwe

Associated Press (AP)	Ghana, Kenya, Nigeria, Senegal, South Africa, Uganda, Zambia, Zimbabwe
United Press International (UPI)	Ghana, Kenya, Liberia, Senegal, South Africa, Zimbabwe
TASS	Benin, Cameroon, Central African Republic, Congo, Ghana, Guinea, Kenya, Mali, Nigeria, Senegal, Sierra Leone, Tanzania, Uganda, Upper Volta, Zambia
Novosti (APN)	Angola, Congo, Ethiopia, Guinea, Madagascar, Mali, Mozambique, Nigeria, Senegal, Tanzania, Uganda, Zambia
Xinhua (NCNA)	Cameroon, Ghana, Guinea, Madagascar, Mali, Sierra Leone, Tanzania, Zaire
Allgemeiner Deutscher Nachrichtendienst (ADN)	Angola, Ethiopia, Mozambique, Nigeria, Tanzania
Deutsche Presse Agentur (DPA)	Ghana, Kenya, Liberia, Nigeria, Senegal, South Africa, Togo, Zambia
Tanjug	Ethiopia, Madagascar, Zambia
Agencia EFE (Spain)	Equatorial Guinea, Nigeria, Zambia
Agenzia Nazionale Stampa Associata (ANSA) (Italy)	Ethiopia, Ivory Coast, Kenya, Mozambique, Senegal, Somalia
Prensa Latina (Cuba)	Tanzania
Československá Tisková Kancelár (CTK)	Kenya, Tanzania
Kyodo Tsushin (Japan)	Kenya
Jiji Tsushin Sha	Nigeria
Central News Agency (Taiwan)	Ivory Coast

Wire Service	*Countries in which News Agencies Maintain Bureaus*
Agencia Noticiosa Portuguesa (ANOP)	Mozambique
Jewish Telegraphic Agency (JTA)	South Africa
Agerpress (Romania)	Madagascar
Ghana News Agency	Kenya, Nigeria
Southern Africa News Agency (SANA)	Zimbabwe

Besides news agencies, *Time, Newsweek,* radio and television networks, and some major world dailies and weeklies maintain correspondents in Africa. However, these can almost be counted on one's fingers. The most popular base for the coverage of the whole of Africa is Nairobi, Kenya. It has the most pleasant climate, the best communication facilities, and one of the least meddlesome governments on the continent. For these reasons, several American publications, such as *The New York Times,* the *Chicago Tribune,* the *Los Angeles Times,* and *Time* magazine have their correspondents there, as do the British, West Germans, Japanese, and others.

PHILOSOPHICAL CONSIDERATIONS

Throughout sub-Saharan Africa, mass media are looked upon both as a help and a hindrance. Without mass communication facilities, governments and leaders cannot hope to fashion coherent nations. Without mass media that can reach all elements of the public, development is at best slow. Everything a nation generally hopes for—strength, prosperity, cohesion, the comforts of technological advancement, peace with one's neighbors, broadened horizons, the personal satisfactions of teamwork, cultural development, and recognition—is in some way connected with communication.

On the other hand, communication is feared by African leaders. Almost without exception, they seek to control it in their countries. For whereas a head of state can rally his people to his support, so can a would-be usurper. Mass media create problems by raising the expectations and frustrations of the public. They highlight and often caricature the mistakes and shortcomings of the government. They split culturally diverse elements of the public by focusing on and even exaggerating their differences. They segment the population by strengthening social, economic, political, religious, linguistic, cultural, and other adherences. Perhaps more than other peoples of the world, Africans feel they are at the mercy of mass communication.

It is not surprising, therefore, that African governments pay such close attention to the role of the mass media. In no African state are the mass media given full freedom of operation. With the authority to govern comes the expectation that all human psychological and physical interaction may be regulated by the government. Most Africans accept government tutelage without question. It is in complete comformity with their tribal past, a system from which they are not too far removed. And it is a philosophy that was perpetuated by colonialism.

The African does not define freedom of the press in terms of an autonomous role for the mass media vis-à-vis his own government, as would most Westerners. He defines it in the context of national independence from outside interference. He looks upon Western press behavior as license, not freedom. "There is such a thing as being too free," one African complained, when told that the United States government could do nothing about the negative opinion expressed in a leading American publication about the president of his country. "My government would never stand for such behavior on the part of our press," he added proudly.

African leaders talk about freedom and independence as though they were interchangeable. "If you want a free press, if you want an independent press—and we want it—I have been asking myself in what sense is a press free, in what sense is a press meant to be free?" Mwai Kibaki, Kenya's minister of finance, is quoted by Frank Barton. "Can it be free? Can you really have an independent press when the people in charge of it, like everyone of us, have their own likes and dislikes." The West, on the other hand, distinguishes between freedom and independence. "You did not gain your freedom in the sixties, as you say," Elliott Abrams, assistant secretary of state for international organization affairs told an African panelist at a State Department function in November 1981. "You gained your independence from foreign rule." By equating freedom with independence, many Africans, whether consciously or unconsciously, try to confuse the two so as to suggest that by gaining independence one has also gained freedom, and that by demanding freedom one is in danger of losing independence.

The role of the mass media, as Africans see it, is to educate the public and to assist in national development, rather than to serve as a watchdog over government. The question one must ask oneself is whether news, and even entertainment, that is to be presented actually advances national development. In the West, a key question is, "Can I sell this? Will people buy it?" By "sell" and "buy," we mean "Will people accept something psychologically?" But behind it all is the profit motive. We mean it literally. News is a commodity, as is entertainment, through which the owner, presenter, or seller makes a profit. The West wants news to be freely accessible and for it to flow freely across boundaries for the same reason that it wants other commodities to move unhampered in trade. Africans do not consider news as a salable commodity but as an instrument for the molding of public attitudes and the development of national identities. They are more concerned about what news can or will do to people than about whether people will or will not want to buy it and read it or listen to it.

If one had to characterize the press theories of sub-Saharan peoples in terms of the four theories popularized by Frederick Siebert, Theodore Peterson, and Wilbur Schramm in their book *Four Theories of the Press*, one would have to say that almost half the countries in Africa have governments that are at least partly authoritarian. Many scholars have pointed out that it is unlikely that a country will subscribe to all the characteristics of a particular theory of the press. Only six countries in Africa may be said to be outright authoritarian, so far as their mass media are concerned.

In Africa, we detect three degrees of authoritarianism—two of these categories being progressively less authoritarian than the first. In other words, one can detect some libertarian tendencies in certain authoritarian governments. In classifying 10 countries under the heading of Soviet-Communist, we must recognize that no country in Africa is anything like the USSR in government or in any other characteristic.

The 10 under this heading merely have socialist leanings, are friendly with the Soviet Union or with China, and have a military or civilian dictator and a single ruling party. A C− means that the country has all the characteristics of a Communist state but also some hint of libertarianism. Although six of the countries are rated libertarian, they cannot be characterized as completely laissez faire. Seven other countries, while libertarian on the whole in their press relations, do exhibit some traces of authoritarianism. Siebert et al. saw an emerging press philosophy in the United States since World War II that they called social responsibility. All African states would feel comfortable with this theory. But they would contend that responsibility of the press should be to society, which means the will of the people as expressed by the government. No press can be called responsible if it betrays the *summum bonum*—the supreme good of the people. The press cannot and must not act selfishly, as a totally free press in the American sense is wont to do.

How the African Press Rates in Terms of the Four Theories*

Country	A	A–	A=	C	C–	L–	L
Angola				X			
Benin				X			
Botswana							X
Burundi	X						
Cameroon		X					
Cape Verde				X			
Central African Rep.			X				
Chad	X						
Comoros	X						
Congo	X						
Djibouti						X	
Equatorial Guinea	X						
Ethiopia				X			
Gabon		X					
Gambia							X
Ghana						X	
Guinea				X			
Guinea–Bissau				X			
Ivory Coast						X	
Kenya						X	
Lesotho							X
Liberia		X					
Madagascar					X		
Malawi			X				
Mali					X		
Mauritania			X				
Mauritius							X
Mozambique				X			
Namibia		X					
Niger		X					
Nigeria							X
Rwanda			X				
Sao Tome & Principe				X			
Senegal						X	
Seychelles		X					
Sierra Leone			X				
Somalia				X			
South Africa							X
Swaziland						X	
Tanzania				X			

Country	A	A–	A=	C	C–	L–	L
Togo	X						
Uganda		X					
Upper Volta						X	
Zaire		X					
Zambia			X				
Zimbabwe			X				

* A: authoritarian; A-: authoritarian with some libertarian traits; A=: authoritarian with even more libertarian traits; C: Communist-Socialist single-party dictatorship; C-: Communist-Socialist single-party dictatorship with some libertarian traits; L-: libertarian with some authoritarian traits; L: libertarian (African style)

EDUCATION AND TRAINING FOR JOURNALISM

One of the many shortages that Africans experienced upon gaining their independence was that of trained journalists. "Some countries (in Africa) cannot claim a single qualified journalist," a 1961 UNESCO report stated. Good copy editors were especially hard to find, according to Frank Barton, an African journalist who played an important role in helping to correct the deficiency. Except in Nigeria, where a few Africans had been working as journalists for some time, whites had been in full control of the press, so that even after independence, newspapers and other media were still forced to bring in Europeans to help run their news operations. But even in Nigeria, the skill gap between editors and their staffs was abysmal. Francophone Africa was probably even worse off than the English-speaking countries. While some Africans had been sent to France for training, they returned with such an elevated command of the language and used such literary styles that they were completely out of touch with the masses.

Entering the breach were a number of organizations that attempted to do for African journalism what defense departments everywhere tried to do for the war machines when World War II broke out. Just as the defense departments trained soldiers in a hurry, these organizations developed intensive condensed training courses during the sixties to produce the necessary cadres of journalists. Among the organizations that came to the rescue were the International Press Institute, with headquarters in Zurich, Switzerland; the International Organization of Journalists (IOJ), of Prague, Czechoslovakia; the International Federation of Journalists, of Brussels, Belgium; the Thomson Foundation in the United Kingdom; the American Press Institute and the African American Institute in the United States; and UNESCO. IPI was especially successful with six-month training programs in Nairobi and Lagos for journalists in East and Central Africa and in West Africa, respectively. Funded by Ford Foundation grants, these courses trained more than 300 African journalists between 1963 and 1968. UNESCO ran training programs for Francophone Africa in Dakar and one for East and Central Africans in Kampala, Uganda, while the East European IOJ conducted courses in Guinea, Mali, and Ghana.

One of the oldest permanent training institutions in black Africa is the Ghana Institute of Journalism, which was founded by Kwame Nkrumah in 1957 as a department of the Accra Technical Institute. It has a two- or three-year diploma course in journalism and a two-year specialist course in public relations. In 1973, Ghana established a School of Journalism and Mass Communications in Legon, outside Accra. It has been active in promoting literacy and rural journalism and offers a masters degree. Ghana also has a National Film and Television Institute, founded in 1978 to offer specialized training in television and film production.

In neighboring Nigeria, a department of journalism was opened at the University of Nigeria, Nsukka, in 1961 along the lines of United States schools of journalism. It was then called the Jackson College of Journalism. The university was closed down in 1967 during the civil war but reopened in 1970. Another program, leading to bachelors and masters degrees, is at the University of Lagos, founded in 1966. Besides these two university programs, Nigerians can get journalism training at the Nigerian Institute of Journalism and at the Nigerian Broadcasting Staff Training School, both in Lagos.

On the East coast, Kenya's School of Journalism at the University of Nairobi was established in 1970 with the assistance of UNESCO, Norway, Denmark, and Austria. In 1975, the government took full financial responsibility for the school. It offered a two-year undergraduate diploma course until 1979, when the program was discontinued in favor of a one-year postgraduate program. Kenya's Ministry of Information and Broadcasting also operates the Kenya Institute of Mass Communication. This started as a training school for broadcast engineering staff in 1961. It still teaches engineering but has since added courses in production. There are also two schools specializing in Christian communication.

The All-African Conference of Churches Communication Training Centre in Nairobi was founded in 1963. It emphasizes broadcasting, while the International Institute of Christian Communications (IICC) is connected with Daystar Communications, an organization that helps churches and missions with their communication problems. Established in 1971 as a four-week seminar, the IICC expanded to a diploma and M.A. degree program in 1976. Uganda attempted a one-year diploma course in journalism at the Institute of Public Administration in Kampala in 1974. The program was closed down the following year, but was reopened as a school of journalism when President Idi Amin was deposed. In 1975, Tanzania's Ministry of Information and Broadcasting opened its school of journalism in Dar-es-Salaam, offering a one-year certificate course and a two-year diploma program in a variety of journalism and mass communication fields. To be eligible for admission, Tanzanians must be members of the Revolutionary Party and have completed their national service. An older school, known as the Nyegezi Institute of Journalism at the Social Training Centre in Mwanza, does not have a college-level program. Zambia has a journalism training program at Evelyn Hone College in Lusaka, with excellent printing and photographic facilities. It also has probably the oldest church-related journalism program at the African Literature Centre in Kitwe, which now offers an annual journalism short course to students in the region.

A regional program for French-speaking Africans is offered at the Ecole Supérieure Internationale de Journalisme de Yaounde in Cameroon. It is part of the Federal University of Cameroon and is financed by the government, with assistance from the Central African Republic, Chad, Gabon, Rwanda, and Togo. Another French program, leading to a diploma in print or electronic journalism, is a three-year course of studies at the Centre d'Etudes des Sciences et Techniques de l'Information (CESTI). The center was founded in 1970 at the University of Dakar, Senegal, and has drawn students from Benin, the Ivory Coast, Mali, Mauritania, Niger, and Upper Volta, besides Senegal itself. An advanced diploma and the third year were added in 1978. A more limited program is offered at the Centre de Formation aux Techniques de l'Information in Niamey, Niger. In Zaire, IPI organized training programs at Kinshasa in 1962 and 1963. There had been a certificate program before independence in 1958–1959 at the former University of Lovanium in Kinshasa; but in 1973, a regular department of journalism was inaugurated at the National University of Zaire. Called the Institut des Sciences et Techniques de l'Information (ISTI), it offers bachelors, masters, and doctoral degrees (graduat, licence, and doctorat) in print and electronic journalism. It has attracted students from Benin, Burundi, Chad, Central African Republic, Rwanda, and Togo.

In South Africa, the Argus Group found a need to train journalists for positions on its various newspapers and in 1956 established the Argus Cadet School of Journalism. It offered a five-month course in Cape Town at its evening paper, the *Cape Argus*. In 1968, it moved the program to Johannesburg. The morning chain of newspapers known as South African Associated Newspapers had a similar program for its staff. University training in journalism did not begin until after a 1967 report by a government-sponsored symposium in Pretoria on the study of communication. The University of Potchefstroom began offering a four-year undergraduate program and a one-year postgraduate diploma plus an M.A. in communications and journalism. Within three years, the University of South Africa in Pretoria, Rhodes University in Grahamstown, and Rand Afrikaans University in Johannesburg were also offering degrees in journalism. Later in the seventies, the Department of Communication was established at the University of Orange Free State, at Bloemfontein.

As is true in the United States, seasoned African journalists who worked their way up from "tea boy" to editor are skeptical about academic programs in journalism. They believe in on-the-job training for reporters and editors. Their prejudice against formal academic training in journalism is bolstered in English-speaking Africa by their British heritage. Britain continues to resist the idea of teaching journalism at a university. Many African leaders of the old school received their apprenticeship in journalism on British or French newspapers; some took correspondence courses, a very common educational alternative in England.

Illiteracy adds to the problem, not only because of the competition for the few educated Africans who are available for responsible positions. That in itself means that journalism, which is poorly paid and low in social standing, frequently has to be satisfied with less than the top talent, since the best minds are attracted to better paying, more prestigious careers. But high illiteracy adds to the problem of communication. It takes a better-trained person to get through to a population with limited education. Radio has been the more prevalent medium of communication in African homes, and it is significant that in Nigeria, for example, it is the newspapers that attempt to recruit former broadcast journalists rather than the electronic media going after print newsmen. This is true despite the fact that there are many more newspaper than radio jobs, and hence more of an opportunity for training in the print media.

RETROSPECT AND PROSPECT

The history of journalism in Africa covers a period of no more than 20 to 25 years. Most of its mass media today date from the 1960s. Whatever journalistic endeavors there were before independence were largely by and for the white settlers many—though by no means all—of whom have left the continent. No one did Africans a favor by engaging in journalism on the continent of Africa. Most of the media ignored the "natives," and the few that included them were mostly out to convert them or to keep them in line.

Missionaries and church-related organizations did address them-selves to the local population. As a by-product of their zeal to bring Christianity to the African peoples, they worked hard at turning oral languages into written ones, then taught as many as would learn the mysteries of reading and writing their own language. The next step was to produce some literature for Africans to read. Much of this literature consisted of translations of the Bible; but some missionaries also started newspapers often filled with church-related announcements.

Such was the first newspaper in Nigeria, *Iwe Irohin fun awon ara Egba Yorubas*, founded by the Rev. Henry Townsend of the Christian Missionary Society (CMS) in 1859. Many other missionaries, some of whose names have been forgotten, produced publications in most African countries. Thus, the CMS mission published *Mengo Notes* in Uganda in 1900, and there was an unnamed mimeographed quarterly even before then in 1897, published by the Rev. A. W. Crabtree. Com-mercial printers were at work early in a few countries, especially South Africa, Sierra Leone, the Gold Coast, and Mauritius. Sierra Leone reputedly had the first periodical in black Africa in 1801 called the *Royal Gazette and Sierra Leone Advertiser*. But most of these publications lasted only a short time, disappearing with the changing character and needs of the population.

From the journalist's viewpoint, the heroes of the African press were not Africans but Europeans. They included men like Charles de Breteuil, who brought newspapers and magazines to Francophone Africa just before World War II. Another was Cecil King, of the London Daily Mirror Group, who influenced press developments in Anglophone West Africa. There was also the Aga Khan and his pub-lisher, Michael Curtis, who established a newspaper empire in East Africa; and Canadian press tycoon, Roy Thomson, with his close adviser, James Coltart, who operated in West, East, and southern Africa.

Among the names of journalists who had an impact on African journalism are both Europeans and Africans. Richard Hall trained many journalists in Zambia, where he was editor of the *African Mail* and the *Times of Zambia*. Norman Cattanach, a Scotsman, was active in Malawi; John Spicer, in Swaziland. Leading African journalists in-clude Hilary Ng'weno and George Githii, both of whom worked for *The Nation* in Nairobi. Ng'weno is an independent publisher of a sophisticated news magazine. Peter Enahoro of Nigeria's *Daily Times* is always mentioned among leading African journalists, and there are others—not too many—including some political leaders such as Azi-kiwe and Nkrumah, who later became presidents of their nations. In South Africa, Tom Hopkinson, editor of the *Drum*, should be mentioned. He trained many African journalists. So should courageous newsmen such as Laurence Gandar, of the *Rand Daily Mail*, and one of his reporters, Benjamin Pogrund. They used their paper to bring South African prison conditions to the attention of the public. Their long-drawn-out trial on charges of publishing false information took a toll on Gandar's health.

Historical highlights, both of the printed media and of the even more recent electronic media, have been discussed under the relevant sections above. It now remains to assess media impact and to make some guesses about their future. Making a judgment about the future of African journalism is like talking about the professional contributions of a young man who is still in junior high school. There are too many unpredictable future influences and environmental factors that could change the course of the young man's career. And so it is with Africa. Literacy is being tackled by all African countries in every way possible within their limited means. Communication instrumentalities other than newspapers, radio, and television, but just as important, are being developed as fast as possible. They include roads, telephone lines, airports, electricity, schools, books, teachers, and informal communication channels.

Literacy must go hand in hand with economic development. One cannot outdistance the other very much. With literacy will come the ability, but not necessarily the desire or even the need, to read printed media. The habit of newspaper reading developed in Europe and the Americas at a time when there was no other link with the outside world. Electronic links today are faster, easier, and even cheaper than the printed media. The need for newspapers is not as pressing today as it was 50 years ago. Although the need and possibly even the desire to achieve and maintain relationships with the rest of the world are stronger than ever, radio and television are less painful channels of communication for this purpose than is print.

By the time independence and self-determination came to most African nations, the civilized world had moved beyond the era of dependence on the printed media and into the age of electronics. Africans were under foreign tutelage and uninvolved in the kind of traffic that required daily printed communications. Their entry into the mainstream of international intercourse was at a time when it was possible for them to skip a stage in the development of many peoples and go straight to electronic communications.

It is unlikely, therefore, that African people will become great newspaper readers. Neither their traditions nor how their institutions have evolved nor, for that matter, their social and psychological needs point to such a stage in African development. Instead there will be a greater use of radio and, with economic growth, television.

For their entertainment, Africans will continue to depend on folk and traditional media, such as dances and plays. When it becomes economically feasible, video disks and recorders will be very popular, as they already are at least in Kenya, where the *Christian Science Monitor* reports some 75,000 video cassette recorders are in use, to the great concern of movie theater owners.

4 LATIN AMERICA

MARVIN ALISKY

A majority of Latin America's newspapers stress views more than news, but a sizeable minority of large dailies with high professional standards—including several of the world's distinguished newspapers —plus a few broadcasting networks manage to maintain an orientation toward information rather than opinion, despite political pressures.

Each Latin American government, whether democratic or dictatorial or somewhere in between, tries to project a favorable image of itself. In stressing achievements and playing down failures, a majority of these governments resort to censorship. A smaller number of Latin American governments rely on media guidance through a variety of mechanisms and pressures. And a few democracies take their chances with press freedom and official public relations to sell the programs of the administration in power.

THE SETTING

Latin America contains 23 nations stretched over 8 million square miles. This continent and a half contained 340 million people in 1981 and keeps adding citizens at a rate of 3 percent a year. The region's number one problem continues to be overpopulation, despite strenuous efforts by the Mexican and Colombian governments to promote birth control. In only two republics, Argentina and Uruguay, have the populations almost stabilized, with annual increases of only 1.7 and 1.2 percent, respectively.

Latin America stretches from the United States border southward to Tierra del Fuego, where Argentina and Chile pinch together into a continental tip near the Antarctic. The Caribbean contains Cuba, the Dominican Republic, and two Commonwealth Dominions, Jamaica and Trinidad-Tobago, both nations of English-speaking blacks in a demographic region where hybrid Spanish Indians, or *mestizos*, dominate.

These 23 nations range from one-third of an island called Haiti (French-speaking) to a half-continent called Brazil (Portuguese-speaking). Argentina, Uruguay, and Costa Rica have populations with white majorities. Brazil, Cuba, and Panama have large black minorities, and Haiti, Jamaica, and Trinidad have black majorities. The typical Latin American is a mestizo.

The Spanish language predominates in 18 of the republics. Yet 121 million Brazilians speak Portuguese and 15 million Indians in southern Mexico, Guatemala, Ecuador, Peru, Bolivia, and Paraguay speak Indian tongues rather than Spanish.

MEDIA DEVELOPMENT

Inasmuch as newspapers and magazines are published in Spanish and Portuguese, the Indians are cut off from the print media. And though Peru does have a limited number of radio broadcasts in Quechua, Paraguay in Guarani, and Guatemala in Maya, monolingual Indians tend to have only minimal contact with broadcasting through music.

In addition to minority languages, a factor limiting newspaper reading continues to be the relatively high prices of dailies within the context of inflation rates and per-capita income. In 1980 big-city dailies sold for the equivalent of 20 cents or more weekdays and 45 cents or more Sundays in the larger, more-developed republics. Rates of inflation in 1980 ranged from 24 to 40 percent in a majority of the Latin American nations and from 50 to 75 percent in a few republics, with Argentina and Uruguay suffering annual cost-of-living increases of more than 100 percent.

Contrasted with most Asian and African nations, the Latin American countries seem relatively prosperous, with the 1980 per-capita income reaching $2,600 in Venezuela, $2,000 in Argentina, $1,700 in Brazil, Chile, and Uruguay, and $1,200 in Mexico. All the Latin American nations but three had per-capita incomes above $600. But when inflation and internal distribution factors are considered, even in the more-prosperous republics, purchasing power remains meager for most citizens, limiting newspaper and magazine sales.

A periodical or metropolitan daily costs more than a loaf of bread. By contrast, the inexpensive transistor radio sells for the equivalent of a couple of dollars and can be maintained for six months with a battery costing approximately 25 cents.

The only factors not fitting this economic profile seem to be television receivers. Despite limited incomes which would logically limit purchases of TV sets, the growth in sales of these appliances during 1970–1980 was phenomenal, doubling the number of sets in use. The family TV set often was the only continuing source of entertainment.

Another factor limiting newspaper reading continues to be adult illiteracy in half of the Latin American nations. Uruguay and Argentina are 92 percent literate, Chile and Costa Rica 91 percent, and Venezuela 88 percent. In those nations, the official literacy rate and the actual functional adult literacy rate match. However, in at least 12 other republics, Census Bureau or Ministry of Education percentages for adult literacy are based on ability to read a limited number of basic words, including the name of each respondent. Functional literacy, which includes understanding a newspaper story, would yield far lower percentages.

Mexico and Peru each claim better than 70 percent literacy, but in each case almost one-third of the adults are functionally illiterate in terms of understanding a news story. Brazil reports 81 percent literacy, but perhaps 40 percent of its adults cannot read a newspaper.

MEDIA USAGE

Mass media abound in Latin America. In 1980 Latin America had 977 daily newspapers, almost 2,000 weekly newspapers, 2,987 standard-band, or AM (540 to 1600 kilohertz), radio stations, 730 short-wave radio stations, 287 FM (frequency modulation) radio stations, and 538 television stations. In addition, eight of the 23 nations had video cable systems which carried programs to communities marginally served by TV stations.

Latin America's total daily newspaper circulation in 1980 reached 22.6 million copies, with 97 million radios and 49.3 million TV sets in daily use. Ministry of Communications, import-export, and manufacturing tax data yield reasonably accurate receiver totals. As for newspaper circulations, the most professional and distinguished dailies authenticate circulation figures with the United States–based Audit Bureau of Circulation (ABC), the Inter-American Press Association's Office of Certified Circulation (OCC), or the Instituto Verificador de Circulaciones (IVC). Many other dailies inflate their circulation totals, but advertising agencies buying space in them are able to estimate circulations realistically, yielding figures used in this study.

Four times as many radios and two times as many TV sets are in daily use than there are daily newspapers sold, making radio Latin America's number one mass medium in terms of quantity. In terms of political impact and social significance, however, the large daily newspapers continue to dominate, for they are read by government and political officials and the civic leaders who shape public life. And only the dailies cover major national news in sufficient detail to be politically meaningful. Latin American broadcasting continues to emphasize entertainment, with news remaining a minimal program offering.

Hundreds of trade and professional journals circulate in Latin America, but general news magazines remain relatively limited in number and readership. No domestic magazine in Mexico exceeds the circulation in that republic of *Selecciones*, the Spanish-language edition of *Reader's Digest*, which in 1980 totaled 500,000 each month. Similarly, *Seleções*, the Portuguese-language edition of *Reader's Digest* in Brazil, at 770,000 circulation, led all Brazilian magazine readerships except that of *Manchete*.

Circulating in every Latin American nation except Cuba, the weekly news magazine *Visión* is read by more than 300,000 Latin American leaders who shape public opinion. Founded in 1950, *Visión* until 1979 was published by Alberto Lleras Camargo, former president of Colombia, and is now published by Mariano Grondona, who continues its traditions of journalistic objectivity, with factual backgrounding of major events in Latin America.

With a *Time* magazine format of news categories—world politics, finance, labor, fine arts—*Visión* usually runs 84 pages. From time to time it may report on criminal justice trends, fuel and energy problems, or foreign trade in Latin America. *Visión* has editorial offices in Mexico City, Bogotá, Buenos Aires, Santiago, and Washington, and for its Portuguese-language edition, *Visão*, in São Paulo.

At least three daily and two weekly newspapers published in English in Latin America have set standards for accuracy and objectivity which have influenced other papers in their respective nations. *The News* in Mexico City, the *Brazil Herald* in Rio de Janeiro, and the *Latin American Daily Post* in São Paulo, have influenced other Mexican and Brazilian dailies in a professional way. The weekly *Tico*

Times in San José has had similar influence in Costa Rica. But the weekly *Lima Times*, while often newsworthy, has not had any similar discernible effect on Peruvian papers. The dean of English-language newspapers in Latin America, the *Buenos Aires Herald*, published since 1876, has earned the respect of Argentine journalists for its continuing struggle to remain independent of governments imposing censorship on and off since 1943. In 1980 the circulations of these English-language tabloids ranged from 25,000 to 37,000, but their influence in setting high journalistic standards loomed large.

Expansion of national advertising in Latin America by advertising agencies in recent years has concentrated in four republics: Brazil, Mexico, Argentina, and Venezuela. Most of the multinational agencies with offices in Latin America are found in these four nations.

Big Brazil became the seventh advertising market in the world in 1979 with more than $2 billion in billings. Of the republic's 773 advertising agencies, nine of the largest are from Europe, Japan, and the United States. Agencies place 85 percent of all advertising in Brazilian media.

Mexico has 177 agencies which place 61 percent of all advertising in that republic. Argentina's 149 agencies place 65 percent of all advertising bought in that nation. Venezuela's agencies place 80 percent of its advertising.

FLOW OF NEWS

Associated Press, United Press International, Reuters of Britain, Agence France-Presse, Efe of Spain, ANSA of Italy, DPA of West Germany, TASS of the Soviet Union, and Prensa Latina of Cuba have client newspapers, broadcasting stations and networks, and magazines all over Latin America. Mexico, Brazil, and Argentina each have national news services. And since 1970, leading Latin American daily newspapers cooperatively have maintained LATIN, a regional news agency serving papers in every Latin American republic except Cuba and Nicaragua. In 1976 the Caribbean News Agency (CANA) began as an independent service with headquarters in Barbados, serving twelve Caribbean nations, including Jamaica and Guyana.

Since 1976, every year conferences by UNESCO have found the Third-World governments of Asia and Africa pressuring Latin American governments to endorse plans to finance a news service and thereby control the content of stories. This proposed official agency would "stress achievements of the Latin American nations instead of the negative emphasis of reporting crises."

The privately owned newspapers and broadcasting stations of the

Western Hemisphere, represented by the Inter-American Press Association and the Inter-American Broadcasters Association, have successfully discouraged this attempt to finance government propaganda in the guise of a news service. At the UNESCO conference in France in May 1980, the free-press nations of the Western world answered the Soviet-bloc and Third-World nations' advocating a program for development of communication in Latin America. The plan called for expanding government controls over the media.

Since its reorganization in 1950, the Inter-American Press Association (IAPA) at its annual meetings each October and its board meetings each March has issued detailed reports from its Freedom of Information Committee. In the case of autocratic governments sensitive to hemispheric and world opinion, the IAPA has been able to help editors and publishers recover from periodic repressions and censorship. In the case of a few powerful rulers—Fidel Castro in Cuba and, in earlier times, Juan Perón in Argentina and Rafael Trujillo in the Dominican Republic—the IAPA was not able to ease restrictions. But it helped end censorship in Brazil in 1978, wrested some minor concessions from the government of Chile in recent years, and in 1980 encouraged the new civilian government of Peru to return seven expropriated dailies to their former publishers.

The IAPA has warned publishers of the potential for governmental control of reporters through the device of licensing news personnel, ostensibly to ensure that professionally educated applicants be hired. In both Chile and Bolivia for awhile all working reporters and editors had to be members of the *Colegiado*, or Professional Association of Journalists. But employers can now hire nonmembers too.

In Costa Rica, Colombia, Honduras, Panama, Peru, and Venezuela, news personnel must get a certificate from a government agency. The problem arises often over educational qualifications. For example, in 1981 in Costa Rica, Stephen Schmidt of the *Tico Times* was sued by the Colegio de Periodistas (Professional Journalists Association) for working as a reporter without having Colegio membership. The Colegio refused to grant him that membership although he holds a journalism degree with honors from the Autonomous University of Central America (Universidad Autónoma de Centro América, or UACA), because UACA is a private institution, founded in 1975. When the licensing law was enacted in 1969, the government's University of Costa Rica was that republic's only university. The Costa Rican Supreme Court agreed to a 1982 review of such problems.

Venezuela passed a Colegio licensing law in 1972 and Colombia in 1975, but in neither nation has the government ever fully applied the law. In both nations journalists with three years of experience but without university training can obtain a license by passing an examination showing competency in grammar, communication law, and national history.

In several Latin American nations, journalist labor unions and professional societies have in recent years been encouraging better training for apprentice news personnel.

When it was established in Lima in 1975, the Latin American Federation of Journalists (Federación Latinoamericana de Periodistas, or FELAP) gave promise of working for higher professional standards for reporters and editors. But late in 1980, when FELAP's secretary general, Genaro Carnero Checa of Peru, died, the group became dominated by Ernesto Vera, head of the Cuban Union of Journalists. In 1981 FELAP took on a Marxist orientation, substituting ideological advocacy for traditional objectivity and press freedom as its major principle. Luis Jordá Galeana of Mexico succeeded in retaining FELAP's headquarters in Mexico City, blocking a move to Havana, but otherwise could not change its new orientation.

The IAPA has been working against the system of *mordidas*, or bribes, which compromise reportorial objectivity in at least 15 Latin American nations, from Mexico southward to Bolivia. But the economic factors extant in Latin America tend to obviate efforts based on ethical philosophy. In most Latin American cities, reporters struggle to live on low salaries in the midst of high annual inflation rates. They attempt to cope by moonlighting, often handling not only a full-time news job but also public relations or advertising jobs or freelance assignments, engendering conflicts of interest.

Governments leery of projecting harsh images by wielding overt censorship often try the alternative of bribery. Yet Latin America has managed to develop and maintain several praiseworthy and trustworthy major metropolitan daily newspapers, some professionally competent radio and television network news departments, and a relatively small number of informative and accurate news magazines.

NEWSPAPERS

Of the 977 daily newspapers in the 23 Latin American republics and dominions, perhaps 20 dailies in 12 countries rate as journalistically first-rate in terms of scope and variety of news coverage of their own nations. Brazil, Mexico, and Argentina can each claim three such papers; Peru and Colombia two each; and Costa Rica, Dominican Republic, Jamaica, Ecuador, and Venezuela one each. In three other nations—Cuba, Nicaragua, and Bolivia—one daily clearly dominates its nation's newspaperdom but is not free to report critically and in depth sufficiently to be included in the first-rate category.

Brazil

Latin America's largest nation, Brazil, is fifth among the nations of the world in land area (3.25 million square miles) and the twelfth largest nation on earth in population, as well as the largest Roman Catholic country in Christendom. Its 1980 population totaled 121 million and increases 3 percent annually. One-fifth of all Brazilians are blacks.

Two-thirds of the citizens are urban, with a dozen gigantic metropolitan areas tending to bunch newspaper circulation. Greater São Paulo and greater Rio de Janeiro are among the world's largest cities and together with the federal capital of Brasília (one-tenth the size of Rio) constitute the three news centers of this republic.

The Census Bureau claims eight out of every ten Brazilians are literate, but the Education Ministry reports only six of them can read a newspaper. In 1981 daily newspaper circulation totaled 5 million for 258 dailies. Three of these papers—*Jornal do Brasil, O Estado de São Paulo,* and *O Globo*—are the leading dailies of Brazil and among the best of the 20 most prominent papers in Latin America.

Brazil's most respected and influential daily, *O Estado,* is published in São Paulo, a city in 1981 with more than 14 million residents in its metropolitan area, in the state of the same name, which contains the republic's largest steel mills, biggest banks, and heaviest industries, including an automobile industry which turns out more trucks and cars a year than either the Soviet Union or Britain.

Estado's more than 450 reporters, editors, and correspondents ensure comprehensive coverage of industry, finance, and the governmental operations in the 22 states of this federal republic. Its sports news emphasizes soccer, Latin America's leading spectator and participant athletic activity. Its agricultural news includes columnists who are experts on coffee, of which Brazil is the world's largest producer.

Censorship ended in Brazil in 1978, but for a decade prior to that, *Estado* displayed courage and suffered fines as it defied government restrictions in covering politics. When it was founded in 1875 by 17 civic leaders, the paper adopted the slogan "representation and justice."

In 1891, two years after the monarchy of Emperor Pedro II had been replaced by a republic, Julio de Mesquita became the crusading publisher and general editor of *Estado.* Since 1969, his grandson, Julio de Mesquita Neto, has been publisher, assisted by his brother Ruy, with O.S. Ferreira as managing editor.

With a daily circulation of 250,000 and a Sunday circulation of 320,000, *Estado* ranks second in Brazil behind *O Globo* in sales and size of readership, but ranks first in quality of readership, being the required morning paper for governmental and civic leaders who shape the public life of the republic. Presidential cabinet ministers, state governors, big-city mayors, members of Congress, industrialists, and labor leaders follow *Estado*'s news and views.

Averaging 48 to 52 pages daily and 150 pages Sundays, *Estado* puts photos and stories of Brazilian events on its front page. Pages two and three carry editorials and letters to the editor. The editorials champion civil rights and democracy, oppose Communist nations' aggression abroad, and support entrepreneurship and the private sector and social reforms.

Estado runs at least six pages of national news, with coverage of the federal government in Brasília impartial, penetrating, and thorough.

This daily never carries fewer than eight pages of world news, giving more space to foreign stories than any other Latin American daily. The International Press Institute, the Inter-American Press Association, the María Moors Cabot awards of Columbia University, and various other entities have honored *Estado* for its excellent international coverage.

Estado maintains its own correspondents in Washington, Moscow, London, Peking, Paris, Rome, Havana, Mexico City, and six other capitals, and sends reporters to wherever events of worldwide significance are taking place. All its reporters have university degrees. The paper owns its own forestry and newsprint company.

Second in prestige to *Estado* is the Rio de Janeiro daily *Jornal do Brasil*, with a daily circulation of 200,000 and a Sunday circulation of 270,000. It runs 60 pages daily and 90 pages Sundays, including its own supplement.

Jornal's distinguished publisher, Manoel do Nascimento Brito, served during 1970–1971 as president of the Inter-American Press Association and continues in the 1980s as a champion of press freedom and quality journalism. Managing editor Walter Fontoura is one of Latin America's most noted journalists.

Founded in 1891 by the writer Rodolfo Dantas and three associates, *Jornal* did not reach its worldwide prestige status until the 1970s. Since 1977 it has resisted carrying government advertising in order to minimize official pressures on its coverage of national problems. *Jornal*'s investigative articles thoroughly expose organized crime, especially embezzlement, smuggling, and narcotics.

Jornal's own correspondents in 14 major cities of the world seek economic and social trends of concern to Latin America, with special emphasis for Brazilian interests. Inasmuch as seven African nations have become coffee exporters on the world market, its coverage of African affairs has intensified and expanded.

The paper's coverage of fine arts and entertainment are especially popular, including its reviews of Brazilian popular and folk music, including the sambas of Carnival time. Its movie, theater, and television reviews have brought success or failure to major productions. All its reporters have university degrees.

Jornal's computer word processors and video display terminals are part of its modern plant. It operates its own news agency throughout Brazil.

Third in importance among Brazilian dailies is *O Globo*, the republic's circulation leader, with 290,000 sales daily and 330,000 Sundays. Like the *Jornal*, only one-third of *Globo's* circulation comes from subscriptions and two-thirds comes from street sales, the reverse ratio from that for *Estado*.

Globo was founded in 1924. Unlike the other two leading dailies, this Rio de Janeiro paper has not remained independently critical of the federal government but since 1964 has given mild support to the successive administrations. It is owned by industrialist Roberto Marinho, who also owns the Globo television and radio networks. He maintains the O Globo Servico (OGS) news service for the affiliates of his networks and the newspaper plus a few other newspaper subscribers.

Video display terminals at *Globo*, at its OGS news bureaus, and its radio and TV stations are linked to computers for background information. *Globo* averages 48 pages daily, 90 pages on Sunday, plus a 20-page supplement on civic affairs on Tuesdays. This paper puts its national and regional news of Brazil on the first eight pages, then runs foreign news, except for a couple of top international stories which begin on page 1. With at least six pages for sports, its sports coverage sometimes takes more space than news of economics and business, and its page on major horse racing tracks has high readership. More consistently than other dailies, *Globo* runs the major stories from the government's National Information Service (Servico Nacional de Informações or SNI).

Globo's popular comic strip, "Beetle Bailey" from the United States, is called "Recruta Zero," with all references changed from the United States to the Brazilian army. The English comic strip "Andy Capp" has been Brazilianized as "Zé do Boné," with the soccer betting especially meaningful to Brazilians.

A Gazeta Mercantil, the nation's business and financial daily, considers itself the "*Wall Street Journal* of South America." It is published in São Paulo, Brazil's financial center. Another daily of national signifiance, the morning *Folha de São Paulo*, maintains editorial independence from the government and an editorial line neutral toward the major political parties. It is owned by a corporation which runs the major bus companies for São Paulo state and six smaller provincial dailies. The corporation also maintains the Folha News Service for its seven papers.

In the federal capital of Brasília, where the seat of national government was moved from Rio de Janeiro in April 1960, no major newspaper has yet evolved. The *Jornal de Brasília*, established in 1972, does an adequate job of covering the government, but the most informative reports about the president, his cabinet ministers, the Congress, and the Supreme Court come from the Brasília bureaus of the three elite papers of Rio de Janeiro and São Paulo.

Among provincial dailies, *Estado de Minas* in Belo Horizonte, capital of the state of Minas Gerais, has won awards for reporting public affairs from the Brazilian Press Association (Associação Brasileira de Imprensa, or ABI). Established in 1928, it serves a metropolitan area of 2.5 million population.

Another city of comparable size, Porto Alegre, capital of the state of Rio Grande do Sul, has *Correio do Povo*, which has been publishing since 1895 as the editorial voice of Brazil's cattle industry.

On the northeast coast, in Recife, another city of 2.5 million, the daily *Diário de Pernambuco*, often editorially expresses the views of the agricultural groups of six northern states.

In the port city of Salvador, the *Jornal de Bahia* reflects the trends in Brazil's fishing industry.

With the exception of *Estado de São Paulo*, which produces its own newsprint, Brazilian newspapers depend on newsprint from Carteira de Comércio Exterior, or CACEX, a foreign trade corporation in which the senior partner is the government's Banco do Brasil. CACEX thus gives the government indirect leverage with newspapers, allowing unstated guidelines beyond which papers cannot stray without running into operational pressures.

Nevertheless, since the end of censorship in 1978, antiestablishment papers have circulated freely, such as the far-left *Tribuna Operária* in Rio de Janeiro, and *Voz de Unidade* of the Communist Party of Brazil circulated in all major cities.

Mexico

Although Mexico's national territory of 750,000 square miles ranks it the third largest Latin American republic, after Brazil and Argentina, its population ranks it second only to Brazil. Its land area is almost one-fourth the size of the United States, but demographic disequilibrium strains its communication facilities, ensuring journalistic as well as political and financial dominance over national life by Mexico City and the two largest provincial cities of Guadalajara and Monterrey.

Despite intensive publicity campaigns in all the media since 1973 for the government's family-planning program, the population reached 70 million in 1980 and continues to increase 3 percent a year, although the increasing use of birth control will reduce that annual increment significantly by the late 1980s.

Half of all Mexicans live in 14 percent of the national territory, the central Valley of Mexico. Although the republic has 240 daily newspapers, provincial papers have grown slowly, reflecting the bunching in the three largest metropolitan areas of industrial payrolls and political controls, with Mexico City dailies circulating nationally among government and civic leaders. The three largest metropolitan centers—greater Mexico City, greater Guadalajara, and greater Monterrey—have 60 percent of the total daily newspaper circulation of the republic but contain only one-fifth of the nation's population.

Mexico's total daily newspaper circulation has leveled off at 5 million, whereas its broadcasting audiences continue to grow. Census Bureau figures show more than 72 percent of the adults to be literate, but one-third of the adults are not functionally literate enough to understand a newspaper story. Government officials and civic leaders, however, at every level of national life down to the local communities read newspapers avidly. And the press they read, while ranging from the Communist left to the rigid far right, in general is centrist and proestablishment, basically supportive of the Revolutionary coalition national leadership regardless of vigorous opposition among interest groups, and against numerous specific government policies. Mexico has developed bandwagon journalism.

Mexican mass media can best be understood within the perspective of the Revolution, always patriotically spelled with a capital "R" to distinguish it from the various revolts and insurrections of the past century. After the fighting of 1910–1920 to rid Mexico of age-old autocratic controls, the Revolution became an institutionalized set of social and economic reforms to which all successive governments have been publicly pledged. The interlocking Revolutionary coalition of reformers, industrialists, labor leaders, business executives, and politicians operate the government through the dominant Institutional Revolutionary Party (Partido Institucional Revolucionario, or PRI), with the press free to cover the opposition leftist and rightist parties.

An amendment to the federal Constitution in 1977 called the "Derecho a la Información" or "Freedom of Information" clause has eased government controls of official news sources somewhat. But counterbalancing that is an agent of the Ministry of the Presidency called coordinator of social communications. Through political patronage, government investments, newsprint distribution, bribes, the dominant political party PRI, and the progovernment Mexican Federation of Labor (Confederación de Trabajadores de Mexico, or CTM), the press remains basically proestablishment with a relatively small number of important papers able to challenge governmental actions without threatening the replenishment of the Revolutionary coalition.

Three Mexico City newspapers—*Excelsior, Novedades,* and *Uno Más Uno*—have the most impact and influence nationally of all Mexican papers and are among the 20 most prominent newspapers in Latin America. Not rating international notice but still significant within Mexico are the Mexico City dailies *El Universal, La Prensa, El Sol, El Día,* and *Ovaciones.*

Despite political pressures by President Luis Echeverría in 1976 which forced the firing of its outstanding editorial staff, *Excelsior* has recovered its prowess and status and in the 1980s remains Mexico's most influential and respected daily. Publisher Regino Díaz has rebuilt an elite corps of reporters for the collective ownership, *Excelsior* being a cooperative in which some 100 of the highest-level editorial and business employees hold a majority of the stock.

Within Mexico *Excelsior* is considered an institution, similar to the position held by *The New York Times* in the United States. Its nameplate carries the slogan "Newspaper of National Life," signifying it as Mexico's newspaper of record. *Excelsior's* weekday editions run 60 to 68 pages and its Sunday edition at least 90 pages plus a 16-page literary supplement called "Diorama de la Cultura" and a 16-page rotogravure feature magazine and a 12-page color comic section.

Those researching national affairs consult this daily's bound volumes or microfilm volumes. Every major library and top government official subscribes to *Excelsior.* Thus, this daily has an impact on Mexican public life far beyond its audited circulation of 190,000 weekdays and 220,000 Sundays. With rapid overnight air service, *Excelsior* circulates in some 70 cities all over the republic each morning. It has the most extensive newspaper home-delivery service in Mexico City, although 20 percent of its circulation comes from street sales.

Excelsior was founded in 1917 by Rafael Alducín to chronicle the new Mexico being shaped by the Revolution. In the 1950s Rodrigo de Llano raised the newspaper's professional level as did Julio Scherer García as publisher from 1968 to 1976. Scherer ended the long-time practice among Mexican papers of accepting *gacetillas,* or paid space in the news columns. A business or labor union or politician could even purchase a front-page story for 100,000 pesos (then $8,000). Since 1974 *Excelsior* has refused paid publicity stories, but many other Mexican papers continue to accept them.

Excelsior under Scherer vigorously investigated and reported on civil rights violations by the Mexican government and did not hesitate to criticize the Echeverría administration directly. At a general meeting of the cooperative stockholders in July 1976, through fraudulent procedures the Scherer staff of editors were fired and replaced by sympathizers of Echeverría. After he was replaced as president of Mexico in December 1976, the daily began to regain its political independence and journalistic stature.

Mexico's second most prestigious newspaper, the morning daily *Novedades*, with a circulation equaling *Excelsior's*, is owned by the O'Farrill family, which also owns part of the four commercial video networks of the Televisa holding corporation. The O'Farrill family also owns the XEX radio network, the English-language *News*, the Mexico City afternoon paper *Diario de la Tarde*, and four provincial dailies in Acapulco, Puebla, Campeche, and Mérida, as well as 20 special-interest magazines.

Novedades was established in 1934 by Ignacio Herrerías and purchased in 1948 by Rómulo O'Farrill, Sr., a leader in the automobile industry. His son, Rómulo O'Farrill, Jr., is executive publisher as well as manager of the other media. *Novedades* exercises care and accuracy in reporting national affairs, with special effort to chronicle the petroleum industry, inasmuch as Mexico is the world's fourth largest oil exporter.

Ranking third among Mexico's dailies in national status is a relative newcomer and the only elite paper in tabloid format, *Uno Más Uno,* founded in 1977 by Scherer García and some of his reporters and editors who had been purged from *Excelsior* in 1976. He went on to devote himself to the independent news magazine *Proceso* while the staffers organized *Uno Más Uno* into a cooperative, electing Manuel Becerra Acosta as executive publisher.

This paper's circulation is a modest 90,000 weekdays and 115,000 Sundays, but its readership includes many influential leaders because it has earned the status of principal responsible journalistic critic of the Mexican government.

In 1978 *Uno Más Uno* broke the news of party disharmony within the PRI and scooped the establishment dailies with the news that Mexican President José López Portillo would replace Carlos Sansores Pérez as head of the PRI. The President commented that the new paper brought responsible and constructive debate into Mexican politics.

In May 1980 *Uno* was the first Mexican paper to point out that Rosa Luz Alegría, then assistant minister of planning and the budget, had been former President Echeverría's daughter-in-law and that her career had survived a divorce and overcome the unpopularity of associating with the controversial former president, who had lost his power in the establishment.

Uno next uncovered the fact that Echeverría had turned over to Ms. Alegría the Cempae educational research institute to be developed as an anti-United States, pro-Third-World entity, but that she changed its orientation to Mexican nationalism and put her brother, Pedro Alegría, in charge of it. Later President López Portillo appointed her as the first woman in a Mexican cabinet as minister of tourism.

Uno uses AP, UPI, AFP, Efe, and LATIN news services and just enough copy from Cuba's Prensa Latina service to satisfy the militant leftists among its readers. It keeps its top reporters at the Ministries of the Presidency, Finance, Planning and Budget, and Commerce.

Formerly one of Mexico's Big-Three dailies, *El Universal* still has some national impact. Its daily circulation of 175,000 puts it in fourth place among Mexican dailies (behind *La Prensa, Ovaciones,* and *Excelsior*). *El Universal* was founded in 1916 by Félix F. Palavicini, who built it into a quality paper. In the 1940s and 1950s Miguel Lanz Duret as publisher made it an elite daily. In the 1960s its reporting prowess began to lessen.

In 1976 Mexican President Echeverría and several of his close associates became major stockholders in the Mexican Editorial Organization (Organización Editorial Mexicana, or OEM) corporation which purchased *Universal*. With Echeverría's former foreign minister, Emilio O. Rabasa, dominating *Universal*'s board, the daily became an apologist for controversial land expropriations and pro-Third-World foreign policies.

By 1981, executive publisher Juan Ealy Ortiz Garza had given *Universal*'s coverage of national affairs enough balance to restore some of its standing among activists of the 1976–1982 López Portillo presidency. However, former President Echeverría writes occasional columns in *Universal* which echo his essays in the Popular Socialist Party magazine *Siempre*, far to the left of the dominant PRI's position on major policies.

La Prensa remains the largest Mexican newspaper, a position it has held since the 1950s, with a daily circulation of 280,000 and a Sunday circulation of 310,000. This tabloid, which averages 52 pages an issue, began in 1928 and is a cooperative. A vigorous supporter of organized labour, *Prensa* is much more critical of the private sector's management than is *Excelsior* or *Novedades* but joins them in supporting the administrators of the government's own corporations. One-third of its news stories deal with government and politics but only 6 percent with foreign news, the latter category being three times as large in the elite dailies.

Another tabloid, *El Día,* is the fourth major daily organized as a cooperative (along with *Excelsior, Uno Más Uno,* and *La Prensa*). Farther to the political left than *Prensa, El Día*, established in 1962, supports some policies of the Popular Socialist, Socialist Workers, and Communist Parties, but rallies to the president and the PRI on key issues.

In 1981 *El Día's* employee assembly elected as its executive publisher Socorro Díaz, making her Mexico's most prominent woman publisher of a major daily.

With approximately the same circulation as *Día's*, 73,000, is the government's Mexico City daily *El Nacional*. In 1929 *Nacional* was incorporated by the dominant party, the PRI, but later the federal government bought majority stock control. Every six years, after a new president of Mexico takes office, he names *Nacional's* publisher. All these publishers have been politicians. For example, Luis Farías went from broadcasting director for the Gobernación Ministry to governor of the state of Nuevo León to *Nacional* publisher, and since 1979 has been leader of the PRI in the Congress. *Nacional* is a valuable source of news about top bureaucrats and federal budget priorities.

The daily *Ovaciones*, established in 1947, second in circulation only to *Prensa* with a daily total of 228,000, thrives on news of sports, crime, entertainment, and sensation.

The other daily with some national significance is *El Sol de México*, established in 1965. Its status comes from being the anchor paper in the capital of Mexico's largest newspaper chain, the García Valseca string of 36 provincial dailies, each named *El Sol de* followed by the name of the city or state or region.

José García Valseca, an army reserve colonel, was an advertising salesman for newspapers and magazines in the 1930s. In 1941 he created *Esto*, a large-circulation sports periodical, and then began to create provincial dailies which gave Mexico its first hinterland papers which were politically neutral in local affairs, proestablishment in national matters, and filled with business and labor stories from all over the republic. His *cadena* or chain, built its own CGV news service.

By 1970, he had spent far beyond his income or earning potential and could no longer make payments on loans from the government's development bank, Nacional Financiera. A government investment corporation, SOMEX, purchased the GV chain, and in 1976 sold minority stock in the CGV to *Universal's* parent corporation OEM. Like *Nacional*, the GV papers support the government which owns them.

Among Mexico's provincial dailies, the outstanding paper is *El Norte* of Monterrey, whose managing editor Ricardo Omana stresses objective coverage of national industrial and business news. Its publisher, Alejandro Junco de la Vega, has never hesitated to criticize federal government policies, even when threatened with temporary curtailment of newsprint by the government's paper importer and distributor PIPSA.

Argentina

Argentina's national territory covers 1 million square miles, but its 26 million citizens crowd into its northeast corner in a few metropolitan areas. Greater Buenos Aires, encompassing suburbs up to 70 miles from its downtown, holds almost 14 million residents, or half of the country's population. The province of Santa Fe, adjacent to the province of Buenos Aires, contains the city of Rosario, whose metropolitan area has 1.5 million residents, and a similar nearby metropolitan area for the city of Córdoba, less than 400 miles from Buenos Aires.

The Federal District and the two provinces hold two-thirds of the republic's people, leaving the other 20 provinces relatively empty. The Buenos Aires daily newspapers easily dominate the nation journalistically.

More than 92 percent literate, Argentina has a daily newspaper circulation total of 4 million for its 120 dailies, giving it the highest ratio of papers per 1,000 persons in Latin America.

Buenos Aires has three leading dailies—*La Prensa, La Nación,* and *Clarín*—which are among the 20 most prominent papers in Latin America.

Argentina's most prestigious newspaper, *La Prensa*, remains one of the best-known dailies in the world because of its many decades of dedication to the principle of objective coverage of world and national news and its long-time struggle for press freedom.

La Prensa was founded on October 18, 1869, by Dr. José Clemente Paz, to be completely independent of government, with a policy of never accepting government subsidies. Its code of ethics was summarized in its slogan "Truth, Honor, Freedom, Progress, Civilization."

His grandson, Alberto Gainza Paz, as publisher during 1943–1977, built *La Prensa* into one of the world's elite dailies, struggling with censorship during the Juan Perón era of dictatorship. The paper was confiscated by the government during 1951–1955. Again during an era of military governments from 1966 to 1973 and since 1976, *Prensa* has suffered fines, harassments, and jail sentences for some of its staffers as it has stretched the limits of censorship as far as possible to report the news. Publisher Maximo Gainza continues the tradition of the Gainza and Paz families of dedication to truthful reporting of the news, even as censorship continues.

La Prensa remains smaller in readership than *Clarín* and *La Nación*, with a daily circulation of 120,000 and a Sunday circulation of 150,000, certified by auditors of the Instituto Verificador de Circulaciones (IVC). Its circulation in the 1980s has shrunk to half of what it was in the 1960s, because military governments have arbitrarily taxed it at maximum rates and withheld substantial government advertising placed in other dailies which are not as adamant in defending criticism of officialdom. Extensive official advertising is placed by the government's news and advertising agency Telam.

Prensa's format continues to be what it has been for decades, running 28 pages daily and 60 pages on Sundays, with well-edited lean verbiage chronicling the highlights of world news. Front-page stories of national life often include wire copy from UPI, Efe of Spain, and Reuters of Britain, because foreign correspondents can file some sensitive reports about Argentine government and economics which domestic correspondents cannot.

This paper assigns trained economists to cover Argentina's stock-market (the Bolsa de Comercio), and most austerity measures of the government, inasmuch as the annual inflation rate has continued to be the highest in Latin America.

Prensa's Sunday literary section reviews articles from the top literary journals of Latin America and its book reviews include a few controversial books. The column "Conferences for Today" alerts the public not only to meetings which they might attend but also to closed meetings affecting public life. Such listings sometimes are the only public reporting of certain government conferences.

Argentina's other elite daily, *La Nación*, was founded in 1870 by Bartolomé Mitre, former president of Argentina. As chief executive of the republic during 1962–1968, Mitre had held regularly scheduled press conferences. As a publisher, he had *Nación* assign a reporter full time to monitoring the daily schedule of the Argentine president.

During World Wars I and II, the Korean and Vietnam wars, and the recent periodic fighting in the Middle East, *Nación* maintained a correspondent in the war zones to find Latin American trade angles. This paper tries to file a story each day on pensioners and the Argentine social security system.

Nación's circulation of 275,000 and 350,000 Sundays puts it in second place to the daily *Clarín*, whose IVC-certified daily circulation of 490,000 and Sunday circulation of 822,000 makes it the largest daily in Latin America and one of the major newspapers of the world in distribution.

A morning tabloid, *Clarín* often features soccer, horse racing, boxing, boating, and other sports, and the entire entertainment spectrum. Politically it supports the government, Argentine nationalism, and the General Federation of Labor (Confederación General de Trabajadores, or CGT), the dominant organization for urban workers. The CGT was the core of Juan Perón's political base and remains a power in public life.

Clarín's Sunday supplement "Cultura y Nación" remains popular with fiction and drama fans. The paper's superficial, neutral coverage of politics makes it innocuous. It remains Argentina's largest paper by entertaining as much as informing, with photos of girls in blue-jeans, coverage of field hockey and South American and European auto racing, and crossword puzzles. Except for *La Prensa's* comic strip from the United States, "Peanuts" ("Rabanitos"), *Clarín* has Argentina's most popular comic strip, "La Vida Cotidiana," drawn by Horacio Altuna. It tells the daily adventures of a 30-year-old bachelor reporter named Loco Chávez, who has romances with glamorous women while observing humorous episodes of Argentine family life.

Raúl Kraiselburd, active with the Freedom of the Press Committe of the Inter-American Press Association, as editor has made *El Día* of La Plata into Argentina's outstanding provincial daily, stressing impartial reporting and wide-range coverage of economics.

During 1981 government corporations, such as the petroleum agency and the railroads, ran huge deficits, as inflation soared and the currency continued to be devalued. *La Prensa's* top columnist, Manfred Schoenfeld, continued to report on these crises, even though police in civilian clothes beat him physically. Through remarkable courage, Argentina's distinguished newspaper kept the nation's reputation for distinguished journalism alive.

Democracies' Dailies

In Latin America's three most democratic nations—Columbia, Venezuela, and Costa Rica—press freedom nourishes some readable and informative dailies.

Colombia, with almost a half-million square miles of territory, by 1981 had a population of 25 million and by 1985 was projected to be larger than Argentina. The nation is three-fourths urban and its capital, Bogotá, dominates the republic politically. Colombia has two elite dailies which are among the top 20 of Latin America, *El Tiempo* of Bogotá and *El Colombiano* of Medellín.

Two major parties, the Liberal and the Conservative, have long dominated Colombia's political system and the major newspapers of the republic have affiliated with one or the other party. In 1911 the Santos family, leaders in the Liberal Party, launched *El Tiempo*. In the 1930s and 1940s Eduardo Santos as publisher built it into the elite paper of Colombia and one of the major dailies in the world. Santos served as president of Colombia during 1938–1942.

El Tiempo's daily circulation totals 190,000 but zooms to 325,000

Sundays. Its Saturday circulation runs 208,000 because of a weekend supplement.

El Tiempo editorially helped rally the nation into adopting a political coexistence to end violence, a plan unique in Latin American history. From 1948 through 1957 the republic suffered civil strife, as the Liberal and Conservative parties battled in hundreds of provincial towns, with 200,000 killed in 9 years. The two parties then amended the Constitution to provide for a National Front 16-year period in which Liberals and Conservatives would alternate in the presidency every four years and share equally seats in Congress. *Tiempo's* editorials, columns, and reports helped bring about that 1958 –1974 National Front. Since 1974, this Liberal paper has continued its fair and accurate coverage of Conservatives, which it stressed during the coexistence period.

Tiempo marshals its reporting strength to expose narcotics smugglers. The large criminal activity in drugs would be worse without *Tiempo's* frequent journalistic indictments.

In the second largest city of Colombia, Medillín, the editorial voice of the Conservative Party, the daily *El Colombiano,* ranks as the republic's second elite paper and one of the 20 best in Latin America. Its coverage of business and industry of the entire nation is first-rate. Established in 1912, *Colombiano's* circulation runs half that of *Tiempo's.*

Also in Bogotá are two dailies of some national standing. Founded in 1887, *El Espectador*, a supporter of the Liberal Party, has Colombia's largest weekday circulation of 250,000 but falls behind *Tiempo* with its Sunday edition of 257,000. It frequently runs essays by Latin America's top writers. The daily *El Siglo*, a supporter of the Conservative Party, was founded in 1936 by Laureano Gómez, who served as president of Colombia durîng 1950–1953. Gómez in the 1940s turned *Siglo* into a profascist organ, cheering the Axis and jeering the Allies. His son, Alvaro Gómez, as publisher has improved *Siglo* into a responsible paper, serving democracy, with a circulation less than half that of *Tiempo.*

Costa Rica in Central America is a democracy with a population of 2 million, some 350,000 of whom live in the metropolitan area of the capital, San José. An open society 91 percent literate, with one of Latin America's best school systems, Costa Rica since 1948 has had the opposition out of power win political control of the government over the incumbents four times in honest elections. Within that democracy press freedom has flourished.

All five of Costa Rica's dailies are published in San José and circulate nationally, with a total circulation of 265,000. One paper, a morning tabloid, *La Nación*, is the leading newspaper and one of the top 20 dailies of Latin America.

Established in 1946 by moderates and conservatives of what later would be the National Unification Party and now is the National Unity coalition, *La Nación* has a daily circulation of 130,000 and 145,000 on Sunday. It is read by all key government leaders even though the opposition National Liberal Party (PLN) holds a substantial number of seats in Congress and posts in the executive branch.

In 1971 the democratically balanced Congress seriously considered a law requiring newspapers of more than 50 pages to give 6 percent of their space to verbatim statements from government officials. *Nación's* persuasive editorial campaign defeated the bill. *La Nación* runs 84 pages daily and 100 pages Sundays.

Nación's vigorous in-depth investigatory reporting in 1978 drove Robert Vesco from his Costa Rican haven. Vesco, American millionaire financier, was a fugitive from justice charged with many stock manipulations in the United States. This *Nación* exposure forced the demise in 1978 of the Vesco-financed San José daily *Excelsior*.

La République, the second most prominent Costa Rican daily, was founded in 1950 by the late Otilio Ulate, who was president of the republic. Inasmuch as it also supports Unity conservatives, *La Nación* makes special efforts to be impartial in its news columns, giving the PLN, the Popular Republicans, and the Christian Democrats the same quality of coverage afforded the Unity coalition.

Costa Rica's oldest newspaper, the daily *Prensa Libre*, founded in 1889, supports the PLN of former President José Figueres. A nationally circulated weekly newspaper, *Libertad*, militantly anti-United States and pro-Cuban, speaks editorially for Marxists and other far left groups.

In the Caribbean, the Dominican Republic after 31 years of censorship under dictator Rafael Trujillo and a 1965 civil war, slowly developed qualified democracy; and under Presidents Joaquín Balaguer and Antonio Guzmán during 1966–1982, press freedom was very rarely abused. In the capital of Santo Domingo, the leading daily is *El Caribe*, published and edited by Germán Ornes, a long-time leader and former president of the Inter-American Press Association. *Caribe* covers all political parties accurately and thoroughly reports on the nation's economy and public works projects.

Also in the Caribbean, with the coming into office of Edward Seaga as prime minister of the Dominion of Jamaica in November 1980, the long-time pressures on the press by the pro-Marxist government of Michael Manley ended. For years the Kingston newspaper, *The Daily Gleaner*, struggled to remain free of government guidance and now flourishes. Its objective—thorough reporting of Caribbean affairs—not only is sought by Jamaica's leaders but is read by key leaders in Trinidad-Tobago and other Caribbean nations.

Not only part of the Caribbean and South America, but also

rivaling Brazil and Mexico as Latin America's major power is Venezuela, with an oil-rich economy which makes it one of the world's five biggest producers and exporters of petroleum. Better than 88 percent literate, Venezuela's 15 million citizens seem lost in a national area of 350,000 square miles, but they are three-fourths urban and crowd into 14 percent of the territory. Almost 3 million live in the Caracas metropolitan area.

With the highest per-capita income in Latin America, Venezuelans have saturated themselves with television and radio receivers. The republic's total daily newspaper circulation of 1.5 million serves 2.5 million households.

Since 1958, honest elections every five years have twice seen the opposition Christian Democrats (COPEI) win the government from the incumbent Democratic Action (AD) party. In this democracy, press freedom thrives.

Venezuela's leading newspaper, *El Universal*, ranks among the 20 top dailies of Latin America. It was founded in 1901 and by the 1940s was featuring the leading Venezuelan intellectuals as columnists, including Rómulo Betancourt, who was president of the republic from 1959 to 1964. The distinguished author Arturo Uslar Pietri has written special columns for *Universal* for more than two decades.

The late Luis T. Núñez Sr. was publisher of *Universal* for 30 years. His son, Luis Teófilo Núñez, the current publisher, was president of the Inter-American Press Association during 1980–1981. Managing editor Luis Alfredo Chávez is one of Latin America's noted journalists.

Universal, a morning Caracas daily, has a daily circulation of 110,000 and a Sunday circulation of 135,000. Its coverage of the petroleum and iron ore industries has been lauded by trade magazines in those fields. *El Nacional*, a Caracas morning daily of comparable circulation, offers good coverage of other major Latin American republics with its own correspondents. The largest Caracas daily, the tabloid *Ultimas Noticias*, with a circulation of 250,000, for a long time was an afternoon paper but now comes out mornings. It was founded in 1941 by Miguel A. Capriles, whose family owns another Caracas afternoon daily, *El Mundo*, as well as several magazines, including the news magazine *Elite*.

Caracas also has the English-language *Daily Journal*, founded in 1945 by its current publisher, Jules Waldman. This tabloid is also read by Venezuelans as well as English-speaking foreign residents, partly for its columnists, ranging from William F. Buckley, Jack Anderson, and Rowland Evans–Robert Novak to Ann Landers.

Cuba

Although Cuba's population totals only 10 million on an island 800 miles long, it rates world attention far more than its size would otherwise indicate. Since 1961 it has been Latin America's full-fledged Communist state and a satellite of the Soviet Union, which spends more than $10 billion a year in subsidies just to keep its economy functioning. With a Russian military brigade and thousands of civilian Soviet administrators entwined in the Cuban government ministries, only 90 miles south of Florida, Cuba's strategic importance will continue.

Cuba's lack of an independent press did not begin with Fidel Castro. During most of its existence as a republic beginning in 1902, Cuba had either a bribed or censored press.

During the dictatorship of Fulgencio Batista from 1952 through 1958, Cuba developed the highest ratio of television and radio receivers in Latin America and a literacy rate of 75 percent. That literacy rate is now 90 percent, but newspaper circulation has not increased accordingly. Castro's charismatic personality and demagogic style of building support through frequent speeches has relied on the broadcast media.

The Communist Party of Cuba (Partido Comunista de Cuba, or PCC) remains the dominant power in Cuban public life, more so even than the government. The few daily newspapers in Cuba all belong to the PCC or its affiliate groups, not the government. No rival political parties, ideologies, or media criticism are allowed. Cuban leaders make no pretense of guaranteeing the right of dissent to challenge their authoritarian government and Marxist social order. The Constitution declares that the press is an instrument for "creation of a collective conscience," not primarily to inform people about what is happening.

One newspaper sets the standards for reporting and commentary for all other Cuban media, the Havana morning daily *Granma*, the official organ of the PCC. In October 1965 *Granma* was founded by a merger of *Hoy*, which had been the organ of the PCC, and *Revolución*, which had been the organ of the "26th of July Movement," Castro's original rebel force which contained some non-Communists when Castro seized government power on January 1, 1959. Not until early 1961 did the Communists purge the non-Communists from the Movement.

Because of a continuing newsprint shortage resulting from the PCC's difficulty in buying expensive imported paper, *Granma*'s daily circulation seven days a week is kept at 600,000. *Granma* also publishes a weekly summary of the daily editions. This *Granma Review* is printed in an English-, a Spanish-, and a French-language edition, with 100,000 copies distributed abroad to groups likely to be sympathetic to Cuba.

Granma's magaging editor, Jorge Enrique Mendoza, was a veteran editor of Communist underground newspapers before Castro took power.

With 12 pages daily and 16 on Sundays, *Granma* carries more foreign than domestic news. It runs reports on Communist nations, Marxist guerrillas and Communist groups in Latin America and the Third World, and highly critical stories about the United States and Western democracies from the Cuban government's news service Prensa Latina (PL). PL has exchange agreements for stories from the news services of the Soviet Union, East European Communist nations, Iraq, and other Third World nations.

Very few of the domestic stories resemble spot news. Most are encrusted with ideological views and speculation. A reader must wade through generalities before actually finding any specifics about a news event. Editorial opinions crowd out statements of fact, with phrases such as "It is a pleasure to announce," "Unworth imperialists took criminal action," and "Heroic struggle by liberation fighters showed courage."

Although there are 23 cabinet ministries and nine other major government agencies, a typical issue of *Granma* will contain no more than reports on four of them, but every issue has a major story from the PCC.

The only other nationally circulated daily is the Havana afternoon paper *Juventud Rebelde*, published by the Union of Cuban Youth of the PCC, with a circulation of 195,000. It echoes *Granma* but features items of interest to young adults.

The PCC also publishes the other nine Cuban dailies, which are provincial newspapers in 9 of the 14 provinces, such as *Guerrillero* in both eastern and western regions. Each of these nine papers circulates within its own province. Each edition runs only eight pages. Circulation for the nine provincial papers totals 122,000.

The Cuban Federation of Labor (CTC) publishes a newspaper three times a week, *Los Trabajadores*, with a circulation of 300,000.

A major obligation of Cuban media is to make nationally known official positions of PCC and government leaders. Editors determine the importance of a story by the person or agency used as its source. Any announcement by Fidel Castro carries more weight than one by a deputy cabinet minister or even another member of the PCC Politburo. Statements by Vice-President of Cuba and PCC Vice-Chairman Carlos Rafael Rodríguez are considered more important news than any statements by the foreign minister or any other cabinet officer.

Peru

After 12 years of governmental guidance of the media, Peru has begun to recover its press freedom. But the elected civilian administration of President Fernando Belaúnde has not dismantled the requirement of all official news sources to emphasize governmental goals. This attunement had been nurtured by the social revolution of the military governments in power from October 1968 to July 1980.

Lima's daily newspapers were expropriated in 1970 and 1971 to bolster support for the institutionalized reforms, and during 1975–1978 were assigned to workers associations in various trades and professions. One daily spoke for agricultural groups, one for industrial workers, and so on. However, within each civil association, rival employee groups could not agree on unified editorial positions for their vocational sector, and the unsuccessful custodial publisher plan was phased out. It was Latin America's only attempt at building a newspaper system in which each paper represented a sector of the economy. The Lima dailies were returned to their original publishers in 1980, but minority percentages of each paper's stock were available on the Lima stock exchange for the paper's employees or other interest groups.

Peru's national territory of a half-million square miles in 1980 had only 18 million citizens, with nine out of ten living on the coastal plain or in nearby cities of the Andes mountains. One-third of the Peruvians speak Quechua or another Indian language rather than Spanish. And despite an official literacy rate of 70 percent, half of the adults cannot read a newspaper.

Of the total daily newspaper circulation of 1.2 million, 88 percent represents sales by the Lima dailies, which also are national papers in that they circulate among civic and government leaders throughout the republic.

El Comercio, founded in 1839, is the second oldest paper in Latin America, antedated only by *El Mercurio* in Chile. Its slogan "Order, Liberty, Knowledge" indicates its orientation. It has always supported tradition over violent change.

A morning Lima daily, *El Comercio* is Peru's leading newspaper and one of the top 20 dailies of Latin America, with a daily circulation of 100,000 and a Sunday circulation of 161,000. During the custodial publisher era it had been assigned to the farm workers sector, but now again speaks for the landowners, the investor aristocratic families, and the exporters.

Oscar Miró Quesada is publisher and Alejandro Miró Quesada is editor in chief. A weekday edition usually runs 52 pages and Sunday editions 70 pages, including a literary supplement.

With the exception of one or two top foreign stories, the front page is usually devoted to national news. News of Lima, major provincial cities, and the national government and economy fill the front half of the first section, with world news coming last. News of fine arts, entertainment, sports, and social events make up the second section.

Editorially *Comercio* supports President Belaúnde's majority coalition of the Popular Action and Popular Christian Parties, the conservatives in Congress, in a multiparty system with leftist minority parties. Editorials often criticize the quality or operations of public utilities, such as telephone or bus services.

Peru's second most prominent paper, the Lima daily *La Prensa*, founded in 1903, was built into an outstanding newspaper by the late Pedro Beltrán, its publisher from 1950 to its expropriation in 1974. His death in 1979 brought nationwide praise from all walks of life. The paper was returned in 1980 to his widow, Miriam Beltrán, as owner. Executive publisher is Arturo Salazar Larraín, who also writes an editorial page column.

With a circulation approximately equal to *Comercio's*, *La Prensa* runs twice as much world news as its rival. Foreign stories make up 20 percent of *La Prensa's* general news, relying heavily on AP, UPI, ANSA, and Efe services. In covering national news, *Prensa* makes a special effort to report on industrial activities, including the processing of fish products, a key factor in the economy. *Prensa* editorially is the voice of importers and retail merchants. Politically it makes a special effort to cover the Aprista party, the centrist-conservative group which remains both prolabor and anti-Marxist, difficult in a nation in which many labor leaders are Marxists.

Lima morning daily *La Crónica*, a tabloid, is owned by the family of the late Peruvian President Manuel Prado, and editorially speaks for financiers.

The daily *Expreso* is owned by Manuel Ulloa, finance minister and chief of cabinet for President Belaúnde. *Expreso* never mentions nepotism in government. *La Prensa* and *El Comercio* both occasionally point out that Ulloa is a cousin of the president's wife. They further mention that the president's brother, Francisco, heads the Chamber of Deputies in Congress. Also, a cousin of the president heads the National Elections Board, two other cousins run the government's electricity corporation Electroperú, and another cousin heads the government's iron ore mining corporation Hierroperú. Informally such nepotism helps maximize support for the government by official news sources.

Since 1981 another Lima daily, *El Diario*, speaks for the Communist and Socialist Parties. This tabloid is published by the leftist magazine *Marka*, whose publisher is also editor of this daily.

Other South American Papers

Of Chile's population of 11 million, almost 4 million live in the greater metropolitan area of Santiago. The five Santiago daily newspapers account for 60 percent of the total 900,000 newspaper circulation in the republic. Better than 91 percent literate, Chileans include almost no Indians or non–Spanish-speaking minorities.

Although press freedom existed from 1925 to 1970, on occasion governments attempted to pressure or restrict newspapers. During the turbulent civil strife of 1970–1973, when Marxist President Salvador Allende faced a citizenry two-thirds of whom opposed him, pressures and counterpressures became fierce. Since a military government took power in September 1973, press censorship has been imposed. A 1981 Constitution continues such military rule to 1989.

Limited criticism of the government is allowed mainly in two news magazines. All the newspapers except one support the government uncritically. That exception, *El Mercurio*, stretches the limits of censorship to report arbitrariness in public administration and economic problems is depth. Chile's leading paper, the Santiago morning daily *El Mercurio*, is one of the 20 outstanding dailies of Latin America. Its daily circulation of 300,000 and Sunday total of 375,000 are the largest in the republic.

El Mercurio in the port city of Valparaíso, owned by the same Edwards family corporation as its more prominent Santiago namesake, was founded in 1927, making it Latin America's oldest existing newspaper. The more prominent Santiago *Mercurio* was founded in 1900. The same corporation also published an afternoon Santiago tabloid, *Ultimas Noticias*.

During the 1960s Agustín Edwards built *Mercurio* into an elite daily. After President Allende threatened *Mercurio* over trumped-up tax irregularies in late 1970, he made a deal with the government to cancel expropriation in return for his resigning as publisher. Politically neutral Fernando Leniz served as publisher until the military government's censorship intensified in 1977. Current publisher, Arturo Fontaine Aldunate, has stood up to the government as best he can without organized political support, as political parties remain suspended. He was winner of numerous journalism awards as an editor in the 1970s.

Mercurio runs 58 pages daily and up to 80 pages Sundays. It publishes a weekly eight-page summary of its daily editions, *Mercurio Internacional,* sold in Chilean provincial cities and in 16 Latin American republics, the United States, and Europe.

Since 1975 the government has published its own Santiago daily,

El Cronista, which reports most governmental activities with glowing enthusiasm. *Cronista* had changed its name to *La Nación*.

Uruguay, 92 percent literate, with a population of 2.7 million which remains stable, finds more than half of its citizens living in the greater Montevideo area. Its capital papers dominate the republic. From 1903 to 1973, a free press nurtured some of Latin America's best journalism. But military intervention came in June 1973 in the wake of runaway inflation, economic collapse, and widespread violence by Tupamaro Marxist guerrillas. Since then, press censorship has lowered Uruguayan journalistic standards.

One elite daily remains. The Montevideo morning paper *El Día* was founded in 1886 by José Batlle. He was president of Uruguay in 1903–1907 and 1911–1915 and the nation's chief social reformer, creating Latin America's first welfare state. For decades *El Día* championed social security, socialized medicine, and public housing, seeing them put into practice. The paper pushed Uruguay into becoming the first Latin American nation with women suffrage 1919. Even with the decline in world prices for wool, mutton, wheat, and beef exports —Uruguay's chief income—in the 1950s and 1960s, *Día* continued editorially to praise subsidies for domestic fuel and commodities.

Still today Uruguay's leading paper, *El Día* has switched its economics from liberal to conservative, preaching against budget deficits. It retains its quality level of writing. The conservative Montevideo morning daily *El País* and the evening tabloid *El Diario* are the circulation leaders with 170,000 daily sales each. A former elite daily, *La Mañana* has been reduced by censorship into a routine paper emphasizing official announcements.

Bolivia has a population of 6 million, with 1 million living in or near its capital of La Paz. Almost two-thirds of the people speak Aymará or Quechua rather than Spanish. Less than one-third of the adults are literate.

Press censorship prevails in Bolivia, but one La Paz daily, the morning *Presencia*, manages to criticize the government. *Presencia*, established in 1952, is owned by the Catholic Church, and is the only church-owned paper in Latin America that is the leading daily of a nation. It runs 14 pages weekdays, twice that Sundays, but has a Monday sports supplement in tabloid form running 32 pages in four colors. The La Paz daily *Hoy*, an evening tabloid, has a similar Monday sports supplement.

Bolivian circulation leader with 100,000 daily and 125,000 Sundays is *El Diario*, a morning La Paz daily founded in 1904. Bolivian papers rely on the Spanish news service Efe for many top foreign stories.

Ecuador has a population of 8 million, with 1 million living in the capital of Quito and a similar number in the port city of Quayaquil. When it ended 8 years of military government in 1979 and returned to elected civilian rule, Ecuador ended formal censorship but still suffers from official restrictions on news sources. Ecuador's leading newspaper is the Quito daily *El Comercio*, established in 1906. Jaime Mantilla is its publisher. *Comercio* rates as one of the 20 most prominent dailies of Latin America.

The largest Ecuadorean daily is in Guayaquil, *El Universo*, with a daily circulation of 170,000 and a Sunday total of 190,000. *Comercio* covers economic problems and social trends in depth, whereas *Universo* stresses sports, entertainment, shipping news, and human-interest stories.

Central America

Central America's land area for six small republics equals California in size, for a population of 22 million. In the discussion of democracies, Costa Rica's press was covered.

Nicaragua suffered press censorship under Anastasio Somoza Sr., sons Luis and Anastasio R., and two other presidents from 1937 to 1979; but for most of that time the Somoza governments had opposition and criticism from the Managua daily *La Prensa* and from a few radio stations. After the Sandinistas won the 1979 revolution and took power, a two year unsuccessful struggle for press freedom ensued, as the Marxists consolidated power and the media lost out. Now even valiant *La Prensa* can chronicle only most public events with great care, avoiding criticism of the government as the price for its existence. All other media follow the guidelines and orders of the Sandinistas.

La Prensa remains the leading newspaper and strives for objective reporting of the major facets of national life. This morning daily was founded in 1926 and remains the republic's circulation leader with 40,000 daily sales, all by street vendors, because the government prevents subscription deliveries. From 1956 to 1978 the late Pedro J. Chamorro as publisher periodically suffered jail terms for defying censorship and consistently criticizing the government in a professional, responsible way.

In January 1978 an unidentified gunman killed Chamorro. Sandinistas blamed supporters of the Somozas. In June 1981 a Nicaraguan court convicted a man who had been exposed by *Prensa* as a smuggler as the person who hired the gunman.

Prensa's publisher is Jaime Chamorro, Pedro's young brother. Editor is Pedro J. Chamorro Jr. Government restrictions on newsprint importation reduced the daily edition from 24 to 16 pages. The paper is forbidden to mention food shortages and the extensive unemployment, plus other sensitive topics on the censor's list.

The government publishes its own daily, *Barricada*, which follows the Marxist line, giving more space to news of Cuba, the Palestine Liberation Organization, and Communist-bloc nations than to Nicaraguan events. Its editorials are violently anti-United States. World news from the Soviet Union's TASS is rewritten under the logotype New Nicaragua News Agency (ANNN). The government also publishes another Managua daily, *El Nuevo Diario*, which echoes the stories in *Barricada*.

El Salvador threw off censorship when a Christian Democratic reform junta overthrew a military government in October 1979. Since 1980, however, the Marxist-led Democratic Revolutionary Front guerrilla warfare has pressured the government into renewing censorship. Three dailies in the capital of San Salvador account for most of the nation's daily newspaper circulation of 270,000. A morning tabloid, *La Prensa Gráfica*, started in 1903, is published and edited by brothers José and Rodolfo Dutriz. Another morning daily, *El Diario de Hoy*, covers agricultural and economic news fully. The afternoon daily *El Mundo* has the most extensive sports coverage. With help from the Copley newspaper chain of California, *Prensa Gráfica* maintains the republic's best makeup and editing standards.

Violence-bedeviled Guatemala has censorship as the government continues to put down guerrilla warfare. More than half of the 6 million citizens speak Indian dialects of Maya, leaving the mass media, except for radio music, more to the Spanish-speaking urban minority. All six of the nation's daily newspapers are in Guatemala City, site of Central America's first newspaper in 1729. The one quality paper is the midday daily *El Imparcial*, established in 1922. For decades it has struggled against censorship and maintained the best journalistic standards in the republic. *Imparcial's* publisher is David Vela. Its circulation is slightly less than the largest paper, the morning *Prensa Libre*, which has a daily circulation of 59,000. *Prensa Libre's* tabloid format features many action photos. It avoids political controversy. Of its 64 pages, usually 12 deal with social events and 8 to 12 with sports. Its most extensive reports are local events in the capital.

Honduras suffers from widespread illiteracy and government censorship. The largest daily in the republic is a provincial paper, the morning *La Prensa* in San Pedro Sula, founded in 1964 and edited by Wilmer Pérez. It has a circulation of 48,000 certified by the Audit Bureau of Circulation. Of the four dailies in the capital of Tegucigalpa, *El Día* and *El Cronista*, both morning papers, do the best job of reporting national news.

Panama ostensibly enjoys press freedom in that there are no official censors stationed at the six newspapers. However, the government continues to hold minority stock in the dailies, and utilizes the threat of tax irregularities and various legal technicalities from compliant politicized courts to guide the media. The morning daily *La Estrella de Panama*, founded in 1853, retains its status as the republic's leading newspaper. Publisher Tomás Altamirano pays the highest reporters' salaries in the nation. Managing editor Juan Carlos Duque emphasizes world news from the AP and Reuters, reflecting Panama's status as a shipping crossroads of the world through its canal.

MAGAZINES

Aside from the *Reader's Digest* Spanish- and Portuguese-language editions and the hemisphere-wide *Visión*, the widest-read magazines in Latin America are in Brazil.

Manchete, Brazil's largest, is a weekly news magazine in Rio de Janeiro with a circulation of 800,000. It has the size format of *Life*, running 138 pages with one-fourth of the news columns devoted to photos. Its publisher, Adolfo Bloch, also owns a television and a radio network and publishes textbooks for public schools in all 22 states.

Manchete's interviews resemble those in *People* magazine. Each issue has eight or nine features on Brazilian national life, usually including something on movie and TV stars, soccer, and industry. Foreign stories often include interviews with a United States entertainer, European government leaders, and the Pope. A recurring feature on consumer goods criticizes questionable advertising campaigns and alerts readers to consumer values.

Almost as large with 750,000 circulation is the weekly news magazine *Veja*, with a *Time* format. It is published by Editôra Abril, a corporation which also owns 100 trade and professional magazines, being the technical publisher for the big republic. Based in São Paula, *Veja* maintains its own daily mail service to the federal capital of Brasília, as well as around-the-clock electronic communication. Its editor, Elio Gaspari, a former leftist militant, has become Brazil's leading establishment critic of the government. *Veja's* book reviews range from popular fiction to scholarly volumes. Its industrial reports are widely read in Brazilian financial circles.

In Mexico, one weekly news magazine, *Tiempo*, serves as a periodical of record of national life and has done so since its founding in April 1942 by the late journalist and author Martin Luis Guzman. Today its publisher, his son Martin Luis Guzman West, continues the tradition of accuracy and detailed background for major national stories. With a *Time* format of standing categories for domestic and foreign news, fine arts, sports, and literature, each issue runs 72 to 80 pages.

Tiempo's weekly overview of the republic's economy, finance, and industry is a treasure-trove for researchers and observers of Mexico's public life. It summarizes major new laws and key statements by cabinet ministers, political and labor leaders, and spokesmen from various sectors of society. It runs texts of vital speeches by the president of Mexico.

Because of a similar physical appearance to *Time, Tiempo* circulates in the United States under the name *Hispano Americano.* Government and civic leaders in all the Latin American republics are subscribers. University libraries throughout the Americas preserve *Tiempo's* back volumes.

Tiempo's coverage of federal, state, and local government provides a precise, concise, detailed presentation. Progovernment *Tiempo* manages to criticize various leaders within the establishment and to report on major problems without attacking the basic positive image of the Revolutionary coalition. It does omit some newsworthy information which would hurt that image.

Two other major Mexican news magazines reflect a proestablishment editorial stance. The weekly *Revista de Revistas*, published by the newspaper *Excelsior*, emphasizes a dozen stories about civic leaders, public works, universities, social security, retail shoppers, and city life. *Impacto* is a weekly published in Mexico City but financed by the Llergo Corporation of Monterrey, with shares held by the Garza Sada and Alfa investor groups. Most of its stories deal with social trends, family life, and entertainment.

Mexico has a growing market for women's magazines, with a Spanish-language edition of *Cosmopolitan* selling 130,000 copies a month. Since 1965 the women's field has been dominated by *Claudia*, a monthly with 150,000 circulation, owned by the O'Farrill family which publishes the daily *Novedades*. Editor Hilda O'Farrill features family life, homemaking, women in careers, and fashions.

Providing responsible antiestablishment criticism is the weekly magazine *Proceso,* founded in 1977 by publisher Julio Scherer García, who had been ousted as publisher of the daily *Excelsior* in 1976 by Echeverría supporters. Many of *Proceso's* staff had worked under him at the paper. *Proceso* editor Miguel López Azuara adapted some of the *Time* format of news categories plus bylined political and economic analyses by intellectuals and philosophers ranging from left to centrist. *Proceso* looks at inflation, unemployment, family planning, slum housing, agriculture, narcotics traffic, government budgets, and foreign debts.

Siempre, a weekly magazine published by the Popular Socialist Party (PPS), is the best-known voice of the Marxist left in Mexico. Nationally it is also read by those in the Socialist Workers Party

(PST), the Communist Party (PCM), and by critics of the establishment of various other affiliations, including dissidents working in the bureaucracy.

In Argentina, a quality news magazine, the weekly *Veritas*, was founded in January 1931 by the late F. Antonio Rizzuto. His son, publisher Francisco A. Rizzuto, stresses economics and finance, with emphasis on industrial and agricultural production, banking, and retail trade. Another leading Argentine news magazine also stresses business affairs. *5 Areas* appears twice a month, covering industry, finance, labor relations, and commerce.

Because of government censorship, general news magazines no longer flourish in Argentina. However, the weekly *Convicción*, published on Sundays, engages in mild criticism of public affairs, its owner being Admiral Emilio Massera, a member of the ruling junta. It also features entertainment, sports, and literary news.

One Argentine weekly magazine with general news coverage is *Análisis-Confirmado*, published by Fernando Morduchowicz. It began in 1961 as *Confirmado* and acquired its current name in 1973. After a military regime closed the magazine *Primera Plana* in 1972 for being effectively critical of government activities, several of its staff were hired by *Análisis*. Its *Time* format of news categories now offers few political stories.

Peru has been enjoying a growth in the quality and quantity of its news magazines since 1980. Its two elite weeklies, *Caretas* and *Oiga*, flourished in the 1960s but contracted in circulation and content in the 1970s under intermittent censorship. Now their circulations are steadily increasing.

Started in 1951, *Caretas* is published by Enrique Zileri, one of Peru's most distinguished journalists. *Caretas* probes economic and social problems and chronicles abuses of civil rights as well as the field of criminal justice. It is politically liberal.

Oiga, published by Francisco Igartua, is to the political left of *Caretas* and a vigorous critic of the government. It interviews officials and politicians with thoroughness.

Peru's weekly news magazine field also has: *Opinión Libre*, politically conservative; *Marka*, which supports the Marxist left, edited and published by Jorge Flores, who also publishes the small daily *El Diario*; and *ABC*, the organ of the Aprista political party, made up of moderates and conservatives who are prolabor.

Venezuela has one of Latin America's leading weekly news magazines, *Resumen*, which is influential in Venezuela's national life and read by leaders of both major political parties as well as civic leaders. Publisher Jorge Olavarría investigates any hints of corruption in government. *Resumen* has an impact greater than its circulation of 170,000 might indicate, because every university, school, and public library preserves its back issues for reference.

Despite censorship of its newspapers and broadcasting, Chile's government allows three weekly news magazines to serve as escape valves for political frustration by running criticism of government within limits. The leading news magazine in Chile, *Qué Pasa*, published in Santiago by Emilio Sanfuentes, carries more details than its rivals do about economic problems and restrictions on opposition politicians. It translates foreign criticism of Chilean policies found in the *Washington Post*. The other two Santiago magazines, *Hoy* and *Mensaje*, are milder in their antigovernment coverage, emphasizing more general news of the republic.

BROADCASTING

With a radio in daily use for each 3.5 Latin Americans and a television receiver in daily use for each 7.5 Latin Americans, the broadcasting media pervade and envelop Latin American life.

Brazil

Brazil's population groups into 25 million households, fewer than the 27 million television receivers in daily use. Some 7 million of these sets are at public sites—bars, schools, community centers—each drawing its own mass audience, projecting some national nighttime total audiences of 80 million televiewers. Brazil has become one of the world's major video markets.

In 1981 Brazil got its fourth commercial television network, the Manchete Television System (SMT) owned by the news magazine *Manchete*, with stations in the 18 largest cities plus affiliates in 12 other cities.

The largest video network, Golobo Television System (SGT), has affiliates in all 22 states. It is owned by the Rio daily *Globo*, and like that paper and like the other networks, is progovernment in its news reporting.

A third network, Brazilian Television System (SBT), has affiliates in the 20 largest cities and in all 22 states. It succeeded the defunct Tupi Network, which took bankruptcy in 1981. SBT is owned by a corporation headed by video entertainer Silvio Santos, the Johnny Carson of South America. A fourth network, SNT, serves affiliates in 17 states live but circulates taped programs to stations in 5 other states. Two nationwide cable systems provide movies and other programs not available on commercial networks for a monthly fee.

Globo TV has the most extensive news coverage. Its 1 P.M. "Hoje" ("Today") news and its 10:30 P.M. roundup, also a half-hour report, draw larger audiences than does news on the other networks. Although censorship ended in 1978, TV and radio news scripts and tapes must be preserved for 30 days in case the government questions violations of national security guidelines or if someone wants to sue for defamation.

An Intelsat satellite provides all Brazilian TV and radio networks with instant global communication for news. Its networks have exchange agreements with networks in the United States, Japan, and Western Europe.

Brazilian television relies not much on information but mostly on entertainment for its large audiences. Music, comedy, variety, and sports events draw millions of viewers. Most popular of all are the daily serialized dramas or soap operas, both daytime and nighttime. A top-rated nighttime soap opera, "The Star", claims Latin America's largest video audience. It focuses on the career of a character who rose from nightclub magician to become industry's most powerful executive. Through psychological tricks, he always defeats his opponents.

The government requires an hour a day from commercial television stations for cultural and educational programs rather than operate its own video transmitters. For radio, however, the government operates 52 standard-band (AM) and shortwave transmitters, and the Rádio Nacional network. There are 579 AM, 139 shortwave, and 63 FM privately owned commercial radio stations. Brazil's eleven largest cities serve Latin America's largest FM audiences with folk, popular, and classical music.

Rádio Educadora, a 50,000-watt station in Brasília, anchors the government's Rural Educational Radio (RER) network. The Ministry of Communications has an agency, Empresa Brasileira de Radiodifusão, or Radiobrás, which produces the "Hora do Brasil," telling of the government's major public works and social services and policies. Originally started in 1936 as a weekly program on a special network of every radio station in Brazil, this "National Hour" became a nightly feature in the 1970s but is now again a Sunday night program.

Through shortwave transmission, Radiobrás broadcasts in English to North America and Australia, in French and English to Europe and Africa, and in Spanish to the other Latin American republics. Radiobrás in Portuguese airs a 15-minute nightly newscast, "Repórter Brasileiro," on four shortwave frequencies for remote jungle and rural areas of Brazil.

In Rio de Janeiro, the station Rádio Jornal, owned by the daily *Jornal do Brasil*, has one of the best-edited and most-popular news programs. In the cities of São Paulo, Porto Alegre, and Rio de Janeiro, respectively, Rádio Continental stations anchor regional networks of the same name with large audiences in seven states.

Mexico

More than 95 percent of Mexican households have radios in daily use and two-thirds of these households have TV sets in daily use. Considering the fact that one-third of the adults are not literate enough to read a paper, a majority of Mexicans hear the news.

The Federal Radio and Television Law includes the federal tax law requirement that every radio and television station must provide up to 12.5 percent of its daily hours of transmission for public-service announcements or other programs from the government. This free air time is defined as a tax on broadcasting paid for in service instead of money. Stations air announcements of educational, cultural, social, political, athletic, and civic events. Government reports tell about commercial development, social security, public health, imports and exports, and production in industry, agriculture, and mining.

The senior cabinet entity, the Ministry of Gobernación (Interior or Internal Affairs) has a Bureau of Radio, Television, and Cinema (RTC) in charge of all government programs aired over privately owned as well as government-owned outlets.

Political campaign broadcasts are limited to four hours of free radio and TV time per month for three months prior to federal elections to be shared by officially recognized political parties. Commercial networks and stations must furnish the air time free but the production costs and operations are handled by the RTC.

The oldest continuing government program, begun in 1937, is the "National Hour," aired each Sunday night over a network of every radio station in Mexico. The RTC hires the leading entertainers and writers to intersperse reports about government activities with songs, comedy routines, and dramatic sketches.

Each radio and television station in Mexico daily devotes 30 minutes to the government's adult literacy programs. Some series offer formal lesson plans, whereas others concentrate on informal lectures.

The government operates 17 AM, 11 shortwave, and 5 FM cultural radio stations. In addition there are 18 radio stations operated by state universities throughout the republic anchored to Radio Universidad in Mexico City, owned by the National Autonomous University of Mexico (UNAM). Although their budgets are administered autonomously, they are funded by the federal government and subject to its guidelines. These stations run four newscasts a day.

The Ministry of Education operates Radio Educación, a Mexico

City station which airs three newscasts daily. News for the non-commercial stations comes mainly from the government's Notimext service.

The leading commercial radio network in Mexico, headed by station XEW in Mexico City, is owned by the Azcárraga family. The XEX, RPM, and smaller tape networks have affiliates all over the country among the 585 commercial radio stations. In Mexico City, the largest audiences for radio news tune to XEW, XEX, and Radio Mil. The most prominent provincial radio station for regional news is XET in Monterrey, which obtains some of its reports from the daily *El Norte*.

The government has reduced its annual increment in population from 3.6 percent in 1976 to under 3 percent currently through its Family Planning Centers. These centers are vigorously promoted on TV talk shows and by radio soap operas produced by the RTC and aired by the commercial networks as well as by the government's Rural Radio tape network.

Three privately owned commercial television stations in Mexico City—Channels 2, 4, and 5—are owned by the O'Farrill and Azcárraga families. A fourth Mexico City commercial television station, Channel 8, is owned jointly by the government and private investors. Each station anchors its own network of provincial affiliates, with the four networks competing for advertising and audiences. However, the four entities belong to a holding corporation, Televisa, with the private investors of the Alarcón Corporation, which publishes the daily *El Heraldo*, owning 25 percent of Televisa's stock. Thus the government is a junior partner of the private sector in Televisa, which oversees the commercial networks.

In addition, the government owns and operates Channel 13 as a Mexico City commercial station and anchor for its own provincial affiliates. Each of the 118 commercial television stations in Mexico affiliates with either one of the four Televisa networks or with the Channel 13 network.

Televisa has a centralized news division headed by Miguel Alemán, Jr., son of the former president of Mexico, Miguel Alemán, Sr. Each network prepares some of its own news programs, and each provincial station prepares some local and regional news reports.

Every night Televisa produces a one-hour news program called "24 Hours," as the most elaborate and best financed video report in Latin America. With correspondents via satellite live or on tape from major Latin American, European, United States, and Mexican cities as the flow of news indicates, "24 Hours" runs on the Channel 2 network and its highlights are repeated the next morning on the Channel 4 network.

The government funds the National Polytechnical Institute's Channel 11 in Mexico City and the University of Sonora's Channel 8, and through RTC operates the Mexican Rural Television (TRM) tape network, which offers public service programs free to all stations.

Two nationwide cable systems offer for a fee television programs from the United States and from Mexican networks in communities where direct reception is not adequate.

Televisa reaches into the United States, owning 75 percent of the Spanish International Network (SIN), which supplies programs to the 11 full-time Spanish-language TV stations in the United States. In addition, Televisa owns one-fifth of each of five of those stations through a subsidiary, Spanish International Communications Corporation. Under the United States Federal Communications Act, the legal limit of foreign ownership of a broadcasting station is 20 percent.

South America

Argentina, with 9 million radios and 5 million TV sets in daily use for its population of 26 million, has both media in almost all its households. Private owners operate 88 AM, 27 shortwave, and 19 FM commercial radio stations. The Belgrano, Mitre, and Splendid radio networks serve every major city in Argentina. Their news programs are censored by the government's Dirección General de Radio y Televisión (DGRT).

The DGRT also runs the Radio Nacional network for the 10 AM and 10 FM noncommercial government stations. The government also owns 26 other AM commercial radio stations which are run exactly like the private outlets, belonging to the CAR radio network.

Government noncommercial AM stations include Radio Municipal owned by the city of Buenos Aires, LY 10 of the National University of Santa Fé, LR 11 of National University of La Plata, and LS LL owned by the Province of Buenos Aires. The government operates FM station Radio Sarmiento in Buenos Aires and FM stations in nine provincial cities.

The Argentine government owns the Buenos Aires television stations Channels 9, 11, and 13, as well as their networks serving 30 provincial TV stations. The government also owns Channel 8 in Mar del Plata and Channel 7 in Mendoza. Seven of the provincial TV stations are owned by public universities or city governments. All television news programs in the republic come under the authority of the DGRT.

In Peru, the government owns 25 percent of the privately operated commercial radio stations. For music and entertainment, including soap operas, Lima's private stations Radio Central, Radio Miraflores, Radio Excelsior, and Radio Crónica compete for the largest audiences. For news, however, the government's Radio Nacional network has more listeners throughout Peru than do the private stations.

The government owns Channel 7 in Lima as well as 51 percent of the 30 commercial television stations of Peru. Channel 13 in Lima is assigned to the public universities as an educational outlet. Lima's four commercial channels and their respective networks have news departments directed by commentators under contract to the sponsors of the newscasts and are not employees of the stations.

In Colombia, the government's National Institute of Radio and Television, called Inravisión, operates the two commercial video networks of 30 provincial stations anchored by Channels 7 and 9 in Bogotá, and the educational network headed by Channel 11. The government operates its own Radio Nacional network and stations. Colombia also has 285 AM, 53 shortwave, and 18 FM privately owned commercial radio stations. The Catholic Church operates the Radio Sutatenza network, emphasizing literacy and basic education.

In Venezuela, with an oil-rich economy and full-scale democracy, 148 AM, 53 shortwave, and 42 FM privately owned commercial radio stations compete fiercely with professionally produced news programs. Caracas's four television channels and their respective networks in the few provincial cities holding most of the population put 1.7 million TV sets in daily use for a republic with 14 million people.

In Ecuador most of the 228 AM, 52 shortwave, and 8 FM radio stations are privately owned commercial outlets. The government's Radio Nacional station in Quito airs frequent news reports. Shortwave station HCJB ("Voice of the Andes") is licensed to the World Missionary Fellowship of Florida and Quito and assigned 15 frequencies. HCJB produces evangelical and educational programs in English, French, German, and Russian aimed at Europe and North America, in Portuguese for Brazil, in Quechua for Indians in Peru and Bolivia, and in Spanish for Central and South America.

Ecuador has 16 television stations, with programming from channels in Quito and Guayaquil serving the republic.

Paraguay has three commercial television stations, Cierrocora and Este in the capital of Asunción and Televisora Itapua in Encarnación. All 32 AM, 7 shortwave, and 2 FM radio stations are privately owned except for the government's Radio Nacional in Asunción. All commercial newscasts are censored. Asunción station Radio Guaraní broadcasts in Guaraní, the Indian language half of the population speaks in addition to Spanish.

In Bolivia, the government owns the ENT network of commercial television stations in La Paz and five provincial cities. The other video network, also with six stations, is the educational chain anchored by the La Paz channel of the University of San Andrés. All but 6 of the 106 AM, 29 shortwave, and 5 FM radio stations of Bolivia are privately owned. In La Paz, the government's Radio Illimani airs extensive newscasts. News programs on private stations are censored.

In Chile, there are 3 million TV sets and 4 million radios for a population of only 11 million. The three television stations in Santiago —Channels 4, 9, and 13—are owned by Valaraíso Catholic University, the University of Chile, and Santiago Catholic University, but the national network of 23 stations covering the republic is owned by the government. Its holding corporation, Televisión Nacional, supervises news but allows other programs to operate as privately produced commercial shows.

The Chilean government's Radio Nacional in Santiago anchors a nationwide network of 25 stations, which function as commercial outlets. News comes from the Orbe News Service, which the government pays to carry its reports. Leaders of the suspended Christian Democratic Party own 29 radio stations in major cities. Some 109 AM, 56 shortwave, and 19 FM radio stations are privately owned and carry censored news. Radio Reloj stations in Santiago, Valparaíso, Viña del Mar, and Concepción have the largest audiences for music and entertainment programs.

Cuba

Cuba has 750,000 TV sets and 2.1 million radios, slightly higher totals than when Fidel Castro ousted Fulgencio Batista on January 1, 1959. With the island saturated with broadcast transmitters and receivers, Fidel Castro has often conducted government by television, using video to rally mass support. Many major policies are first aired by him on television and then rubber-stamped by the Council of Ministers, the Central Committee of the Communist Party of Cuba (PCC) already having formulated them.

The government owns the two television networks, with the two Havana channels each anchoring a network of 13 provincial stations. The PCC designates the editors of the government's Institute of Radio and Television (IRT) who produce TV and radio news, not primarily to inform but to support development of a Marxist state.

Although IRT obtains considerable film coverage of world news from Soviet Union and Eastern European broadcasting systems, it buys additional tapes and films from Mexico, Italy, and France. IRT then rewrites the narration from the Cuban government's Prensa Latina news service to conform to PCC guidelines.

The IRT operates the government's three national radio networks. The Radio Liberación network (formerly the CMQ chain) with a 50,000-watt Havana station and affiliates in 9 other cities, blankets the republic from Piñar del Río to Santiago. The Radio Rebelde network connects Havana with 11 provincial stations across the island. And the Radio Reloj network links Havana with stations in 12 other cities.

In addition, two regional networks connect to anchor stations in Havana. Radio Revolución (formerly the "26th of July" chain) connects five cities in western Cuba, and Radio Progreso links six cities in eastern Cuba.

Via shortwave, RHC (Radio Havana Cuba) broadcasts in eight languages on four frequencies eight hours every night. RHC broadcasts in Spanish, English, French, Portuguese, and Arabic. It beams commentary in Quechua to Indians in Peru and Bolivia, and in Guaraní to Indians in Paraguay, and in Creole to peasants in Haiti. Stories claim PCC achievements in Cuba, in African nations, in Nicaragua, and encourage Marxist guerrilla warfare in the Third World.

Central America

In Nicaragua, the Sandinista Marxist government controls all broadcast news. It operates the three television channels which, with three repeater transmitters, blanket the republic. The official Dirección Nacional de la Radio y Televisión (DNRT) also runs Managua radio stations Voz de Nicaragua, Radio Maravilla, and Radio Sandino. Each of these anchors a network of affiliates in the seven largest provincial cities. The Catholic Church owns Radio Católica but its news is prepared by Sandinista laical reporters working with Maryknoll priests and nuns who publicly support Marxist liberation theology.

In Guatemala, the government operates radio station TGW and its repeater transmitters, whereas the other radio stations are privately owned. Two national networks are Radio Cadena Popular and Radio Reloj. The government censors news on radio and the Guatemala City television channels which, with repeaters, also serve the republic.

In Costa Rica, all stations are privately owned except for the government's Radio Universidad owned by the National University. Radio station Foro del Caribe airs religious programs. Radio Cadena Nacional connects Radio Reloj in San José with affiliates in the six largest provincial cities. The four television channels in San José anchor three affiliates each in the other regions of the small republic. Radio Noticias del Continente is a tape service which airmails taped news about Costa Rica to subscriber stations in Mexico, South America, and Western Europe.

In El Salvador, the Catholic Church owns radio station YSAX, and private owners run Radio Cadena Central stations and other major stations, as well as the seven television channels of the nation.

GOVERNMENT-PRESS RELATIONS

Counting the dominions of Jamaica and Trinidad as part of this geographic region, Latin America has 23 nations. Of these only Costa Rica, Colombia, Venezuela, Jamaica, and Trinidad enjoy full press freedom without any significant official restrictions.

Mexico, Peru, Brazil, Ecuador, the Dominican Republic, and Panama are free of government censors and enjoy relative amounts of media autonomy but suffer enough official pressures and guidelines that they must be classified as having press systems with guidance.

Cuba, Haiti, Guatemala, El Salvador, Honduras, Nicaragua, Guyana, Bolivia, Chile, Argentina, Uruguay, and Paraguay suffer government press censorship.

In Mexico, the press remains basically proestablishment through political patronage, the entwinement of government contracts and services and the dominant PRI political party, government investments, newsprint distribution, and bribes.

Under Mexican law, all production, importation, and distribution of newsprint comes under authority of the public-private corporation PIPSA (Producer and Importer of Paper, Inc.). PIPSA subsidizes the price of imported and domestic newsprint. If a publisher tried to buy paper directly from a foreign producer, he would have to pay an 80 percent ad valorem tax, whereas publishers pay a 5 percent tax on less expensive PIPSA newsprint. Publications receive paper quotas based on their circulations and the number of pages of each issue.

PIPSA's ability to extend credit to periodicals with cash-flow problems ensures self-restraint among most papers when criticizing governmental actions. PIPSA's board of directors consists of publishers of Mexico City's major dailies and magazines plus the head of the Association of Newspapers of the States. The government employs three commissioners to run PIPSA and to administer a Publications Classification Commission (CCP), which enforces a code of ethics.

A Mexican newspaper inciting a breakdown of law and order would be a violation of that code, prompting suspension of newsprint, pending a federal court hearing. Since PIPSA's establishment in 1935, fewer than a dozen times has it permanently withheld newsprint from publications, the most celebrated case being the closing of the Communist magazine *Política* in 1968 after that periodical called for riots to try to cancel Mexico's hosting of the Olympics.

By investing in the García Valseca newspaper chain and the television networks of Channels 13, 11, and 8, the Mexican government influences journalism. By being able to get up to 12.5 percent of radio and TV air time of private stations, the government exerts even greater influence. By paying reporters bribes (*igualas*) in the form of public relations consultant fees, officials guide media coverage of public affairs. And the interlocking governmental and political hierarchy of cliques (*camarillas*) ensures Mexico a bandwagon journalism of widespread voluntary proestablishment viewpoints in reporting and editing.

In Peru, the government corporation National Industrial Commercialization Enterprise (ENCI) administers all importation, production, and distribution of newsprint. ENCI under a 1971 law has authority to end the supply of paper to any publication which incites the overthrow of the government.

From 1974 through 1978, Peru attempted a system of Custodial Publishers whereby the government assigned expropriated newspapers to workers associations each daily representing a different trade or profession. With the return of elected civilian government in 1980, these papers were returned to their private owners, with the proviso that employees of a paper can purchase minority stock in it.

Reform laws of the social revolution of military governments during 1968–1980 are still administered by the civilian government, which exerts pressures through patronage and government investments to get favorable media coverage. The president of Peru appoints a director for the National System of Information (SINADI), who serves as liaison between cabinet ministers and reporters covering the national government.

Peru's government owns 51 percent of each television station and 25 percent of each radio station, in addition to operating its own radio network which dominates broadcast news. Through extensive nepotism and political alliances, the administration of President Fernando Belaúnde effectively influences official news sources.

In Brazil, the government's Banco do Brasil owns the newsprint corporation CACEX (Portfolio of Foreign Trade), distributing newsprint to the newspapers and magazines. CACEX sets limits on journalistic attacks on the government. Any which would curtail operations of a key agency would bring restrictions in paper supplies to the offending publication.

All four of Brazil's national television networks are licensed to progovernment corporations. Other media find that if they are supportive of key administration policies, government development agencies will extend them loans and subsidies.

In Argentina, the Ministry of Press and Broadcasting (Secretaría de Estado de Prensa y Difusión, or SEPYD) maintains a 14-point *Procedures Code for the Media*, requiring the promotion of national identity, an orderly society, and the family as an institution, in the selection of news stories. Censors at newspapers, magazines, and broadcasting stations eliminate words they consider obscene and censure stories highly critical of the government whose sources are persons without specific authority or expertise on the subjects at issue. In other words: no freedom of speech for citizens who oppose the government.

In Chile and Uruguay, censors eliminate stories from the media coming from Communist, Marxist, and far-left sources. Media censors suppress stories which challenge the legitimacy of the military-backed governments or call for their ouster, and stories which demand an end to major public policies.

In Cuba, the Communist Party (PCC) dominates the government and the media. Fidel Castro, his brother Raúl, Carlos Rafael Rodríguez, and 18 other men hold the top posts in the PCC Central Committee and in the government's Council of Ministers, with these 21 leaders simultaneously each holding three or more government and party offices. Through the Radio and Television Institute, the government's news service Prensa Latina, and the PCC newspapers and magazines, 24 editors work with those 21 top government-party officials to shape each day's budget of national and foreign news. Politics, not traditional news values, set priorities and define what constitutes news in Cuba.

In Nicaragua, the Sandinista government similarly sets news values and priorties based on political objectives.

In Guatemala, El Salvador, and Honduras, governments censor the media primarily within a framework of military security, in response to continuing guerrilla warfare by radical groups trying to seize power by force.

In Bolivia, Paraguay, and Guyana the governments censor the press and broadcasting to minimize political opposition and to bolster the regime in power. The media are not utilized to spread the prevailing ideology and nullify opposing ideology—as in Cuba, Nicaragua, Chile, and Uruguay—but rather to promote government programs and silence opponents who might become a threat if given sufficient exposure in the media.

REGIONAL AND NATIONAL NEWS AGENCIES

UPI with 500 newspaper and broadcast subscribers and AP with 300 subscribers are the largest international news agencies in Latin America. Throughout the region, Agence France-Presse, Reuters, Efe of Spain, ANSA of Italy, and DPA of West Germany have hundreds of subscribers. Even in the 12 republics with formal censorship of domestic reporting, foreign correspondents for the international news service are able to file numerous stories of political and economic significance to their home countries for global distribution.

This candid coverage has prompted various Latin American governments to encourage a news service which they could control and thereby enhance their images by playing down or eliminating stories telling of their failures. With this propagandistic entity as a goal for the mid- or late 1980s, 13 Latin American governments since 1980 have funded the Action of National Information Systems (Acción de Sistemas de Información Nacional, or ASIN). Presidential press secretaries and directors of governmental information bureaus make up this ASIN planning association. ASIN leader is Luis Javier Solana, coordinator of social communication for the Mexican Ministry of the Presidency.

In Mexico, the government funds Notimex as a service providing national news to media subscribers for a nominal subsidized fee. The García Valseca chain of newspapers operates its own news service nationwide, controlled by the government corporation SOMEX. Mexico's privately owned news agencies, cooperatively operated by member newspapers and magazines, include the Asociación de Editores de los Estados, or AEE (Association of Editors of the States), the Asociación de Periódicos Independientes, or API (Independent Newspapers Association), and the Agencia Mexicana de Información, or AMI (Mexican Information Agency). Seven Mexican feature syndicates provide sports news to subscribers nationwide.

In Argentina, the government owns and operates Telenoticiosa Americana, better known as the Telam news agency. Telam has a majority of the newspapers, news magazines, and radio and television stations of the republic as subscribers. Telam also administers government advertising in all the media, and state-owned industries often approach private industrial and business advertising in monetary value. Once a large service, the Saporiti News Agency, founded in 1900, now has relatively few subscribers.

In Brazil, the Diários Associados Serviço, or DAS, is a news agency originally formed to serve the Assis Chateaubriand corporation newspapers and broadcasting stations. DAS now serves 100 other media subscribers in addition to the DAS' 6 papers, 3 radio stations, and 12 TV channels. Folha News Service has media subscribers in all major cities of the seven largest states where the bulk of the population reside. The Rio daily *O Globo* OGS news agency has subscribers in 22 states. The Rio daily *Jornal do Brasil* JBS news agency has many radio station subscribers. The Abril corporation, which publishes the magazine *Veja*, operates the Abril News Agency for trade magazines. The government's National Information Service (Serviço Nacional de Informações, or SNI) provides official news to all media about public projects and policies.

The Cuban government's Prensa Latina, or PL, news agency is the required service for all Cuban media. It receives foreign news from TASS of the Soviet Union, INA of Iraq, WAFA of the Palestine Liberation Organization, Newspool of India, TAP of Tunisia, MAP of Morocco, and Tanjug of Yugoslavia. PL distributes Marxist interpretations of world news to 200 leftist newspapers, magazines, and broadcasting stations in other Latin American nations, with its largest concentration of subscribers in Nicaragua and Mexico, and to 700 clients in Communist and Third-World nations, being the principal news service in Angola and Mozambique. In Radio Libya, PL is the only authorized source of information about Latin America.

Noticias Aliadas, established by Maryknoll Catholic priests in 1964 in Peru, remains headquartered in Lima although its Marxist-line propaganda in place of straight news reporting causes Peruvian media to ignore it. NA has 300 subscribers in Cuba, Nicaragua, El Salvador, Panama, Mexico, and elsewhere in Latin America, including many leftist religious magazines.

Funded by TASS, the New Nicaragua News Agency, or ANNN, serves the media of Nicaragua except for *La Prensa*, and a few leftist media in other Central American and Caribbean nations.

The cooperative news agency LATIN, founded in May 1969 by 13 leading Latin American dailies, became a full regional service in 1970 with an exchange agreement with Reuters trading top Latin American stories for world news gathered by the British agency. LATIN now has subscribers in 20 Latin American nations, its daily budget stressing the top economic and political events in those same nations.

PHILOSOPHICAL CONSIDERATIONS

UPI's *Manual de Estilo y Referencia*, a 63-page style book, has encouraged other news agencies in Latin America as well as the media they serve to strive for cogent and concise news writing, until recently a rarity in the entire region. Literary phraseology often prevails, with concise prose found in a minority of the papers. But more objective writing slowly continues to spread among media not politically committed to political propagandizing as their primary mission.

Only one Latin American nation, Cuba, supports outright the Marxist theory that the mass media primarily function to develop a socialist economy and a political system in which no opposition political parties can exist. The Communist Party of Cuba (PCC) in its 1965 statutes states that the PCC must tell the media what to publish to mobilize support for the government "and create within the public an identification with the administration and the party."

The 1975 Cuban constitution states: "The press, radio, television, and cinema are the instruments of ideological education for creation of a collective society." Each Cuban government ministry's operational regulations includes the principle that mass media cannot be left to chance or used without government direction. Media are required to make known official positions and programs, to support the government at all times, and to attack anti-Marxist statements and actions both domestic and foreign even when they involve legitimate criticism of Cuba.

Nicaragua is the other Latin American nation with a government embracing censorship to instill Marxist principles but without officially labeling its policy positions as Marxist.

Argentina, Uruguay, Chile, Paraquay, Bolivia, Haiti, Guatemala, El Salvador, and Honduras censor the media officially to put down military challenges to the governments in power. Unofficially, their governments censor to minimize effective political opposition. Periodic insurrections bring curtailment of press freedom. But reports of public life get abridged because of unstable domestic political and economic institutions.

The libertarian theory of press freedom, in which a democratic government does not interfere with daily operations of the press, can be found only in Costa Rica, Colombia, and Venezuela. However, minimal government interference and oblique guidance allows considerable press freedom in Mexico, Peru, Brazil, Ecuador, and the Dominican Republic.

Extensive government investments in radio and television stations are found in Mexico, Peru, Bolivia, Panama, Colombia, Chile, and Argentina in systems in which privately owned commercial outlets and networks not only coexist but also flourish in terms of income and audiences.

Concentration of private ownership of newspapers can be found in powerful chains in Mexico, Brazil, and Chile. Excessive dominance of national newspaper circulations by a relatively few dailies in the national capital can be found in a majority of the Latin American nations.

Government advertising as a significant influence of the media can be discerned in almost all Latin American countries. Only in Costa Rica, Colombia, and Paraguay is government advertising small enough in monetary value to be an insignificant percentage of media income.

A majority of the Latin American republics continue to have editors and reporters basically oriented to the principle that the media should inform the public about newsworthy events regardless of the prevailing political and governmental priorities. In practice, however, sufficient pressures on news sources, government loans and subsidies to publishers, bribes to reporters, and broadcasting regulations constrict the free flow of news to various degrees.

EDUCATION FOR JOURNALISTS

In the 23 Latin American nations there are 163 schools of journalism, varying in title. For instance, at the National Autonomous University of Mexico, the College (Facultad) of Political and Social Sciences has a Department of Communication Sciences offering a journalism degree. In Mexico City the private Ibero-American University has a Department of Communication. In Peru, the National University of San Marcos offers a journalism degree from its Department of Literature, Linguistics, Journalism, and Philology.

In Caracas, the government's Central University has a School of Social Communication. The University of Puerto Rico has a School of Public Communication. The National University of Uruguay has a Journalism School. The University of Costa Rica has a School of Mass Communication Sciences.

In Brazil, universities have colleges, schools, or departments of social communication. São Paulo has an independent School of Public Relations and Advertising. None of the Brazilian journalism schools have the word "journalism" in their titles any more.

In Argentina, National Universities in Zamora, Mendoz, and Rosario and Catholic University in Salta each have a School of Journalism. In the 1970s, most of the Latin American journalism schools changed their names to "social communication" schools, indicating news curriculums in broadcasting, public relations, advertising, and public opinion polling. Of the 163 schools, 118 have "communication" in their titles.

Of the 163 Latin American journalism schools, only 13 of them are not affiliated with a university, being vocational schools. Most of the schools have deemphasized news reporting in favor of marketing research, opinion surveys, public relations, and broadcasting production. This change came because the older journalism schools could not place their graduates in newspaper jobs at salaries appropriate for university graduates. More of these graduates become government administrators or employees than working journalists. A large majority of these graduates work for the government, industry, or commerce in nonmedia jobs.

UNESCO in 1959 founded in Quito the International Center of Advanced Studies in Journalism for Latin America (Centro Internacional de Estudios Superiores de Periodismo, or CIESPAL). With funds from UNESCO, the Ecuadorean government, and Central University of Quito, CIESPAL offered its first courses in 1960. For more than 20 years it has promoted the establishment of journalism schools. In 1960 Latin America had only 44 such schools, most of them with tiny enrollments. Yet even today most of these schools rely on working reporters, editors, and broadcasters to teach one course on a part-time basis. One-fifth of the schools do not have one full-time teacher and only two of the Latin American journalism schools have an entire full-time faculty.

The theoretical nature of much of the instruction and lack of practical experience in their training continues to reinforce the tendency of Latin American journalism school graduates to go into nonjournalism work.

HISTORICAL HIGHLIGHTS

Printer Juan Pablos began operating the first printing press in the Western Hemisphere in Mexico City in 1535. The second printing press was introduced in Lima, Peru, in 1581, and the third one in Puebla, Mexico, in 1636. As early as the 1640s in a few cities of the Spanish American empire one-page announcements of one major event, called *Relaciones*, would appear rarely but without any publication name or any attempt to produce a genuine newspaper.

The first genuine newspaper in Latin America, the *Gaceta de México*, a monthly, began in 1722 in Mexico City. Latin America's second newspaper, also a monthly, the *Gazeta de Goatemala*, began in 1729 in Guatemala City. Like almost all other Latin American newspapers before the struggle for independence from Spain began in 1810, these pioneer papers were licensed by the royal government.

An exception appeared in 1807 in Montevideo, Uruguay. British troops landed unchallenged by the Spaniards and established a trading post and the first unlicensed newspaper in Latin America, *La Estrella del Sur*. This weekly was suppressed by Spanish officials in 1808, but a precedent for press freedom had been established.

Latin America's oldest newspaper still in existence is *El Mercurio* of Valparaíso, founded on September 12, 1827. The second oldest extant newspaper in Latin America is *El Comercio* of Lima, founded in 1839.

In Brazil, in 1808 when Napoleon's French army temporarily occupied Portugal, the Portuguese court moved from Lisbon to Rio de Janeiro. The king's ministers immediately began printing court news in the official monthly *A Gazeta do Rio de Janeiro*. In 1808 the monthly *Correio Brasiliense*, printed in England and smuggled into Brazil, became the first widely distributed unlicensed opposition paper to a colonial government in Latin America.

In 1785 the newspaper *Aviso* began in Bogotá, a monthly circulating among civic leaders in what is today Colombia, Venezuela, and Ecuador. *Aviso* was the first genuine newspaper for the entire northwestern portion of South America.

In 1876 the emperor of Brazil, Dom Pedro II, visited the World's Fairs in Boston and Philadelphia celebrating the centennial of United States independence. Dom Pedro discovered at the fairs the newly invented telephone and took a telephone system back to Rio. Thus Brazil got Latin America's first telephone service and its capital newspapers became the first to use the device in gathering and transmitting news.

In 1886 in Montevideo, José Batlle started the daily *El Día*. He went on to become president of Uruguay during 1903–1907 and 1911–1915 and the creator of Uruguay's modern welfare state. His paper has remained preeminent among Uruguayan media.

In 1869 in Buenos Aires, Dr. José Clemente Paz, writer and physician, started Latin America's world famous daily *La Prensa*. The next year a leading statesman, Bartolomé Mitre, who had been president of Argentina during 1862–1868, started another quality daily, *La Nación*. Mitre had originated the first regularly scheduled presidential press conferences in Latin America during his own six-year term. His paper encouraged this practice to continue not only in Argentina but also in neighboring Uruguay and Chile.

From 1885 to 1910, President Porfirio Díaz ordered Mexico City newspapers to utilize the telegraph wires from Texas to obtain world news from New Orleans and New York.

Broadcasting began in Latin America in.1920. From 1912 on, pioneer amateur broadcasters substituted radiotelephony for radiotelegraphy, talking person-to-person through the air without ground-wire connections. But mass electronic communication from a microphone to a scattered audience with receivers began in Buenos Aires on August 27, 1920, when a private corporation headed by

Horacio Cháves in partnership with the Marconi Company put Radio Argentina on the air, with music, literary readings, and civic announcements every night.

The Brazilian government issued a license on August 2, 1920, to the French news agency Havas for station SAH in Rio de Janeiro, but nightly broadcasts did not begin until August 30, making SAH the second Latin American radio station on the air.

Verdadero Bank put station PWX in Havana on the air October 10, 1922. Also in 1922 pioneer commercial radio stations began in Santiago at the University of Chile, in Caracas at station AYA, and in San José at the Liceo de Costa Rica station. On April 23, 1923, General Electric opened station Radio Sud América in Montevideo.

In Mexico City, government station JH began daily broadcasting June 16, 1923. Mexico's first private commercial station, CYL, owned by the newspaper *El Universal*, went on the air in July 1923, managed by Luis and Raúl Azcárraga. In 1930 their younger brother, Emilio Azcárraga, revived CYL with the call letters XEW after a brief shutdown. Today the XEW network dominates Mexican radio.

In Lima Cesar Coloma, Luis Tirado, and four partners founded the Peruvian Broadcasting Company and on June 20, 1925, inaugurated Lima's first station, OAX, with a concert. By 1926, at least one full-time commercial radio station could be found in every major city and every nation of Latin America.

Television came to Latin America when station XHTV or Channel 4 went on the air on the evening of August 31, 1950. Owned by Rómulo O'Farrill Sr., publisher of the daily *Novedades*, Channel 4 broadcast a musical variety program. The next morning it aired the "Informe Presidencial" (or "State of the Union") address of President Miguel Alemán. In March 1951, XEW-TV, or Channel 2, owned by the late Emilio Azcárraga Sr., began operations. In August 1951 electronics engineer Guillermo González Camarena started Mexico City's Channel 5. In 1972 the networks of these three channels became part of the Telesistema Mexicano corporation, and in 1977 these networks plus those of Channel 8 became part of the Televisa holding company.

In early 1951 Argentina and Brazil became the second and third Latin American republics with television, as Buenos Aires got Channel 7 and Rio de Janeiro got Channels 4 and 6.

In 1952 Cuba got CMQ-TV and by 1953 four Havana commercial video stations anchored island-wide networks with affiliates in all major cities. After Castro installed communism, television shrunk to two networks in 1960.

In 1956 Guatemala, El Salvador, Costa Rica, and Panama got their first television stations. When Peru inaugurated television in

1958, only Paraguay, Bolivia, and Haiti among all Latin American nations were still without TV stations but had already issued licenses for them.

From 1905 to 1915 linotype machines spread among the major dailies of Latin America. From 1916 on, United Press popularized wire service usage among Latin America's major newspapers. In the late 1970s electronic high-speed printing spread throughout the region.

A LOOK TO THE FUTURE

During the 1970s a majority of the Latin American dailies converted from letterpress printing to high-speed offset presses. In the 1980s the major Latin American dailies use electronic word processors and video display terminals.

Even provincial radio stations in the smaller Latin American nations now utilize multideck tape recorders and automated control panels. The 10 largest Latin American republics have cable video systems plus satellite communications for television news. Every major Latin American city has a growing FM radio market. As Latin American mass media look to the 1990s, adequate technology seems assured.

The problems confronting the media are political and economic. Inflation continues to increase newspaper, magazine, television, and radio production and operation costs. Increasing populations and unemployment continue to put economic and political strains on governmental stability, reinforcing the reliance on censorship in more than half the Latin American nations. Marxist ideology radiating from Cuba and Nicaragua challenges the traditional democratic role of the media to remain independent of government and to function as sources of information rather than indoctrination.

Nevertheless, a healthy number of journalists and broadcasters still cling to their journalistic mission of informing their fellow citizens, of defending the people's right to know what goes on in their own country. After eight years of governmental attempts to utilize the press as a device to bolster social revolution in Peru, the Lima dailies returned to their primary task of chronicling the news as soon as they were given the chance. After decades of censorship, the press of the Dominican Republic has embraced press freedom as if it had been a long-time heritage.

Once government shifted from military to elected civilian status in Ecuador, the media responded with responsible efforts to truly report the major events of national life. Despite newsprint control, government investments, and other institutionalized guidelines making for bandwagon journalism, Mexico's newspapers manage to report extensively on national problems, social inequities, and economic crises. A similar inclination of the media to circumvent official pressures retains journalistic prowess among Brazil's major media.

The unfettered free flow of news, found in Costa Rica, Colombia, and Venezuela, will not likely spread to a majority of the other Latin American nations in the 1980s. But the relative flexibility found in Mexico, Brazil, and Peru may be copied to various degrees in a few other republics as political pressures lessen. Even the strong censorship in Argentina, Chile, and Uruguay has not erased from the collective psyche of publishers, broadcasters, and politicians in those republics their long-time tradition of press freedom. The communicators do not stop trying to communicate.

5 NORTH AMERICA

RALPH D. BARNEY
DEANNA NELSON

The North American countries of Canada and the United States have shared many commonalities over the years. Having similar borders, languages, heritage, money, and social press systems, they are connected in more than geography.

Historically, Canadian society has lived in the shadow of more powerful societies. French dominance of Canada was succeeded by British influence, only to be followed by that of the United States. With its close proximity, larger population, and greater economic power, the United States has clearly dominated Canada both culturally and economically for decades.

Canada's significantly smaller population has been important in Canadian social development and in development of small media systems. The 220 million United States citizens overshadow Canada's 24.5 million in relatively the same amount of territory, giving Canada few alternatives to dominance by its southern neighbor. The concentration of 90% of the Canadian population along a 200-mile-wide strip adjacent to the United States border compounds the problem.

The United States, on the other hand, has had the resources and the populations to develop overwhelming mass-media systems that create what is perhaps a unique situation in the world, virtually complete penetration of mass media in a national population exclusively by media of that country. Most countries in the world have at least a signal overlap for the electronic media of radio and even television and many have significant levels of foreign media within the country. In neither of these cases is this so in the United States.

Thus, the two countries of North America have, emerging from the similarities listed above, a startling dissimilarity in mass-media structures. That is, the United States is dominated by its own media systems and Canada is substantially affected by a foreign media system, particularly television from the United States.

While Canada and the United States have many interactions, commonalities, and similarities, Canada has been increasingly concerned with her own identity and the maintenance of it. External forces have made it difficult for Canada to establish her own unique character. Therefore, a strong feeling of nationalism has emerged and Canadian society seeks not comparative power in the world arena but greater control over herself.

While United States culture and society has often been referred to as a melting-pot society, Canada has prided herself on its mosaic, or patchwork, society. Canadian society supposedly has greater tolerance for ethnic identities and traditions—particularly since government policy encourages the maintenance of cultural differences, with laws requiring bilingual labels and signs, among other requirements. Such a condition accounts for an absence of a dominant Canadian way of life, of a culture into which ethnic groups can melt.

The ethnic groups that make up Canada's population are united either by race, language, or religion or some combination of the three. All these variables have been a significant means of social differentiation in Canadian society. However, while these variables keep the various ethnic groups together, one in particular seems to have caused conflict in Canada as a whole.

Language seems to make little conscious impact on the United States. There is only one official language—English. Yet Canada has a unique situation in that there are two official languages—English and French. The official Language Act of 1969 guarantees all Canadians the right to communicate with the national government in either French or English. About 67 percent of the Canadian people speak only English, about 18 percent speak only French, and more than 13 percent speak both languages. The rest of the people speak other languages.

Most of the approximately 6 million French-speaking Canadians live in Quebec. As a result, Quebec's French-speaking citizens, called Quebecois, consider themselves the guardians of the French language and culture in Canada. During the 1960s, many Quebecois began to campaign to make French the sole official language of Quebec. In 1977, Quebec legislature passed a law that restricted the use of languages other than French in Quebec. In 1980, the independence movement suffered a setback. That year Quebec voters refused to empower the provincial government to negotiate with the national government for sovereignty association with the rest of Canada. Such an arrangement would have given political independence to Quebec, but maintained the providence's economic ties with Canada.

One can see, then, that as Canada tries to loosen its dependence on America and develop her own unique culture, it must also adjust to problems of language that periodically threaten to split the country.

In these circumstances of slight internal disarray, much cultural activity that originates outside the country has become part of Canadian society. The underdeveloped nature of the visual media in Canada, the lack of variety of printed media, and resultant flooding of the Canadian market with foreign films and magazines have created a dependence on foreign culture and its media. It's here that the United States and its mass communication system become significant, exerting influence, in time, on Canada's communication system.

Geographical proximity permits Canadian reception of American radio and television signals. Placement of the vast majority of Canada's population forces Canadian broadcasters to compete for the attention of their own national population. Depending on broadcasting choice, many Canadians may be more attuned to events occurring in the United States than to activity in their own country. Because Canadian broadcasters have often found it easier and perhaps cheaper to buy successful American programs, the Canadian Radio-Television Commission began to formulate Canadian content regulations or quotas insisting that stipulated percentages of broadcast time be devoted to Canadian programming.

Canada has done much in the area of broadcast and print journalism in recent years to help in the preservation of her unique culture. But Canada's most fundamental concern is its independence and nationhood in the face of growing American presence in all sectors of Canadian life. Canadians are trying to maintain control of their economy and safeguard their identity, and they are attempting this through their own unique approach to the area of press.

This chapter will look at the interaction and independence and yet at the same time the separateness of the North American neighbors, Canada and the United States.

It is probably among newspapers that there is the least international overlap between the United States and Canada; therefore, since each newspaper has a fairly well defined circulation area, it is easy to consider the newspapers of Canada and the United States separately, with Canada discussed first.

PRINT MEDIA

Canada

Because of its relatively small population and its proximity to the highly developed media of mass communications in the United States, Canada has often found itself at a disadvantage in building a flourishing native industry in mass communications. Since World War II, however, there has been marked growth, both in quality and quantity, in publishing and broadcasting.

Daily Newspapers. After more than two centuries of growth, printing has been transformed from a weak pioneer venture of unassociated and isolated units into a centralized and consolidated segment of the national life, powerful commercially and culturally important.

There are over 120 daily papers in Canada at the present time. Over 100 of these are in English and at least 12 are in French. Although daily newspaper circulations have risen steadily since 1900 and the number of daily newspapers has grown gradually since the low year of 1945, the number of publishers in the daily field has decreased. In 1930, 99 publishers owned 116 dailies; in the mid-1970s, three major English-language publishing groups owned 56 of the 120 dailies. The groups' share of total circulation has risen from 25% in 1958 to 52 in the mid-1970s.

The foremost daily newspaper publishing groups are Free Press publications, Southern Company, and Thomson of Canada in the English-language area, and Les Journaux Trans-Canada Limited in the French-language area. Economic factors are the chief cause of these publishing groups' consolidation and centralization. The costs of operating a daily newspaper have accelerated so much that publishing units must be wealthy and stable if they are to survive. In some cases, even the rich entrepreneur has had to join larger groups to protect his paper from destructive competition and the sometimes disastrous effects of death duties.

The leading English dailies in Canada are the *Globe and Mail* and the *Toronto Star* of Toronto; *The Province* and *The Sun* of Vancouver; and *The Gazette* of Montreal. The leading French dailies include *Le Devoir* and *La Presse* of Montreal and *Le Soleil* of Quebec.

The Globe and Mail. In 1963, George McCullagh bought first the *Globe*, owned by William Gladstone Jaffray, a straight-laced individual who refused to permit the *Globe* to carry advertisements for cigarettes, girdles, whisky, and cheap clothing, and the *Mail and Empire*, a newspaper owned by Isaac Walton Killam. Money to buy the two newspapers, which were immediately combined as the *Globe and Mail*, was provided by William Henry Wright, millionaire mine owner. About the only evidence of the mining magnate's direction of policy and content of the newspaper was to be in the unusual number of pictures of horses it carried in deference to the owner's interest in the animals, and the reinstatement of the cartoon "Gals Aglee" as a result of Wright's mild inquiry about why the panel had been dropped.

At the time of the merger, the newspaper began a long-lasting support of the Conservative Party. The newspaper thus perpetuated a long tradition of political opposition. During the nineteenth century, it had been a vigorous Liberal paper consistently opposed to the Conservatives. By mid-twentieth century it was a forthright Conservative news organ adamantly against the long-lived Liberal administration.

A. A. McIntosh edited the *Globe and Mail* from 1936 to 1948. Highly respected managing editor during much of this period was R. A. Farquharson, prime mover in establishing the Canadian Managing Editors' Conference.

In 1955, R. Howard Webster purchased the daily, then expressed disenchantment with John Diefenbaker by switching its support from the Conservatives to the Liberals in the 1963 federal election. By the 1965 election, it had also lost its pro-Liberal enthusiasm. However, in a lukewarm editorial, it advised voters to vote Conservative. When it joined F. P. Publications in December 1965, it apparently sacrificed none of its independence. It still maintained its long-established reputation of being one of Canada's best newspapers of record.

The Toronto Star. It was Joseph Atkinson, Sr., who transformed the *Toronto Star* from a struggling journal into one of the most valuable newspaper properties in North America. Appointed in 1899 to run the paper, he soon acquired a controlling interest. In 1911, Harry C. Hindmarsh, the man who was to become Atkinson's able lieutenant and son-in-law, joined the *Star*. The two men used methods which earned the distinction "the last home of razzle-dazzle journalism." They hurled battalions of reporters into big stories to gain saturation coverage, hired trains and airplanes for news-staff use, and spent money lavishly to provide a news treatment of overwhelming impact. A penchant for cheesecake, huge headlines, full-page pictures, charitable activities such as the Santa Claus Fund, startling newspaper stunts, and off-trail and frequently left-wing causes gave the paper a liveliness and variety that readers could not ignore.

It was Atkinson who imbued the paper with the Liberal philosophy which has persisted since his death in 1948. Such Liberalism usually meant support of the Liberal party but such support was not automatic. Nor was a Liberalism of the laissez-faire kind, containing a strong infusion of social-welfare thinking, consistent with the *Star's* concern for the underprivileged, the handicapped, and the victims of injustice.

The Toronto Star of the late 1950s and 1960s became markedly different from the *Star* of the 1930s. Without abandoning its role as alert news gatherers, it has come to place greater emphasis on in-depth reporting. News of long-term significance is being presented in well-backgrounded detail, makeup has been made more tasteful and discriminating, and writers with considerable specialized knowledge are writing authoritative features on subjects of national and international importance. In 1961, an American survey which purported to list non-U.S. newspapers in order of merit ranked *Star* fourth after *La Prensa* of Buenos Aires, The *Times of London*, and the *Guardian* of Manchester.

The Vancouver Province. Although traditionally conservative in editorial policy, the *Province* showed itself to be imaginative and energetic in meeting newspaper competition. It proved itself to be adaptable and adventurous in such matters as revamped makeup and aggressive news coverage. This sort of hard-hitting journalism has flourished particularly when the *Province* was fighting its most spirited circulation battles with the *Sun*. A 1957 publishing agreement seemed to take the sharp edge off such uncompromising competition, however.

The Vancouver Sun. Until the 1950s, Vancouver was, with the possible exception of Toronto, Canada's most competitive newspaper city. The rivalry between the *Sun* and *Province* had been tremendous. The *Sun* was the product of many amalgamations, starting as the *News-Advertiser*, then becoming the *Morning Sun*. In 1944, publisher Donald Cromie started making for the *Sun* a name for itself. By insisting on vigorous coverage, emphasizing bright and readable local stories, hiring a battery of interesting, controversy-seeking columnists, sending his reporters on globe-trotting assignments, and taking advantage of his chief rival's misfortunes, Donald Cromie turned the *Sun* into an unrepressed, enterprising newspaper.

The *Sun* had a reputation for flamboyance, and although the newspapers of this period had a reputation for neglecting national and world news for provincial and local happenings, the *Sun* gave expression to many varying viewpoints. Nominally liberal in political sympathy, it allowed its columnists considerable freedom, and was notable for its generous treatment of labor news. It now has the second largest circulation among Canadian dailies.

The Montreal Gazette. The biggest Montreal English-speaking daily at Canada's centennial year was the *Star*, the *Gazette's* rival for many years. However, the *Star* recently has become the first fatality in an increasingly vicious duel between Canada's two biggest newspaper chains. Montreal could no longer support two English dailies because of the minorities' slow strangulation by Quebec language law and the flight of Anglo-owned business. Therefore, the *Gazette*, the *Star's* older rival, has become Montreal's biggest daily.

Started in 1890 by Richard and Thomas White, the *Gazette* has been a consistent Conservative supporter, but its support has not been of the doctrinaire kind. The *Gazette* has gained an enviable reputation as an excellent newspaper of record.

Le Devoir. *Le Devoir* came into existence in 1910. Henri Bourassa held controlling interest and was editor in chief from the outset. One of his staff writers, Oliver Assel, a giant of journalism in French Canada, was an ardent nationalist and leader of French-Canadian thought. Bourassa was one of the most influential men of his time. He served in both the House of Commons and the Quebec legislature, where he strengthened his reputation for impassioned oratory. He was an uncompromising opponent of imperialism and an eloquent champion of the rights of French Canadians in Quebec and in other provinces. He made his journal a newspaper for the intellectually elite rather than a mass-circulation organ, and his successors continued the tradition. *Le Devoir* has been called the best-written newspaper in Canada.

La Presse. This paper had the largest circulation of any Canadian daily in 1900. Until the 1920s, *La Presse* practiced dazzlingly lurid journalism. Stories of murders and lesser crimes filled its pages. Its reporters engaged in bizarre and attention-getting stunts. Reporter Septime LaFerriere dragged into the newsroom a corpse he had discovered in a back alley behind the *La Presse* building, identified him from papers found in the dead-man's pockets, and wrote his story before turning the body over to police. On another occasion he stole a bloodstained axe from a murder scene and photographed it for his paper before the police recovered it. In 1904, he reputedly provoked a mutiny at sea to get the biggest story of his career.

While La Presse was gaining a reputation for unorthodox enterprise the newspaper was doing its part to further good causes. The journal strongly supported the Liberal Party and advocated road construction, the acceptance of trade unionism, and the establishment of employment exchanges, night schools, children's aid societies, and a house of refuge for the destitute.

United States

While there are around 119 daily newspapers in Canada, the United States produces more than 1700 dailies.

Daily Newspapers. The top daily newspapers in the United States by circulation are, respectively, *The Wall Street Journal, The New York Daily News, The Los Angeles Times, The New York Times*, and the *Chicago Tribune*. Other newspapers high in circulation and prestige in the print-media arena include the *Christian Science Monitor* and the *Washington Post*. A few of these outstanding papers will be discussed briefly in the following paragraphs.

The Christian Science Monitor. This is an international daily newspaper published by the Christian Science Publishing Society in Boston, Massachusetts. Since its founding in 1908, it has sought to provide, a constructive, solution-oriented journalism for the nation and its people. In a sense, the *Monitor* was founded as a protest against the sensationalism of some early twentieth-century American newspapers and the emphasis which many gave to news of crimes, accidents, and disasters. But it has been more concerned with the unfolding of good and of progress in human experience, a policy that probably reduces the breadth of its appeal.

Its founder, Mary Baker Eddy, said that "the object of the *Monitor* is to injure no man, but to bless all mankind." Erwin D. Canham, who served as editor from 1945 to 1964, said that its mission was to "help give humankind the tools with which to work out its salvation." These tools included information, explanation of that information, and the arousing of dormant thinking. The *Monitor* has pioneered in interpretive reporting and analysis of national and world affairs. Numerous recognitions and awards document the success of the *Monitor* in carrying out its mission. It has won hundreds of journalistic awards, including several Pulitzer prizes and a wide variety of others. Recently, the *Monitor* has emphasized a problem-solving journalism that seeks not only to inform its readers about issues and problems but also to analyze those problems and focus on possible solutions. The paper seeks to assure readers that problems can be attacked systematically and intelligently by citizens with proper information.

Wall Street Journal. This is a national daily that specializes in the coverage of business but also includes summaries of important national and international news and other features. Published by Dow Jones & Co., it was founded by Charles H. Dow and Edward T. Jones as a financial news service for private clients in 1882. The service originally consisted of handwritten news bulletins that were delivered to clients in New York's financial district at intervals throughout the day. In time the bulletins were summarised in a two-page printed sheet called *Customers' Afternoon Letter*, and in 1889 this was enlarged, improved, and turned into a newspaper.

The *Journal* was essentially a financial newspaper until about 1940 when it broadened its concept of business news, or what constitutes news of importance to its readers. The new concept defined business news to embrace all topics that somehow relate to making a living. Lucid summaries of major news were included, and in-depth trend stories about business and related matters were emphasized.

Editors William H. Grimes and, later, Vermont Royster played key roles in the *Journal's* rise to national prominence during the 1950s and 1960s. Both won Pulitzer Prizes for editorial writing. As the 1970's ended, the *Journal* ranked second only to the *New York Daily News* in circulation among United States dailies. It has approximately 1.6 million readers in the United States and more than 90 foreign countries. The *Journal* continues to expand its already strong coverage of business and government news and it has increased its coverage of arts and leisure activities. Of particular note is the resources it routinely devotes to multiplying the number of sources contacted for stories.

The New York Times. This highly regarded newspaper seeks to provide complete and thorough coverage of national and international affairs without neglecting its responsibilities to its city and state of publication. It has often been ranked first among American dailies and is considered a national and world leader in the area of journalism. Because of its thorough coverage, the *Times* has been regarded as a principal newspaper of record in the United States.

The *Times'* tradition of thoroughness has been developed by a series of responsible owners and publishers. The pattern was set by its founding editor, Henry J. Raymond, and continued by Adolph

Ochs, who acquired the paper in 1896. Ochs was succeeded by Arthur Sulzberger in 1935, who was succeeded by Orvil Dryfoos in 1961. When Dryfoos died in 1963. Arthur Ochs (Punch) Sulzberger assumed full command and serves as chairman, president, and publisher.

The *Times*, in an effort to stimulate thought and provoke discussion of public problems, introduced in 1970 the Opposite Editorial Page. The idea was not new, but the *Times* approach is different in that it doesn't rely on syndicated columnists to help fill its two pages. Instead, the *Times* runs guest articles by government officials, scholars and others. The guest columns and additional letters were expected to provide an improved forum for the exchange of opinions on important issues. While the news sections maintain the traditional *Times* approach, the special sections include a variety of features often accompanied by splashy graphics not associated with the *Times* until recent years.

The Washington Post. This daily has improved rapidly in recent decades to become one of the nation's most highly regarded daily newspapers. It should be considered a newspaper of national orientation and influence because of the national government and its publication seat in the nation's capital. Yet, it must also be considered a newspaper of local and regional impact because of its services to its adjacent areas.

Founded in 1877 by Stilson Hutchins, the early years of the paper showed that it was lively and combative and crowded with news and features. But in the 1920s and 1930s, it was unable to pay its bills and was put up for auction. Eugene Meyer purchased it, and for the next 15 years the newspaper improved editorially but not financially. In 1948, Philip and Katherine Graham acquired the voting stock and set out to expand the economic base.

First, the Post Company acquired radio and TV interests and in 1954 purchased the *Post's* remaining morning competitor, the *Washington Times-Herald*. In 1961, it acquired *Newsweek* magazine, and in 1963, it joined in the creation of the *Los Angeles Times/ Washington Post* News Service. It has acquired other interests in subsequent years.

The *Post* has been especially noted in recent years for its editorial and investigative reporting. Under Philip Geyelin the editorials have been long and stimulating. They seek to support viewpoints with evidence and often contain fresh reporting. He won a Pulitzer prize for his efforts in 1970. The *Post's* investigative reporting achievements are perhaps best typified by its exposure of the Watergate scandal in 1972. Reporters Bob Woodward and Carl Bernstein won numerous awards for their efforts in uncovering the Watergate story, and the newspaper received the 1973 Pulitzer Prize for distinguished public service.

Both the *Washington Post* and the *New York Times* have fallen victim to the problems of news coverage in a competitive and complex world, however. A Pulitzer prize was returned after a story written by a *Washington Post* reporter was found to be fabricated, and in early 1982 the *New York Times* was severely criticized for publishing a story that also appeared to have been careless with information.

The Los Angeles Times. This daily newspaper has improved dramatically in the past 20 years to rank high among the nation's leading newspapers. The newspaper has established itself as a leader in circulation, advertising linage, the amount of space devoted to news, and the type of coverage and commentary provided in that space. Its image has been remade from ultraconservative and often unfair to independent and responsible.

Started in 1881, the *Times* has been successful under the guidance of the Otis and Chandler families. Under these families, the paper developed a strong tradition of conservatism. It strongly favored Republicans and tended to be antilabor. But the paper participated in numerous service activities and earned Pulitzer prizes in 1942 and again in 1960.

In the early 1960s, the *Times* had one foreign correspondent and three reporters in a Washington bureau; by the early 1970s it had 18 bureaus overseas, seven bureaus in the United States, and more than 20 reporters in Washington. By the early 1970s, the *Times* had greatly increased its interpretive and background reporting, and its editorial pages provided good balance of columnists as well as thought-provoking institutional editorials and cartoons. In addition, the *Times* developed a Sunday tabloid magazine called *Calendar* to expand coverage of drama, the arts, and literature, and added a new rotogravure magazine called *West* to serve the area.

There are about as many types of newspapers in the United States and Canada today as there are newspapers. No two are exactly alike, even though they may be part of the same group or one of two jointly owned newspapers in the same city. Most will differ primarily because their purposes and audiences are different.

Many groupings can be employed, however, to place newspapers into better perspective. They may be grouped according to frequency of publication, such as daily, which has just been discussed, weekly, semiweekly and biweekly. As weeklies, specialized newspapers and alternative or underground newspapers will be discussed. Also, the ethnic and international aspects of weekly newspapers in Canada are worthy of some explanation.

Weeklies and other nondailies serve a variety of special-interest groups, as well as the residents of cities, suburbs and small towns throughout North America. In the late 1970s, there were approximately 7,500 nondaily paid circulation newspapers in the United States and another 6,000 free papers and "shoppers," which often have some characteristics of newspapers and at times are published by newspapers. In Canada, there are more than 900 weeklies that serve the small communities and certain areas of major Canadian cities. Also, about 275 foreign-language papers are read by the many Canadian ethnic groups. Of these foreign-language papers published in Canada, there are 153 languages represented, with the largest published in French, Italian, German, Ukranian, and Arabic.

Weeklies best compete with the metropolitan newspapers by providing detailed local coverage in areas outside the particular primary coverage area of daily newspapers. The large newspapers usually do not become involved in issues at the community level as do the community newspapers.

A few general-interest weeklies reached national audiences in the 1970s in the United States. The most significant was the *National Observer*, published until 1977 by Dow Jones and Company.

The *National Observer* was designed to present information about worldwide events and cultural developments in an attractive newspaper format. It had a strong cultural and educational flavor and included many in-depth reports designed to help readers with basic problems such as health, jobs, and education.

Weekly tabloids such as the *National Enquirer* and its competition the *National Star* have achieved economic success with a somewhat different approach. Stories that appear in tabloids such as these consist of UFO visits, sex scandals, prophecies, and other provocative topics. Groups such as Accuracy in Media, Inc., question the accuracy of some reporting and some say the publications are not in good taste. Whether in good taste or not, the popularity cannot be ignored, nor can weekly newsstand sales in the millions.

Canadian weeklies are very similar to those found in the United States. They consist of community journals which focus attention on local happenings, leaving the reporting of national and international news, for the most part, to their big-city contemporaries. Editors of such papers are in many ways counterparts of eighteenth-century printer-editors—remarkable for their jack-of-all-trades versatility. There are over 900 Canadian weekly newspapers, and over 500 of these belong to the Canadian Weekly Newspapers Association.

Black Newspapers. Black newspapers were started in the United States during the nineteenth century to oppose exploitation of black people and to work for their equal rights and opportunities. The newspapers have continued, at least in part, because blacks have continued to feel a need for such publications. Basically, a black newspaper is one owned and operated by blacks, intended primarily for a black audience, and concerned with the black struggle for equality and justice in society.

The New York City Amsterdam News is the largest of the black newspapers in the nation's major cities. Though the outlook for black newspapers appears uncertain because of inflation, the rising cost of newsprint, and ballooning energy costs, most feel that as long as black communities exist, there will be a market for black newspapers.

Canadian Ethnic Press. There are over 100 ethnic publications in Canada which are published monthly or more frequently. More than half these are weeklies. The foreign-language publications are read by roughly a million and a half people. It is through these small ethnic presses that Canada reaches out to its many language groups represented in its mosaic society.

The Underground Press. An alternative "underground" press was developed in the United States in the late 1950s and 1960s to express and reflect the views of some Americans, especially young Americans, who felt alienated from the mainstream of national life. This other press developed in part because those disenchanted with the existing social system or establishment found little encouragement to express their views and feelings in existing media.

Benjamin Franklin, who helped operate what was probably the first underground paper in America, employed wit and cleverness in drafting satirical letters against the establishment of his time. However, the modern-day underground press has suffered from serious faults, one of which has been its indulgence in vulgar language. Other faults include biased reporting and the subsequent confusion rather than clarification of issues, and indiscriminate use of sexual themes.

Notwithstanding its faults, it also has strengths—at least a transitory ability to attract and hold youth while regular newspapers are floundering with that audience, enough inventiveness in layout and design to influence professional media, and an ability to provide access for dissenters to the marketplace of ideas after press experts had decreed the libertarian principle dead.

By the late 1970s, it appeared that the underground press movement which had flourished in the late 1960s with over 450 papers was over. The significant underground papers of the 1960s and 1970s, the *Berkeley Barb*, the *Los Angeles Free Press*, and others were either dead or had turned somewhat conservative in efforts to attract broad audiences.

News Magazines. A flood of American periodicals in Canada, estimated to consist of about four out of five magazines read by Canadians, takes two forms: first, the so-called American magazine overflow, an essentially unrestricted volume of imported American editions which, since 1965, are required by the customs act to be free of advertising directed specifically at the Canadian market. About 90 percent of Canada's total import of periodicals comes from the United States, representing nearly 70 percent of United States periodical exports to all countries.

Second, and more acutely at issue, has been the dominating presence, by special dispension, of the Canadian editions of *Time* and *Reader's Digest*. The latter has had a widely read edition in French as well as English. Until recently, Canadian periodicals publishers were inclined to live with the special status of *Time* and *Reader's Digest*. Yet their presence and dominance, along with other American periodical imports, has been viewed increasingly by many nationalists as a threat to the integrity of Canadian culture. *Time* halted publications of its Canadian editions in 1976. *Reader's Digest* still publishes special editions in Canada.

In 1970, a special committee of the Canadian Senate produced a strongly stated affirmation of the critical importance to Canadian nationhood of Canadian-owned periodicals: "Magazines are special. Magazines are the only national press we possess in Canada.... In terms of cultural survival, magazines could potentially be as important as anything in Canada."

Nearly four out of ten Canadians over age 15 receive a newsmagazine; over half of them read *Time*. *Newsweek*, which unlike *Time* and *Reader's Digest* has no Canadian edition, has about one-seventh of *Time's* readership with its imported American edition.

Other Magazines. There are only two large-scale Canadian publishing companies—the Maclean-Hunter organization and Southam Business Publications, each of which produces more than 50 Canadian magazines. Maclean-Hunter relies heavily on profitable trade and business publications to subsidize *Chatelaine*, a general-interest magazine, and *Macleans*, which in 1975 abandoned its general-interest format to become Canada's first indigenous newsmagazine. The Southam organization and Canada's many small publishers are exclusively concerned with special-interest periodicals.

Chatelaine with an English and French edition and a circulation of 1.5 million is considered one of Canada's best magazines. *Macleans*, with a circulation of around 700,000, is a weekly with a format comparable to the United States' *Newsweek.*

In the United States, magazines have flourished and readership has increased. *Time* remains the healthiest of the American newsmagazines since its founding in 1923. It has been described as "curt, clear, complete." *Newsweek* and *US News and World Report* followed *Time* a decade later, and have continued to be popular weekly newsmagazines, offering a new dimension to the printed media.

Special-interest magazines are developing more and more to handle the consumer's requests for specialized media. Women's magazines are among the top circulation leaders with *McCalls, Ladies' Home Journal, Better Homes and Gardens*, and *Good Housekeeping* all in a healthy state. Both the United States and Canada share in the need for specialized magazines to satisfy their varied publics. The incursion of American magazines into Canada may continue to cause controversy. However, as Canada develops its own magazine industry, the quality of Canadian magazines should increase with readership.

The importance of specialized magazines needs special emphasis, since the cornerstones of the American magazine industry for decades were general-circulation publications. The spread of television as an entertainment and advertising medium seems to have sounded the death knell of those publications, shifting emphasis to the specialized.

The foremost newspaper publishing groups in Canada are Free Press Publications, Southam Company, and Thomson of Canada in the English-language field, and Les Journaux Trans-Canada Limitée in the French-language field. Most publishing takes place in Toronto and Montreal, with some being done in Vancouver.

The United States has publishing centers distributed by population. Wherever population concentrations are, the printing industry is present in proportion. Major cities such as Los Angeles, New York, Chicago, and Washington, D.C., contain the majority of the publishing and press facilities in the country.

BROADCAST MEDIA

As in most of the Western world, Canadian broadcasting has experienced the most rapid and costly development, as well as the most abrupt transformations in technology under the impact of the electronics revolution. This medium could hardly be expected to fit into the community without dramatically reshaping its culture, economy, and politics. Consequently, it is not surprising that since the start of publicly owned or regulated sound broadcasting in the early 1930s and the start of television at the end of World War II, the electronic media of radio and television have been the center of constant agitation and virtually unceasing inquiry into the policies, programs, and administrative structure deemed most appropriate for a country of continental dimensions.

The fact that Canada, faced by a wealthier and more populous nation on its southern border, has consciously sought through these media to identify and preserve a national image has accentuated the significance of broadcasting to the community. The price of achieving a peculiarly Canadian broadcasting system has been high. And the special form assumed by that system is a strictly Canadian solution that in broadcasting as well as in other means of communication has evolved into a genuinely mixed enterprise, with publicly owned components operating parallel to privately owned establishments. These sometimes complement but often compete with one another. Canadian broadcasting thus falls somewhere between the nationalized British system and the regulated free-enterprise arrangements in the United States.

For nearly two decades radio in Canada developed as an aid to trade, commerce, and transportation rather than as an entertainment and information device for the general public. Voice radio began in 1919 when Marconi Wireless Telegraph Company experimental station XWA in Montreal received the first license for a wireless telephone transmitter. In 1922, provisions for licensing commercial broadcasting stations was made. Within the year, 34 stations began operating. Every Canadian province except Prince Edward Island and Nova Scotia were served.

During the pioneer period, Canadian broadcasters often found interference-free broadcasts impossible because stronger unregulated American stations were using every wavelength of the limited broadcast band. A Canadian-American agreement to assure Canada of six clear channels came to nothing because an American court decision ruled that government allocation of wavelengths was unconstitutional in a free-enterprise economy. A 1927 Washington conference provided for the first frequency allocations under the International Telecommunications Union which Canada had entered in 1906. In 1929, Ottawa joined Cuba, Newfoundland, and the United States in trying to regulate frequency assignments in North America. Despite such endeavours, and despite a further agreement in 1932, interference from American transmitters continued, and was compounded by strong Mexican stations which jammed Canadian channels in the evening. It was not until implementation of the Havana Convention in 1941 that Canada was assured of a fair share in hemispheric frequency allocations.

In the 1920s, radio broadcasting developed in Canada on much the same basis as it did in the United States. Privately owned commercial stations were licensed to use certain frequencies in given areas and were free to carry on their activities with few restrictions. They grew rapidly in number and output. A federal royal commission, under the chairmanship of Sir John Aird, examined the development of Canadian radio at the end of the decade and found that broadcasting was tending to become a mere extension of the American system. A very high proportion of the program material on Canadian transmitters was being brought across the border by recording or line connections. Some Canadian stations in major centers had become affiliates of American networks. There seemed little hope, therefore, for the development of Canadian programming or for east-west network connections that would link the regions of the country. Although there were many divergent views, the royal commission united on one basic point: Canadian listeners want Canadian broadcasting.

In response, Parliament passed the Broadcasting Act of 1932. The act established the Canadian Radio Broadcasting Commission which was required to set up a national service. But the main purpose of the commission—establishment of a nationwide broadcasting service—was not achieved. Full-scale coverage obviously required time, experience, and money, but during the prolonged depression of the 1930s only time was available in quantity. In 1936 commission broadcasting was effectively reaching less than half the Canadian people. So in that same year, a new Canadian Broadcasting Act was passed replacing the Canadian Radio Broadcasting Commission by the Canadian Broadcasting Corporation.

Radio

Canada. The Canadian Broadcasting Corporation (CBC) was founded in 1936 and is presently headquartered in Ottawa, Ontario. It receives most funds from the Canadian government, but it also derives additional income from advertising revenue. The CBC operates radio and TV networks and other broadcasting services throughout Canada. It operates two AM radio networks, one French and one English, and FM radio stations in several major cities. These AM networks furnish 150 Canadian stations with programs. The CBC owns about 50 of these stations and another 100 are privately owned. The CBC also provides medium- and short-wave services to northern areas in English, French, Eskimo, and Indian languages, and it operates the CBC Armed Forces Service that broadcasts to Canadian troops abroad. Finally, the CBC operates Radio Canada International, short-wave service that broadcasts in 11 languages all over the world.

The Canadian Radio-Television and Telecommunications Commission (CRTC) is a government agency that regulates all electronics communication systems in Canada. The CRTC issues licenses to radio and TV stations and makes sure that Canadian content accounts for certain percentages of their programs. These Canadian content quotas are intended to help maintain a Canadian cultural identity in the face of United States influence. They are designed to create jobs in Canada by encouraging production of TV and radio shows.

United States. Although educational and other noncommercial stations share the airwaves, the American broadcasting system for the most part is a commercial system. In this respect it is supported by revenue from those who advertise goods or services to the audience. Advertising messages are presented as commercial spot announcements before, during, and after programs, or as a part of sponsored programs.

Broadcasting stations are licensed to serve the public interest, convenience, and necessity. Because radio channels are limited and are part of the public domain, stress is placed on entrusting them to licensees with a sense of public responsibilities. By law, each license must contain a statement that the licensee's right to operate the station or use the frequency does not extend beyond the terms of license. The maximum license is three years.

Identity of the first American broadcasting station is a matter of conflicting claims, mainly because of development of some pioneer AM broadcast stations from experimental operations. Although KDKA Pittsburgh did not receive a regular broadcasting license until November 7, 1921, it furnished programs under a different authorization before that date. Records of the Department of Commerce, which then supervised radio, indicate that the first station issued a regular broadcasting license was WBZ Springfield, Massachusetts, on September 15, 1921.

In 1926 the National Broadcasting Co. (NBC), a subsidiary of RCA Corp., started the first regular network with 24 stations. In that same year, the Columbia Broadcasting System, first called the Columbia Phonograph Broadcasting System, was organised.

For some years NBC operated two networks, the Red and the Blue, but FCC adoption of chain broadcasting rules in the early forties forbade one organization from operating two networks serving the same area at the same time. RCA sold the Blue Network to Edward J. Nobel in 1943. It ultimately became today's American Broadcasting Co.

Regulation of broadcasting began with the Radio Act of 1912, which was the first domestic law for general control of radio. It made the secretary of Commerce and Labor responsible for licensing radio stations and operators.

Early broadcasting was experimental and also noncommercial. In

1919 radiotelephone experiments were enabled to operate as "limited commercial stations." In 1922 wavelengths were assigned for the transmission of important news items, entertainment, lectures, sermons, and similar matter.

Recommendations of the first National Radio Conference in 1922 resulted in further regulations by the Secretary of Commerce and a new type of AM broadcast station came into being. So rapid was the development of broadcasting that a fourth National Radio Conference asked for a limitation on broadcast time and power. The Secretary of Commerce was unable to deal with the situation because court decisions held that the Radio Act of 1912 did not give him this authority. As a result, many broadcasters changed frequencies and increased power and operating time at will, regardless of the effect on other stations, thereby producing chaos on the air in the United States and Canada.

The Radio Act of 1927 created a five- member Federal Radio Commission to issue station licenses, allocate frequency bands to various services, assign specific frequencies to individual stations, and control station power. The same act delegated to the Secretary of Commerce authority to inspect radio stations, examine and license radio operators, and assign radio call signs.

Much of the early effort of the Federal Radio Commission was needed to straighten out confusion in the broadcast bans. It was impossible to accommodate the 732 broadcast stations then operating. New regulations caused about 150 of them to surrender their licenses.

The Communications Act of 1934 created the Federal Communications Commission to regulate all interstate and foreign communication by wire and radio. The FCC began operating on July 11, 1934, as an independent federal agency headed by seven commissioners appointed by the president with the advice and consent of the Senate.

One of the FCC's major activities is the regulation of broadcasting. This is summarised in three phases: first, allocation of space in the radio frequency spectrum to the broadcast services and to many nonbroadcast services which also must be accommodated; second, assignment of stations in each service to frequency bands, with specific location, frequency and power; third, regulation of existing stations. This involves inspection to see that stations are operating in accordance with FCC rules and technical provisions of their authorizations, modifying the authorizations when necessary, assigning station call letters, licensing transmitter operators, processing requests to assign the station license to another party, and processing applications for renewal of license. At renewal time, the FCC reviews the station's record to see if it is operating in the public interest.

In 1981, there were 8,933 radio stations operating in the United

States. Of these, 4,575 were commercial AMs, 3,272 were commercial FMs, and 1,086 were noncommercial FMs. In 1980, 78.6 million homes had radios in them. There are 456 million radio sets with 333 million in homes and 123 million outside homes. Radio spot advertising costs range from $300 or more in major markets for 60-second commercials to less than a dollar in small towns.

Television

Television is seen and heard in nearly every Canadian and American home. People who watch TV include virtually all the possible combinations of race, age, sex, background, and education. America's system of broadcasting is free and competitive, and the programs it offers tend to not only reflect the influence of established institutions that shape values and culture but also expose the dynamics of social change which bear upon the lives of its residents.

Canada. Television developed about the same way as did radio. In Canada, the CBC established its own stations in some areas and obtained network coverage in others through private affiliates, and later other private stations and private networks were licensed. Because all television costs are much higher than are those for radio, pressures for importation of programs from the United States have been very strong. Even the CBC, with its public funding, has had to take more American programming than it wished to in order to survive and satisfy the Canadian audiences.

In 1976, the CRTC reported that the audience share of the CBC-TV network had declined by 12 percent since 1967. This resulted mainly from the spread of cable systems and the increase in the use by private stations of American programming during prime time. Given the choice between the CBC and United States programming, the Canadians have usually opted for the latter. Because of vast audiences in the United States, far more resources are devoted to the average network production than is possible in Canada. Canada has therefore been concerned about. producing better programs in a few critical areas to keep its people tuned to Canadian-based television. One example of the improvement of Canadian TV is in the area of educational television.

At its birth, educational television typically presented a "talking head"—a speaker staring straight into the camera. But as provincially run educational television rounds out its first decade in Canada, matters have changed and some commercial broadcasters are looking twice and are concerned that these educational networks may in fact be cutting into their audience by presenting entertaining programs.

Since the provinces were formally allowed into the field of educational broadcasting in 1972, Ontario, Quebec, and Alberta have established networks that work under a definition of education that goes beyond the classroom. TV Ontario (TVO), for instance, has received more than 140 international awards for programming, design, and acting in the past 10 years, and it has even managed to make money.

Presentation of old movies, discussions of public affairs, and popular music has drawn criticism that the network is competing unfairly with the advertising-supported networks. But legislation simply provides a general guideline to the educational channels to produce programming that must aim at the acquisition of improvement of knowledge and must be "distinctly different" from the CBC and private stations. Thus, educational channels appear to be on the rise and to be setting an example of Canadian programming that the CBC and the other private stations might do well to emulate.

Canada's programming has powerful competition from Hollywood and New York. And, as has been mentioned earlier, the Canadians seem to prefer these prime-time programs to their own home-grown programs. This daily diet of United States programming had most recently been strengthened by the growth of cable television systems. In the past few years, Canada has become a leading country in coverage by cable television systems, largely because many Canadians want to have available to them full American as well as Canadian television services.

The CRTC has ordered United States commercials stripped from broadcasts simultaneously carried on Canadian channels and replaced with domestic advertising. (In the United States the CRTC's counterpart, the FCC, has just freed cable interests from all but minimal strictures.) But many say the CRTC has outlived its purpose, and that a review of the Canadian-content regulations enforced by the CRTC are not achieving their purpose. Canadians still choose to watch United States–produced programs.

Not only are the cable systems bringing in more American-produced programs, but many say pay-TV is within five years of hitting Canadians, and some say less than a year. Canada's largest cable company, Canada Cablesystems Ltd, says, "Pay TV is already here. Saskatchewan already has it and there will be an increasing demand for it on the part of the Canadians."

Pay TV was available in Canada on an experimental basis in 1960; but starting in 1981, the CRTC will probably allow its development on a national scale. In the United States nearly 6 million viewers watch this new home entertainment. But for Canada, the introduction of Pay TV brings as many problems as opportunities. Two criteria have been determined essential in any plan to wire Canadian homes with this new medium: most of the revenues produced should be funneled into the production of Canadian films and other programming; and whatever new CRTC regulations govern its use should be designed to guarantee the continuing viability of the CBC.

In the eyes of CBC and CRTC executives, Pay TV is not simply a more expensive way to watch better television. It could be the final blow to the dream of developing a distinctive Canadian culture, according to many Canadian nationalists.

Also, northern Canada makes it through the long winter on more than CBC's Northern Service, with the help of Canadian Satellite Systems. All across northern Canada, aluminum dish antennas are aimed heavenward to get signals from the RCA satellite 22,000 miles above the earth. The problem is that this practice is illegal and the northern earth-receiving stations cannot be licensed now because they are in violation of a 1972 "exchange of letters" between the United States and Canada that stated that Canadians could not pull United States television signals off United States satellites, and vice versa. (So far the United States has not considered the unpaid use of its signals widespread enough for concern.)

Canada, it appears, is not doing too well competing with America's big TV business. However, with the recent introduction of Canada's first hour-long local TV news program on CTV called "Newshour," the dream of producing good programming for the home culture may still come true.

One final note on Canadian television. The programming situation with the United States has never been a serious threat to the French-speaking Canadians because of the language difference. The 6 million French-speaking Canadians enjoy programming that is much more home-produced than is that for the English-speaking majority. A certain amount of United States television material is available in dubbed form, but French-language operations have had to rely heavily on production in Quebec. This has been true of both the CBC-Radio Canada in its French form and the private operators. Therefore, French-language television has developed in Canada with a high degree of creativity and a strong appeal to the audience it serves. It is patently more effective than is English-language television in drawing out talent and providing a means of communication among the members of its society.

United States. In the United States, the Federal Radio Commission (predecessor of the FCC) reported that a few broadcast stations were experimenting with television in 1928. By 1937, there were 17 experimental TV stations operating. The Journal Company of Milwaukee, now licensee of WTMJ-TV, filed the first application to broadcast TV on a commercial basis. At a 1940 hearing, the FCC found the industry divided on technology and standards, but on April 30, 1941, the commission authorized commercial TV operations to start the following July on 10 commercial stations.

By 1945, the commission allocated 13 VHF channels for commercial television. That same year, as part of an extensive revision of frequency allocations, the commission reserved 20 FM channels for noncommercial educational stations. Stations in the educational service are licensed principally to school systems, colleges, and universities for student-teacher programs as well as for public education and information. The first educational TV station to go on the air was KUHT Houston in 1953. The first state educational TV network was established in Alabama on April 28, 1955.

A 1962 law enabled the Department of Health, Education, and Welfare to make matching federal grants of money to build educational TV stations, and a 1967 law extended these to radio. In 1980, there were a total of 267 noncommercial TV stations in operation.

American television programming some years ago was referred to as a "vast wasteland." However, one cannot deny that the United States commercial TV stations produce enormous amounts of programming each season, and competition between the three major networks is fierce enough to make all three networks, as well as other organizations, strive constantly for available audiences.

ABC, NBC, and CBS are the three major networks. Programming by these networks is strongly influenced by the Nielsen ratings and other audience analyses. Most programming is produced either in Hollywood or in New York for general distribution not only nationwide but also worldwide.

Greater emphasis has been placed lately on developing better programs, more diversity, and better news programs for the general population. Broadcasters have adopted the NAB Television Code with its specific guidelines for treatment of news and public events. For instance, a news program's schedule should be adequate and well-balanced. Many stations are changing to one-hour evening newscasts instead of the previous half-hour approach. Also, as in all reporting, the code says that news should be factual, fair, and without bias. This last criterion has been the object of some controversy because it has been recognized increasingly that all news and information has some bias. However, the news programs are urged to make efforts to be objective.

Since American broadcasting is funded not by the government but from advertising funds, commercial television relies on the positive response to its programming from its viewers to succeed. Television broadcasters are responsible for programming and advertising on their stations, yet the advertising messages must be presented with honesty, responsibility, and good taste. Advertisers should support the endeavors of broadcasters to offer a diversity of programs that meet the needs and expectations of the total viewing audience.

In 1981, there were 1,020 operating television stations in the United States: 519 were commercial VHFs, 233 were commercial UHFs, 106 were noncommercial VHFs, and 162 were noncommerical UHFs. Most commercial TVs are network affiliated, but approximately 150 operate as independents.

In 1980, there were 77.8 million homes with television sets, which is 99% of all United States homes. As of January 1, 1981, 66.25 million homes with television sets had color sets. This is 85% of all homes in the United States.

According to 1979 statistics, the broadcasting business is producing revenues of approximately $10.6 billion. Of that, television had $7.9 billion, or 74.5% of the revenues, and made $1.7 billion, or 89.5% of the profits. Broadcasting is a big business in the United States. With advertising costing $150,000 for a 30-second spot, one can see that advertising is the key source of broadcast income.

United States homes spend an average of 6 hours a day in front of the television set. Sixty-seven percent of the United States public turns to TV as a major source of news, and 47% ranks it as the most believable news source available.

Cable TV

A quick word should be said about the expanding area of Community Antenna Television. CATV was developed in the late 1950s in communities unable to receive TV signals because of unfavorable terrains or distance from TV stations. Cable systems located their antennas in areas having good reception to pick up broadcast station signals and distribute them to cable subscribers for a fee.

In 1950, cable systems operated in only 70 communities. However, at the beginning of 1981, there were approximately 4,400 cable systems serving over 17.2 million people in over 10,400 communities in every state across the country. The FCC has had jurisdiction over cable TV since 1962. Rules for cable TV systems were adopted in 1972 and were the most comprehensive compilation of regulations ever issued on cable television regulation. Although the commission has amended the 1972 rules numerous times, the basic framework has remained unchanged.

Cable reaches 22% of the nation's TV households. Most systems offer 12 channels. But systems constructed after March 1972 must have a minimum 20-channel capacity. Most cable systems derive less than 5% of their gross revenues from advertising. Basic income is from monthly set-connection fees.

Pay TV or pay cable is on approximately 2,500 systems and reaches close to 5 million subscribers in 50 states. Home Box Office Inc. initiated the first national satellite interconnected pay network in 1975, using transponder time leased on the Satcom satellite. Pay TV offers first-run specials and motion pictures for a monthly fee. This system seems to have revolutionized the broadcasting industry inasmuch as it indicates that people are willing to pay for entertainment. Also, other special cables such as an all-sports network and also an all-news network have been set up and both seem to be providing programming that is attractive to consumers.

GOVERNMENT-PRESS RELATIONS

Nothing attests to the vitality of the United States Constitution more than the continuing argument about what it means, particularly with respect to the first ten amendments embodied in what is called the Bill of Rights. There is agreement that the Constitution is a unique political document in the history of Western civilization, and that the First Amendment itself has given the press in America a privileged position not held by the communications media in any other country.

In the 1980s, American newspapers exercised a considerable amount of freedom to publish news and commentary, thanks to the foresight of the drafters of the Constitution, court decisions, and editors and publishers fighting for press and public rights. The right to publish without a license and the right to comment on public activities in a fair and reasonable manner seem to be generally well-established. However, other rights are less secure. These include such areas as prior restraint, access to information and the media, protection of sources, free press versus fair trials, libel, and privacy. The First Amendment that restrains the federal government from passing free-speech laws, and the Fourteenth Amendment that prohibits states from passing laws against free speech have been tested again and again. Let us look at the less secure rights listed above to see what direction the relations between press and government seem to be taking.

In the area of prior restraint, there appears to be fairly constant tension between the government and the press. However, as the 1970s began, it appeared that the right of the press to publish information without prior restraint was generally well accepted. The case of *Near versus Minnesota* is the landmark that was set in 1931 by the Supreme Court to eliminate prior restraint, although many attempts to challenge this concept have recently shown up.

The case of the Pentagon papers in 1971 again strengthened the case for the free watchdog press. Although government officials tried to ban the publication of these documents, the Supreme Court decided that the government could not prevent publication because it had not demonstrated that their publication threatened national security. The Court said that any system of prior restraints of expression bears a heavy burden of showing justification for the enforcement of such a restraint.

In another prior restraint case in 1979, the government sought and obtained a preliminary injunction against the publication of a *Progressive Magazine* article describing how to build a hydrogen bomb. In September 1979, after a Wisconsin newspaper, the *Madison Press Connection*, published a letter to the editor containing information similar to that in the *Progressive* story, the government announced that it was abandoning its efforts to prevent publication of the story. It did warn the press though that it wasn't giving a green light to anyone to violate the Atomic Energy Act of 1954 by revealing national security secrets.

The media and others have sought to establish the right to know along with the right to publish as fundamental guarantees of democratic government. Under this concept a number of groups have sought legislation at both federal and state levels to assure them access to the records and meetings of public bodies. In 1957 only 21 states had laws guaranteeing citizens the right to inspect the records of their government and only 11 states had laws requiring that meetings of governmental bodies be open to the people. Fifteen years later, 41 states had open-record laws, and 38 states had open-meeting laws; 30 of the states had both.

Efforts to assert the public's right to know about their federal government also have been successful to some extent. After a decade of discussion, Congress in 1966 passed a Freedom of Information Act designed to open many records of the federal bureaucracy to public inspection. In 1974, Congress adopted 17 amendments designed to close loopholes in the Freedom of Information Act. Since then, steps have been taken to reduce the number of documents that are classified unnecessarily.

With the passage of the Sunshine Law in 1976, Congress took another important step toward providing public access to the government. This law opened the meetings of about 50 boards and agencies, while still providing for exceptions when meetings could be closed. These included discussions that might affect "interests of national defense or foreign policy."

Access to the Media

Many persons today agree that individual freedom and democratic government are fostered by laws that assure the public and press access to information about public and government matters. Some say that to further these goals requires laws that guarantee public access to the media: that is, the right of individuals to express views in the media. They argue that the cost of engaging in media operations had become so great and the number of media units so small that existing media must assume the role of common carriers. They must be open to divergent views if the individual's right to speak and the public's right to hear divergent views are to be realized.

Newspaper officials argue that public-access laws would violate their rights to control their products and invite further governmental interference in the press. They argue that such laws could discourage newspapers from speaking out on issues and reporting election campaigns and would open up a flood of irrelevant material which could crowd out important news. They also note that newspapers already provide adequate access through Letters to the Editor columns, news stories, and advertising.

Chief Justice Warren Burger, in a Supreme Court ruling in 1974, called a Florida law unconstitutional because

> a newspaper is more than a passive receptacle or conduit for
> news, comment, and advertising. The choice of material to go
> into a newspaper, and the decisions made as to the
> limitations on the size of the paper, and content, and
> treatment of public issues and public officials—whether fair
> or unfair—constitutes the exercise of editorial control and
> judgment. It has yet to be demonstrated how government
> regulation of this crucial process can be exercised consistent
> with First Amendment guarantees of a free press as they
> have evolved to this time.

Reporter Privilege

Some newsmen assert that protection of confidential sources of information is essential to the free flow of information. They contend that forced disclosure of information about these sources to grand juries or other government bodies would dry up the sources and deprive the public of useful information. They argue that investigative reporting which exposes corruption and other questionable practices in government and in the private sector often depends on protecting sources; to insist on disclosure of these sources would eliminate them and greatly reduce the potential of investigative reporting.

At present, news reporters have failed to establish protection of sources as a constitutional right through court action, though there are continuing efforts to obtain statutory immunities at both federal and state levels. The United States Supreme Court in 1972 held that requiring newsmen to appear and testify before state or federal grand juries is not an abridgement of the freedom of speech and press guarantees of the First Amendment. Cases following that decision have affirmed that newspapers and reporters cannot withhold identity of their sources. So the struggle of information flow and right to know, along with reporter privilege, continues to be a major struggle in the 1980s.

Another controversy involving freedoms has evolved between the First and Sixth Amendments. At stake are the individual's rights under the Sixth Amendment to a fair trial and the public's rights under the First Amendment to receive information about crime and administration of justice. Press and lawyers agree that the two rights were intended to be complementary, not contentious, and the Supreme Court has refused to say one has primacy over the other. However, there are disagreements over specific procedures to follow in administering the rights and the extent to which reports concerning crimes, persons accused of crimes, and judicial procedures can prejudice juries and make fair trials impossible.

This conflict has been receiving increased attention since 1959 when the Supreme Court ruled that a defendant had not received a fair trial because of prejudicial newspaper publicity despite statements of jurors that they would not be influenced by news articles. In five subsequent cases, the courts reaffirmed this rule that prejudicial publicity may be grounds for setting aside convictions.

In 1968, a statement called the Reardon Report set guidelines to help in improved news coverage of trials and arrests while protecting freedom of the press and ensuring fair trials. The danger for members of the press is that they must be careful in considering press-bar guidelines and not bargain away the people's rights. The press was encouraged to work with the courts and lawyers in efforts to resolve differences. Finally, the making of a case to the people whose support can assure that the people's right to know and the individual's right to a fair trial are complementary, not exclusive, interests, was encouraged.

It is clear that the First Amendment does not protect cases of libel, obscenity, and sedition. However, court decisions in the past decade have dramatically changed the status of libel laws in the United States and markedly changed the status of those concerning invasion of privacy.

Libel laws vary from state to state. But prior to 1964, any published statement about an identifiable person held up to public contempt, scorn, or ridicule or one that tended to injure him in his business or professional standing probably would have been considered libelous in most states. The primary defenses against libel suits were truth, fair comment, and criticism of public persons acting in their public capacities, and the fair and accurate reporting of privileged materials such as court and legislative records.

The Supreme Court's decision in 1964 in *New York Times Co. v. Sullivan* redefined libel and transferred the burden from the defendant to the plaintiff. The Court held that the First Amendment guarantees prohibit a public official from recovery for a defamatory falsehood unless he can prove "actual malice"—that is, that it was stated with the knowledge that it was false or reckless.

In 1971, this new approach to libel was extended to the private person involved in matters of public or general interest. However, in 1974, the court modified its position on libel to draw a sharp distinction between public officials and public figures on the one hand and ordinary citizens on the other. The court held that an ordinary citizen could recover actual damages in cases involving matters of public interest by showing that a false statement was published negligently. It appears, in the future, that state courts will be called upon to define the boundaries of negligence and determine who is an ordinary citizen as opposed to a public figure.

Four types of privacy cases have evolved over the years; those dealing with the truthful disclosure of private facts; ones involving physical intrusions; cases of appropriation of a name or likeness; and instances of placing someone in a false light. By the late 1970s, most states had privacy laws, and Congress was considering legislation to give individuals increased privacy guarantees for personal medical, financial, and insurance records. Newsworthiness was still a good defense for the press in privacy cases, but it can be used only with information that the press can obtain; narrowly interpreted privacy laws and regulations could become another form of prior restraint.

It appears that newspapers and other media have made considerable progress in their efforts to assert the right to publish and to know. Still the struggle continues and the press in the United States is left to convince the people that the fight for a free and uncensored press is their right too.

CANADA AND GOVERNMENT-PRESS RELATIONS

In Canada, the law is a critical factor in preventing journalistic freedom from degenerating into journalistic license. The law can protect the citizen from abuse by the mass media and assure him redress when the media wrong him.

To the journalist, the most important laws are the laws of defamatory libel. Every province has some sort of libel and slander act, but perhaps the most consequential change in Canada's civil laws of defamation occured in the 1950s and 1960s when six provinces made broadcast defamation the offence of libel rather than of slander even though communication by radio is exclusively oral and that of television largely oral. Manitoba is unique in being the only Canadian province which permits legal action against persons accused of libeling a race or religious creed. Ontario and Nova Scotia have adopted a provision of the British Libel Act of 1952 which makes it unnecessary for a defendant using a plea of justification (i.e., of truth) to prove the truth of every allegation made against him.

The laws of contempt of court are considered second to the laws of defamatory libel in providing legal guidelines for the conduct of the press in Canadian society. Such regulations are designed to ensure fair trials for those who come before the courts to receive justice as well as to preserve the dignity of the court and the respect the court enjoys. Contempt of court decisions related to such matters involve a balancing of society's interest in a fair trial with society's interest in maintaining a free press. In the United States, the scales are weighted in favor of the press, with the media allowed wide leeway in the reporting of trials so long as the reportage does not violate another's rights. In Canada the law is much more clearly on the side of the court and its members.

Contempt of court in Canada may be of two kinds: contempt in the face of the court or contempt not in the face of the court. The first might be explained as that of a wildly abusive outburst on the part of a witness during a trial. The other form of contempt could be a newspaper editorial about a trial in progress, or newspaper accusations questioning the integrity of the judiciary. A criminal code amendment designed to give additional assurance of fair trials was put on the statute books in 1959. It banned news report references to admissions or confessions made at preliminary hearings. Many critics of press privileges felt that a similar prohibition should apply to coroner's inquests. More objections were raised over the right to report preliminary hearings: the argument offered was that such reportage would be unfair to defendants because the law requires that only the prosecution case be presented at preliminary hearings, with the result that only the prosecution case gets reported, creating a predisposition in the mind of the public.

Contempt of court rulings are also associated with the question of photography in courts of law. The problem of permitting such photography is that proceedings of the court might be interfered with, and that defendants might not be able to get a fair trial because they are confused and made nervous by the disturbing presence of cameras and related equipment. In Canada, judges have full jurisdiction over their courtroom and its precincts. Theoretically they might allow pictures, whether still or television, but they have usually declined to do so. (Recent court cases in the United States have allowed the use of cameras in the courtroom, although this issue is still being debated on a state-by-state basis.)

Revealing sources is another matter related directly to contempt of court citations. Confidentiality is respected by the courts if four conditions, known as Wigmore's canons, are adhered to. Apparently solicitor-and-client and husband-and-wife relations are recognized in all Canadian law courts. In Quebec, there is a statutory recognition of the relation of doctor and patient.

However, the Canadian journalist as journalist enjoys no similar protection. The most important situations in which he or she may be called upon to reveal sources are: when he appears to have information pertinent to a properly constituted commission of public inquiry, etc.; when he publishes information alleging that a crime has been committed which appears pertinent to the determination of the guilt of particular persons; and when he is accused of libel as a result of publication of information and bases his defense on an assertion of honest belief in the truth of the matter published.

In any of these situations a journalist may be called on as a witness and asked the sources of his information. If he refuses, he may be held in contempt and imprisoned (theoretically until he produces the information sought).

There seems to be one basic dilemma related to disclosure of sources in the case of journalists on trial for libel. On the one hand, if a reporter cannot guarantee the anonymity of his informants, then his sources will probably dry up, and he will lose his usefulness as a reporter. On the other hand, when a reporter is on trial for libel, it might be grossly unfair to the person about whom he has written if the reporter is not required to say who has originated the potentially libelous statements he has passed on.

Generally speaking, Canada's working journalists run little daily danger of violating laws governing obscenity and indecency. Problems in this area are more likely to arise in connection with books rather than family-interest newspapers and periodicals.

The interest of the practicing journalist in laws governing blasphemy is even more academic than is his concern with obscenity laws. Section 246 of the criminal code's main provision is that "everyone who publishes a blasphemous libel is guilty of an indictable offence." Also, no one can be convicted of an offence under that section for expressing in good faith and in decent language an opinion upon a religious subject. The fact seems to be that the section of this Canadian law dealing with blasphemy is pretty well dormant. Public opinion appears to be a far stronger weapon of control in this area than are courts and laws.

Sedition is also covered in Canada's criminal codes that were revised in 1954. Section 60 deals with seditious words, seditious libel, and seditious conspiracy. Each is defined in terms of seditious intent. Seditious intent in the seditious libel context (which refers to journalists) is described as follows: everyone shall be presumed to have seditious intention who publishes or circulates any writing that advocates the use, without authority of the law, of force as a means of accomplishing a governmental change within Canada.

As Canada looks at its freedom of the press, the question is asked, "Who controls and who should control the press?" In the case of print media, years of struggle had already established, without authoritarian shackles, the private-enterprise control basic to the libertarian system. In the case of the electronic media, Canada had early decided that the social-responsibility philosophy of public enterprise was a necessary ingredient of Canada's dual broadcasting system, although the ideal was to preserve the practices of freedom in both the public and private sectors. In neither case, however, was there universal satisfaction with the position reached. Canada's press is not as free as that of the United States; however, as in the United States, there is a constant vigil over freedoms and a struggle to maintain freedom of information in both societies.

REGIONAL AND NATIONAL NEWS AGENCIES

The two news services which have dominated the United States are United Press International and the Associated Press. Both have interesting histories and both are global in their coverage. Early competitive pressures for news discouraged cooperative efforts. In the early 1800s, for example, the Exchange Coffee House in Boston provided news for its patrons as a means of attracting them. Gathered by Samuel Popliff, Jr., who boarded incoming ships, the papers were brought to the reading room at the coffee house. Similar operations were later used in Charleston, South Carolina, and other communities. Pigeons, trains, and other means of news dissemination eventually were used by individual newspapers to overshadow their competitors. Many of these operations developed into full-service operations which supplied the needs for large and small papers.

The Associated Press is traced to the pre-Civil War era. The New York Associated Press (NYAP) was formed in 1848 and included six papers. These were the *Sun, Herald, Journal of Commerce, Tribune, Express, Courier and Enquirer*. The *Times* was admitted when it was founded in 1851. Soon news service was being sold to papers in other cities, correspondence expanded, and in 1855 a monopolistic contract was made with the Western Union Telegraphic Company for news transmission.

Regional groups challenged the NYAP control and made secret deals that eventually split up the association. Western Associated Press (WAP) came into being in 1862, with Melville Stone as manager, leaving several strong eastern papers to operate under the name United Press for four years. Regional groups formed throughout the country, such as New York State AP, New England AP, etc. The American Press Association was organized in 1871 with Henry George as one of the promoters. But in 1900, an antimonopoly decision of the state's supreme court caused dissolution of the AP of Illinois and the removal of the organization to New York.

Associated Press organizations consisted of participating papers that exchanged stories among members and paid fees for coverage of areas not served by a member newspaper. Competitive pressures generally led to exclusive memberships for areas and a strong monopolistic flavor emerged.

In 1945, the United States Supreme Court ordered the AP to halt the barring of franchises from competitive media. AP first sold its news reports to radio stations in 1940. AP newsfeatures had started in 1927, with wirephotos emerging in 1935 and photofax being used in 1954.

In 1907, E. W. Scripps bought the independent Publishers Association and combined it with his Scripps-McRae Press Association and Scripps News Service. He called it United Press Associations and shortly thereafter made Ray W. Howard general manager. Scripps was suspicious of AP, and thought its publishers were capitalistic and conservative. Unlike the cooperative AP, the UP organization sold its services only to its clients. It prospered, becoming a formidable rival of the older organization. In 1935, five years before AP, UP sold news reports to radio stations. It instituted Unifax in 1954.

The International News Service founded by William Randolph Hearst in 1909 never gained leadership over AP or UPA. Its foreign service was considered good by the 1930s and it won a Pulitzer prize for its reporting in 1956 of a Russia trip by the vice-president of the United States. However, in 1958, UP absorbed Hearst's news service and renamed itself the United Press International, the name it bears today.

In Canada, there are two chief wire services: the Canadian Press and the United Press International of Canada. The Canadian-Pacific Telegraphs withdrew from the field of news-gathering in 1910 and left the way open for expansion of the news service cooperative. The Canadian Press Limited was formed that same year to serve as a national holding company for AP rights, and almost every Canadian daily was a member of the organization. In 1917, the regional components of Canada's daily press—the Central Provinces, the Western Associated Press, and the Eastern Press Association—were merged under the title of Canadian Press Limited. In 1923, the organization was reincorporated and renamed the Canadian Press.

Since 1917, the agency had received an annual parliamentary subsidy of $50,000 to help pay the cost of bridging three geographical gaps in its wire services. However in 1923, some felt that acceptance of this annual grant obligated the organization to report the news in a way acceptable to the government. Faced with what the Canadian press considered to be a threat to its independence, the agency debated the wisdom of depending on government support and seemed relieved when the subsidy was discontinued. Now the agency is financed by annual fees paid by member newspapers, assessments being proportional to the size of the community the contributing paper serves.

The CP has exchange arrangements with AP and with Reuters, the British agency. Before World War II, Agence France-Presse shared a similar arrangement with CP. Up until 1951, French-language newspapers had to do their own translations of CP copy from English, but in that year a French-language service was established. In 1941, a subsidiary, Press News Limited, was created to provide news for radio stations. In 1966, CP was serving the Canadian Broadcasting Corporation and many privately owned radio and television stations.

The United Press International of Canada had its beginnings in 1922, when Charles Crandall advocated that a privately owned and operated news agency be set up. In 1923, the British United Press was established as the British Commonwealth branch of the American organization, the United Press. One reason the word British was chosen was to play down the company's American connection because the United States was unpopular in some quarters then, as it has been in other periods of Canadian history.

In 1958, United Press and INS joined forces to form UPI. Although the credit on the copy originated by the Canadian organization was changed from BUP to UPI, the official name of the Canadian affiliate continued to be British United Press until January 1, 1964. The name was then changed to United Press International of Canada. Head office of the UPI of Canada is in Montreal, and bureaus are located in Halifax, Quebec City, Ottawa, Toronto, Winnipeg, and Vancouver. The company distributes a news report, a telephoto picture service, and a spots wire and television film service as well as allied services in these fields.

PHILOSOPHICAL CONSIDERATIONS

The ability of newspapers and other media to perform the vital roles expected of them is determined to a great extent by the degree of freedom they have from government or other interference. Only a free press can effectively serve free, participating people and help them maintain their freedoms. The press must continue to be free to publish without government license or other undue restriction. It must be free to criticize fairly and truthfully the performance of public officials, and it must have access to information about the activities of government at all levels. In return, the press must act responsibly in exercising its freedoms. A nation's press must be both free and responsible.

United States and Canadian papers, as well as other media, operate under what has been termed by Siebert, Peterson, and Schramm as the social-responsibility theory of the press. The philosophy grew out of an older philosophy known as the libertarian view, which evolved from and in opposition to the authoritarian concept that prevailed from introduction of the printing press in the fifteenth century until the eighteenth century.

Briefly, the authoritarian concept of the press was born around 1450. At that time, an individual was regarded as only a member of the community, serving the state. Truth was restricted and the state's ideals became the standard for everyone. Autocratic leaders sensed that the press could be dangerous to them, and so they controlled it through licensing, censorship, and threat of punishment, thereby keeping it from developing freely. This approach was somewhat the global norm until the second half of the eighteenth century in North America.

The libertarian philosophy of the press grew out of increasing dissatisfaction over the control and suppression caused by the authoritarian concept. It was based on the philosophy of rationalism and natural rights. Its chief purpose was to inform, entertain, and sell; but its main purpose was to discover the truth and check on the government. Reason was used to distinguish between truth and error, and the value of a free marketplace of ideas was urged. Party subsidies financed many of the early papers under this philosophy, but by the middle of the nineteenth century, advertising provided the main financial support. The libertarian philosophy emphasized free expression of ideas, easy access to the means of publication, and the ultimate self-righting process of truth. But the United States and other countries, including Canada, have modified this philosophy in forming the social-responsibility theory.

The press philosophy of the twentieth century seems to be the social-responsibility theory which is based on changes in media, such as consolidation of newspapers and concentration of newspaper ownership and new thinking by communicators, commissions, and philosophers. Some felt that the objective reporting of the libertarian era was irresponsible and urged that background material be included along with the raw facts of news stories to provide an adequate perspective. The absolute freedom of the libertarian society was to change with a new emphasis on responsibility. Today the press is not only free for the publication of information vital in a democratic society. It seeks to inform, entertain, and sell as it did under the libertarian philosophy, but its chief purpose is to convert conflict into public dialogue.

Many authors have sought to define a "free and responsible press" and in 1947, the Commission of Freedom of the Press came up with the following five ideal demands of society for the communication of news and ideas: a truthful, comprehensive, and intelligent account of the day's events in a context which gives them meaning; a forum for the exchange of comment and criticism; the projection of a representative picture of the constituent groups in the society; the presentation and clarification of the goals and values of society; and full access to the day's intelligence. The Commission also asked that the mass media accept the responsibilities for financing new, experimental activities in the field, engage in vigorous mutual criticism, and increase the competence, independence, and effectiveness of their staffs.

As has been mentioned, both the United States' and Canada's press philosophies fall generally under the category of social responsibility. However, some in both countries feel that the press should still be libertarian. Some say that each philosophy has its own weaknesses. To the social-responsibility adherent, the libertarian falls into error by placing the greater emphasis on freedom with the result that responsibility is sacrificed to irresponsibility. To the libertarian, the social-responsibility practitioner errs in invoking government as the guarantor of freedom, with the result that the authoritarian system will inevitably result. It is worth noting that both the libertarian and social-responsibility theories are normative theories of the press, in that they are not merely descriptive but prescriptive, and are as much ideologies as they are philosophies.

All this suggests that neither the libertarian nor social-responsibility theory is likely to win enough converts and make the other theory obsolete, at least in the United States and Canada, where there still appear to be conflicts over which philosophy the press should adhere to. However, both theories concern themselves with the interrelations of the government, the press, and the public. If each of these had been a single, unified entity, always behaving with consistent, concerted action, the story of the press in the twentieth century would undoubtedly be rather boring. But press, government, and public have separate components and take different forms. Sometimes the elements work together, while at other times they sharply oppose one another.

To Canadians, there are many sharp reminders that the press is never able to take its freedom for granted, and the authoritarian concept is, it appears, waiting for its chance to take over the press theory once more. Three instances in particular that have shown them the press must be alert include a restrictive Alberta Press Act, a "Babies For Export" trial, and a Quebec Padlock Law. Each of these cases in their own way helped to strengthen the argument for the necessity of the freedom of the press in Canada as well as to emphasize that one cannot take press freedoms for granted.

Now that the freedoms of the press have been emphasized and the concepts of the press discussed, one needs to turn to the basic responsibility of the press in the twentieth century. Newspapers vary in responsibilities as they vary in size, frequency of publication, and intended audience. Each must determine its role and then perform to the best of its ability. However, there seem to be some basic responsibilities of the press that can be applied to all, according to one observer.

First, newspapers must lead in the search for truth. They should do more than disseminate information; they must seek to explain the meaning of the information they provide and must seek to provide understanding and expand knowledge. And while newspapers have to accept the impossibility of achieving complete objectivity in their reporting, they should keep it as a goal. They must remain as fair and impartial as possible in the presentation of the news, and correct distortions when and if they occur. Clearly, they must endeavor to provide information and perspective so that readers can make their own determinations about what is truth.

Second, newspapers in a democratic society have a responsibility to help make democracy work. This involves providing information not only for the common people but also for legislators and governmental officials and seeking out truth about the government at all levels. Information is necessary for a free society. Newspapers must therefore serve as a check on or watchdog of those who exert power and influence in the government.

Third, newspapers have a responsibility to help individuals and communities adjust to change and improve themselves. Nothing remains the same and nothing is certain except change. Man's information about the world around him will be doubling every few years and discoveries and new inventions will be occurring every day rather than every 20 years.

The press will need to keep up with this rapid growth and do things to meet the challenge of change. For instance, media can provide greater exposure for different ideas and groups in society and greater coverage of minorities. They can also seek for greater diversity in their staffs, adding new members who can bring new ideas. They can use special teams to do more in-depth reporting and can take more interest in understanding and reporting the processes of change in the complex social systems that are evolving. In all, newspapers must realize that as society changes, so must they. This is a challenge for any institution.

Fourth, newspapers have a responsibility to improve themselves. At all times they should follow the "Canons of Journalism" and be accurate, truthful, fair, decent, and sincere in their reporting. They should seek to improve themselves by conducting and encouraging research; improving their staffs, improving their content and appearance; and establishing definite procedures to resolve complaints, correct mistakes, and engage in vigorous self-criticism.

Finally, newspapers have a responsibility to remain free, independent, and solvent. Newspapers must seek to remain free and independent so they can carry out their many basic responsibilities in the face of continuous threats both from government and from forces within the economic structure of society. Governments pose a threat to press freedom when they withhold or manage news and restrict the rights of newspapers or force reporters to reveal confidential sources. Dangers to press freedom from within the economic structure of newspapers themselves are less obvious but no less serious. Press freedom is threatened by publishers whose first concern is making money. Too great a concern on profits can lead to censorship or policy-setting by advertisers. Information that might reflect adversely on advertisers must not be withheld for that reason. Fair and accurate reporting is essential no matter who is involved. Solvency in the 1980s and beyond will be a challenge for newspapers even if government and internal pressures are reduced. To succeed economically, newspapers must adjust to a rapidly changing society and provide new as well as traditional services for readers. The concept of the newspaper industry as an information source for information consumers must be explored. Newspaper readers today are less loyal and more demanding than those in the past. People are less likely to read newspapers out of habit or a sense of duty. Audiences are more fragmented. Nevertheless, the need for good newspapers is as great today as at any time in history. Those which adjust to change and carry out their other basic responsibilities should not simply remain solvent; they should do well economically.

Newspapers need the understanding and support of the public if they are to carry out their responsibilities successfully. Newspapers can effectively serve individuals, communities, and the nation only if they are willing to be served. Newspapers can survive rising costs and increasing competition only if the public understands its own needs for newspapers and supports them. Newspapers should seek renewed public confidence through the exploration of press councils as well as the operation of their own accountability procedures. The people need newspapers to help them adjust to change, improve themselves and their communities, and make democracy work effectively.

ADVERTISING

Advertising is a basic function of any newspaper in a free-enterprise system. Not only does it provide about three-fourths of the revenue to operate the newspaper, but it also provides a valuable service for readers who want to buy something, sell something, hire someone, or find a job. Simply stated, the function of advertising is to persuade people to buy products or services.

The media of the United States rely almost totally on revenues obtained for advertising, while some Canadian media are subsidized by the government. America's exception to total support from advertising is in the area of educational television, which is in part funded by the government. However, media in both countries rely heavily on funds obtained from their advertisers.

Advertising revenues were up during the late 1970s as a result of rate increases and an apparent determination by consumer products companies to maintain or increase advertising-to-sales ratios in the battle of the shares of the market. Newspapers got approximately 55.2% of revenues spent at the local level from advertising; television got 27.1% of those spent at the national level. An estimated 70% of radio's advertising is local, but most of magazines' advertising is national. A breakdown of newspaper advertising for 1978 showed 55% retail, 31% classified, and 14% national. Based on assumptions concerning inflation, advertising rate increases, advertising page gains, and circulation growth, some observers have estimated that newspaper advertising revenues could grow 10% or more a year through 1985.

Rising costs, distribution problems, and media competition could cause the downfall of individual newspapers in the 1980s; but if the newspaper industry itself falters, it more likely will be the result of a failure to understand and adjust to changes that have taken place in society in the past 25 years. Newspapers can profit from expanding their own delivery systems to deliver magazines and other products. They can use computers, lasers, and other new technology to better their product, the press package.

Some believe that independent ownership and competition are vital to good press. Others say that some outstanding press units enjoy monopoly status in their communities, are parts of groups, or are both. Whoever is right, locally originated newspaper competition has declined drastically in the United States, joint operating agreements between competing newspapers have been sanctioned, group ownership has expanded rapidly, and cross-media and conglomerate ownerships have evolved. In Canada, the media are either privately owned or government-owned. Cross-media owners control more than a third of the daily newspapers, a fourth of the television stations, and almost a tenth of the AM and FM radio stations. The combined holdings of groups, cross-media owners, conglomerates, and firms related to the mass media encompassed almost three-fifths of the daily newspapers, slightly more than three-fourths of the television stations, and slightly more than one-fourth of the AM and FM radio stations.

Many believe the government should discourage media involvement in conglomerates. They see such involvement as a distinct threat to the free flow of information vital to the public. The free flow of information could face an even more subtle threat from ownership if the movement toward public ownership started in the late 1960s continues to expand. Some problems encountered in going public include the considerable expenses involved as well as other financial matters. However, the potential economic values of public ownership are considerable.

In summary, it appears that some fairly definite patterns of press ownership have evolved over the years. Because of the large amounts of operating capital required, most daily newspapers today are corporations. Individual ownership and partnership approaches are no longer practicable for most dailies. Some newspapers and other press units are employee-owned, and an increasing number have been opened to public ownership. The integrated communications-companies concept appears to be gaining strength and many companies are involved in cross-media ownerships and conglomerates. Under this total communications approach, companies own newspapers, broadcast stations, and other media to broaden their revenue bases and develop related activities. Such combinations almost certainly will be good for business. Whether they will be also good for the public will depend on the companies involved, the public's reaction to them, and government regulation of their activities.

EDUCATION AND TRAINING FOR JOURNALISTS

Specialized university training for journalism has not had a long history. In Canada, the idea of special training for journalists started in 1902, when the Queen's University of Kingston, Ontario, sponsored a prize essay competition. The essays were on the topic of how Canadian universities can best benefit the profession of journalism as a means of elevating public opinion. The best entries were collected and published in 1903. However, not until after World War II had ended did the first journalism school start in Canada.

It began because some returning veterans were seeking a journalism education. In 1944, H. M. Tory, president of Ottawa's Carleton College, decided to offer a course in journalism to former servicemen. In 1946, three were awarded bachelor degrees in journalism. In 1964, Carleton University's journalism school began to offer graduate courses in journalism. The University of Western Ontario started offering journalism courses in 1945; and the Ryerson Institute of Technology (later renamed Ryerson Polytechnical Institute), established in 1948, included courses in printing in the curriculum. These were later converted to journalism courses in 1958; and by 1964, a three-year diploma course in journalism was offered. Other ventures into journalism instruction in Canada have not provided programs as complete or durable as those offered at Carleton, Western Ontario, and Ryerson. Other schools are St. Clair College of Applied Arts and Technology, Windsor, Ontario, and the University of Windsor.

In the United States, the first full-fledged journalism school was established at the University of Missouri in 1908. However, in 1903, Joseph Pulitzer first submitted to the board of governors of Columbia University plans which were to launch the Columbia School of Journalism in 1912.

In the wake of these two schools of journalism, many other colleges and universities across the United States offered bachelor, associate, and graduate degrees in journalism. Also, many journalism associations were formed in these schools to add a bit of professional training and information to students interested in careers in journalism. Such associations include the following (these are student and professional organizations): Agricultural Communicators of Tomorrow (ACT), American Advertising Federation (AAF), Alpha Epsilon Rho (AER), Beta Phi Gamma (BPG), Kappa Alpha Mu (KAM), Kappa Tau Alpha (KTA), National Association of Black Journalists (NABJ), National Press Photographers Association (NPAA), National Academy of Television Arts and Sciences (NATAS), Public Relations Student Society of America (PRSSA), Society for Collegiate Journalists (SCJ), Society of Professional Journalists, Sigma Delta Chi (SPJ/SDX), and Women in Communications, Inc (WICI).

The Accrediting Council on Education for Journalism and Mass Communication, representing both educational and professional media organizations, is the agency formally recognized by the Council on Post-Secondary Accreditation and government agencies for accreditation of programs for professional education in journalism and mass communications in institutions of higher learning in the United States. Canada has a similar accreditation process. Accreditation means that the overall unit and the program or programs to which that term is applied have been evaluated by a team of educator and media and industry professionals and they have agreed that the overall unit and the programs meet the standards set up by the ACEJMC.

Other associations that faculty and others are affiliated with include the American Association of Schools and Department of Journalism (AASDJ), the American Society of Journalism School Administrators (ASJSA), and the Association for Education in Journalism (AEJ).

Specifically, Canadian press organizations include the following: Canadian Daily Newspapers Association, which was the Canadian Daily Newspaper Publisher until 1954; Periodical Press Association; Canadian Industrial Editor's Association; the Agricultural Press Association of Canada; Business Newspapers' Association of Canada; Magazine Publishers' Association of Canada; and Magazine Advertising Bureau of Canada.

L'Union Canadiennes des Journalistes de Langue Francaise was created in 1954 by les Syndicate de Journalistes Francophones. Its purpose was to consider such matters as the establishment of journalism as a profession, the development of a code of ethics, and the creation of standards of performance and journalism education for French-speaking journalists.

Training programs that have been instituted by the UPI and AP and other organizations, including most if not all newspapers, include internships. These are jobs offered to students in various areas of the mass media that give them the necessary outside-the-classroom experience they need in order to become effective professionals in their fields. These internships have proved to be excellent opportunities for students as well as a benefit to the organization that acts as sponsor.

Listings of journalism schools may be found in the current year's editions of the *Editor and Publisher International Yearbook*, published in New York City, and in a special annual issue of *Journalism Educator*, published by the Association for Education in Journalism.

HISTORICAL BACKGROUND

The history of Canadian journalism is divided into four time periods: the transplant, 1752–1807; thickening growth, 1807–1858; Western transplant and spreading growth, 1858–1900; and the mutation, 1900–1967. Each will be discussed briefly in the following paragraphs.

Transplant, 1752–1807

The British North American pioneer newspapers began as transplants from the New England colonies. It was the preconditioning in the colonies that kept the Canadian press alive. Also, journalism, which seems to be remarkably hardy, survived with encouragement from the government. The first Canadian paper was issued March 23, 1752, by John Bushell. It was the *Halifax Gazette*. This news sheet had evolved from the Royal Letters days of Agincourt, and the introduction of England's first true newspaper, the *Oxford Gazette*, in 1655.

These early papers had long, dull columns, broken only rarely by monotonous label heads. The paper editors were known as the King's Printers and were controlled by the government. Government was authoritarian during this period. Newspaper editors knew that government patronage was vital for the paper's existence, and revenue-producing government announcements, proclamations, orders, and enactments made up a large part of their content. Foreign news was the second main ingredient of these papers, but the news was usually months old. There was no competition at that time between papers, and all the news sheets were read from beginning to end. The magazine press had a token beginning during this period, with Rev. Wm. Cochran as the first editor and John Howe as the printer of the *Nova Scotia Magazine and Comprehensive Review of Literature, Politics and News*. This was started in 1789 and ended March 1792. The second magazine to appear was the *Quebec Magazine*, which printed half in English and half in French.

Thickening Growth, 1807–1865

Six provinces had papers during the first period; and during the second period, no new colonies gained newspapers, but the original six added to their newspaper numbers. The growth in population and economic and social institutions accelerated press growth. In 1813 there were 20 newssheets; by 1857, there were 291. Production improved as roads were built, so that news could be gathered and distributed better, and increased literacy enlarged readership.

A responsible government was the theme new-style editors gave most of their attention to. The struggle started with the Constitutional Act of 1791 and ended or climaxed with passage of the Rebellions Losses Act in 1849. There was press warfare between government and antigovernment papers. Individual newspapers were labeled according to the stand they took on the responsible government issue. They were either reform or antireform.

The papers contained not only political news but also local news and long abstracts from literary classics; and in 1817, the press started reporting about parliament. The format changed also, with boldface headlines and exclamation points used occasionally. Also, advertising gained in prominence and importance, with items sometimes subject to extravagant claims.

Joseph Howe's 1835 libel-trial victory provided the most momentous freedom of the press precedent during this period. Howe wrote and published an offending letter about Sir Colen Campbell in a newspaper. He was found guilty, but was acquitted 10 minutes later.

The Hallowell Free Press imported the first iron printing press in 1832, but others still used the flat wooden press. Also, in 1833, the *Daily Advertiser* became the first daily paper. However, the weekly was still more important for some time than the daily. The *Morning News* was the first penny newspaper, started in 1839 on a triweekly basis. The magazine press was more active during this period, but it still struggled.

Western Transplant and Spreading Growth, 1858–1900

This period began with the establishment of a British Columbia newspaper in Victoria, which started the Western pioneering phase and closed with the founding of Dawson City and Whitehorse news organs. The arrival of settlers brought the press to the Pacific Coast region. At that time, most settlers came West in search of gold. With the new settlements came newspapers. Railways and steamboats shortened the distance to the Western lands.

British Columbia was the first western province to acquire a newspaper, the *Victoria Gazette and Anglo-America*, in 1858. This appeared first twice and then five times a week because of demand. Alberta's first newspaper preceded its formation as a province by 25 years. Frank Oliver published this *Edmonton Bulletin* in 1880 and it lasted until 1951. The *Yukon Midnight Sun* was the first paper published in the Yukon territory during gold rush days.

With respect to content in the papers, the events of the days determined the subject matter. Confederation was the main theme, and Canada's independence came on Dominion Day, July 1, 1867. Reporters included little editorial opinion in the writing of their stories, but they often engaged in careless libel. Inflation of advertising claims grew, and newspaper content became more departmentalized. Illustrations greatly improved; and in 1871, *Canadian Illustrated News* carried a photograph of Montreal's new customs house. This was a first in the field of photojournalism. Most important, the paper's content was moving to the day-to-day news with competition growing.

New inventions helped the Canadian press improve continually. United States companies such as Hoe Co. of New York introduced innovations to speed printing. With the telephone in 1876 and the typewriter in 1868, journalists had good tools to work with. Also, the first use of the rotary press was in 1888 by the *Vancouver News-Advertiser*. The Canadian Press Association was organized in 1859, and several other journalism organizations sprang up.

The development of a freer press came with John Stuart Mill's essay *On Liberty*, published in 1869. His thesis was from the unrestricted clash and interplay of opinion in the free marketplace of ideas, and through the operation of what was called a "self-righting process," truth would become known to all men and would carry the day. However, acts began to appear on statute books that certainly limited the freedom of journalism. Press control was rampant with acts such as the Fox's Libel Act of 1792, Lord Campbell's Act of 1843, the Newspaper Libel and Registration Act of 1881, and the Law of Libel Amendment Act of 1888. What these laws did was define what a newspaper was and what privileges and responsibilities it had in relation to libel, defamation, and related matters.

Mutation, 1900–1967

During this time, the daily, the most important component of Canada's press, had grown rapidly. Dailies became larger, far more heavily capitalized, and far more dependent on an impressively massive technology. Also, between 1901 and 1911, Canada was the fastest growing country in the world. Many ethnic groups moved in until World War II stopped immigration. 1921–1931 began and ended in depression.

In 1900, the daily French and English press had an estimated 650,000 subscribers. Circulation of dailies grew at a faster rate than did the overall population. In 1967, a number of dailies about equal to the 1901 total served nearly seven times as many subscribers as in 1901. There were speedier and more complex presses, teletypes, teletypesetters, scan-a-gravers, klischographs, telephones, and computers that all permitted dailies to meet new subscribers needs.

The twentieth century press was also a story of consolidation and centralization. The strongest Canadian holdings in 1966 were by the Free Press Publications. Papers became depersonalized as they became unprovocative, impartial, standarized, and public-oriented in order to get more readership.

UNITED STATES PRESS HISTORY

The Canadian and United States press histories are very similar. Their beginnings are the same, in that they dealt mainly with commerce and overseas events, and the changes that occurred in each happened about the same time.

Colonial papers in America were a branch of English journalism, printed after London models. Early papers were printed on a single sheet of paper on hand presses. However, by 1765, many papers had four pages that contained such things as news-items from English papers, reports from sea travelers, private letters, and information about local events—and essays and occasional poems, as well as advertising (though scant).

The first printing in the American colonies took place in 1638. However, the first continously published American paper was founded by John Campbell in 1704 and was called the *Boston Newsletter*.

Newsletter

As in England, the press in colonial America was under authoritarian control. Papers were subject to suspension, and printers were jailed for offence to authority and the government. During the American Revolution, 37 colonial papers were in publication and 33 new ones developed during the war. Papers grew in prestige because of the growth of popular literacy, bold editorial leadership, and cooperation of Patriot leaders. Patriot papers at that time included the *Boston Gazette, Connecticut Courant, Massachusetts Spy*, and others. Popular papers included the *New York Gazetteer*, the *Boston Chronicle*, and the *Georgia Gazette*.

Dailies were first published to compete with coffee houses for providing news of ship arrivals and descriptions of their cargos. Most had the word "advertiser" in the title or subtitle and most were priced at 6 cents. In an era of bitter partisanship, all had strong opinions. By 1820, 42 of the 512 newspapers in the United States were dailies. Benjamin Towne was the first daily publisher with his *Pennsylvania Evening Post*, in 1783. The first paper to be founded as a daily was the *New York Daily Advertiser* in 1785.

Partisan journalism began with John Fenno's *Gazette of the United States*, which was founded in 1789 as the organ of Washington's administration. The Federalists kept a majority of papers with them until about 1810, when the disintegration of the Federalist party and the founding of a new Republican (Democratic) paper west of the Alleghenies gave the latter a press majority. Andrew Jackson exercised stricter control over his party's press than did any other president. The *United States Telegraph* founded in 1826 was the administration organ until Jackson found it leaning toward his rival, John Calhoun. The Whig party generally had minority press support with the exception of W. H. Harrison's campaign in 1840. Some leading Whig papers included the *National Intelligencer,* and *Boston Daily Advertiser,* and the *Albany Evening Journal.*

The Penny Press was the cheap-for-cash daily that was an outgrowth of the Industrial Revolution. The first daily published north of Boston, was small in size and sold for $4 a year. It was the *Portland Daily Courier* and it was founded in 1829. However, the first successful penny daily, called the *New York Sun,* was founded by Benjamin Day in 1833. Another penny daily, the *New York Herald,* was founded in 1835 by James Bennett. It flourished so that in 1836 it raised its price to 2 cents. By 1860, the *Herald* had the world's largest daily circulation (77,000). The last of the great papers to be launched at 1 cent before the Civil War was *The New York Times.* Founded in 1851 by Henry Raymond, George Jones, and Edward Wesley, the *Times* gave much attention to political activities.

Pioneer papers were developed in the west to promote settlement, support political parties, and provide news, features, and advertising. Such notable papers included the *Pittsburgh Gazette,* the *Missouri Gazette,* the *Chicago Daily Tribune,* and the *Moniteur de Louisiane.*

During the Civil War era, papers were choosing sides, with some supporting the secessionists and others supporting the north. Many papers proved fickle, first siding with one philosophy but later switching loyalties. Confederate papers suffered from paper shortages, lack of printers due to army service, and destruction, suspension, and censorship by Union occupation forces. Also, coverage of the war by the northern papers was thorough, even though the transmission of news was often difficult. The Civil War saw the first substantial numbers of United States war correspondents in the battle fields.

After the war, there was a phase of expansion for papers and they increased in number and circulation. The number of newspapers doubled in the 1870s, while the population increased only 30%. The *New York Daily News* was claiming circulations of 175,000 at a penny a copy. The causes of this growth were expansion of the west, economic improvement in the south, boom times in the east, and a growing variety of the content and independence from party control on the part of the newspapers. As in Canada, as dependence on political subsidies declined and advertising revenue increased, United States newspapers turned increasingly objective to broaden their appeal.

A name imbedded in American journalism is that of Joseph Pulitzer. This Hungarian immigrant came to St. Louis, Missouri, in 1865 and worked in the *Westliche Post* for seven years before buying a partnership in the paper. In 1878, he acquired the *Dispatch*, a lively young paper founded in 1875, and merged it with the *Post*. The *Post-Dispatch* became the leading newspaper in the St. Louis area.

When Pulitzer was 37, he decided to try his luck in the main newspaper center of the United States and bought the *New York World* in 1883. Pulitzer made the *World* a fresh, newsy, sensational crusading paper at 2 cents a copy, and circulation doubled in four months and continued to skyrocket, reaching 300,000 by 1884. The new journalism that Pulitzer introduced was a spectacular success because of the alert and colorful news policy he used, the editorial page of high character, the many crusades and stunts, an increasing number of illustrations, an increasing size that reached 16 pages in 1890, the building up of the Sunday edition, and an active promotion policy.

William Randolph Hearst is another name associated with journalism, particularly yellow journalism. Hearst studied the *New York World's* methods and having successfully experimented with its techniques in San Francisco, he bought the *Journal* in New York in 1895. In its second year under Hearst, the *Journal* overtook the *World* in circulation. Hearst used such techniques of sensationalism as large type, lavish use of pictures, colored comics, and a stress on promotion. The term yellow was derived from a comic picture first drawn for the *World's* Sunday edition by Richard Outcault caricaturing amusements of kids from the tenements and called "Hogan's Alley." When the dress of the central kid was printed in yellow, the series became a hit as the "Yellow Kid." When Hearst hired Outcault for the Sunday *Journal*, George L. Lukas took over the feature for the *World*, and the toothless grinning figure on city billboards and popularized on the stage became the symbol of the yellow press.

When war with Spain broke out, a spectacular and persistent propaganda campaign to force United States interference on behalf of Cuban rebels to overthrow Spanish control was led by the *New York Journal* and the *World*. Some 500 writers, photographers, and artists covered the war with Spain for United States newspapers and magazines. Most papers, however, lost money during the war, even though circulation increased.

The decline of yellow journalism started in 1910, because of a growing distaste on the part of readers for the overplay of crime and sex and distrust of fakery for the sake of excitement. Also, Pulitzer started disapproving of this type of journalism and changed his *World* policy. Finally, the success of the *Christian Science Monitor* as a daily newspaper that played down crime and disaster news showed that it could be successful in emphasizing foreign news and culture.

A LOOK TO THE FUTURE

Dramatic changes that cannot be fully covered in a short chapter have profoundly affected the mass media in North America over the 40 years since World War II. Introduction of the new medium of television, which grew from infanthood to what is probably currently a lusty adolescence, has revolutionized the news, or journalism, industry. Television has tended to become the spot news medium and newspapers have joined magazines as the reflective, interpretive medium.

Technology now in use, and that waiting in the wings to storm media processes, is revolutionary in itself. Most unpredictable of all, however, is the technology not yet discovered and destined to have its impact on the media within the next two decades.

Probably the greatest changes in the media are yet to take place, as microchip technology, lasers, and other devices create serious questions about how long media in the United States and Canada will remain in the forms that are familiar in the early 1980s.

There is a substantial chance that the forms will change for virtually all media existent today. The rapidity with which even predictions have changed, however, can be illustrated by guesses during the late 1970s and early 1980s that newspapers would retain their present form while incorporating computer and laser technology into their production. Then came development of videodisc— a small plastic disc with a capacity of upwards of 52,000 frames of information, which could be presented either still or in movement, either in color or black and white. The entire 52,000 frames could be indexed and any frame found instantaneously.

With such videodiscs costing less than 25 cents and easily recycled, newspapers produced by such means were visualized, reducing the need for a "forest of trees" daily for newsprint needs in the United States and Canada. Hardly had that idea been tested, however, when home computers suddenly made first possible, then very feasiible, the data bank newspaper that allows a home computer owner to not only bring great quantities of current news into the home but also to get printout, or facsimile, copies.

With the great versatility and freedom offered to the householder by the new technology, it may well be that newspapers as they are known today will become very rare by the end of the twentieth century. Such an eventuality is, of course, resisted by current print journalists, but there are a number of striking parallels that need to be considered between development of newspapers in the United States and the current development of computer information systems.

It was mentioned earlier that the first newspapers in the American colonies were commerce- or business-oriented, dealing with information about ship arrivals, cargoes, and prices. Such newspapers were very expensive and appealed only to a special-interest audience— the businessman with a considerable vested interest in current commercial information.

Following the commercial newspaper into the market was the political paper, generally subsidized by a political party or special interest group, which had the basic function of disseminating partisan information.

The common characteristic of each of these was the relatively narrow, and dedicated, audience each commanded. The commercial paper was distributed to businessmen and the partisan paper was designed to strengthen the resolve of ideological supporters and to gather new converts who might be exposed to the message.

Today a similar phenomenon is occurring relative to the spread of data banks: their early content is heavily oriented to specialized information for which there is a market. Farm information services, as one example, are springing up to provide updated information several times a day that will assist the farmer in his decision making. His home computer, sometimes as simple as an inexpensive leased keyboard that connects to his television set, allows him to make a telephone connection at his convenience with the master computer half a continent away.

Such a system enables the farmer rapidly to bring large quantities of current information into his computer's memory by toll-free telephone lines for the price of a monthly fee. He can then, also at his convenience, recall the information from memory, read it, and either erase it or store it for future reference.

Subscribers to various business services find themselves in a similar situation, and scholars, libraries, researchers, and others are subscribing in increasing numbers to the large number of vast data banks that have been set up to meet the demands for rapid, comprehensive topical information. Many of these data banks operate on an as-used fee basis for subscribers, eliminating even the set monthly fee.

It is not difficult to see such services projecting themselves, as demand occurs, to providing current information and even photographs and moving pictures of current news events. With such development could easily come the mass audience, with very low subscription fees.

Thus, it may not be unusual for a reporter in the near future to file a story in the computer so it can be made available instantly to homes in the community or to viewers across the nation or around the world.

Such an electronic newspaper provides the maximum flexibility of constant editing and usage at the reader's convenience rather than the current scheduled delivery of the television or radio station. It also reduces or eliminates many costly production and distribution expenses.

Probably the great question in the equation at the moment is that of economic support. With newspapers and electronic media outlets currently dependent on advertising for the vast majority of their revenue, effective ways of working advertising into the scheme have yet to be found. But there is increasing evidence that audiences are willing to pay for their mass media in many instances. Such television offerings as Home Box Office and other pay-TV services seem to be competing effectively with so-called free network television by providing first-run movies, sports events, and other programming at a fee. Perhaps computerized news services will also develop a broad popular appeal.

Such discussion of the form news will take has, however, little to do with the problems of news collection and of freedom of information over the next decades. What will influence these areas is the rising education levels of both Canada and the United States, expanding the populations of people who will insist on access to the vast quantities of information they will need in order to participate in determining their own destinies.

These people are likely to require substantial numbers of a new breed of journalist, one who is able to translate events of the world around him and to make projections that will help people understand what is happening and what is likely to happen. His job will be, simply, to reduce the number of unpleasant surprises his audience confronts by preparing that audience for the events. Such skills will require educated, thoughtful journalists and inexhaustable and comprehensive information systems throughout the world.

The technology exists, but men seem to be lagging in its usage. At the moment, virtually any spot in the world is readily and instantaneously reachable by satellite communications. Yet history shows that events continuously catch journalists by surprise. Some are the product of ignorance and insensitivity—the reactions to United States involvement in Vietnam and the rapid rise on the best-seller lists of Ralph Nader's first consumer safety book, *Unsafe at Any Speed*, or Rachel Carson's pioneering work on environmentalism, *Silent Spring*. Others are the result of distance and isolation, such as the devastating droughts in central African countries, the periodic bloody religious wars in some African countries, Central American guerrilla uprisings, the Argentine invasion of Britain's Falkland Islands, and other remote events that tend to explode into world consciousness only when need for worldwide attention is irreversible.

In order to do these things, journalists will still find themselves fighting government leaders and others who take a proprietary interest in the affairs of their governments, and facing the physical dangers of such combat situations as Central America, Southern Africa, South and Southeast Asia, and other troubled world spots.

SELECTED BIBLIOGRAPHY

General

Abshire, David M. *International Broadcasting*. Beverly Hills: Sage, 1976.
Batscha, Robert. *Foreign Affairs and the Broadcast Journalist*. New York: Praeger, 1975.
Boyd-Barrett, Oliver. *The International News Agencies*. Beverly Hills: Sage, 1980.
Browne, Donald R. *International Radio Broadcasting*. New York: Praeger, 1982.
Buzek, Antony. *How the Communist Press Works*. New York: Praeger, 1964.
Casmir, F. L., ed. *Intercultural and International Communication*. Washington, D.C.: University Press of America, 1978.
Cherry, Colin. *World Communication: Threat or Promise?* New York: Wiley, 1978.
Cooper, Kent. *Barriers Down: The Story of the News Agency Epoch*. Port Washington, N.Y.: Kennikat Press, 1942.
Curry, Jane, and J. Dassin, eds. *All the News Not Fit to Print: Press Control Around the World*. New York: Praeger, 1982.

Dake, Anthony C. A. *Impediments to the Free Flow of Information Between East and West.* Paris: NATO, 1973.

Davison, W. Phillips. *International Political Communication.* New York: Praeger, 1965.

Dizard, Wilson. *The Coming Information Age.* New York: Longman, 1982.

Desmond, Robert. *The Information Process: World News Reporting to the Twentieth Century.* Iowa City: University of Iowa Press, 1978.

————. *Windows on the World.* Iowa City: University of Iowa Press, 1980.

Emery, Walter B. *National and International Systems of Broadcasting.* East Lansing: Michigan State University Press, 1969.

Fascell, Dante B., ed. *International News: Freedom Under Attack.* Beverly Hills: Sage Publications, 1979.

Fischer, H.-D., and J. C. Merrill, eds. *National and International Communication.* New York: Hastings House, 1976.

Fisher, Glen. *American Communication in a Global Society.* Norwood, N.J.: Ablex, 1979.

Gastil, R. E., ed, *Freedom in the World: Political Rights and Civil Liberties.* Westport, Ct.: Greenwood Press, 1981.

Hachten, William. *The World News Prism: Changing Media, Clashing Ideologies.* Ames: Iowa State University Press, 1981.

Hardt, Hanno. *Social Theories of the Press: Early German and American Perspectives.* Beverly Hills: Sage, 1979.

Hohenberg, John. *Foreign Correspondence: The Great Reporters and Their Times.* New York: Columbia University Press, 1964.

Koszyk, Kurt, and Hugo Pruys. *Handbuch der Massen Kommunikation.* Munich: K. G. Saur, 1981.

Kurian, George, ed. *World Press Encyclopedia* (2 vols.). New York: Facts on File, 1982.

Lehman, Maxwell, and T. J. M. Burke, eds. *Communication Technologies and Information Flow.* Elmsford, N.Y.: Pergamon Press, 1981.

Lendvai, Paul. *The Bureaucracy of Truth: How Communist Governments Manage the News.* New York: Westview Press, 1981.

Mankekar, D. R. *One-Way Flow: Neo-Colonialism via News Media.* New Delhi: Clarion Books 1978.

Martin, L. John, and Anju Chaudhary, eds. *Comparative Mass Media Systems.* New York: Longman. 1983.

Merrill, John C. *The Elite Press: Great Newspapers of the World.* New York: Pitman, 1968.

Merrill, J. C., Carter Bryan, and Marvin Alisky. *The Foreign Press.* Baton Rouge, La.: LSU Press, 1970.

Merrill, J. C., and Harold A. Fisher. *The World's Great Dailies.* New York: Hastings House, 1980.

Murphy, Sharon, E. Atwood, and S. Bullion, eds. *International Perspectives on News.* Carbondale: Southern Illinois University Press, 1982.

Nascimento, C. A. *The World Communication Environment.* Georgetown, Guyana: Ministry of Information, 1981.

Pelten, Joseph. *Global Talk.* Brighton, U. K.: Harvester House, 1981.

Pollock, John C. *The Politics of Crisis Reporting: Learning to Be a Foreign Correspondent.* New York: Praeger, 1982.

Richstad, Jim, ed. *New Perspectives in International Communication.* Honolulu: East-West Communication Institute, 1977.

Robinson, G. J. *News Agencies and World News.* Fribourg: University Press of Fribourg, Switzerland, 1981.

Rogers, Everett, and Lawrence Kincaid. *Communication Networks.* West Drayton, Middlesex, U. K.: The Free Press, 1981.

Seymour-Ure, Colin. *The Political Impact of Mass Media.* Beverly Hills: Sage Publications, 1974.

Siebert, Fred S.; Theodore Peterson; and Wilbur Schramm. *Four Theories of the Press.* Urbana: University of Illinois Press, 1956.

Snow, Marcellus S. *International Commercial Satellite Communications.* New York: Praeger, 1975.

UNESCO. *World Communications: A 200-Country Survey of Press, Radio, Television and Film.* New York: UNESCO, 1975.

Wells, Alan, ed. *Mass Communication: A World View.* Palo Alto: National Press Books, 1974.

Wicklein, John. *Electronic Nightmare: The New Communications and Freedom.* New York: Viking Press, 1982.

Africa

Ainslie, Rosalynde. *The Press in Africa: Communications Past and Present.* New York: Walker, 1968.

Ansah, Paul, Cherif Fall, Bernard Chindji Kouleu, and Peter Mwaura. *Rural Journalism in Africa.* Paris: UNESCO, 1981.

Barton, Frank. *African Assignment: The Story of IPI's Six-Year Training Programme in Tropical Africa.* Zurich: International Press Institute, 1969.

———. *The Press of Africa: Persecution and Perseverance.* New York: Africana, 1979.

Behn, Hans Ulrich. *Die Presse in Westafrika.* Hamburg: German Institute of African Studies, 1968.

Bokonga, Botombele E. *Communication Policies in Zaire.* Paris: UNESCO, 1980.

Boyd-Barrett, Oliver. *The International News Agencies.* Beverly Hills: Sage, 1980.

Broughton, Morris. *Press and Politics of South Africa.* Capetown: Purnell & Sons, 1961.

Feuereisen, Fritz, and Ernst Schmacke, eds. *Die Presse in Afrika: Ein Handbuch fuer Wirtschaft und Werbung.* Munich: Pulloch, 1968.

Gale, W. D. *The Rhodesian Press.* Salisbury: Rhodesian Printing and Publishing Co., 1962.

Gastil, R. D., ed. *Freedom in the World: Political Rights and Civil Liberties, 1981.* Westport, Ct.: Greenwood Press, 1981.

Hachten, William A. *Mass Communication in Africa: An Annotated Bib-*

liography. Madison: University of Wisconsin, Center for International Communication Studies, 1971.

————. *Muffled Drums: The News Media in Africa*. Ames: Iowa State University Press, 1971.

Head, Sidney W. *Broadcasting in Africa*. Philadelphia: Temple University Press, 1974.

Hopkinson, Tom. *Two Years in Africa*. Zurich: International Press Institute, 1965.

Huth, Arno G. *Communications Media in Tropical Africa*. Washington: International Cooperation Administration, 1961.

Katz, Elihu, and George Wedell. *Broadcasting in the Third World: Promise and Performance*. Cambridge: Harvard University Press, 1977.

Kitchen, Helen. *The Press in Africa*. Washington: Ruth Sloan Associates, 1956.

Kucera, G. Z. "Broadcasting in Africa: A Study of Belgian, British and French Colonial Policies." Unpublished Ph.D. dissertation, Michigan State University, 1968.

Legum, Colin. *Africa: A Handbook to the Continent*. New York: Praeger, 1966.

Mwaura, Peter. *Communication in Kenya*. Paris: UNESCO, 1980.

Pinch, Edward T. *The Third World and the Fourth Estate: A Look at the Non-Aligned News Agencies Pool*. Washington: Senior Seminar in Foreign Policy, 1977.

Potter, Elaine. *The Press as Opposition: The Political Role of the South African Newspaper*. London: Chatto and Windus, 1975.

Scotton, James. "Growth of the Vernacular Press in Colonial East Africa: Patterns of Government Control." Unpublished Ph.D. dissertation, University of Wisconsin, 1971.

Sommerlad, E. Lloyd. *The Press in Developing Countries*. Sydney: Sydney University Press, 1966.

Stokke, Olav, ed. *Reporting Africa*. New York: Africana, 1971.

Ugboajah, Frank O. *Communication Policies in Nigeria*. Paris: UNESCO, 1980.

USICA. *Country Data Papers: Africa*. Washington: U. S. International Communication Agency, 1981.

USIA. *Mass Media Habits in West Africa*. Washington: U. S. Information Agency, March 1966. R-64-66.

Wilcox, Dennis L. *Mass Media in Black Africa: Philosophy and Control*. New York: Praeger, 1975.

Asia and the Pacific

Burr, Trevor. *Reflections of Reality: The Media in Australia*. Adelaide: Rigby, 1977.

Chu, Godwin C. *Radical Change Through Communication in Mao's China*. Honolulu: University Press of Hawaii, 1977.

Desai, M. V. *Communication Policies in India*. Paris: UNESCO, 1977.

Gunaratne, Shelton A. *The Taming of the Press in Sri Lanka.* Lexington, Ky.: AEJ Journalism Monographs 39, 1975.

Ghose, H. P. *The Newspaper in India.* Calcutta: University of Calcutta, 1952.

Hanazono, Kanesada. *Development of Japanese Journalism.* Nichi, Japan, 1934.

Hattori, Yoshio. *Study of Local Newspapers in Contemporary Japan.* Tokyo: Information Science Research Institute, 1980.

Howkins, John. *Mass Communication in China.* New York: Longman, Inc., 1972.

Holden. W. Sprague. *Australia Goes to Press.* Detroit: Wayne State University Press, 1961.

Kato, Hidetoshi. *Communications Policies in Japan.* Paris: UNESCO, 1977.

Lee, Wen-yi. *The Press in China.* Hong Kong: International Studies Group, 1964.

Lent, John A., ed. *Asian Newspapers: Reluctant Revolution.* Ames: Iowa State University Press, 1971.

———. *Broadcasting in Asia and the Pacific.* Philadelphia: Temple University Press, 1978.

Lerner, Daniel, and Jim Richstad, eds. *Communication in the Pacific.* Honolulu: East-West Communication Institute, 1976.

Markham, James W. *Voices of the Red Giants.* Ames: Iowa State University Press, 1967.

Mayer, Henry. *The Press in Australia.* Melbourne: Lansdowne Press, 1968.

Mehta, D. S. *Mass Communication and Journalism in India.* Beverly Hills: Sage, 1980.

Moses, Charles, and Crispin Maslog. *Mass Communication in Asia: A Brief History.* Singapore: AMIC, 1978.

Nayar, Kuldip. *The Judgement: Inside Story of the Emergency in India.* New Delhi: Vikas, 1977.

Richstad, Jim, and Michael McMillian, eds. *Mass Communication and Journalism in the Pacific Islands: A Bibliography.* Honolulu: University Press of Hawaii, 1978.

Schramm, Wilbur, and L. Erwin Atwood. *Circulation of Third World News: A Study of Asia.* Hong Kong: Press of the Chinese University of Hong Kong, 1981.

Tiffen, Rodney. *The News from Southeast Asia: The Sociology of Newsmaking.* Singapore: Institute of Southeast Asian Studies, 1978.

Wolseley, Roland E., ed. *Journalism in Modern India.* Bombay: Asia Publishing House, 1964.

Yu, Frederick T. C. *Mass Persuasion in Communist China.* New York: Praeger, 1964.

Europe and the Middle East

Duesenberg, Albert. *The Press in Germany.* Bonn: Buchdrukerei M. Scholl, 1960.

Emery, Walter B. *Five European Broadcasting Systems.* Austin: AEJ Monograph 1, 1966.

Freiberg, J. W. *The French Press*. New York: Praeger, 1981.

Gustafsson, Karl, and Stig Hadenius. *Swedish Press Policy*. Stockholm: The Swedish Institute, 1976.

Inkeles, Alex. *Public Opinion in Soviet Russia*. Cambridge: Harvard University Press, 1950.

Harasymiw, Dohdan, ed. *Education and the Mass Media in the Soviet Union and Eastern Europe*. New York: Praeger, 1976.

Kaplan, Frank. *Winter into Spring: The Czechoslovak Press and the Reform Movement, 1963–1977*. Boulder, Colo.: East European Quarterly, 1975.

Katz, Elihu, and Michael Guerevitch. *The Secularization of Leisure: Culture and Communication in Israel*. Cambridge: Harvard University Press, 1976.

Kottyar, A. *Newspapers in the USSR*. New York: USSR Research Council, 1955.

McFadden, Tom J. *Daily Journalism in the Arab States*. Columbus: Ohio State University Press, 1953.

Mickiewicz, E. P. *Media and the Russian Public*. New York: Praeger, 1981.

Nasser, Munir K. *Press, Politics, and Power: Egypt's Heikal and Al-Ahram*. Ames: Iowa State University Press, 1979.

Olson, Kenneth E. *The History Makers: The Press in Europe from Its Beginnings Through 1965*. Baton Rouge: LSU Press, 1966.

Robinson, G. A. *Tito's Maverick Media: The Politics of Mass Communications in Yugoslavia*. Urbana: University of Illinois Press, 1977.

Said, Edward W. *Covering Islam*. Henley, Oxfordshire: Routledge & Kegan Paul, 1981.

Sandford, John. *The Mass Media of the German-Speaking Countries*. London: Oswald Wolff, 1976.

Schlesinger, Philip. *Putting 'Reality' Together: BBC News*. Beverly Hills: Sage, 1979.

Schneider, Maarten. *The Netherlands Press Today*. Leiden: E. J. Brill, 1951.

Shulte, Henry F. *The Spanish Press, 1470–1966*. Urbana: University of Illinois Press, 1968.

Smith, Antony. *The British Press Since the War*. Plymouth: Latimer Trend, 1974.

Thorsen, Svend. *Newspapers in Denmark*. Copenhagen: Det Danske Salskab, 1953.

Weber, Karl. *The Swiss Press: An Outline*. Bern: H. Lang, 1948.

Williams, Francis. *Dangerous Estate*. London: Longmans, Green, 1957.

Latin America

Acosta, Miguel, ed. *Libertad de Prensa*. Caracas, Venezuela: Universidad Central, Facultad de Humanidades, 1969.

Alexander, Robert J. "Freedom of the Press." In *The Tragedy of Chile*. Westport, Conn.: Greenwood Press, 1978.

Alisky, Marvin. *Latin American Media: Guidance and Censorship*. Ames: Iowa Sate University Press, 1981.

Artega, Carlos, and Carlos Romero. *Communication Policies in Peru.* Paris: UNESCO, 1977.

Beltrão, Luiz. *Jornalismo Interpretativo.* São Paulo, Brazil: Falco Masucci, 1969.

Carty, James W., Jr. *Cuban Communications.* Bethany, W. Va.: Bethany College, 1978.

―――. *Working with the Latin American Press.* New York: Algonquin Press, 1963.

Comisión de Derechos Civiles. *La Prensa en Puerto Rico.* San Juan: Civil Rights Commission of Puerto Rico, 1977.

De Camargo, Nelly, and Virgilio Noya Pinto. *Communication Policies in Brazil.* Paris: UNESCO, 1975.

De Noriega, Luis Antonio, and Frances Leach. *Broadcasting in Mexico.* London: Routledge & Kegan Paul, 1979.

Cuthbert, Marlene. *The Caribbean News Agency.* Minneapolis: AEJ Monograph 71, February 1981.

Dominguez, Jorge I. *Cuba: Order and Revolution.* Cambridge, Mass.: Harvard University Press, 1978.

Gardner, Mary. *The Press of Guatemala.* Minneapolis: Association for Education in Journalism Monograph 18, 1971.

―――. *The Press of Latin America: Selected Bibliography in Spanish and Portuguese,* Austin: University of Texas Institute of Latin American Studies, 1973.

―――. *The Inter-American Press Association.* Austin: University of Texas Press, 1967.

Hester, Albert L., and Richard R. Cole, eds. *Mass Communication in Mexico.* Brookings, S. Dak.: South Dakota State University for the International Communication Division of the Association for Education in Journalism, 1975.

Knudson, Jerry W. *Herbert L. Matthews and the Cuban Story.* Minneapolis: Association for Education in Journalism Monograph 52, 1978.

―――. *The Press and the Bolivian National Revolution.* Minneapolis: Association for Education in Journalism Monograph 31, 1973.

Lent, John A. *Caribbean Mass Communications : A Comprehensive Bibliography.* Waltham, Mass.: Brandeis University Crossroads Press, 1981.

―――. *Third World Mass Media: The Commonwealth Caribbean, 1717–1976.* Lewisburg, Pa.: Bucknell University Press, 1977.

Merrill, John C. *Gringo: The American as Seen by Mexican Journalists.* Gainesville: University of Florida Press, 1963.

Nixon, Raymond B. *Education for Journalism in Latin America: A Report of Progress.* Minneapolis: Minnesota Journalism Center, 1981.

―――. *Education for Journalism in Latin America.* New York: Institute for International Education, 1971.

Pierce, Robert N. *Keeping the Flame.* New York: Hastings House, 1979.

Timerman, Jacobo. *Prisoner Without a Name, Cell Without a Number.* New York: Alfred A. Knopf, 1981.

North America

Barnouw, Erik. *A History of Broadcasting in the United States.* New York: Oxford University Press, 1966.

Blanchard, Robert O. *Congress and the News Media.* New York: Hastings House, 1974.

Cater, Douglas. *The Fourth Branch of Government.* Boston: Houghton Mifflin, 1959.

Clery, Val, ed. *Canada from the Newsstands: A Selection from the Best Canadian Journalism of the Past 50 Years.* Toronto: MacMillan of Canada, 1978.

Commission on Freedom of the Press. *A Free and Responsible Press.* Chicago: University of Chicago Press, 1947.

Dennis, Everette E., and William L. Rivers. *Other Voices: The New Journalism in America.* San Francisco: Canfield Press, 1974.

Diamond, Edwin. *The Tin Kazoo: Television, Politics, and the News.* Cambridge: MIT Press, 1975.

Dickey, John S., and Whitney H. Shepardson. *Canada and the American Presence.* New York: New York University Press, 1975.

Emery, Edwin, and Michael Emery. *The Press and America: An Interpretative History of the Mass Media.* Englewood Cliffs, N. J.: Prentice-Hall, 1978.

English, H. Edward, ed. *Canada-United Sates Relations.* New York: Praeger, 1976.

Fisher, Glen. *American Communication in a Global Society.* Norwood, N. J.: Ablex, 1979.

Franklin, Marc. A. *The First Amendment and the Fourth Estate.* Mineola, N.Y.: The Foundation Press, 1977.

Gramling, Oliver. *AP: The Story of News.* New York, Toronto: Farrar and Rinehart, 1940.

Head, Sydney W. *Broadcasting in America: A Survey of Television and Radio.* Boston: Houghton Mifflin, 1956.

Hiebert, Ray Eldon; Ungurait, Donald F.; and Bohn, T. W. *Mass Media: An Introduction to Modern Communication.* New York: David McKay, 1974.

Hiller, Harry H. *Canadian Society: A Sociological Analysis.* Scarborough, Ontario: Prentice-Hall of Canada, 1976.

Hohenberg, John. *The Professional Journalist: A Guide to the Practices and Principles of the News Media* (4th edition). New York: Holt, Rinehart and Winston, 1978.

Hynds, Ernest C. *American Newspapers in the 1980s.* New York: Hastings House, 1980.

Kesterton, Wilfred H. *A History of Journalism in Canada.* Toronto: McCleland & Stewart, 1976.

Merrill, John C., and Ralph L. Lowenstein. *Media, Messages and Men: New Perspectives in Communication.* New York: Longman, 1979.

Mott, Frank Luther. *American Journalism: A History, 1690–1960.* New York: Macmillan, 1962.

Pollard, James E. *The Presidents and the Press.* New York: Octagon Books, 1973.

Rivers, William L. *The Adversaries: Politics and the Press.* Boston: Beacon Press, 1970.

Rosenblum, Mort. *Coups and Earthquakes: Reporting the World for America.* New York: Harper & Row, 1979.

Rosewater, Victor. *History of Cooperative News-Gathering in the United States.* New York: D. Appleton, 1930.

Rosten, Leo. *The Washington Correspondents.* New York: Arno Press, 1974.

Rubin, Barry. *International News and the American Media.* Washington Paper 49. Beverly Hills: Sage, 1977.

Small, William J. *Political Power and the Press.* New York: Norton, 1972.

Tebbel, John. *The Media in America.* New York: New American Library, 1974.

Tunstall, Jeremy. *The Media Are American.* New York: Columbia University Press, 1977.

Wolseley, Roland E. *The Journalist's Bookshelf: An Annotated and Selected Bibliography of United States Journalism* (7th edition). Philadelphia/ New York: Chilton, 1961.

Third World and UNESCO

Altbach, P. G., and Eva-Maria Rathgeber. *Publishing in the Third World.* New York: Praeger, 1980.

Gerbner, George, ed. *Mass Media Policies in Changing Cultures.* New York: Wiley, 1977.

Gunter, Jonathan F. *The United States and the Debate on the World Information Order.* Washington, D. C.: Academy for Educational Development, 1979.

Heacock, Roger. *UNESCO and the Media.* Geneva: Institut Universitaire de Hautes Etudes Internationales, 1977.

Hedebro, Goran. *Communication and Social Change in Developing Nations: A Critical View.* Stockholm: Economic Research Institute, University of Stockholm, 1979.

Horton, Philip C., ed. *The Third World and Press Freedom.* New York: Praeger, 1978.

Jamison, D. T., and Emile G. McAnany. *Radio for Education and Development.* Beverly Hills: Sage, 1978.

Katz, Elihu, and Tamas Szecsko, eds. *Mass Media and Social Change.* Beverly Hills: Sage, 1981.

Katz, Elihu, and George Wedell. *Broadcasting in the Third World: Promise and Performance.* Cambridge: Harvard University Press, 1977.

Lee, Chin-Chuan. *Media Imperialism Reconsidered.* Beverly Hills: Sage, 1980.

MacBride, et al. *Many Voices, One World.* London: Kogan Page; New York: Unipub; Paris: UNESCO, 1980.

McAnany, Emile G., ed. *Communications in the Rural Third World.* New York: Praeger, 1980.

McPhail, Thomas L. *Electronic Colonialism: The Future of International Broadcasting and Communication.* Beverly Hills: Sage, 1981.

Mankekar, D. R. *Media and the Third World.* New Delhi: Indian Institute of Mass Communication, 1979.

Masmoudi, Mustapha. *The New World Information Order.* Paris: UNESCO, 1978.

Nordenstreng, Kaarle, and H. I. Schiller, eds. *National Sovereignty and International Communication.* Norwood, N. J.: Ablex, 1979.

Pinch, Edward T. *The Third World and the Fourth Estate: A Look at the Non-Aligned News Agencies Pool.* Washington: Senior Seminar/Foreign Policy, 1977.

Richstad, Jim, and Michael Anderson, eds. *Crisis in International News: Policies and Prospects.* New York: Columbia University Press, 1981.

Righter, Rosemary. *Whose News? Politics, the Press and the Third World.* London: Burnett Books, 1978.

Robinson, Gertrude J., ed. *Assessing the New World Information Order Debate.* Grand Forks, N. D.: ICD Publications, University of North Dakota, 1982.

Rogers, Everett M., ed. *Communication and Development: Critical Perspectives.* Beverly Hills: Sage, 1976.

Schramm, Wilbur and Daniel Lerner, eds. *Communication and Change: The Last Ten Years and the Next.* Honolulu: University of Hawaii Press, 1976.

Smith, Anthony. *Geopolitics of Information: How Western Culture Dominates the World.* London: Faber & Faber, 1980.

Sommerlad, E. Lloyd. *The Press in Developing Countries.* Sydney: Sydney University Press, 1966.

Sussman, Leonard R. *Mass News Media and the Third World Challenge.* Washington Paper 46. Beverly Hills: Sage, 1977.

ABOUT THE CONTRIBUTORS

MARVIN ALISKY, who holds an M. A. in journalism and a Ph.D. in Latin American politics from the University of Texas, is a professor of political science at Arizona State University, where he has also chaired the department of Mass Communications and founded the Center for Latin American Studies. He has also taught at Indiana University, Princeton University, the Hoover Institution of Stanford University, and the University of California, Irvine. He has been a Fulbright professor at the Catholic University of Peru and the National University of Nicaragua.

He has served as a news correspondent for NBC in Latin America and as a parttime summer correspondent for the *Christian Science Monitor* and the Copley News Service.

Mr. Alisky was a U. S. delegate to a UNESCO conference in Ecuador and the liaison media aide for Presidents Jerry Ford and Luis Echeverría at a 1974 summit meeting on the Arizona—Mexico border. He has also lectured for the State Department in Peru and Mexico. The author of 200 articles in magazines ranging from *Arizona Highways* to *Inter-American Economic Affairs*, he is the author or co-author of 16 books and monographs, including *Latin American Media, Historical Dictionary of Mexico, Peruvian Political Perspective,*

The Foreign Press, Political Systems of Latin America and *Uruguay: A Contemporary Survey.*

RALPH D. BARNEY, a professor in communication at Brigham Young University, received his journalism Ph.D. from the University of Missouri. His main area of research and teaching are in journalism ethics and international communication. In 1981–82 he was a Fulbright-Hays Fellow establishing journalism courses in the South Pacific through the systems of the University of the South Pacific in Fiji.

He has been editor and publisher of his own weekly newspaper, as well as reporter and copy editor for the *Deseret News* of Salt Lake City, Utah, and the *Honolulu Star-Bulletin*. In addition, he has some experience with radio and television news. He has been a Fellow of the East-West Communication Institute in Honolulu and was a Founding Member of the Honolulu Community-Media Council.

Recent research has explored development of ethical values among journalists. He has written a number of articles, papers and book chapters, co-authored *The Pacific Islands Press* and, with John Merrill, edited *Ethics and the Press.*

As a private consultant and researcher, he has examined the community newspaper field and audience loyalties among radio, television, metropolitan newspaper and community newspaper audiences.

DEANNA GEDDES NELSON holds a Master of Arts degree in communication from Brigham Young University. As an undergraduate student at Brigham Young University and in Hawaii she was a newspaper editor and reporter.

JOHN LUTER, professor of journalism and chairman of the Journalism Department at the University of Hawaii, is a graduate in economics from St. Mary's University of Texas (where he also completed three years of law school) and was a fellow at the School of Advanced International Studies in Washington, D.C.

Mr. Luter administers the University of Hawaii Journalism Department's special training program for young journalists from China and is a member of the planning and selection committees for the university's Gannett Fellowship Program in Asian Studies. He has also taught at the Columbia Graduate School of Journalism, where he coordinated the Ford Foundation program in Advanced International Reporting, and directed the Cabot Prize Program in inter-American journalism.

Mr. Luter has worked as a professional journalist for the *San Antonio Light*, the *Washington* (D.C.) *Star, Time* and *Life* magazines,

CBS News and *Newsweek* magazine. He was a Time correspondent in the Pacific toward the end of World War II and served eight years as a Time-Life foreign correspondent in Southeast Asia, Japan, the Middle East and Italy. He has twice been elected president of the Overseas Press Club and has served as chairman of the Advisory Screening Committee on Communications for the senior Fulbright program.

L. JOHN MARTIN is professor of journalism at the University of Maryland, where he teaches courses in comparative journalism, international communication, public opinion, and research methods in mass communication. A former foreign correspondent and newsman in the Near East, he has worked for the *Detroit Free Press*, the Rochester *Democrat & Chronicle*, the Louisville *Courier-Journal*, and the St. Paul *Pioneer Press*. During the 1960s, he was a research administrator in the U.S. Information Agency, first as chief of the Near East and South Asia Division and later as head of all overseas research.

Besides teaching journalism at the universities of Florida and Nebraska, he was a research fellow in journalism and political science and assistant director of the International Relations Center at the University of Minnesota. He is author of *International Propaganda*, editor of *Propaganda in International Affairs*, and co-editor of *Comparative Mass Media Systems*, among other books, and has contributed articles to a number of periodicals and encyclopedias, and chapters to books. He is editor of the *International Communication Bulletin*, and associate editor of the *Journalism Quarterly*.

He earned his Ph.D. in political science and an M.A. in international relations and area studies from the University of Minnesota, and his B.A. from the American University in Cairo, Egypt. He has traveled and lectured extensively in Africa and is external examiner for the M.Sc. degree in Mass Communication at the University of Lagos, Nigeria.

JOHN C. MERRILL, editor of and contributor to this volume, is a professor of journalism at Louisiana State University. He holds a Ph.D. in mass communication from the University of Iowa and has been an active scholar-teacher-lecturer, and writer on international communication since the early 1950s.

He has taught at the University of Maryland, the University of Virginia, California State University at Long Beach, Texas A&M University, and National Chengchi University in Taiwan. He was on the journalism faculty at the University of Missouri for 15 years. He has also lectured, taught, and conducted workshops and seminars in some 50 countries.

Dr. Merrill is the author or co-author of a dozen books, including the *Elite Press, International and Intercultural Communication, The World's Great Dailies*, and the *Foreign Press*. He has also written widely in U.S. and foreign periodicals.

Dr. Merrill has worked in various capacities for weeklies and as a reporter, copy editor, columnist, and feature writer for daily newspapers.

JIM RICHSTAD is a professor of journalism and mass communication at the University of Oklahoma. Previously, he was a research associate at the East-West Center's Communication Institute in Honolulu, where he specialized in journalism training and education and mass communication in Asia. In addition, he coordinated the center's Jefferson Fellowships, a mid-career study program for Asian, Pacific and American journalists. He directed a Pacific Basin flow-of-news study, out of which have come several journal articles.

His publications, alone and jointly, include *Crisis in International News: Policies and Prospects; Mass Communication and Journalism in the Pacific Islands: A Bibliography; Communication in the Pacific; Evolving Perspectives on the Right to Communicate; New Perspectives on International Communication*. He contributed to the International Commission for the Study of Communication Problems (MacBride Commission), and has served as a consultant to Unesco and to The Asia Foundation. He has taught journalism at the University of Hawaii and the University of Washington, and has worked for the Honolulu *Advertiser*, the Seattle *Times* and the Decatur (Ill.) *Herald and Review*.

He holds a Ph.D. in journalism and mass communication from the University of Minnesota and a B.A. in journalism from the University of Washington.

PAUL S. UNDERWOOD began his newspaper career with *The Cincinnati Enquirer* after attending Ohio Northern University and the University of Cincinnati. He worked for the Associated Press for 12 years, including a four-year stint in London. He joined the *New York Times* as a foreign desk editor and then spent six years as a correspondent in Eastern Europe.

Mr. Underwood is now a professor specializing in international communications on the faculty of the School of Journalism at Ohio State University. He has written a number of books and articles dealing with both journalism and Eastern Europe, and is the recipient of a citation for foreign reporting from the Overseas Press Club of New York and an honorary Doctor of Letters Degree from Ohio Northern University.

INDEX

368